Marcella's Italian Kitchen

MARCELLA'S
ITALIAN KITCHEN

By Marcella Hazan

ALFRED A. KNOPF   NEW YORK   1987

THIS IS A BORZOI BOOK
PUBLISHED BY ALFRED A. KNOPF, INC.

Copyright © 1986 by Marcella Polini Hazan and Victor Hazan
Photographs copyright © 1986 by David Massey

All rights reserved under International and Pan-American Copyright Conventions.
Published in the United States by Alfred A. Knopf, Inc., New York, and
simultaneously in Canada by Random House of Canada Limited, Toronto. Distributed
by Random House, Inc., New York.

Library of Congress Cataloging-in-Publication Data

Hazan, Marcella.   Marcella's Italian kitchen.

Includes index.
1. Cookery, Italian.   I. Title.   II. Title: Italian kitchen.
TX723.H3424   1986   641.5945   86-45268
ISBN 0-394-50892-0

Manufactured in the United States of America

Published October 15, 1986
Second printing, January 1987

For my star pupil

His enthusiasm at the table has fed mine in the kitchen; in the kitchen beside me, as my official taster, his judgment has never failed me; of his own cooking, the only thing I regret is that I am not around to have it more often: my son, Giuliano Hazan.

In Appreciation

Of Craig Claiborne, whose work has helped open America wide to cooks, to teachers, to writers, to good food from all peoples. To his interest and encouragement I owe the start of my career in cooking.

Of Judith Jones, editor incomparable, whose firm yet gentle guidance has steered me toward clarity, on whose all-encompassing understanding of good cooking I have had the comfort to rely, whose unstinting patience and confidence replenished mine whenever they were waning.

Of Robert Lescher, peerless author's paladin, without whose support I might never have cooked my way to the end of this book.

Of all the cooks, students, friends on whose knowledge and experiences I have drawn.

Contents

What This Book Is About

There are nearly 250 recipes here, encompassing every aspect of Italian home cooking, from appetizers to ice cream. As you might expect in an Italian cookbook, there is a generous selection of first courses, more than 60 new pastas, *risotti,* and soups. The fish, chicken, and veal dishes are the most varied and, I think, among the most flavorful I have ever done. For the first time, I have included some recipes for ingredients that have recently become more available to American cooks, such as *radicchio,* yellow bell peppers, fresh *porcini* mushrooms, and white truffles. To take advantage of the good tomatoes that are beginning to appear in farmer's markets throughout the country, I have given many examples of that light touch with fresh tomatoes which is one of the wonders of Italian cuisine. Moreover, I have described a method I have developed for making frozen ripe tomato purée to use as an off-season alternative to canned tomatoes. I am particularly pleased with the ice creams, sorbets, and *semifreddi* in this book, which seem to me to capture better than ever before the taste of the Italian originals.

Although I first cooked most of the dishes in my Venice and Bologna kitchens, I have included none that, when tested later in New York, were not equally successful with American ingredients. Some of the recipes were drawn from the inexhaustible store of oral and written tradition. A great many were devised by me and by other contemporary Italian cooks whose work is firmly rooted in that tradition.

I have recorded here only such recipes that, both individually and taken as a whole, would reflect my lifelong attitude toward cooking. Even though nearly two decades of teaching and writing have transformed Italian cooking for me into a profession, when I step into my kitchen I am still the woman who learned to cook to please her family and her friends. The only kind of cooking I have ever cared for is relaxed and unpretentious; bringing satisfaction to those moments when we are most comfortably ourselves; producing food that becomes a part of our lives and of our warmest memories, food that we want to go back to again and again, simple food that has only one objective: to taste good.

This is likely to be the last general cookbook I shall be persuaded to write.

I hope that the recipes I have put into it, the discussions of principles, and the descriptions of methods succeed in demonstrating what constitutes good Italian cooking, as I understand it.

                                                              Marcella Hazan

Venice
December 1985

Marcella's Italian Kitchen

Good Italian Cooking

Words are capable of mysterious chemistry. Taken singly, the three common words in the title above appear plain enough in their meaning. We can use any one of them in ordinary conversation, confident we'll be understood. But put just two of them together and you can set off a debate. Ask what is good cooking and you may get as many conflicting replies as you have people willing to offer a definition. Italian cooking? Ask a Neapolitan, a Roman, a Florentine, a Bolognese, a Genoese, a Venetian. Each will describe something different. Good Italian cooking? Who is to say? Let us pull the words apart again, turn them around, and see what is behind them.

COOKING: A LANGUAGE

To understand what the uniquely human act of cooking represents, it helps to take a quick, far look back. As our biped ancestors were evolving into the human species, two things happened that distinguished them from other animals: They formed closely knit social groups whose members were mutually dependent for procuring food, and they addressed each other in spoken language.

To wander deeper into anthropology is beyond the scope of this cookbook and of my competence. But it is no coincidence that the campfires where human words were first exchanged also witnessed, at some point, the change from merely eating food that was gathered or caught to preparing it. Language has been described as a loom on which the fabric of society has been tightly woven. To a narrower, but none-theless significant extent, the same can be said of cooking. The evocations of flavor of shared cooking, like the familiar accents of a common tongue, established one's identity, formed tribal bonds, chased solitude.

Since then, written and oral language has grown to encompass all of man's feelings, experiences, perceptions. The languages of cooking have also developed so that we use them now to express ourselves subtly or boldly, elaborately or simply, extravagantly or frugally, with elegant restraint or rustic forthrightness, in the context of innovation or of tradition. But all of cooking's infinite varieties of expression still take their meaning from a single, deep, ancestral emotion: the pleasure that is aroused by flavor.

All that really matters in food is its flavor. It

matters not that it be novel, that it look picture-pretty, that it be made with unusual or costly or currently fashionable ingredients, that it be served by candlelight, that it display intricacy of execution, that it be invested with the glory of a celebrated name. Such incidentals may add circumstantial interest to the business of eating, but they add nothing to taste and signify nothing when taste is lacking.

Taste is produced by the expressive use of the cuisines that have come down to us. One becomes fluent in a cuisine as in a language, steeping oneself in its idioms, getting its accents right. Cooking well is very like the telling use of language: Expression must be vigorous, clear, concise. There can be no unnecessary ingredient or unnecessary step. A dish may indeed be complicated, but in terms of taste every component, every procedure must count.

Do not strain for originality. It ought never to be a goal, but it can be a consequence of your intuitions. If the purpose of flavor is to arouse a special kind of emotion, that flavor must emerge from genuine feelings about the materials you are handling. What you are, you cook.

Do not arbitrarily shuffle the vocabulary of one cuisine with that of another in an attempt to make your cooking "new." There is no more use for such a hybrid than there is for Esperanto. The cuisines available to us have all the flexibility we can handle with felicity, and more variety than our invention can exhaust.

I am not suggesting that one must cook in pedantic submission to unalterable formulas. I hope the recipes in this book demonstrate that I do not. I am suggesting that the discipline of a cuisine's syntax, cadence, native idiom can make invention and improvisation eloquent rather than contrived.

❧ THE ITALIAN LANGUAGE OF COOKING ❧

The cooking of Italy is part of that large group of cuisines usually described as ethnic. A more appropriate term, I think, would be vernacular. It is colloquial family cooking, spontaneous, pithy, spirited, direct.

The originals of many dishes the Italians—or, for that matter, the French—cook today were created in the courts of the Medicis in Florence, the Sforzas in Milan, the d'Estes in Ferrara, of Venice's doges and Rome's Renaissance popes. In France they have led to the formal vocabulary and structure of *haute cuisine*. In Italy, they have long since been mingled with the earthier, plainspoken accents of regional kitchens and rephrased to suit everyday, popular usage. Italian cooking owes its vitality, its constantly fresh appeal to this potent mixture of the patrician with the humble.

Because it is straightforward, Italian cooking appears simple and invites one to take many liberties. It can be and one should. But if one does not pay close attention to its idiomatic flavors, the rendition can easily slip into parody. I have tried to collect and develop only such recipes as clearly enunciate those flavors, in the hope that cooking from this book may lead to convincingly Italian expressions of taste.

❧ *THE TASTE OF ITALIAN COOKING* ❧
Elementary Rules

I wish I could take you into my kitchen and say: Look, this is how it's done; here, taste this sauce, that is what I mean by fresh and light; bite into that chicken, see how tender it is all the way through. We meet, however, only in these pages, which, I hope, can connect my kitchen with yours. I shall try to make that connection a good one, to be clear about the principles of taste that guide me as an Italian cook, to set down those recipes that seem best to exemplify such principles, and—through the introductions to the recipes—I hope to communicate some notion of their flavor, to show how the dishes evolved, what choices were made, and why.

Let us begin with basic rules of usage. Some may coincide with or differ from those of other cuisines, but all are fundamental to the practice of good Italian cooking.

• Use no Parmesan that is not *parmigiano-reggiano*. (See the discussion of *parmigiano-reggiano* on page 11.)

• Never buy grated cheese of any kind; grate cheese fresh when ready to use it.

• With exceedingly rare exceptions, do not add grated cheese to dishes or sauces cooked with olive oil.

• Use only extra virgin olive oil. (Please see Olive Oil on pages 7–10.)

• Dress salads with no other oil but olive.

• Do not use prepared salad dressings, even if prepared at home. Mix the condiments into the salad when you are tossing it. Toss salads just before serving.

• Use herbs and spices sparingly. Think of them as a halo, not a club.

• Do not confuse stock with meat broth. Meat broth (page 73) is what goes into Italian cooking.

• When ripe, fresh tomatoes are in season, do not use the canned. (Out of season, see the recommendations on pages 12–13.)

• Abstain from frozen vegetables, except for frozen leaf spinach, which can be substituted for fresh in making green pasta.

• Do not overcook pasta.

• Do not precook pasta.

• Do not esteem so-called fresh pasta more than the dry, factory-made variety. (Please see discussion of homemade and factory-made pasta on pages 90–6.)

• Match the sauce to the pasta, taking into account the shape and texture of pasta.

• Do not buy prepared pasta salads, precooked or frozen pasta, or stuffed pasta.

• Do not turn heavy cream into a warm bath for pasta or for anything else. Reduce it, reduce it, reduce it.

• Vegetables and beans are, on occasion, passed through a food mill. Do not process them to a cream. In Italian cooking there is no cream of anything soup.

• Do not serve fowl rare. Italian birds are cooked through and through.

• Do not clarify butter. (See Cooking with Butter at High Temperature, page 16.)

• When making *risotto*, use only Italian varieties grown for that purpose. (Please see *Risotto*, pages 153–5.)

• Find a butcher who will cut *scaloppine* across the grain from the top round.

• Unless you are on a medically prescribed diet, do not shrink from using what salt is necessary to draw out the flavor of food.

❧ *THE INGREDIENTS* ❧

One can cook almost anything in an Italian style, but there are a few ingredients—some with special applications, others more versatile—that are indispensable to a clear articulation of Italian flavor. Some are more widely distributed than others, but most of the ones described below are now available in good food stores throughout the country's major markets. Where there is no satisfactory local source, mail order houses abound that carry a substantial assortment of Italian specialties.

BALSAMIC VINEGAR
Aceto Balsamico

WHAT IT IS. Aceto Balsamico is a pure, naturally sweet grape product that has been made since the Middle Ages in the country houses of the province of Modena, in Northern Italy. A glimpse of its deep, charred brown color, a sniff of the spice and honey in its aroma, a sour-sweet drop of it on the tongue quickly reveal that it is unlike any other wine vinegar. To understand how it got to be that way, it is useful first to review how wine turns to vinegar.

It all begins with grape sugar. When certain yeasts feed on the sugar in grape juice, they transform it into alcohol, and the juice becomes wine; when another type of organism is allowed to feed on wine's alcohol and transform it in turn into acetic acid, the wine becomes vinegar.

All conventional wine vinegar is started with dry wine, with no residues of sugar. The *aceto balsamico* process gets under way one step earlier. The juice of a white grape, *trebbiano,* is boiled down until it is a sweet syrup that is then poured into a wood barrel, filling it not quite to the top. Slowly, wine yeasts nourish themselves on the sugar, converting it into alcohol. Even more

slowly, acetic bacteria consume the alcohol, gradually transmuting it into acetic acid. The original quantity of sugar is so high that the yeasts cannot consume it all: What remains sweetens the vinegar.

From the time that grape juice is boiled down for *aceto balsamico* until the day vinegar is drawn from the barrel, it is not months or years that go by, but generations. When, after ten to fifteen years, much of the contents of the original barrel has evaporated, what is left is poured into a smaller barrel. After another decade or so, as the vinegar continues to evaporate, it is decanted into a third, even smaller cask. And so it continues, from father to son to grandson, until only a few priceless pints of *aceto* come to rest in the last container, perhaps the fifth or sixth of the series, a diminutive barrel usually made of juniper wood.

That is the traditional homemade method. Commercially produced *aceto balsamico,* the only one of which most of us are likely to have any experience, is made within a drastically reduced time span, sometimes not longer than five years, but following exactly the same principles.

HOW TO USE IT. In earlier centuries, it was believed that *aceto balsamico* possessed medicinal qualities and that a small amount rubbed on the forehead or chest would chase away fevers, colds, and other ailments. That is the reason it is called *balsamico,* a balsam. But it was then, as it is now, the finest of condiments. A few drops, added to a regular olive oil and vinegar dressing, ennobles any salad. It can be used on meat dishes or in a pasta sauce. It should cook briefly, however, or not at all; otherwise much of its aroma will be snuffed out. One of the most remarkable uses of *aceto balsamico* is on strawberries, when even those that are pale and tasteless are magically invested with the flavor of the ripest berries. The recipe is on page 313. Other recipes in this book with *aceto balsamico* are on pages 129, 202, and 232.

AN ANECDOTE. This is a true story. My husband and I were guests one evening of a woman who lived on a farm outside Modena. When she poured some drops of her own *aceto* out of a perfume-size bottle into the salad, we remarked how precious such a substance must be to those whose families had devoted the better part of a century to making it. She agreed and proceeded to give us an illustration of the value the Modenese place on *aceto balsamico.* "During the war," she said, "my brother moved out of the city, which was being periodically bombed, to this house, where he felt his family would be safer. One day, the bombs inexplicably came much closer, and the siren sounded. If you have never been in an air raid," she went on, "you cannot know, in those moments, what emotions will rise from the depths to drive your actions. When he heard the alarm, my brother remembered that, in case of danger, we had planned to use the cellar as a shelter. As the planes rumbled overhead, he flew to the attic, where we keep the *balsamico,* and moments later he was in the cellar, gently putting down the juniper cask containing the nearly finished vinegar. When he looked up, he realized what he had forgotten, and he rushed out again, this time to look for his wife."

PARSLEY

In Italy we say of someone whom we seem always to run into that he is "like parsley—he's found in every sauce." There are dishes beyond counting, in the Italian repertory, whose base is garlic, olive oil, and parsley: the starting point for a soup, a pasta sauce, a stew, a vegetable. When vegetables are sautéed in garlic, oil, and parsley they are called *trifolati,* from the Piedmontese for truffle, *trifola,* because it is the classic preparation for truffles.

Once you feel so at ease with the indivisible garlic, oil, and parsley trio that you work with it instinctively, not only will the preparation of many basic dishes become second nature but you will be drawn toward improvisations that express an authentically Italian flavor.

Many markets sell the sweet, mild Italian parsley and, if it is available, that is the variety to use. Its leaf is broad and flat, with jagged edges rather than curly and crinkled. Do not confuse it with coriander, which it resembles in appearance. Coriander's leaves, although flat, have rounded points, and its flavor is pungent in a distinctly non-Italian way.

Chopped parsley in a recipe means chopped parsley leaves. Use the stems only when a fainter aroma is desired, as in boiling fish or making *ossobuco.*

Before chopping the leaves, wash them in several changes of cold water, then shake them thoroughly dry in a towel. If you chop them when they are wet they become mush. For chopping fresh parsley fine, nothing rivals the food processor.

Once chopped, parsley can be wrapped in plastic wrap and kept in the refrigerator for a few hours, if necessary, but not longer. Washed, dried whole leaves can be refrigerated for three to four days. If the parsley is very fresh when you buy it—bright green and unbowed—keep it on the stems, snip off a little bit from the ends of the stems, and place it in a glass or a jar of cold water, as you would a bunch of flowers. It will stay fresh in the refrigerator for a full week.

OLIVE OIL

In an obscure alley in Venice, well askew of even the most inquisitive visitor's course, there is the

Corte Sconta, a *trattoria* whose butcher-paper table mats and naked light bulbs might make you think you'd stepped into the Venetian equivalent of a truck stop. Yet it is the most celebrated place for fish in the city, and the flavor of its cooking draws to it food enthusiasts from all over the world.

My husband and I were lunching there one day. We finished late, steadily keeping up with a prodigious procession of sea creatures boiled, stewed, fried, and grilled. As the end came, Gianni Tegon, one of the partners, sat down with us to chat. My husband asked him, "What is it that gives your food that extraordinary taste?" Gianni, a quiet-spoken man with a quizzical, self-deprecating air, blinked, squinted, and replied, "I'd like to claim it was the fish or our cooks, but there are others who buy fish as we do and cook it with care. The real difference between our cooking and that of most of our colleagues is in the olive oil."

He was understating his case, but not by much. No other ingredient is so critical to the good taste of Italian cooking. I happen to like butter and I use it more liberally than many Italian cooks, but if I were commanded to eliminate either butter or olive oil from my kitchen, it's butter I would drop. Olive oil is the first ingredient to think of when cooking fish in any manner, streaming it over boiled seafood, using it to stew, or brushing it on a whole fish hot from the grill. It is olive oil that gives slow-cooked vegetables, beans, mushrooms, and most pasta sauces that sunny Italian taste. It is matchless in bringing out garlic's sweet aroma. Without olive oil there could be no pesto, no *bagna caôda,* no *salsa verde,* no *peperonata.* Salads without olive oil are unthinkable.

Olive oil is capable of four degrees of virginity, and the Italian law defines them thus:

Extra Vergine Olive Oil is obtained from olives that have been crushed solely by mechanical means and that have not been subjected to

chemical treatment of any kind. It may contain no more than 1 percent oleic acid.

Sopraffino Vergine Olive Oil, Fino Vergine, and Vergine are made exactly like Extra Vergine, but their acidity, in terms of oleic acid, is permitted to reach 1½ percent, 3 percent, and 4 percent, respectively. An oil with more than 4 percent oleic acid is not suitable for consumption.

Oil that exceeds 4 percent oleic acidity may be rectified with such solvents as trichloroethylene to reduce the acid to edible levels, then blended with some virgin oil to improve its taste. It can then be called Olio d'Oliva or, as most makers choose to label it, Pure Olive Oil.

THE MEANING OF EXTRA VIRGIN. In this book all recipes that require olive oil specify extra virgin. A dedicated cook should use no other. In my previous books I regretfully avoided emphasizing the point because it could only have been frustrating to readers to be instructed to look for something they were not likely to find. Now that extra virgin olive oil appears even in supermarkets and, if there is no alternative, can easily be ordered by mail, there is no reason to encourage people to settle for anything less.

WHICH OIL TO CHOOSE. The best Italian olive oils have no close rivals: they are not as pungent as the Spanish, as unctuous as the Greek, as weightily fruited as the California, or as bland as the French. But just because it's Italian doesn't necessarily mean it's good. Sometimes myths cloud our choice. A venerable one tells that the best oil comes from Lucca, while a more recent belief assigns greatest merit to the murkiest, most impenetrably green oil we can find. Neither is necessarily true. In fact, some of the dreariest oil I have ever had would answer to one or the other of the descriptions.

When choosing an extra virgin Italian olive oil, the first thing to consider is regional character. Most of Italy's choicest oils come either from the southern region of Apulia or the central regions of Latium, Umbria, and Tuscany. Apulia's greatest oil—velvety, full, and spicily aromatic—is grown in a zone in the province of Bari known as Andria. The premium zone in Latium is Sabina, spread between Rome and Rieti, making a clean-tasting, fragrant, round-bodied oil that is finer than any produced farther south, with the exception of Apulia's. The oils of Tuscany and Umbria—the first from the Chianti zone, the latter from the hills outside Perugia and Spoleto—are the best known and most widely admired. The Tuscan is strongly vegetal in odor and flavor, with nutty, scratchy backtaste. I prefer the more delicately fruity, warm-tasting Umbrian.

The production of olive oil in the north is smaller, but not necessarily lesser in quality. To my mind, the most perfectly balanced oil is one from the Veneto, grown on the luminous eastern shore of Lake Garda in the same estates that make that other celebrated product of Lake Garda, Bardolino. It packs in all the flavor one can hope for, yet it is fresh and light on the palate. It is the oil I use regularly at home. Some of it, I have been told, also goes to the Vatican.

Perhaps the most fascinating of all olive oils, the rarest jewel of Italian production, is made from the olives of centuries-old trees growing in Brisighella, a hill town in Romagna. It is called Brisighello, after the town name. Small quantities are occasionally exported, and part of the production, in recent years, was reserved for the Four Seasons restaurant in New York.

From the Italian Riviera in the Liguria region comes a mild oil similar to that produced in Southern France, golden green, satiny, sweetly fruity. Unfortunately, Italian law does not yet require that an olive oil packer use only the oil produced in his area. The geographic name on a label may sometimes correspond only to the address of the plant, not to the zone of produc-

tion. The contents of the bottle or can, although legitimately labeled extra virgin, could well be the mediocre product of the south, or some of it might even come from North Africa.

Until proposed changes in the law are adopted, making it easier for consumers to identify the source of production, you must gather such information for yourself. Try different oils, possibly sharing them, along with the cost, with friends. Your palate will tell you which flavor suits you best. When you find one or two you really like, stay with them. An Italian wine maker friend uses a definition of good olive oil you may find helpful: It must *condire, non ungere* —coat with flavor not with grease.

STORING OLIVE OIL. In an Italian kitchen it isn't keeping olive oil that is a problem but rather always having enough on hand. Nevertheless, if you do not use it that frequently, it is important to bear in mind that olive oil does not improve with age; with exposure to air and heat it turns rancid. Do not buy oil that is stored near hot lights or in a window. At home, keep it in a cool cupboard in a tightly closed bottle. If you are going to be away for an extended time, decant an opened container of olive oil into smaller bottles, filling them to the top. Use oil within two years of purchase, preferably within one.

IS IT HEALTHY TO USE OLIVE OIL? I prefer, and I am better equipped, to talk about taste than about health, but those who might be concerned about the effects of olive oil in the diet may be comforted by the following facts:

• Olive oil does not contain cholesterol.

• A University of Texas study indicates that olive oil does no damage to HDL, the good cholesterol that protects the heart.

• A ten-year investigation conducted by doctors from the University of Minnesota into the relationship between heart disease and the fat in seven national diets revealed that Italians and Greeks, heavy consumers of olive oil, had one of the lowest rates of heart disease of the groups surveyed.

• The calories in a tablespoon of olive oil are approximately those of an equivalent amount of other vegetable oils, but that tablespoon of olive oil goes farther because it has taste.

• Of all oils, olive has the percentage of linoleic acid that is closest to that of mother's milk, making it the most completely digestible.

• No chemicals are used to extract extra virgin olive oil—it is simply crushed from the fruit.

Pancetta

Pancetta is Italian bacon, an essential component of cooking throughout Italy, a fundamental element in many a *soffritto*—the flavor base—of pasta sauces, stews, roasts, fricassees, and vegetable dishes. There are five types of *pancetta,* of which the most important ones to a cook have their equivalent abroad in most Italian delicatessens, pork butchers, and other food shops.

Pancetta arrotolata. It is the basic *pancetta* for nearly all Italian cooks. It is part lean meat, part fat taken from the pig's belly, seasoned with salt, pepper, and spices, and rolled up—*arrotolata*—into a salami shape to cure. It is not smoked; smoked bacon is not a satisfactory substitute in those dishes that call specifically for *pancetta.*

Pancetta affumicata. Affumicata means smoked. In the Veneto, when you ask simply for *pancetta,* what you get is very much like the choicest-

quality smoked American bacon. It was during the nineteenth century, I am given to understand, under Austrian rule that the Venetian preference for smoked *pancetta* established itself. Although I was frustrated when we first lived in Venice to have to hunt for the unsmoked product that abounds elsewhere in Italy, I was pleased in the end to find that something so close to the common American bacon could fit so well into Italian cooking. In this book you will find several recipes calling for *pancetta affumicata.* In Venice it is sliced to order, as thick or thin as one needs, from a slab. It tastes much better than the packaged presliced kind, so, to duplicate the results, try to find a source for good-quality slab bacon to slice.

Pancetta stesa. It is slab bacon—*stesa* means spread out—to which only salt has been added. It is somewhat like a lean cut of salt pork. Its flavor is far more subdued than that of standard *pancetta*; it would be used only when one needs some *pancetta* in the dish but prefers to tone down its presence.

Pancetta fresca. It is raw bacon, uncured, unsalted, unsmoked, used to add a minimum of pork flavor while utilizing its fat as part of the shortening.

Pancetta coppata. It is cured, unsmoked *pancetta* rolled up with a piece of *coppa*—pork butt, the solid muscle at the back of the pig's neck. This is the same part of the pig that is used to make *coppa* cured with salt, pepper, and hot pepper, known sometimes as *capocollo. Pancetta coppata* is not so much an ingredient in cooking as it is a cold meat, usually served sliced as one would salami or prosciutto.

Parmigiano-Reggiano

In the list of ingredients that precedes each recipe of this book, whenever Parmesan is called for, I have specified *parmigiano-reggiano*. It would be simpler to use the shorter name—Parmesan— but those who do are usually shortchanged. There is irony in that fact. The qualities of a cheese that for 700 years has been the finest of its kind have made Parmesan a universally familiar word; yet the product it describes is almost invariably a substitute, at its best no better than tolerable.

The taste and consistency of true *parmigiano-reggiano* are matchless. The fundamental reasons are two. The first is the milk of which it is made, whose flavor issues from the distinctive environment of its production zone in Emilia-Romagna, a zone whose boundaries are inviolably fixed by law. The second is the stern production code, perpetuating a centuries-old tradition that admits no additives, no antifermentatives, no substances other than milk and rennet, and that requires for each wheel of cheese eighteen months of constantly monitored maturation. The only change in more than seven centuries took place in 1984: in the past, only cheese made between April and November could be branded *parmigiano-reggiano*; now the entire year's production is entitled to the controlled name.

Parmigiano-reggiano keeps for quite a long time in a refrigerator. If you buy a large piece, divide it into wedges each big enough to last you about two weeks. Cut it so that some crust remains attached to each wedge. Wrap the wedges separately with two or three thicknesses of aluminum foil. Make sure no part of the cheese pierces the wrapping and protrudes. Refrigerate on the bottom shelf.

From time to time, unwrap and check the stored cheese. If it has begun to dry, its golden color turning to white, wrap it in cheesecloth that has been moistened and wrung out until it is just damp. Wrap foil around the cloth and refrigerate the cheese overnight. The following day, remove the foil, discard the cheesecloth, pat dry with a clean towel the moist surface of the cheese, rewrap it in foil, and return the cheese to the refrigerator.

Following this uncomplicated procedure will help you stay supplied with fresh, tender *parmigiano-reggiano*. If I did not have a hunk of it always available in my refrigerator, I'd feel lost. In my entire life as a cook, I have never spent a day without it on hand.

Pecorino

The emotions roused by food are not exclusively connected to what happens on the taste buds; they are sometimes fed by sources deeper than consciousness. *Pecorino* provides an example. It is sheep's milk cheese whose name is derived from *pecora*, the Italian word for sheep. Its power to satisfy those who respond to it indubitably depends on its flavor, but it is rooted also in its origins, which have a significant place in the story of Western man. It isn't necessary to be a historian to realize that, in the civilizations of the Mediterranean, the raising of sheep meant more than just the production of wool and food; it is sufficient to recall the uses that the sacred texts of the Jews and Christians made of the words flock, shepherd, lamb.

For most of Italy's history, some kind of *pecorino* has been its preeminent cheese. Sixteenth-century records show that one pound of *pecorino* cost twice as much then as one pound of Parmesan or one pound of beef. Even today, a choice *pecorino* is expensive, and Italians with a fine appreciation of cheese are likely to prize it above all others.

Although cow's milk now dominates cheese

production and the solitary life of the shepherd is attracting few new recruits, dozens of varieties of *pecorino* are still being made. Regrettably, the one best known abroad, *romano,* is also the crudest. *Pecorino* can be a milk-white mild cheese a month old or less and nearly spoon soft, but it can also be a hard Sardinian cheese called *fiore,* amber in color and spicy, aged one year or more, and used mainly for grating, particularly in making pesto.

Pecorino served as table cheese is generally older than three months and younger than nine, in color it is eggshell white to pale straw, and it tends to crumble slightly when cut. There can be notable differences in taste, depending on the sheep's pasture and on the techniques of the cheese maker, but whatever the variations, there is always a nippy pungency and something of a bite to a good *pecorino.*

Excellent cheeses are produced throughout Italy, particularly in Sardinia, but the consensus is that the finest *pecorini* for the table are made in Umbria and in Tuscany. Especially good are the *caciotte*—the name given to small drum shapes about 8 inches in diameter and 2½ inches high—from the zones of Pienza and Monte Amiata near Siena. A slice of such a *pecorino,* ¼ inch thick, sprinkled with black pepper and anointed with a few drops of excellent extra virgin olive oil, accompanied by a liberal supply of thick-crusted bread and young red wine, may bring one as close as any food can to perfect contentment.

TOMATOES

Cooking in Italy is far less red than it is thought to be; most of it, in fact, is not red at all. When tomato does appear, however, it never swamps the dish, nor does it have the cloying or acrid, boiled-down, pungent flavors that too often still characterize expatriate Italian food. The Italian tomato taste is neither sharp nor watery; it is sweetly fresh and fruity, a taste that depends on both the main ingredient and how it is handled.

CANNED TOMATOES. I have worked with every kind of canned tomato, but the only ones that produce the taste I look for are the Italian-packed whole plum tomatoes of the San Marzano variety grown near Naples. They are deep red, firm and meaty, with hardly any seeds, they are low in acid and high in fruitiness because they are handpicked when fully ripe, and they are firm because they have been scalded just long enough to loosen and remove the skin.

When sauces or dishes with tomato—such as *ragù bolognese* or a meat stew—are cooked a long time, use both the tomato pulp and its juice, cooking over low heat, allowing the juice to bubble away at a slow pace.

But there are many instances in which tomatoes are cooked for a short time. In such cases, drain the tomatoes, discarding the juice and keeping only the pulp. In the south, where many tomato sauces undergo the shortest possible cooking, one speaks of *sugo al filetto di pomodoro,* sauce with tomato fillets, because one uses the drained whole tomato sliced into wedges and cooks it too briefly for it to dissolve completely.

Concentrated tomato paste can be a useful product. It serves to make homogeneous sauces that usually accompany meat dishes such as stuffed veal rolls. It is customarily diluted first, either with water or wine, depending on the recipe.

Tomato paste is packed in both cans and tubes. Cans are a nuisance because a small amount goes far: What is left over must be transferred to a jar and topped with olive oil before refrigerating, to keep it from forming a surface mold. Even so I end up throwing some of it away. The paste in the tube is much more practical. It squeezes like toothpaste and, refrigerated, it keeps as long.

FRESH TOMATOES. It's easy for us to forget that, however good canned tomatoes may be, they are a substitute. The real thing is the true, fresh, ripe tomato.

I know Italian cooks who never use tomatoes from a can, even in winter. Late in the season they stock up on firm, ripe tomatoes, choosing a variety slightly larger than a cherry tomato, attached in clusters to its vine from which they will be hung in a cool, dry, airy place. They will keep until the first tomatoes come on the market the following year. They taste marvelous. Try it, if you have a cool cellar. A pity it's not a practice suitable to apartments or to the overheated houses in which most of us live.

In this book there are several recipes that call for fresh tomatoes. Until recently at least, genuinely ripe tomatoes have been such a rare item in American markets that I thought hard about suggesting canned tomatoes as an alternative, or dropping the recipes altogether. In the end I decided to keep them in as they are. I rejected the canned tomato alternative because it would have failed to deliver the vital fresh taste required by the dish. However infrequently good tomatoes turn up, they do appear, in their season. I know, because I have cooked with them in America. Therefore, on the understanding that only fully ripened seasonal tomatoes are used, the recipes seem to me to be worth proposing.

When the season reaches its peak, it is desirable to buy fresh tomatoes in quantity and freeze their purée for use in colder months. It will taste sweeter than the best canned tomatoes. Occasionally you may chance on a bargain, a case of tomatoes so ripe they have been marked down for quick sale, or one the vegetable man may have withdrawn from display because the toma-toes are overripe, split, or blemished. I remember buying such a lot once on Long Island for $2.00 and cooking from it for months.

Preparing fresh tomato purée for freezing. Wash the tomatoes thoroughly in cold water, discarding only the rotten or moldy ones and any that smell sour or rancid. Cut them in pieces of 2 to 3 inches. Put them in a pot without adding butter, oil, or seasoning of any kind. Cover the pot and turn on the heat to medium. Cook the tomatoes for 10 minutes after they begin to boil.

Insert a disk with small holes in a food mill and mash the tomatoes through the mill (see page 23). Let the purée cool thoroughly in a bowl. If the tomatoes were somewhat watery, a nearly white liquid will float to the surface. You have the choice of either returning the tomatoes to the pot and boiling the liquid away or scooping it off with a spoon.

When the purée is cold, pour it into ice cube trays and freeze it. As soon as it is frozen, remove the cubes from the tray, seal them in airtight plastic bags, and return them to the freezer.

Use the purée for making sauce as you would use canned tomatoes, with any of the olive oil or butter flavor bases you will find in the recipes of this book. Do not use for any recipe that specifies only fresh tomatoes.

DRIED PORCINI MUSHROOMS

At last, fresh *porcini*—wild *boletus edulis* mushrooms—are occasionally available in some markets in the U.S. The recipes on pages 85-6 describe ways to cook them. But even if they were as plentiful and as cheap as beans, fresh *porcini* would still not make the dried kind obsolete.

Dried *porcini* are an ingredient on their own, different but no less fascinating than the fresh. As the mushrooms dry, all the luscious, moist texture disappears of course, but what is left behind is a concentrated, musky, powerfully rousing forest scent. Thus the role of dried *porcini* is that of a unique aromatic agent, a part it plays with much variety in pasta and *risotto,* with all meats and some fish, and with many vegetables.

You will find that the recipes in this book direct you to soak the mushrooms at length, to retain and filter the water they have soaked in, and to wash the reconstituted *porcini* in many changes of water. Do not look for shortcuts. There is a notable quantity of grit embedded in the mushrooms that only prolonged soaking will loosen and nothing but patient filtering and thorough washing can carry away.

If you are inexperienced at buying dried *porcini,* bear in mind that their quality can be variable. Those produced from selected, firm, healthy mushrooms are sliced into larger pieces whose color is light, mainly cream or fawn, with patches of deep brown. Packets that seem filled with blackish, crumbly bits are of inferior stock, weak in aroma. But you can expect even the best-looking packets to contain some lower grade pieces, stuffed where they won't show through the cellophane. I have never seen exported *porcini* that were quite of the lovely, uniform quality one can buy in good food shops in Italy. No traveler interested in good cooking should pass them up. Customs admits them without fuss, and they keep indefinitely. If the quantity is large or the consumption infrequent, they should be kept in a tin box in the refrigerator.

PROSCIUTTO

Take the Italian word *prosciugato,* which means dried up, cross it with its colloquial version, *presciutto,* and you have prosciutto, a salted and air-cured ham. Although its original, and still primary, meaning applies to the end result of the curing process, in common usage prosciutto now refers to ham, however it has been treated.

For the sake of clarity, descriptive qualifiers are usually added to the word.

Prosciutto fresco. Raw ham bought whole or by the slice for cooking.

Prosciutto crudo. Literally it means raw ham, but it is not raw at all; it is the familiar cured ham one eats sliced—alone, with melon, or with ripe figs.

Wherever pigs are raised in Italy, *prosciutto crudo* is made, but there are three areas where the hogs, the air, the traditional skills produce prosciutto of surpassing excellence. They are Langhirano, in Emilia-Romagna, where hogs are fed the rich whey left over from the making of Parmesan cheese; San Daniele, in Friuli; and Carpegna, in the Marches.

Langhirano prosciutto is better known as Parma ham and, at its best, it is the sweetest, juiciest, most refined of the three. More of it is produced, however, than is consistent with unvarying standards of quality, and some Parma hams can be disappointingly bland. The flatter, compact hams of San Daniele, cured without removing the hoofs, can be depended on for somewhat deeper and more uniform flavor. The most savory and perhaps most deeply satisfying of all is the Carpegna, whose velvety meat is fragrant and tasty, yet not too salty.

Prosciutto made in America is better than it used to be, but up to the present only the one produced by John Volpi compares creditably with the taste and texture of a good Parma ham.

Prosciutto crudo is made from salted, hind hams cured in fresh, dry air for as long as a year and a half. It is never smoked. The salt in fine prosciutto is never obtrusive, the flesh is firm, not slick and flabby, its color ranges from salmon pink to pale red. It must be well ringed with fat, which ought never to be trimmed away.

The perfectly balanced flavor of prosciutto is a combination of the firm, drier, saltier lean meat with the moist, sweet, satiny fat. To trim the fat away is comparable to taking the bubbles out of a superior champagne with a swizzle stick.

Another common practice that diminishes the flavor impact of prosciutto is slicing it paper thin by machine. If the ham cannot be sliced manually, the machine should be regulated to cut it no thinner than the slice a skilled carver produces by hand.

Prosciutto cotto. It is boiled or baked fresh ham. Like *prosciutto crudo,* it is not smoked. Except for a minimum of salt, it should have no other flavors than its own natural ones. There is ordinary *prosciutto cotto* made from the pig's front leg, but the choicest, just like *prosciutto crudo,* utilizes only the hind. Its meat should be solid and gristle-free, nicely rimmed by glossy white fat. The color of good *prosciutto cotto* is a lively flesh pink, never flat or dull.

COOKING WITH PROSCIUTTO. Prosciutto crudo, cured ham, and *prosciutto cotto,* boiled, unsmoked ham, are frequent ingredients in pasta sauces, stuffings, meat dishes, and some vegetable preparations. They yield different results that one should keep in mind when choosing which to use. *Prosciutto crudo* has much more flavor to start with than boiled ham and, as its sweet fat melts and its moisture evaporates in the cooking, that flavor and the saltiness of the lean meat become concentrated. When cooking with *prosciutto crudo,* one usually adds no other intensely flavored ingredient and little, if any, salt. Boiled ham is mild and is more suitable to light cream sauces and delicate stuffings.

❦ *COOKING AND PREPARATION* ❧

Just as in a language words and phrases are joined to form idioms peculiar to that language, in a cuisine there are procedures that transform ingredients in a manner that is characteristic of that cuisine. To spell out what I mean, I have used this section to call attention to some of the fundamental cooking methods and preparatory techniques that help state Italian flavor idiomatically. You will come across them often throughout the recipes that follow, together with other procedures incorporated into the recipes themselves.

They are far from daunting, but, because they are simple, they ought not to be underestimated. Simple does not mean easy. All are within the reach of any cook who uses care, taste, and common sense: elusive ingredients that can't be measured out in cups or teaspoons but that no cook can be without.

THE FLAVOR BASE
Battuto and Soffritto

Ask an Italian cook the recipe for the soup, or meat sauce, or chicken fricassee, or veal stew you have just had and her answer is likely to begin: "Make a *battuto,* then . . ." *Battuto* is a combination of all or some of the following—parsley, celery, garlic, carrot, onion, and lard—chopped more or less fine. The name comes from the verb *battere,* which means strike or, in this case, chop. The chopping board itself is called *battilardo,* lard chopper, from the time when lard was a more commonly used ingredient than it is today. Now the place of lard is often taken by other shortenings but, whether one uses lard, *pancetta,* oil, or butter, the *battuto* remains one of the foundation stones of Italian cooking.

On rare occasions the *battuto* is used *a crudo*— raw, that is—which means that the principal ingredient of the dish, for example a roast of lamb, is put into the pot at the same time as the *battuto,* before the latter sautés.

It is customary, however, for the *battuto* to become a *soffritto.* This means that, before any other ingredient is added to the pot, the *battuto* is sautéed over lively heat until it becomes lightly colored.

Here you have one of those significant and recurrent moments in the kitchen when the savor of the dish depends less on the directions of the recipe than on your judgment: What must the *battuto* do for you, what intensity of flavor must it deliver? It is through the transformation of *battuto* into the flavor base that is a *soffritto* that a cook achieves part of that unmistakable taste that can be identified as Italian.

WHERE FLAVOR STARTS
Insaporire

My Italian-English dictionary translates *insaporire* as "make tasty," which renders the meaning if not the native force of the word. The expression *insaporire* comes up in Italian oral or written recipes dealing usually with vegetables that are tossed with sautéed onion or garlic or both during the first cooking stage. Examples are:

• The sauce known as *primavera.* In such a sauce one sautés chopped onion in butter and vegetable oil until it becomes translucent, then adds a variety of vegetables diced small, and cooks over very lively heat, turning them again and again in the onion until every part of their surface is coated with flavor. Only then does one add cream and reduce it. If the vegetables

are not first "made tasty" in this manner, they will have that boiled-in-cream flavor that is exactly what most restaurants' vegetable sauces on pasta taste like to me.

• A *risotto* with artichokes. Chopped onion is cooked in butter and vegetable oil until translucent gold, then the artichoke is tossed with the hot fat and onion. When you determine that sufficient flavor has been passed on from the sautéed onion to the vegetable, you add the rice and make the *risotto.*

• Smothered cabbage, in the Venetian style. First chopped onion is sautéed in olive oil until it becomes colored a deep gold, then shredded cabbage is tossed with it over lively heat for a few minutes. After that the heat is lowered, the pan covered, and the cabbage allowed to cook down slowly until very tender.

• Spinach and rice soup. In this case, whole spinach is first cooked briefly in its own moisture, squeezed dry, added to chopped onion sautéed in butter, and tossed over high heat for a few minutes. Only after that step does one combine it with broth and rice and make the soup.

• Also see the Vegetable *Lasagne* on pages 120–2.

"Making tasty" works when carried out briskly and decisively to make sure that the vital transference of flavor from the sautéed onion to the vegetable is rich and complete. When certain Italian soups or sauces or vegetable dishes taste bland, when their flavor lacks brightness, the cause often is that the cook either skipped the *insaporire* process or executed it too timidly, too briefly, at too low heat, or with the onions insufficiently sautéed.

COOKING WITH BUTTER
AT HIGH TEMPERATURE

French cooks clarify butter to remove substances that burn at high temperature. It may be that Italian cooks are lazier or perhaps less inclined to manipulate ingredients, but they solve the problem in another manner: To the butter in the pan they add one-third part vegetable oil. The oil's burning temperature is much higher, so the mixture can tolerate cooking at high heat. Moreover, since the oil is tasteless and nothing has been done to the butter, the butter's natural flavor comes through virtually unimpaired.

COOKING WITH CREAM

Once, to be recognizably Italian, dishes had to be suffocated with tomato. Recently, to fit the currently fashionable Northern Italian image, they float in cream. Neither way resembles the way Italians cook.

Cream has a connection with some Italian cooking, in particular the cooking of the rich agricultural plain in which the provinces of Bologna, Modena, Parma, and Reggio Emilia are dominant. In that cooking, however, cream is thought of not as a rich soak but as a barely perceptible binding agent in generally skimpy sauces.

We usually add cream at the final stage of preparation and reduce at high heat until it is no longer runny. In *fettuccine alla panna* cream is put in a skillet or a flameproof dish in which the *fettuccine* will later be tossed; butter, nutmeg, and pepper are added, the heat is turned up to high, and the cream cooked down to no more than one-third its original volume.

When making veal *scaloppine* with cream, the *scaloppine* are removed from the pan in which they were sautéed, cream is added to the pan and cooked at high heat until the fat separates and floats free. Only then is the veal returned to the pan briefly to warm it and coat it with the small amount of cream sauce produced. Other examples can be found throughout this book.

Always reduce cream over high heat; don't let it die over a slow fire. High heat doesn't curdle cream, if it is perfectly fresh. In all my years of cooking, cream has never curdled while I was reducing it.

Buy only the best-quality fresh heavy cream you can find, preferably not ultrapasteurized. It is the same product you would use to make dense whipped cream. For some time, in Italy, an ultrapasteurized product has been marketed as "cooking cream." It is, alas, as awful as it is popular. The consistency is that of greasy shaving cream and the taste not much better. Stay away from any so-called cooking cream. Nothing needs to be done to heavy cream to make it suitable for cooking except to be sure it is as rich, and good, and fresh as one can.

COOKING WITH WINE OR BROTH AND WATER

Wine and broth have a double function: they provide liquid with which to conduct the cooking and they add flavor. No more wine or broth should be used than is necessary to fulfill the flavoring portion of their roles. It is quite possible that the quantity indicated by the recipe is not sufficient to last to the end of the cooking time. In such cases one adds water because it is neutral in flavor. If one were to add wine it might add sourness to the dish or load it with astringency. If one were to add broth it might make it too salty, or simply overemphasize the broth's flavor.

It is unnecessary for wine used in cooking to be very expensive, but it should not be any less good than what you drink at the table.

Broth should be homemade meat broth, which is not stock. It is straightforward broth made with meat, some bones, and a few vegetables: please see page 73. Do not depend on substitutes for homemade broth. If, on occasion, you must use one, try bouillon cubes. If substituting canned broth, do not use it straight from the can. Dilute it with water to blunt the edge of its sharpness.

COOKING WITH GARLIC

No seasoning in the Italian kitchen has as much to say as garlic, nor can any other match an expressive reach that extends from tantalizing whisper to clarion call. Garlic also has a strident top register that too often emerges in misguided interpretations of Italian cooking. To modulate its flavor in harmony with the style of the dish, it is sufficient to bear in mind this simple principle: the finer garlic is chopped and the darker it is allowed to become in cooking, the sharper it will taste. In no instance must garlic ever be cooked to a dark brown, or it will become offensively pungent, even bitter, and indigestible.

To obtain the most reticent, subtle scent of garlic, peel it, taking care not to cut it, sauté the whole clove until it becomes colored a very pale gold, then remove it from the pan before adding other ingredients.

To step up its intensity slightly, mash it gently to peel it. After it becomes lightly colored, remove it from the pan. In both these procedures, more distinct garlic flavor emerges by allowing the garlic to simmer slowly with the other ingredients. You can remove it at any time during the cooking or just before serving, depending on how much flavor you need to extract from it.

If in a sauce, a vegetable dish, a stew, you want, in addition to the scent, delicately sweet but perceptible garlic flavor, cut the peeled clove in very thin slices, cook it very briefly until it begins barely to sizzle but before it becomes colored, then add all the other ingredients.

When a dish requires lustier garlic aroma and more explicit flavor, chop the garlic fine, cook it until it becomes colored a pale gold, then add the other ingredients.

Extracting garlic's oily juice through a press produces the most pungent flavor. It is not suitable to careful cooking.

Not all garlic is alike. In Italy, in the spring, we have tender, fresh, very sweet garlic that we use with abandon. As it ages and dries, garlic becomes sharper. Beneath the flakes of brittle skin, cloves of old garlic are the color of yellowed ivory, their surface is pitted and wrinkled, and when cut, they do not appear moist. When garlic reaches this state, use less of it. The large kind from California known as elephant garlic is often available fresher, and it is milder and sweeter. A cook can work with any kind of garlic, adjusting the cooking method to draw from it just the right measure of aroma and flavor.

ROASTING OVER A BURNER

Reliable home ovens did not appear in most Italian kitchens until after World War II. Dishes that required a proper oven, such as *lasagne* or cakes, were taken to the local baker. In fact, these dishes are not intended to be consumed piping hot. I remember waiting with my bicycle at the baker's; as soon as the *lasagne* came out of the oven, I quickly pedaled them home. By the time we were all at our places at the table and the *lasagne* had been portioned out, all the fierce baking heat had subsided, clearing the way for a glorious revelation of flavor and fragrance.

The lack of an oven at home generated one of the most distinctive Italian cooking methods. I call it pan roasting. To roast meat in a pan over a burner, one begins by browning the meat on all sides in an uncovered pot together with the appropriate flavor base (please see *Battuto and Soffritto* on page 15). Then one adds wine or what other liquid may be required, reduces the liquid slightly, turns the heat down to low, and covers the pot, setting the lid slightly ajar.

The meat cooks, surrounded by heat, while the vapors—which would otherwise, by condensing, dilute the flavor—slowly evaporate. In this manner, meat and birds retain tenderness while developing exceptional tastiness. I know no other cooking method that can produce, to give an example, a roast of veal as moist and savory.

ON USING SALT

When I have salted a dish that is cooking, to judge whether the salt is sufficient, I do not taste, I sniff. For many years, the only person who knew of this peculiar practice was my husband, Victor. He was skeptical, but noninterfering. For me, it worked, but I was careful not to let others, who might have been less understanding, know what I was doing. During one of the trips my husband took when he was doing research for his wine book, the conversation with a wine producer turned to the variety of substances the sense of smell is capable of distinguishing. "You may find it hard to believe," Victor said, "but my wife claims she can detect by smell the presence of salt in food." "It isn't hard to believe at all," the man replied. "I can give you a demonstration of it right now." He thereupon poured equal quantities of the same wine into two glasses and asked my husband to look away while he sprinkled salt into one of them. He then let Victor sniff, asking him to say whether one glass of wine had a richer, fuller aroma than the other. One did; it was the one with salt.

Salt is a magnet. When used judiciously, it draws fragrance from food. Bear in mind that virtually all sensations of taste are odors that, through the mouth, reach our olfactory or smelling nerve. It is a phenomenon confirmed each time that that same smelling nerve is shut off by a cold and we detect no taste in the food we eat. To shrink from an adequate use of salt is to leave unmined the deep-lying flavors of food. A pernicious consequence of the unjustified fear of salt is that our sense of taste, through lack of exercise, becomes atrophied and we fail to reject, as resolutely as we ought, the savorless food we are served or led to prepare.

Salt also draws out and deepens color. It is useful to recall this when cooking green vegetables: The emerald in spinach, green beans, and Swiss chard emerges with a glow if they are cooked with salt. The white in vegetables such as cauliflower, however, will stay clearer if no salt is added until they are done.

Liquid also follows salt's compelling pull. Season a salad with salt only when ready to serve it, unless you like tomatoes, cucumbers, or greens a little soupy. When cooking any legume such as chick-peas, kidney beans, peas, or fava beans, add salt only after cooking; otherwise their skins will stiffen and crack. In the preliminary preparation of eggplant for cooking, salt is indispensable: As the sliced eggplant steeps in salt, it sheds its bitter juice.

If one is making a meat broth and wishes to flavor the broth rather than the meat, salt helps by forcing out the juices of the meat. Omit the salt during cooking, and the broth will be blander, but the meat juicier. As an illustration of the same principle, when sautéing or roasting meat, salt it only after it has browned, whereas, if you are making a sauce Bolognese, put in salt at the very beginning to obtain a sauce saturated with meat flavor.

The undiscriminating condemnation of salt is one of the least savory manifestations of gastronomic fashion. My arguments in defense of this vital substance have long been on record. I'd like to rest my case now by borrowing the words of Robert Farrar Capon, an Episcopal priest and food writer. They are excerpted from his *New York Times* article of September 8, 1982.

... This penchant for discrediting the dietary wisdom of the race is not, for all its scientific trappings, a nice habit. Oh yes, there's a skin of reason on it: there are, quite plainly, people with exceptional physiologies who must not eat this or that; there are obviously certain things that no one should eat at all; and there is certainly no earthly substance that is not liable to misapplication or abuse.

But what a thin, elementary skin it is, and what a volume of mean-spirited hot air it encompasses. All too often, it is a cloak for dispositions that would rather borrow trouble than behold goodness —that relish theoretical bogeymen more than any real creature in this grandly material world.

Consider salt then. Without it we would not only have difficulty being well, we would not be here at all. All life came from the salt sea, and all our history has been salted as well. Salt's preservative properties made it a symbol of enduring compacts (the Old Testament records a "covenant of salt"). Its necessity in climates without ice made it precious (salt was offered in sacrifices to God); its preciousness made it a measure of labor (he who earns a salary is worth his salt); its sovereign use as a seasoning—its ability to sharpen and define, to give balance and point to the taste of food— made it the perfect metaphor for all that is unmistakable in life (a salty character, a salacious dance); and to think of life without it was the very antithesis of wisdom (if salt "loses its savor," it becomes, literally, foolish: the Greek is *moranthe*). [In Italian as well, insipid food is described as foolish: The word is *sciocco*. M.H.]

. . . To cook without salt (save for sound and personal medical reasons), or to undersalt deliberately in the name of dietary chic, is to omit from the music of cookery the indispensable bass line over which all other tastes and smells form their harmonies . . .

Amen, Father.

COATING WITH BREAD CRUMBS OR FLOUR

To brown, sauté, or fry meat, fish, or vegetables it is necessary to have them as dry as possible on the outside, because when moist nothing can brown—it simply steams. One often uses a coating of bread crumbs or flour to dry the surface of the ingredient to be cooked. It is a simple procedure, basic to good Italian cooking, but, like many other simple techniques, it can be done badly and often is, even by professionals. The mealy texture of so many veal dishes and the thick bread coating that falls away are evidence of failure to observe fundamental principles of breading and flouring.

BREADING. Breaded food is usually coated with eggs and bread crumbs, in that order. Spread the bread crumbs on a platter. Beat the eggs lightly in a deep dish. Hold the ingredient to be breaded by one end between thumb and forefinger and dip it into the egg, turning it several times. Lift it away, holding it above the dish, until all excess egg has flowed back, leaving but a filmy coating on the meat, fish, or vegetable. Now drop it into the bread crumbs and turn it over two or three times. When crumbs are sticking to both sides, press it firmly against the bread crumbs, using the flat of your hand. Turn it over and do the other side. Your palm should come away dry. Hold the ingredient between thumb and forefinger and shake it smartly to cast off loose crumbs. If at all possible, cook it immediately before the coating begins to be soggy. If you have absolutely no alternative, you can do the breading 1 to 2 hours ahead of time, but the food will lose some crispness.

FLOURING. It must be done fast and with a light touch. Spread the flour on a platter. Dredge the meat, fish, or vegetable in the flour, coating it on all sides. Do not let it rest in the flour or pat flour onto it: It would absorb too much flour and acquire a pasty texture when cooked. Do shake it well to remove all excess flour. Proceed immediately with the cooking, otherwise the floured surface will become moist and defeat your purpose.

TOASTING BREAD CRUMBS

Bread crumbs are as vital to many Italian dishes as mortar is to bricklaying. Crumbs are applied to the surface of food, as in a cutlet *milanese,* or added to a marinade, like the one used on the Adriatic when grilling fish, or mixed into a meat loaf: They are there to absorb excess moisture and to retain the appropriate amount of butter, oil, or other cooking fat.

If crumbs are too soft, they do not produce ideal results because they become soggy and pasty. To obtain fine texture and correct absorption quality from crumbs, I prepare them as follows:

• In a tin box I store any leftover non-sweet white bread, provided it has no extraneous flavors, such as those of herbs or seeds. When I have enough bread available, and time, I cut it into 1-inch pieces, then grind it in the food processor.

• I pass the crumbs through a strainer with not too fine a mesh.

• I put about 1 cup of crumbs in a medium-size skillet with a heavy bottom and turn on the heat to medium. I move the crumbs around frequently, bringing to the top the ones on the bottom, until they all become colored a light nut brown.

• I transfer the toasted crumbs to a large baking sheet and spread them out. I repeat the procedure with the rest of the crumbs, in batches of 1 cup.

• When the crumbs have cooled completely and all moisture has evaporated, I store them in a jar to use as needed.

THE FINE ART OF PEELING

The peel, since it rarely has anything desirable to contribute to the taste of food, interests us in only one way: how to get it off. In many circumstances, it can be pulled away easily enough when the ingredient has been cooked or blanched. Examples are potatoes that are skinned after boiling, peppers after roasting, tomatoes and almonds after blanching. There are occasions, however, when it is to our advantage to skin a vegetable or fruit while it is raw. If you are sautéing peppers for a sauce or a meat dish, you want the peppers to be firm and dry. If you roast them first to peel them, they will become moist and soft, and impossible to brown. If you leave the skin on, it will slip off during the cooking and mingle with the other ingredients—and there is nothing interesting about chewing on bits of vegetable peel.

The same applies to tomatoes. When cooking fresh tomatoes fast for a light sauce, one can't blanch them to peel them because they become watery and will therefore take longer to cook. Moreover, when preparing tomatoes for salads, removing the peel also removes some of the sourness, which makes them taste sweeter and riper. Peeling is also useful when marinating fruit such as peaches, or making *macedonia,* the Italian fruit salad.

Skinning one's way around the folds of a pepper or over a soft tomato or a ripe peach is troublesome unless one knows how to use a peeler. To my surprise, considering it is a tool produced by the millions, most people do not know how to use it properly and efficiently—at least, most of the people who have come to my classes did not. A cooking teacher once wrote to say that of all the techniques she had acquired in my class, none had proved more useful than having learned to use the peeler.

The tool I have in mind is the one whose blade looks a little like a long buttonhole, with parallel cutting edges facing each other on the inside rims. The blade is not set in the handle in a fixed position, it swivels. The error I have seen students make is to use it like a paring knife, pressing the blade against the vegetable or fruit, sometimes even blocking its action with a fingertip. That is not peeling, it is whittling. It removes pulp along with the peel and, eventually, will blunt the blade.

The peeler must be used with a sawing movement, left to right, side to side, and it must be left free to swivel. No pressure at all needs to be applied. When used correctly, the cutting edge slips under the skin and separates it neatly from the ingredient, without biting into the flesh. When practiced correctly, peeling is effortless and fast and, in many cases, indispensable.

RAW ONIONS MADE SWEET

Raw onions are delicious, provided the sharpness of their bite is blunted. The following method is the most successful I have found in achieving the objective. Ideally, one starts with a naturally sweet onion, such as the Bermuda red, or, in Italy, with the young onions of Tropea in Calabria, which look like very fat purple scallions. But even the common white onion responds to the treatment.

Begin about 1 hour before you plan to use the onion. Cut it into the thinnest possible rings and put these in a bowl with an ample quantity of cold water. Squeeze the rings under water, closing your hand around as much onion as it can hold, then letting go. Repeat it seven or eight times. You will notice the water becomes slightly milky from the acid that is forced out.

Drain the onion through a strainer, refill the bowl with fresh cold water, return the onion to the bowl, and repeat the entire procedure once or twice. After squeezing and draining the onion for the last time, place it in a fresh change of cold water to soak. At 10-minute intervals drain the onion and change the water three or four times.

When ready to serve, drain, gather the onion up tightly in a towel, and squeeze all the water out of it. It will be delightfully mild, perfect for salads and sandwiches, and so digestible that there will be no reminders of it to trouble you later.

∾э TOOLS ℘

The more I cook, the less equipment I want to be bothered with. The pleasure of collecting a variety of handsome cooking implements can be irresistible, and I confess I have resisted it less often than I should. But it easily becomes an end in itself, it is extravagant, it causes clutter, and it doesn't have much to do with good cooking.

I cook best, I find, with a few well-made things whose properties have become so familiar that I use them as uncalculatingly as I do my hands.

I have nothing to add to the ample information already available from so many sources on the basic pots, knives, and other tools every cook needs. Special tools, such as pasta and ice cream machines, are discussed in the logical context of the recipes for which they are required. Here, I shall limit myself to listing a few implements useful to Italian cooks that might not be considered standard equipment in other kitchens.

THE FOOD MILL

In *The Classic Italian Cook Book* I gave a recipe for fish soup. Part of the recipe requires that the heads be separated from the fish, cooked in a flavor base of olive oil, onion, garlic, parsley, wine, and tomatoes, and then mashed through a food mill. A few years after publication, a man telephoned to say he had a complaint about my fish soup recipe: Although it was very tasty, it was full of little bones. "Little bones?" I asked. "Did you follow the instructions?" "Of course," he replied, "even to puréeing the heads." "You puréed them through a food mill?" I inquired. "I don't have a food mill," he said. "I put them in the blender."

Since that time, I have discovered that there are many cooks who don't have this simple, yet intelligent tool. If I had to choose, I would sooner give up my food processor, because what the food mill does, no processor or blender can. The best a processor can do is chop things infinitesimally fine. The food mill goes further, separating unwanted strings, skins, seeds, and small bones from the desirable pulp of food going through its disks. Moreover, it does not entirely break down the texture of the pulp, conserving the interesting consistency essential to the Italian style of cooking.

A food mill is a truncated cone-shaped container with a perforated disk fitted at the narrower end; a two-armed propellerlike blade clamps tightly over the disk and, as one turns its handle, scrapes the food across the surface of the disk and forces only the pulp through the holes. There are American, French, and Italian mills. The American model has just one disk, permanently attached. The French and Italian models have interchangeable disks with small, medium, and large holes that mill food fine or coarse as desired. In addition, they have practical fold-away clamps on the bottom that allow you to rest the food mill securely over a bowl or a pot while it does its work.

French and Italian mills are made of either plastic or stainless steel. Although more expensive, the steel model is to be preferred because it will never warp or crack and it is easier to maintain. Whether plastic or stainless, for anyone doing Italian cooking a food mill has to be on the list of indispensable equipment.

THE SAUTÉ PAN

A sauté pan, 10 to 12 inches in diameter, with either flaring or straight sides between 2 and 3 inches high, and a close-fitting lid, would probably be all one needs to cook a majority of the recipes in this book. Add to it a sturdy stockpot that could double as a *risotto* pot, and you could handle virtually any kind of Italian dish that is cooked over a burner. It is cooking over a burner, the direct and continuously responsive management of heat—as distinguished from oven baking, remote and preset—that is the main act in the Italian kitchen. The sauté pan can take on most of it: It can fry, simmer, sauté, stew, and fricassee, it makes sauces, and it even blanches skinny vegetables like asparagus.

THE PASTA COLANDER, SLOTTED SPOONS AND SPATULAS, THE CHEESE GRATER

Some of the tools most essential to an Italian kitchen are full of holes. To begin with, there is the perforated half sphere that rests, curved side down, on little feet: the pasta colander. When pasta is done, it must be drained, tossed with sauce, and served without delay. The colander starts that process quickly and efficiently. It drains, of course, not only pasta but any other ingredient cooked in water, or in its own moisture, such as spinach. Its usefulness does not stop there. When eggplants are sliced and salted before cooking, the most convenient place to stand them to purge them of their bitter juices is around the inside of a colander. Before stuffing tomatoes, I split them in half and spread them along a colander's inner face to let their excess moisture run off. To exploit the full versatility of the colander, it is good to have two or three of them, possibly in different sizes so they can be stacked, taking up little room.

In many of the recipes here, the instructions, at some point, say "transfer with a slotted spoon or spatula." The occasion may be when one must lift food from a pan without taking up any of the cooking fat, or when the pan juices need to be reduced, or when wine must be added and boiled down and one wants to remove the food temporarily from the pan while it is being deglazed. A pierced spatula is good for flat long things such as *scaloppine,* while a slotted spoon is more practical for handling smaller, chunky shapes, such as meatballs or stew.

A good cheese grater, simple tool though it is, is hard to find. Properly grated cheese should not be in the form of pellets, such as those produced by a food processor, because they do not dissolve satisfactorily. Nor should it be in the form of shavings, which dissolve too slowly on pasta. Nor should it be pulverized, because it will dry out almost instantly. The ideal consistency is that of medium-fine grains. The holes of a grater, therefore, should be neither too large nor too small.

With pasta, Parmesan tastes best when grated at the last moment over the dish. For that purpose I use a flat, triangular grater whose shape helps direct the gratings where one wants them—inside the dish. To grate cheese efficiently for cooking, I rely on the French Mouli grater for a good, quick job; its design—a grating drum with a handle, held between two clamps—allows one to utilize even pieces of cheese too small to hold by hand.

THE PEELER

The useful technique of peeling is discussed on page 21. The peeler alluded to there is that familiar tool whose double-edged blade pivots on pins set at each end. There are two versions of it: In one the blade extends away from a straight handle, in the other it is slung between the two ends of a triangular handle. They are equally efficient, but the latter model, which is the one used in Italy and is available also in the United States, permits a more comfortable grip and is easier to work with.

❧ *COMPOSING AN ITALIAN MENU* ☙

In simpler times, planning a menu did not require hard thought. Each season had its products, and cooks had a modest stock of reassuringly familiar recipes that could be arranged to suit most circumstances: a casual dinner for friends or a fancy one for important guests; a celebration; the everyday family meal, when it was still the custom to produce one.

Today, in the market, it appears to be spring and summer all year long. Moreover, there is such an abundance of recipes available to Americans, most of them derived from other heritages, that picking one's way among them is like sorting out the many and tangled strands of a thick skein. The trick is to find the principal thread, the one that, as it unwinds, shakes free all the others.

When I am deciding on a menu, no matter if it is for the family, for guests, or for one of my demonstrations, I start thinking not of a specific dish, but of what ingredients may be timely. Nearly always, the first ones I look at are the vegetables. I know that now one can find almost all grown things almost all the time, but until one has seen them, no one can tell which are the freshest, ripest, youngest. No preparation, however skillful and elaborate, can compensate for indifferent produce, nor can the most brilliantly conceived menu divert attention from its shortcomings.

Vegetables are the main line to which the several courses of an Italian meal connect. The choice of vegetable will determine with which pasta, *risotto,* or soup you will begin, which in turn affects the decision on the second course, the side dish, and, eventually, the salad. The process unrolls just as naturally from the other end, by choosing the second course that is flattered best by the accompanying vegetable, then settling on a first course that will lead gracefully to the second.

Once the theme of the menu is established, its evolution is guided by principles of harmony and good sense that are common knowledge to most cooks. One takes care to avoid conflicting, or mutually obfuscating sauces: If the meat course is sauced, the vegetable is not, and vice versa. Nor does one repeat sauces with tomato or cream. A desire for balanced diversity will suggest not to duplicate dishes that are markedly spicy, or starchy, or runny, or dense, nor to let exuberant flavors precede and overshadow soft-spoken ones.

It is acceptable — even necessary — to spend some time in the kitchen away from one's guests, but the menu could include one course that can be prepared in advance and baked at the last minute, such as *lasagne*; that can be reheated without loss of taste, such as a stew or a fricassee; that can cook on its own with a minimum of supervision, such as a roast. On the other hand, one of the principal courses should be prepared,

at least in its final steps, just before serving to brighten the meal with the sparkle of fresh, immediate flavor.

When invited to give a class for a benefit or as guest teacher in another cooking school, I decline, despite my hosts' sometimes tearful entreaties, to supply a menu in advance. How can one put together a natural sequence of dishes without a sense of the place and its market?

Of course, we all like to plan ahead as much as possible, drawing on experience to work out tentative choices. But once we are in the market, we must be willing to revise or abandon those choices. A menu ought never to be jammed into an arbitrarily established scheme. One takes one's cues from what the ingredients themselves suggest, as though one were listening to a story unfold. A sensitively assembled Italian menu has no set pieces; it may be meticulously wrought, but conveys no sense of fabrication; it speaks not of the cleverness of the cook but of the character of its components; it is derived each time from a true, sweetly seasonal moment of which it is the faithful depiction.

THE CLASSIC ITALIAN MENU AND ITS ALTERNATIVES. Most Italians expect their principal meal to begin with a soup, pasta, or *risotto,* succeeded by a fish or meat course accompanied by a vegetable, and followed by a salad. They take dessert on special occasions and in restaurants, but at home they usually end the meal with fruit.

Nearly all the recipes of this book are grouped into categories that correspond to the different stages of an Italian meal. You can compose your own Italian menu choosing from each category the dish that is most compatible with the season, with the occasion, and with the harmonious sequence of flavors you wish to establish.

I am convinced that a succession of small courses is the most interesting and balanced way to experience Italian food. There is no question, however, that eating patterns are changing, even in Italy, even in my own home. We may want sometimes to follow a pasta with nothing more than a salad or to skip the first course altogether and begin with the fish or meat course, possibly preceded by a small appetizer. On occasion, we could even be satisfied with just one of the more substantial vegetable dishes. Any of the recipes in the main body of the book may be used in this manner. The choice is obviously the reader's; therefore no set menus have been suggested.

The yields of the recipes have been calcu-lated on the assumption that they would be used as part of a traditional menu with two or more courses. If you depart from that format or if you have teenagers at the table, you should consider increasing the amounts.

The first recipe section is a group of dishes that would not necessarily fit into the formal Italian dinner pattern. Some are single-course meals, some are replacements for either the first or the second course, some are simply savory condiments, others would be more appropriate outside the dinner table. For all of these, to avoid confusion, serving suggestions are given.

Appetizers and Dishes
for Buffets and
One-Course Meals

L'Aperitivo di Victor

VICTOR'S POTION

*B*EFORE we get into the recipes, let us start the juices flowing with a drink. This is our house *aperitivo* concocted by my husband when we were living in Milan. It has a beautiful coral red color and is smooth, fragrant, refreshing, and potent. Here is Victor's description of how he goes about making it. *Salute!*

1 part well-chilled Campari
½ part vodka kept in the freezer
½ part chilled, aromatic, sweet white wine, possibly Moscato Naturale from Piedmont, or a Late Harvest Riesling from California, or a German Beerenauslese

or Trockenbeerenauslese, or a French Sauternes
A sprig of fresh mint
1 part freshly squeezed orange juice, possibly using blood oranges, if available
A thin slice of lemon for each glass

1. Combine the Campari, vodka, and wine in a pitcher, and stir.
2. Add the mint, stir, cover the pitcher with plastic wrap, and place it in the refrigerator for 30 minutes.

3. Remove from the refrigerator, discard the plastic wrap, add the orange juice, and stir several times. Remove and discard the mint.
4. Place a slice of lemon in each guest's glass, and serve.

Noci in Camicia

WALNUTS IN PARMESAN BUTTER

*W*ALNUTS with Parmesan are a hallowed, but never palling, coupling of tastes. In Emilia-Romagna, while waiting for the first course to arrive, a platter of shelled walnuts with slivers of tender, young Parmesan may be

Walnuts in Parmesan Butter (continued)

passed around to soothe impatient appetites. It is likely to be washed down with a fresh, prickly white wine. The order is sometimes reversed, the offering coming at the end rather than at the beginning of the meal. Then, with the nuts, one might serve an older, firmer, more savory Parmesan and finish off with it the last glass of the deepest, most complex red served with dinner.

It occurred to me that binding the two ingredients would make an elegant and tasty biteful to serve with an apéritif before going to the table. I grated the cheese and added just enough butter to hold the mixture together, with a little basil to contribute a cool, fresh accent.

For convenience's sake you can use shelled walnuts. If you take the trouble to shell them yourself they may taste fresher. The trick in shelling walnuts without breaking the meat into bits is one I learned in Sorrento, where the sweetest, thin-shelled walnuts come from. Put away the nutcracker; stand the walnut on its rounded base, its pointed end facing up, and give the pointy tip a few sharp raps with a heavy knife handle or similar object. When the shell begins to crack, pry it apart and extract the meat whole, or in two separate halves.

For 6 to 8 persons

⅓ cup freshly grated *parmigiano-reggiano* (Parmesan)
1 tablespoon butter, softened to room temperature

1 teaspoon chopped fresh basil
¼ pound shelled walnut halves

1.   In a bowl combine all the ingredients, except for the walnuts, until they are thoroughly amalgamated into a smooth paste.
2.   Scoop up some of the cheese and butter mixture with your fingertips and apply it to the walnuts, sheathing each half only partially, leaving about one-third exposed.
3.   Place the coated walnuts on a dish without overlapping them and refrigerate until ready to serve.

AHEAD-OF-TIME NOTE: You can prepare the cheese and butter mixture in the morning for the evening, but it is best to coat the walnuts not earlier than 1 or 2 hours before serving.

SERVING SUGGESTION: Serve with a glass of dry sparkling wine or other apéritifs before dinner or at other suitable times outside meals.

Tartine di Mortadella e Cetriolini

CANAPÉS WITH WHIPPED MORTADELLA AND PICKLES

*T*WO aspects of our life in Venice led to this recipe: There are eighty-two steps from ground level to our floor (our sixteenth-century house has no elevator), and the telephone is always ringing, announcing visitors. One day the call came late in the afternoon, and the only time we were free to see the callers was immediately. I had nothing in the house to serve with drinks and, having been out several times that morning, I felt running down to the shops—and back up—was out of the question. The only thing the refrigerator offered was *mortadella*, the Italian sausage. To serve it as I found it, sliced, seemed unsuitable, so I processed it into a foam, mixed it with chopped pickles, and presented it over rounds of good but tender bread. It was so warmly received that it has since become a fixed part of our welcome.

16 canapés

Enough good-quality, firm white bread or its equivalent to make 16 squares or rounds about 1¾ inches square or in diameter

4 ounces *mortadella*

1½ tablespoons butter

1 tablespoon *cornichons* or similar cucumber pickles chopped fine, plus 2 or 3 pickles sliced into thin rounds

1. Trim the bread of its crust and cut the slices into 16 squares or make 16 rounds.
2. Peel away the casing from the *mortadella* and put the *mortadella* and the butter in a food processor or blender. Process to a creamy consistency. Remove it from the processor's or blender's bowl.
3. Mix the chopped pickles—the pieces should be no bigger than one-third of a grain of rice—with the *mortadella*.
4. Place enough of the mixture over each square or round of bread to make a mound about ½ inch high.
5. Top the mound with a single disk of the sliced pickle.

AHEAD-OF-TIME NOTE: The mixture of *mortadella* and chopped pickles can be prepared a day in advance and refrigerated. Remove it from the refrigerator in sufficient time before serving so that it is soft enough to spread. The canapés can be completed fully 1 hour before serving and kept at room temperature.

SERVING SUGGESTIONS: With wine or other apéritifs, along with or in place of Walnuts in Parmesan Butter (page 29). It can also be an appealing addition to a buffet.

Bruschetta al Pomodoro

GRILLED BREAD WITH OLIVE OIL, GARLIC, AND TOMATO

*W*HEN, many years ago and newly arrived in America, I was asked at the table of friends if I'd like some Italian garlic bread, I thought, as I accepted, how nice that they know about *bruschetta*. After a while, a warm bundle in a napkin was brought to the table and unwrapped to disclose a steaming loaf of bread, split in two, its redolently garlicky inside drenched in butter. I rethought, no, they don't know about *bruschetta*.

Garlic bread in Italy, *bruschetta*, is never made with butter but with fruity extra virgin olive oil. It isn't heated in an oven: It is sliced, crusty bread that is grilled—preferably, if possible, over charcoal. It must be crisp, never steamy. The garlic is rubbed lightly over the hot bread after it is removed from the grill. Then it is drizzled with olive oil and is deliciously complete.

This version goes one step further, featuring tiny cubes of ripe, firm, fresh tomatoes and the added fragrance of basil or oregano.

Up to 6 portions

4 fresh, ripe, firm plum tomatoes
4 large or 6 small fresh basil leaves, or a few pinches oregano
Six ½-inch-thick slices good, crusty country-style bread

A hot charcoal grill
3 or 4 garlic cloves, peeled and mashed
Salt
Black pepper in a grinder
3 tablespoons extra virgin olive oil

1. Wash the tomatoes, split them in half lengthwise, pick out as many seeds as possible with the tip of a paring knife, and dice the tomatoes into ¾-inch cubes.

2. Wash the basil leaves, shake them thoroughly dry, and tear them by hand into tiny pieces. (For more pungent flavor, a few pinches of oregano can be substituted for the basil.)

3. Grill the bread on both sides. While still hot from the grill, rub one side of each slice with the mashed garlic. Spread over it the tomato and basil (or oregano), sprinkle with salt and a grinding of pepper, and top with a trickle of olive oil. If the olive oil is truly choice, you can increase the amount. Serve at once.

AHEAD-OF-TIME NOTE: Bruschetta is best when served hot from the grill, as described above. If it is necessary to grill it in advance, however, rub it with garlic while it is still hot, then add all the other ingredients when ready to serve.

SERVING SUGGESTIONS: As an appetizer, when making a barbecue; as part of a buffet; if cut into bite-size squares, with drinks before dinner. It would be inappropriate at table for a formal sit-down meal.

Pomodori Perini Farciti

PLUM TOMATOES STUFFED WITH EGGS, ANCHOVIES, AND CAPERS

I HAVE been stuffing tomatoes this way for so long that I no longer remember if it is my idea or if it has always been done. In any event, it's obvious that one can't go wrong with such naturally complementary components as eggs and anchovies and capers.

In this, as in any other recipe that calls for anchovies, a substantial improvement in flavor is achieved when whole, salt-cured anchovies are used instead of canned fillets. Their salt has to be rinsed off, and they must be skinned, boned, separated into fillets, and placed under olive oil—undeniably a chore. It can be done a week or more ahead of time, and the reward is ample: a taste so astonishingly good that the anchovies become irresistibly appetizing just as they are, on a thickly buttered piece of good bread. Keep the anchovies refrigerated when not using them.

For 6 to 8 persons

3 extra large hard-boiled eggs
8 to 10 flat anchovy fillets
4 tablespoons capers

6 to 8 fresh, ripe, firm plum tomatoes
2 scallions, chopped fine

1. Shell the hard-boiled eggs. Put the shelled eggs, the anchovy fillets, and 3 tablespoons of the capers into a blender or food processor and purée to a creamy consistency.

2. Wash the tomatoes, cut them in half lengthwise, remove all the seeds and the central partition to make a hollow in each tomato half.

Place them cut side down in a dish to allow any juice to run off.

3. Mix the chopped scallions with the puréed eggs, anchovies, and capers. Stuff the tomatoes with the mixture. Top with the remaining whole capers. Serve at room temperature.

SERVING SUGGESTIONS: As part of a buffet or as an appetizer taking the place of a first course before a fish course.

Pomodori Ripieni con Formaggio Caprino ed Erba Cipollina

TOMATOES STUFFED WITH GOAT CHEESE AND CHIVES

*F*OR this recipe, I have combined two ingredients that had long been a part of the Italian larder, but that today in Italy have almost been forgotten. True, tender goat's milk cheese still exists but, except for the kind packed in olive oil, is seldom found outside its few, hilly production areas. Chives are located more frequently in private herb gardens than in a vegetable market. They are both firmly attached, however, to Italian concepts of flavor. The sweet pungency of goat's milk works well, I find, with the onionlike reminiscences of the chives. Nor does it hurt that the presentation—which evokes the Italian colors through the tomato red, the white of the cheese, and the green chive—is as pretty as it is good.

Plum tomatoes are the ones I prefer because they have enough firm meat to balance the creamy cheese stuffing and their cavities are not too large.

For 6 to 8 persons

9 ripe plum tomatoes about 2 inches long
1/2 pound goat cheese, mild and creamy
    rather than sharp and crumbly
Heaping 1/3 cup chopped chives, keeping the
    tips of 2 spears for each tomato

4 or more tablespoons extra virgin olive oil,
    depending on the creaminess of the goat
    cheese
Black pepper in a grinder

1. Rinse the tomatoes in cold water. Cut the tomatoes in half lengthwise and scoop out all the seeds and inner partitions. Place them cut side down in a colander. Let drain for at least 30 minutes.

2. Put the cheese, chopped chives, olive oil, and a liberal grinding of pepper in a bowl. Using a fork or wooden spoon, mash all the ingredients together to form a smooth, creamy mixture.

3. Divide the cheese mixture roughly into as many parts as you have tomato halves. Spoon the mixture into the tomatoes, heaping it into a mound, if there is enough of it. In the center of the mound embed the tip of a chive spear, the sharp end pointing up. Serve at room temperature.

SERVING SUGGESTIONS: As a lively and very pretty appetizer, either before the first course or replacing it, in any meal that includes a meat course and in which tomato is not prominent. Serve also as part of a buffet.

Caprino ai Ferri Avvolto nella Foglia di Vite

GRILLED GOAT CHEESE IN VINE LEAVES

WHEN I cook a full meal on the charcoal grill, goat cheese in a vine leaf wrapper is one of my customary appetizers. The zestful fragrance of the leaf diverts some of the cheese's sharpness, making it taste sweeter. No other seasoning is required, except for olive oil and black pepper. Grilling over coals is the most desirable way of doing this recipe, but one can manage satisfactorily with an indoor broiler.

For 6 to 8 persons

6 vine leaves, either fresh or packed in brine, 6 to 7 inches broad, if possible
1/3 cup extra virgin olive oil

1/2 pound goat cheese
Black pepper in a grinder

1. If using fresh vine leaves, wash them thoroughly, trim the stems down to 1 inch in length, then place them in a bowl of cold water to soak for at least 30 minutes. If using leaves packed in brine, rinse them well, then pat thoroughly dry.

2. Light the coals or turn on the broiler.

3. Choose a plate a little bit larger than a vine leaf and pour the olive oil onto it.

4. When the fresh leaves have soaked the required amount of time, drain them and pat them thoroughly dry with kitchen towels. If using brine-packed leaves, they are ready for the next step if you have rinsed and dried them.

5. Place a leaf on the plate with the oil, turning it over once or twice so that it is well coated.

6. Divide the cheese into 6 equal portions. Turn the vine leaf so that its duller, rougher side faces up, because it is the side that retains more oil. In the center of it place one of the portions of cheese, sprinkling over it a generous grinding of pepper.

7. Fold the sides of the leaf toward the center and over each other. Over them fold first the stem end and then the bottom end of the leaf. Fasten securely with a toothpick.

8. When all the leaves have been stuffed, place them on the hot grill with the side pierced by the toothpick facing down. If using an adjustable charcoal grill, try to keep the wrappers about 8 to 9 inches from the fire.

9. When the leaves begin to blacken and become charred in spots, turn them over on the other side until it also becomes dark. Remove from the grill then, and serve immediately.

AHEAD-OF-TIME NOTE: The vine leaves may be stuffed with cheese 1 to 2 hours before cooking and placed on the grill when the coals are well lit and have formed a white ash or when the broiler is hot.

Tartine con il Gorgonzola e i Pignoli

CANAPÉS WITH GORGONZOLA AND PINE NUTS

*T*HE idea for these canapés has a double origin: in the classic combination of Gorgonzola and nuts that in Italy is served at dinner's end and in the fact that the oven is very kind to Gorgonzola. The winning fresh-out-of-the-oven tastiness of these canapés conceals the fact that all the preparation can be done ahead of time.

12 canapés

4 tablespoons butter, softened to room
   temperature
5 ounces creamy Gorgonzola, cut into small
   pieces
2 tablespoons chopped fresh basil or parsley

1½ tablespoons chopped pine nuts
Black pepper in a grinder
1½ tablespoons whole pine nuts
6 slices good-quality, firm white bread trimmed
   of its crust

1. Turn on the oven to 400°.
2. Put the butter, Gorgonzola, basil or parsley, chopped pine nuts, and several grindings of pepper in a bowl. With a wooden spoon, mash all the ingredients until they form a smooth, dense cream. You can use a food processor, but it is likely to liquefy the mixture too much.
3. Mix the whole pine nuts into the creamy mixture.

4. Spread the mixture over the bread slices, leaving a rim of about ⅛ inch uncovered.
5. Place the bread on a baking sheet and toast in the upper level of the preheated oven until the bread becomes colored a light brown at the edges.
6. Cut each slice of bread diagonally into 2 triangles and allow to cool for a moment or so before serving.

SERVING SUGGESTIONS: Before dinner, with wine or other apéritifs, or as part of a buffet.

Uova Sode con Salsa Rossa

HARD-BOILED EGGS UNDER RED SAUCE

I AM EQUALLY fond of hard-boiled eggs and tomato sauce and, on a day that I felt like having nothing else, I put the two together.

Simple and straightforward as it is, the dish has turned out to be quite versatile. One can make of it, as I originally did, a light but satisfying lunch, or serve it as warm *antipasto*, or include it in a buffet.

4 or 8 portions

4 tablespoons extra virgin olive oil
½ cup chopped onion
1 cup chopped celery
1½ cups canned Italian peeled plum
    tomatoes, cut up, with their juice

Salt
Black pepper in a grinder
2 tablespoons fresh basil leaves, washed,
    shaken dry, and torn into small pieces
4 extra large hard-boiled eggs

1.   Choose a sauté pan that can subsequently accommodate the 4 eggs sliced in half in a single layer. Put in the oil and chopped onion, and turn on the heat to medium high.

2.   Sauté until the onion becomes translucent, then add the celery. Cook, stirring from time to time, until the celery is tender.

3.   Add the tomatoes with their juice and cook for 15 to 20 minutes, stirring occasionally, until you see the fat separating from the sauce. Add salt and liberal grindings of pepper. Stir, add the basil, and stir again.

4.   Shell the hard-boiled eggs, slice them in half lengthwise, and place them in the pan, yolk facing up. Spoon enough sauce over them to cover. Turn the heat down to medium, cover the pan, and cook for 2 minutes. Serve when lukewarm.

SERVING SUGGESTIONS: As part of a light, summer lunch or brunch. Also as part of a buffet.

Tonno sott'Olio Mantecato

TUNA SPREAD WITH CAPERS

A PAINTER friend who is as gifted a cook as he is an artist had asked me to have tea with him at a smart new Italian place on Madison Avenue. With tea we had little soft rolls with a buttery spread. My friend marveled over the spread, asked what it was and could I get him the recipe. "But it's so simple," I said. "It's just good canned tuna beaten with butter and capers." "Why have you never put it in a book?" he asked. "It's so simple that I paid no attention to it," I explained, "but if you like it that well, I'll put it in my next book."

This is the next book. The recipe is for Hector.

For 8 to 10 persons

Two 6½-ounce cans Italian-style tuna packed in olive oil
3 tablespoons capers

8 tablespoons unsalted butter, softened to room temperature

1. Drain the tuna of all the olive oil in which it was packed.
2. Put the tuna, capers, and butter in a food processor or blender and whip to a creamy consistency.

NOTE: Although this spread can be served in a bowl, it is more appealing when presented already spread on small rounds of soft bread. It should not be spread more than 30 minutes before serving. If it is made ahead of time and refrigerated, it should be taken out of the refrigerator at least 45 minutes ahead of time so that it can soften to its original creamy consistency. I like to garnish each canapé with a strip of raw red bell pepper or of tomato in the center, flanked with a caper on each side.

SERVING SUGGESTIONS: I usually serve this with a glass of wine to afternoon callers, or with a before-dinner apéritif. It makes a memorable tuna spread for sandwiches. It is fine enough for the table, as an appetizer.

Tortino di Melanzane col Pesto di Olive

FRIED EGGPLANT SLICES LAYERED WITH A PESTO OF GREEN OLIVES AND CAPERS

*E*GGPLANT is a marvelous mixer, maintaining its own identity while blending agreeably into almost any company. Here, layers of sweet fried eggplant are spread with a faintly tart, piquant coating with which they briefly macerate. Once fried, the dish is easily assembled.

For 4 or more persons, depending upon whether it is served as an appetizer or a vegetable course

About 2 pounds medium eggplants
Salt
Vegetable oil for frying
1 extra large hard-boiled egg
6 or 7 green olives, pitted

2 tablespoons capers
2 tablespoons chopped parsley
1 tablespoon wine vinegar
2 tablespoons extra virgin olive oil
Black pepper in a grinder

1. Peel the eggplants and cut them lengthwise into slices about ¼ inch thick. Spread them along the inside of a large colander set over a bowl and sprinkle generously with salt. Allow to stand for at least 1 hour to permit as much of their bitter liquid as possible to drain away. After 1 hour or more, remove the eggplant slices from the colander and pat thoroughly dry with paper towels.

2. Put enough vegetable oil in a skillet to come ⅓ inch up the side of the pan and turn on the heat to high. When the oil is hot, slip in as many eggplant slices as will fit without crowding. Fry them until they become colored a rich gold on both sides, but do not turn them over too often as they fry. When done, transfer them to a platter lined with paper towels to blot, and con-

tinue slipping more slices into the pan and frying them until all the eggplant is done. Allow to cool completely.

3. Shell the hard-boiled egg and chop it briefly in a food processor or blender. Add the pitted olives, capers, parsley, vinegar, oil, and several grindings of pepper. Do not chop too fine: the mixture should not be creamy but slightly chewy, composed of tiny bits bound by the puréed egg.

4. Line the bottom of a serving dish with a layer of cold fried eggplant. Spread over it a thin layer of the olive and capers mixture. Cover with another layer of eggplant topped with more mixture, and proceed thus until you have used up both eggplant and mixture. Serve at room temperature.

AHEAD-OF-TIME NOTE: The entire dish may be made a day in advance and refrigerated, but always bring to room temperature before serving.

SERVING SUGGESTIONS: As part of a buffet, as an appetizer before the first course, or to replace the first course of a fish dinner. As a vegetable side dish for a pork roast.

Sugo di Melanzana e Peperoni per Spaghetti Freddi

EGGPLANT AND PEPPERS DRESSING FOR SPAGHETTI SALAD

*I*F I HAD invented pasta salads I would hide. As it is, I am uncomfortable in recalling that it was after a recipe for pasta salad appeared in my preceding book, nearly a decade ago, that the item became a fixture of delicatessens and take-home food shops everywhere.

It is not the dish itself that is at fault. It is the use that has been made of it. Salads of homemade egg pasta, and particularly of any kind of stuffed pasta, are most of all abominable: only dry, factory pasta has the firmness required for salads. And any such salad that has first steeped in its condiments at the shop and is likely to steep hours more before it is consumed at home, one that has known the inside of one or more refrigerators before reaching the table, defeats the essence of pasta, which is immediacy of preparation and freshness of taste.

Here, for the record, is a version faithful to the original principles. The sauce is a zesty, lemon-accented mixture of roasted eggplant and roasted peppers. It would make, by itself, a savory appetizer, spread over grilled bread. As a condiment for pasta it works best with thin *spaghetti*, but could also be good with *fusilli*.

For 4 to 6 persons

1 medium eggplant
1 small to medium sweet red bell pepper
4 small scallions
¼ cup extra virgin olive oil

Salt
Black pepper in a grinder
2 tablespoons freshly squeezed lemon juice
1 tablespoon chopped parsley

1. Turn on the oven to 425°.
2. Wash the eggplant and place it on a baking sheet in the uppermost level of the oven. Turn the eggplant after 15 to 20 minutes, taking care not to puncture the skin. You do not want to lose any of the juices that help to make the eggplant tender and sweet as it cooks. Check the eggplant for tenderness after another 15 to 20 minutes. If it feels soft when pressed with a spoon, remove it from the oven.

3. As soon as the eggplant is cool enough to handle, cut off the stem and peel the eggplant. Starting at the cut end, separate the eggplant flesh into lengthwise strips, exposing the seeds. Remove as many of the seeds as come away easily.

4. Put the eggplant with its juices into a bowl and mash it with a fork to a creamy consistency.

5. Turn on the broiler and put in the red pepper (you can use aluminum foil over the broiling pan to keep it from becoming sticky with juices from the pepper). Turn the pepper from time to time until its skin is charred on all sides. Do not overcook because you want the pepper's flesh to be as firm as possible. When charred all around, put the pepper in a bag of heavy plastic or brown paper, close tightly, and set aside for 20 to 30 minutes, until the pepper is cool enough to handle.

6. Pull off the skin, split the pepper, remove the core and seeds, and cut the flesh into ¼-inch squares. Add these to the mashed eggplant.

7. Trim the root ends from the scallions, wash them, and chop them fine, including the green tips. Add them to the eggplant, together with the olive oil, salt, a liberal grinding of black pepper, lemon juice, and chopped parsley. Mix all the ingredients thoroughly.

NOTE: If you have a gas stove, both the eggplant and the pepper can be roasted directly over the burner. This quicker and tastier method is described on page 289.

AHEAD-OF-TIME NOTE: The dressing is best served the same day it is made because the longer it sits the less sweet and more sharp it becomes. If it is going to be served several hours after it is made, do not add anything to the mashed eggplant but the lemon juice. Mix in the other ingredients just before serving.

SERVING SUGGESTIONS: The eggplant and peppers mixture can be served on its own as a spread with drinks, or as an appetizer at table, or as a between-meals snack.

Putting the salad together:

1. Drop 1 pound thin *spaghetti* or *fusilli* into 3 to 4 quarts boiling salted water.

2. Cool a serving platter under cold running water for a minute or more. Wipe it completely dry, then moisten the bottom with a filmy coat of extra virgin olive oil.

3. When the pasta is done *al dente*—firm to the bite—drain immediately and transfer to the platter. Toss it repeatedly, thoroughly coating it with olive oil until it glistens. If necessary, add a few more drops of oil. Set aside to cool, but do not refrigerate.

4. When completely cool, toss the pasta with the sauce. Do not, however, toss with sauce much earlier than 30 minutes before serving.

NOTE: Rinsing pasta after cooking does its flavor and texture no good. I do not recommend it.

SERVING SUGGESTIONS: As the main course of a light summer lunch or as part of a buffet.

Zucchine all' Amalfitana con l'Aceto e la Menta

ZUCCHINI, AMALFI STYLE, WITH VINEGAR AND MINT

W*HAT* I find particularly appealing about this appetizer is the chewy, compact consistency of the zucchini rounds and the trio of heady, herbal, and tart fragrances issuing from the garlic, mint, and vinegar.

Pierino Jovene of Amalfi, whose recipe this is, would say that it could not be made with any mint except the small Neapolitan variety whose fine aroma highlights much southern cooking. Neapolitan mint would be my first choice, too, if I had it. Since I rarely do, nor, I imagine, do many of the users of this book, I am willing to compromise with any fresh mint rather than forgo the pleasure of the dish.

For 4 to 6 persons

2 pounds fresh, firm zucchini, as young and small as possible
Salt
4 garlic cloves, peeled and lightly mashed
1 to 2 tablespoons fresh mint leaves, torn by hand into bits

Vegetable oil for frying
3 tablespoons wine vinegar
2 tablespoons extra virgin olive oil
Black pepper in a grinder

1. Soak the zucchini in a large bowl of cold water for at least 20 minutes.
2. Rinse them thoroughly under running water, rubbing them briskly with your hands or a kitchen towel to remove any grit sticking to the skin.
3. Cut off and discard both ends of each zucchini and slice the zucchini into very thin rounds.
4. Place the zucchini slices in a colander over a platter or basin and sprinkle with 2 tablespoons fine salt. Mix well and allow to stand for at least 30 minutes to give the zucchini time to throw off as much liquid as possible.

5. Put the mashed garlic and crumbled mint leaves in a bowl large enough to contain all the zucchini later.
6. Put enough vegetable oil in a skillet to come ½ inch up the side of the pan and turn on the heat to medium high.
7. Remove the zucchini from the colander and pat them dry with kitchen or paper towels. When the oil is very hot, put as many of the sliced zucchini in the pan as will fit without much overlapping. Cook the zucchini rounds on both sides until each side has become colored a light golden brown.
8. Transfer them with a slotted spoon or

spatula to the bowl containing the garlic and mint and sprinkle with a little vinegar. Put another batch of raw zucchini in the pan and repeat the whole process. As you put more cooked zucchini in the bowl, sprinkle with more vinegar and mix well.

9. When all the zucchini are done and in the bowl, add the olive oil, mix well, taste and correct for salt, and sprinkle with 1 or 2 grindings of pepper. Serve lukewarm or at room temperature. The zucchini may also be served a day later, but they will have acquired a slightly sharper flavor.

NOTE: The zucchini can also be cooked over a charcoal grill. If grilling them, cut them into long, thin slices rather than into rounds. Place them in a tightly closing hinged double grill to make it easier to turn them over. They cook very quickly, so watch them carefully. As soon as they become spotted with brown specks on the side next to the fire, turn them over. Remove from the grill when they are lightly speckled on both sides, and marinate them as described above.

SERVING SUGGESTIONS: As an appetizer or even as a side vegetable dish in a meal featuring grilled or fried fish. As part of a buffet. If you are barbecuing, as part of an assortment of appetizers, along with *Bruschetta al Pomodoro* (page 32) and Grilled Goat Cheese in Vine Leaves (page 35).

Barchette di Zucchine Ripiene di Gamberi

ZUCCHINI BOATS STUFFED WITH SHRIMP

ZUCCHINI is the most talented vegetable. It can do nearly everything any other vegetable can do, often better, and besides it can turn into the most delectable container for a variety of stuffings: meat, rice, even other vegetables. I have found, through experimentation, that it has an elegant affinity for shellfish, compensating with its spry flavor for the slightly cloying touch of sweetness that characterizes the flesh of shrimp and lobster.

You'll find here that the zucchini are hollowed out, blanched, and split in two to resemble toy boats. The stuffing is chopped raw shrimp seasoned with garlic, olive oil, and parsley. It is all popped into the oven and in just minutes it is done, a grand little dish requiring only moderate effort and no particular skills.

For 4 to 6 persons

Zucchini Boats Stuffed with Shrimp (continued)

2 pounds small to medium young zucchini

1 pound shrimp, in their shells

½ cup toasted, unflavored bread crumbs

1 teaspoon garlic chopped very fine

2 tablespoons chopped parsley

⅓ cup extra virgin olive oil

Salt

Black pepper in a grinder

1 large egg

1. Soak the zucchini in cold water for 20 minutes. Drain and rinse well under cold running water, rubbing off any residue of soil from the skin with your hands. If you find there is still some soil embedded in the skin, peel the outer layer of skin lightly.

2. Drop the zucchini into boiling salted water. The moment the water returns to a boil, drain the zucchini, removing them gently from the pot with a large slotted spoon or spatula. Set aside to cool completely.

3. Trim the ends off and with a corer, or other narrow-bladed tool, scoop out the insides, taking care not to puncture the skin. Leave a wall about ¼ inch thick.

4. Turn on the oven to 450°.

5. Rinse the shrimp in cold water, shell them, and remove the dark vein from each. Chop them into pieces not bigger than a large pea.

6. Put the chopped shrimp in a bowl together with ¼ cup of the bread crumbs, the garlic, parsley, 2 tablespoons of the olive oil, salt, and grindings of pepper.

7. Separate the egg, set aside the white, and add the yolk to the bowl. Mix all the ingredients thoroughly.

8. Cut the zucchini in half lengthwise.

9. Choose a shallow baking pan that can accommodate all the zucchini in a single layer. Grease the bottom of the pan lightly with olive oil and place the zucchini on it cut side up. Sprinkle them lightly with salt.

10. Beat the egg white lightly and brush the insides of the zucchini with it.

11. Stuff the zucchini with the shrimp mixture, heaping them full enough, if possible, to form a slight mound.

12. Sprinkle the top of each boat with the remaining bread crumbs and pour the remaining olive oil over in a thin stream.

13. Place the boats in the uppermost level of the oven for 6 to 7 minutes, until the tops form a light, pale gold crust. Serve when lukewarm.

SERVING SUGGESTIONS: It takes the place of a first course in a fish dinner or, in a more elaborate meal, it can precede the first course. It is also an ideal buffet dish and, for a light lunch, it can serve as the principal course.

Maiale Tonnato

PORK LOIN WITH TUNA SAUCE

ONE is always learning, sometimes in unexpected ways. Some years ago, at a *trattoria* in the country, near Bologna, I called the owner over and berated him: "How dare you serve this as *vitello tonnato*!" I exclaimed. "It isn't veal, it's pork!" "Of course," he coolly replied. "I always make it with pork—it's tastier." I pointed out at the time that the fact that pork is also considerably cheaper must have entered his consciousness, although the questionable integrity of selling it as veal obviously did not. When I went home, however, I thought the idea intriguing enough to try it for myself, and indeed I found the result very good.

As I worked with it, I made changes from the classic veal recipe to suit the different taste of pork. I eliminated mayonnaise and, instead of blending anchovies into the sauce, I studded the pork with them. The fusion of pork and anchovy is so natural that it manifests itself as a single coherent flavor.

Distressed as I was by my experience at the *trattoria*, I am pleased by the dish that came out of it. I don't advise passing it off for what it isn't: veal's flavor is gentler and its texture markedly finer. But pork, if coarser, is undeniably more savory and, as long as one doesn't fob it upon one's friends or patrons as *vitello*, one can justifiably claim it is an admirable *tonnato*.

For 6 persons

2 to 2½ pounds boned pork loin
8 to 10 flat anchovy fillets
A larding needle or other long, narrow,
   pointed tool
1 medium onion, peeled
2 celery stalks, washed

1 medium carrot, peeled
21 ounces canned Italian-style tuna packed
   in olive oil
½ cup tiny capers
¼ cup freshly squeezed lemon juice
1½ cups extra virgin olive oil

1. Stud the meat deeply in several places with the anchovy fillets, using a larding needle or other long, narrow, pointed tool.

2. Choose a pot in which the meat will subsequently fit snugly. Put in enough water to cover the meat later, add the onion, celery, and carrot, turn on the heat to medium, and cover.

3. When the vegetables have cooked for 15 minutes at a low, steady boil, add the meat and cover the pot again.

4. When the water returns to a boil, turn the heat down to low. Simmer the meat for 1½ hours, then turn off the heat and allow the pork to cool completely in its liquid.

5. Drain the tuna and put it in a blender or

food processor together with the capers, lemon juice, and olive oil. Process to a runny consistency. Add more olive oil if too dense.

6. When the meat is cold and firm, cut it into slices as thin as possible.

7. Spread a tablespoon of the tuna sauce over the bottom of a deep serving platter. Cover with a layer of sliced pork and top the pork with a thin, covering layer of tuna sauce. Repeat the procedure until you have used up both the pork and the sauce, making sure that the topmost layer is sauce with no meat protruding.

8. Cover with foil or plastic wrap and refrigerate for at least 24 hours. Return to room temperature before serving.

SERVING SUGGESTIONS: Like *vitello tonnato*, this is perfect as the principal course of a summer lunch. Keep it in mind also when planning a buffet.

Sfogi in Saor

FRIED SOLE FILLETS MARINATED WITH ONIONS, VINEGAR, RAISINS, AND PINE NUTS

IMAGINE a summer night in Venice when fireworks spill out of an indigo sky as though they were fiery strands of gems tumbling from a great, overturned coffer. Imagine the lagoon beneath teeming with boats—gondolas, barges, rowboats, powerboats, ferries, yachts—glowing with thousands of trembling colored lanterns. It is the most glorious night of the year, the night of the Redeemer, *il Redentore*, when all Venice turns out to recall its deliverance from the plague, as it has always done on the third Saturday of July since the end of the sixteenth century.

Everyone who can get on a boat does. While waiting for the fireworks, which begin just before midnight, they dine on board their craft, no matter how small or crowded. Among the many dishes that will be laid out—some of the traditional ones are cold pasta and beans soup, *polenta*, roast duck—one that is a must on this night is *sfogi in saor*.

Sfogi is Venetian for *sogliola*: the small, firm-fleshed Adriatic sole, the world's finest flatfish. It is fried, then macerated for many hours in a marinade— *saor*—of browned, smothered onions, olive oil, vinegar, pine nuts, and raisins. It is one of the most savory inventions of the Venetian cuisine, itself a cause for celebrating.

The sole to choose should be the least flaky, most firm fleshed you have available. (If you have a copy of *More Classic Italian Cooking*, see the similar recipe for sardines on page 89.)

For 4 to 6 persons

1/4 cup seedless raisins
1 pound sole fillets
Vegetable oil
1 cup flour, spread on a platter or on a sheet
    of aluminum foil or wax paper
Salt

2 tablespoons extra virgin olive oil
1 large onion, sliced very thin, about 1 1/2 cups
1/2 teaspoon granulated sugar
1 cup red- or white-wine vinegar, diluted with
    1 tablespoon water
3 tablespoons pine nuts

1. Put the raisins to soak in a bowl with enough lukewarm water to cover.

2. Separate the sole fillets in half lengthwise, then cut them into 2 or 3 shorter pieces so that each piece is approximately 3 inches long.

3. Put enough vegetable oil into a frying pan to come 1/2 inch up the side of the pan, and turn on the heat to high.

4. Dry the fish fillets thoroughly with paper towels, then turn them lightly in the flour, shak-

ing off all excess flour. When the oil is hot, put them in the pan and brown them on both sides to a deep gold color. Using a slotted spatula or spoon transfer them to a platter lined with paper towels. Sprinkle with salt.

5. Discard the oil from the pan, wiping the pan clean with paper towels.

6. Put the olive oil in the pan, add the sliced onion, the sugar, and salt, cover, and turn on the heat to low. Cook for 15 to 20 minutes, stirring from time to time, until the onion is completely limp and fully cooked, but still pale in color. It will probably have thrown off some liquid.

7. Uncover the pan, raise the heat to medium, and boil off the liquid while cooking the onion further until it becomes a light nut brown.

8. Add the diluted vinegar, turn the heat up to high, and boil the vinegar for 3 to 4 minutes. Turn off the heat.

9. Drain the raisins and pat them dry with a kitchen towel.

10. Choose a deep dish in which the fish will fit snugly, even overlapping, and narrow enough so that the vinegar marinade won't be spread out too thin. Place the fish on the bottom, then, using a slotted spoon or spatula, transfer the onion from the pan, spreading it over the fish. Over the onion sprinkle the pine nuts and raisins, then pour over these all the contents of the pan. Cover the dish with plastic wrap.

11. Allow the fish to marinate for at least 12 hours before serving, but if you wait a full day it will taste even better. If serving within 12 hours, do not refrigerate. If serving the following day (it will keep perfectly for several days), put the dish in the refrigerator, but be sure to take it out 1 to 2 hours ahead of time so that it will be at room temperature when it is served.

SERVING SUGGESTIONS: Serve as an appetizer in a seafood meal if sole does not appear in other courses. It is a splendid buffet dish. For a light but savory lunch it can be the only dish, followed by salad and fruit.

Carciofini sott'Olio al Miele

PRESERVED ARTICHOKE HEARTS COOKED IN HONEY

*E*IGHT miles outside Bologna, in the farming town of Castel San Pietro, the Piana family makes some of Italy's finest honey. On a tasting call there, I was surprised not by the variety and quality of the honeys, of which I had had some prior knowledge, but by a family specialty served later at table: artichoke hearts cooked with vinegar and honey, then packed in olive oil. They are luscious beyond comparison with any other preserved artichokes I have known. They are ready to eat almost immediately or they will keep for months, if one can save them for that long. I have retouched the Pianas' original recipe, eliminating the white wine they add to the vinegar and honey. I find it diminishes the sumptuously mellow quality of this preparation.

Preserved Artichoke Hearts Cooked in Honey (continued)

3 medium artichokes

Freshly squeezed juice of ½ lemon

1 cup red-wine vinegar

2 tablespoons salt

2½ tablespoons honey

Extra virgin olive oil

1.   Trim the artichokes of all their tough leaves and tops, as described on page 80. Cut each trimmed artichoke into 6 sections, putting each wedge, as you cut it, into a bowl of water acidulated with the lemon juice.

2.   Put 2 cups water and the vinegar in a saucepan and bring them to a boil.

3.   Add the salt and the artichoke wedges and cover the pan. When the liquid resumes boiling, let it boil for 2 to 3 minutes, then put in the honey.

4.   Boil the artichokes for 4 more minutes, then drain them, and squeeze them thoroughly dry with kitchen towels. Set them aside to cool completely.

5.   Choose a screw-top jar (about 1 cup) in which the artichokes will fit tightly packed, put in the artichokes, pour in enough olive oil to cover, wait for it to settle, and add more oil if necessary. Screw on the top tightly.

NOTE: If you repeat the recipe within 10 to 14 days, save the oil and use it again, adding what fresh oil may be necessary.

STORING NOTE: Keep the jar in the refrigerator. The artichokes are ready to eat within a day, or they will easily last for 2 months or more. Remove them from the refrigerator in sufficient time before serving to allow the congealed olive oil to liquefy.

SERVING SUGGESTIONS: Serve alongside boiled or grilled meats. Place them in the center of a plate of cold meats served as an appetizer or making part of a buffet. Slice very thin and add to prosciutto in a sandwich. Also see Bolognese Pickled Onions (page 49), Pickled Raw Eggplant (page 51), and Eggplant Preserved in Oil (page 52).

Peperoncini sott'Olio

HOT RED PEPPERS PRESERVED IN OIL

*T*HESE peppers in oil provide a more succulent alternative to dried peppers, when fresh hot peppers are not available. Use them in any recipe of this or other Italian cookbooks that call for hot peppers. To the flavors of stews and pasta sauces, the tiny, tender rings of peppers add a high-pitched accent that will jab a nodding palate to attention. They can also be used as a condiment at the table whenever appropriate, as in a salad, for example. A few drops of only the olive oil in which they are put up often will supply all the fire one wants.

About 1 cup

½ pound fresh, hot peppers, preferably the small, red Italian ones, but also other varieties, such as *jalapeños*
2 tablespoons salt
A 1½-cup pickling jar with a tightly closing cover
A jar or water tumbler taller than the

pickling jar, but narrow enough to fit inside it
A weight, such as a heavy meat pounder or a stone
Extra virgin olive oil, if planning to use them within 6 months or, to keep them longer, vegetable oil

1.   Wash the peppers and remove their stems.
2.   Slit them lengthwise along one side to expose their seeds. Remove and discard as many of the seeds as you can.
3.   Cut the peppers crosswise into open rings about ⅛ inch thin.
4.   Place the rings in a bowl, add the salt, and mix well.
5.   Transfer the peppers to the pickling jar. Put the tumbler or narrower jar into the pickling jar, inserting it bottom end first. Turn both jars upside down over a bowl or deep dish.

Place the weight on top of them. The weight will press the contents of the pickling jar against the bottom of the narrower one, forcing liquid out of the peppers. Let stand for 24 hours.
6.   After 24 hours, turn the 2 jars right side up, remove the narrower one, and pour enough oil over the peppers to cover amply. Screw on or clamp on the cover of the jar. The peppers are ready to eat, but they are better after 1 week. You may refrigerate them, but they will also keep well in a cool, dark cupboard.

Cipolline sott'Aceto alla Bolognese

BOLOGNESE PICKLED ONIONS

WHEN serving Bologna's magnificent pork specialties—prosciutto, salami, *mortadella*—as *antipasto*, one usually accompanies them with an assortment of vegetables pickled in vinegar or preserved in olive oil. One of the most pleasing of such accompaniments are these home-pickled onions. There is a lively crunch to their consistency, and they have a judicious measure of tartness, enough to freshen the palate between helpings of meat, yet not so much to sting it. They are so easy to take that we even eat them on their own

Bolognese Pickled Onions (continued)

with good crusty bread. The onions are good within 48 hours of making, but they are even better after a month, when they are fully pickled and become colored an appealing purple.

13 to 14 small, flat white onions,
    1 to 1½ inches in diameter,
    about 6 ounces

1 quart water
2 tablespoons salt
Red-wine vinegar

1. Peel and wash the onions.
2. Bring the water to a boil. Add the salt.
3. When the water returns to a boil, put in the onions.
4. When the water begins to boil again— and make sure the heat is high enough so it doesn't take too long—cook the onions for less than 1 minute, at most 50 seconds.
5. Drain the onions, pat them thoroughly dry with kitchen towels, and allow to cool completely.
6. Choose a glass jar with a tight closure. When the onions are cold, put them in the jar, adding enough vinegar to cover amply.

❧ *PICKLED EGGPLANTS I &II* ❧

One of the vast and largely unexplored resources of Italian cooking are the home-pickled specialties of southern cooks. They merit a volume apart, which I leave to some future researcher. The following two recipes for eggplants and the preceding one for hot red peppers are a sample. I prepared them originally with the guidance of Elisa, a woman from Benevento who settled in my hometown of Cesenatico.

Eggplant recipe no. 1 yields a moister, spicier, more vinegary product, excellent as an accompaniment to boiled meats and quite zesty on its own.

Recipe no. 2 produces strips of eggplant that taste remarkably like wild *porcini* mushrooms and, besides being a lively accompaniment for a meat dish, they are delicious on their own, as an appetizer.

Both can be quite peppery, depending, of course, on the fieriness and quantity of the peppers you use. Elisa herself makes them blazing hot.

Neither of the two recipes works as well with the large eggplants as they do with the sweeter, skinny variety found in Italian, Chinese, and other markets.

Melanzane Conservate a Crudo

PICKLED RAW EGGPLANT

About 2¼ pounds eggplant, the long, skinny
   variety
5 or 6 small, hot, fresh red peppers,
   about 2½ inches long and ½ inch thick
About 2 dozen fresh mint leaves
6 garlic cloves, peeled and mashed
A 3-cup pickling jar with an opening large
   enough to push your fist through

Salt
A jar or tumbler taller than the pickling jar,
   but narrow enough to fit inside it
A weight, such as a heavy meat pounder or
   a stone
1 cup red-wine vinegar
Extra virgin olive oil

1.   Wash the eggplants in cold water, remove the stem, cut the eggplants into pieces about 3 inches long, and slice these lengthwise as thin as possible: The slices should be less than ¼ inch thick.

2.   Wash the peppers, remove their stems, and cut them into 1-inch lengths.

3.   Wash the mint leaves and shake them as dry as possible.

4.   Cover the bottom of the pickling jar with a layer of eggplant, 1 or 2 mint leaves, a piece of pepper, and a bit of garlic. Sprinkle with salt. Repeat the operation, sprinkling salt over each layer of eggplant. As you build up the layers, press them hard toward the bottom of the jar with your fist or fingers. You will soon see that the eggplant begins to shed water.

5.   When you have used up the eggplant and all the other ingredients, place the second jar or tumbler into the pickling jar, putting it in bottom end first. Turn the 2 jars upside down over a bowl and put the weight on top of them. The weight will press the contents of the pickling jar against the bottom of the narrower, taller jar, forcing them to shed their liquid into the bowl. Let stand for 24 hours.

6.   After 24 hours, turn the 2 jars right side up, remove the narrower one, and pour the vinegar over the eggplant. Place the narrower jar inside the pickling jar, turn them upside down again, put the weight on top, and let stand for 12 hours, allowing excess vinegar to run off into the bowl.

7.   After 12 hours, turn the jars right side up, remove the narrower, taller jar, pour enough olive oil over the eggplant to cover amply, and cover the pickling jar tightly. Refrigerate.

NOTE: The eggplant is ready to eat the moment the process described above is completed, but it will keep perfectly in the refrigerator for several months.

Melanzane sott'Olio

EGGPLANT PRESERVED IN OIL

2 pounds eggplant, the long, skinny variety
Salt
Cheesecloth
2 to 3 tablespoons chopped fresh mint leaves
1 tablespoon chopped garlic, or more to taste
1 teaspoon oregano

2 tablespoons wine vinegar
A pickling jar
2 small, hot, fresh red peppers, or more
   to taste
Extra virgin olive oil

1.   Detach the stem from the eggplants and peel them. Cut the flesh into strips 2 to 3 inches long and ¼ inch thick. Place them in a bowl together with ¼ cup salt. Toss thoroughly and set aside to steep for 12 to 16 hours.

2.   When the eggplant has macerated the recommended length of time, it will have thrown off much liquid. Drain it, place it in cheesecloth, and twist tightly to force out all liquid still in the eggplant.

3.   Remove the eggplant from the cheesecloth and put it in a bowl. Add the mint, garlic, oregano, and 1 tablespoon of vinegar. Toss thoroughly and at length.

4.   Place the eggplant in a pickling jar, laying the strips flat facing the bottom of the jar. If the diameter of the jar cannot accommodate the strips lying completely flat, it does not matter; allow their ends to curve up along the sides of the jar. Any seasoning left over in the bowl should go into the jar along with the eggplant. In between several layers of eggplant, place the hot peppers.

5.   With a pestle or the back of a spoon gently press the eggplant down a little. Add the remaining tablespoon of vinegar and enough olive oil to cover amply. Cover tightly and place in the refrigerator. If after a few hours you find that the olive oil level has dropped below the topmost layer of eggplant, add more oil.

NOTE: The eggplant is ready to eat the moment it is done, but it becomes richer in flavor with time. It can keep in the refrigerator 3 to 4 months, but always return it to room temperature before using. If you are making a larger quantity than the recipe and would like it to keep for as long as a year, substitute a good vegetable oil, such as safflower, for olive oil.

Insalata di Gamberi

SHRIMP SALAD WITH CELERY, OLIVES, AND TOMATOES

*C*ELERY, its stalk cut into skinny strips, makes this one of the freshest tasting of shrimp salads. The tomato is also cut into strips, matching the celery.

For 4 to 6 persons

2 dozen medium shrimp, in their shells
Salt
3 tablespoons wine vinegar
2 cups celery stripped of its strings and cut into strips about 1½ inches long and ¼ inch thick
1 cup fresh, ripe plum tomatoes peeled as suggested on page 21, seeded, and cut into strips similar to the celery
6 to 8 Greek-style olives, pitted and cut into strips about ¼ inch thick
2 tablespoons chopped parsley
Black pepper in a grinder
⅓ cup extra virgin olive oil

1. Wash the shrimp in cold water.
2. Bring a pot of water to a boil. Add 1 tablespoon of salt and 1 tablespoon of the vinegar. Put in the shrimp. One minute after the water returns to a boil, drain the shrimp. As soon as they are cool enough to handle, shell them, devein them, and put them in a serving bowl.

3. Add the celery, tomatoes, olives, and parsley to the bowl. Season with a liberal grinding of pepper, the olive oil, and the remaining 2 tablespoons of vinegar. Toss thoroughly. Add salt to taste only when ready to serve; otherwise the salt will draw too much juice from the tomatoes and make the salad watery.

AHEAD-OF-TIME NOTE: Except for the addition of salt, the salad can be prepared several hours in advance and, if necessary, refrigerated. It should, however, be brought back to room temperature before serving.

SERVING SUGGESTIONS: It makes a most refreshing one-course lunch, but it is also an elegant replacement for a first course in a seafood meal, as long as the second course does not have shrimp.

Insalata di Riso e Gamberetti

RICE AND SHRIMP SALAD

To the natural coupling of shrimp and rice one adds tomato, bell pepper, and cucumber. The vegetables are all diced small to favor maximum absorption and interaction of flavor, a feature of this salad that becomes even more prominent if it is allowed to macerate for 1 hour or more. Add the salt only just before serving.

For 6 persons

2½ cups long-grain rice
Salt
½ cup extra virgin olive oil
1 pound tiny shrimp, in their shells
2 tablespoons wine vinegar
1 large ripe, firm tomato; or 2 medium
   tomatoes, enough to yield, when diced,
   about 1½ cups

1 sweet bell pepper, preferably yellow, but if
   unavailable, red
1 cucumber
3 tablespoons capers
Black pepper in a grinder

1.   Pour the rice into a pot of boiling salted water and cook, stirring from time to time, until tender yet firm to the bite. Drain and place in a bowl, mixing in 2 tablespoons of the olive oil. Set aside to cool.

2.   Rinse the shrimp in cold water. Bring a pot of water to a boil, add 3 tablespoons of salt and the vinegar, then put in the shrimp. If the shrimp are very tiny, they will be done a moment before the water begins to boil again. If slightly larger, wait until the water has resumed a full boil. Drain and set aside to cool.

3.   Wash the tomato or tomatoes in cold water and cut it into ½-inch cubes, discarding all seeds. You need about 1½ cups.

4.   Wash the bell pepper, open it, remove the stem and the core with all its seeds, and cut the flesh into ½-inch squares. The yield should be approximately 1⅓ cups.

5.   Peel the cucumber, split it in half to scoop out the seeds, and dice it into ½-inch cubes. It should yield about 1⅓ cups.

6.   Shell the shrimp and remove the dark vein. If tiny, leave whole. If a little larger, split in half lengthwise.

7.   To the bowl containing the rice add the shrimp, tomato, pepper, cucumber, and capers. Toss thoroughly with the remaining olive oil. Just before serving, add salt and grindings of pepper to taste, and toss again.

SERVING SUGGESTIONS: See preceding recipe.

THE VEGETABLE TORTA:
TWO VERSIONS WITH SPINACH

A *torta* can take a vegetable dish well on the way to being a complete meal. The two examples given here are both made with spinach and rice and would appear to be quite similar. Yet they illustrate what small adjustments need to be made in the *torta* method to achieve substantial differences in result.

The first *torta* starts with a flavor base of diced tomatoes sautéed in butter, *pancetta,* and garlic to which one adds the spinach raw. After a few minutes' cooking, one puts in the rice, which is cooked like a *risotto* until it is partly done. When cool, the rice, spinach, and toma-toes are mixed with egg, Parmesan, and nutmeg, and the *torta* is ready for baking.

In the second recipe, a Piedmontese specialty, spinach or chard is blanched and the rice is boiled separately. They are then *insaporiti* together—coated with a flavor base of onion sautéed in butter and olive oil. When cool, they are mixed, like the batch from the preceding *torta,* with egg, Parmesan, and nutmeg, but some Parmesan is held back for sprinkling on top of the *torta* when it goes into the oven.

The first is somewhat moister and more savory. The second is subtler, less rustic in taste.

Torta di Spinaci

SPINACH TORTA

For 4 to 6 persons

1½ pounds fresh spinach
4 tablespoons vegetable oil
5 tablespoons butter
1 large or 2 medium ripe tomatoes, skinned raw with a peeler and diced into ¼-inch cubes; or 1 cup canned Italian peeled plum tomatoes, drained and diced
¼ cup chopped *pancetta*
1 teaspoon chopped garlic
Salt

⅔ cup raw rice, unwashed
1½ cups Homemade Meat Broth (page 73), or ¾ cup canned beef broth diluted with ¾ cup water
A 10-inch springform pan
½ cup toasted, unflavored bread crumbs
4 eggs
½ cup freshly grated *parmigiano-reggiano* (Parmesan)
¼ teaspoon grated nutmeg

1. Trim away the thicker part of the spinach stems. Soak the spinach for 5 to 6 minutes in a large basin of cold water. Scoop the spinach out, throw out the water and the soil deposit, refill the basin with fresh water, and put the spinach back to soak. Continue to soak in fresh

Spinach Torta (continued)

changes of water until no more soil settles at the bottom of the basin. Drain, cut the spinach into large pieces, and set aside.

2.   Choose a pot that can subsequently accommodate the spinach, tomatoes, and rice, put in the vegetable oil and 2 tablespoons of the butter, turn on the heat to high, and put in the tomatoes. Sauté the tomatoes for about 2 minutes.

3.   Add the *pancetta* and the chopped garlic and continue sautéing for 2 to 3 minutes, stirring frequently.

4.   Add the spinach and salt and cook, stirring from time to time, until the spinach wilts.

5.   Add the rice. Cook it in the uncovered pan, stirring frequently and moistening it from time to time with a little broth, until the rice is half done, about 15 minutes. It should be tender enough to be chewable, but with a hard, chalky core. Pour the entire contents of the pot into a bowl and allow to cool completely.

6.   Turn on the oven to 375°.

7.   Smear a 10-inch springform pan with a tablespoon of butter and dust with 2 tablespoons of the bread crumbs.

8.   When the ingredients in the bowl are cold, add the eggs, beating them in thoroughly one at a time. Add the remaining tablespoons of butter, grated cheese, and nutmeg and mix well. Taste and correct for salt.

9.   Transfer the contents of the bowl to the springform pan and sprinkle the top with 2 tablespoons of the bread crumbs. Bake in the uppermost level of the preheated oven for 50 to 60 minutes. The *torta* is done when a toothpick poked into it comes out dry.

10.   Unhinge and remove the side band of the pan. When the *torta* becomes a little cooler and firmer, loosen it from the bottom piece of the pan and transfer it to a serving platter. Serve lukewarm.

SERVING SUGGESTIONS: A delicious choice for a simple lunch, preceded by a plate of good, cold, boiled ham or prosciutto, mild salami, or other cold meats accompanied by pickled vegetables. It is clearly a good choice for a buffet.

La *"Turta" di Spinaci e Riso*

SPINACH AND RICE TORTA

For 6 persons

2 pounds fresh spinach, or young, narrow-stalked Swiss chard, or the leaves from mature Swiss chard
Salt
1 heaping cup long-grain rice
4 tablespoons butter, plus additional butter for smearing the baking pan
¼ cup extra virgin olive oil

½ cup chopped onion
½ cup freshly grated *parmigiano-reggiano* (Parmesan)
⅛ teaspoon grated nutmeg
4 eggs
Black pepper in a grinder
A 10-inch springform pan
¼ cup toasted, unflavored bread crumbs

1. If using spinach, first cut off and discard the root end holding the leaves together. Soak spinach or chard in a basin full of cold water for 5 to 6 minutes. Lift the greens out of the water, empty the basin, and refill the basin. Wash the greens in several changes of fresh cold water, always lifting out the leaves before pouring out the water, until no more soil settles to the bottom.

2. Put the clean spinach or chard in a pot with no other water than what clings to the leaves, add salt, cover, and turn on the heat to medium. Cook until tender, drain, and, when cool enough to handle, squeeze dry with your hands and cut up into coarse bits.

3. In another pot bring water to a boil and add salt. When the water resumes boiling, drop in the rice and cook until tender but still a bit firm. Drain and set aside.

4. Turn on the oven to 450°.

5. Put 2 tablespoons of the butter, the oil, and the chopped onion in a sauté pan and turn on the heat to medium. When the onion becomes colored a pale gold, add the cut-up greens and the rice. Cook, stirring frequently, for 3 to 4 minutes, until all the ingredients are coated thoroughly, then transfer the contents of the pan to a bowl and let cool.

6. When cool, add ¼ cup of the grated cheese, the nutmeg, and the eggs, mixing these in one at a time. Mix in several grindings of pepper, then taste and correct for seasoning.

7. Smear the inside of the baking pan with butter and sprinkle with the bread crumbs. Turn the pan upside down and rap it against the work counter to shake off excess bread crumbs. Add these crumbs to the remaining ¼ cup of grated cheese.

8. Put the rice and spinach or chard mixture into the pan, leveling it off evenly. Sprinkle the grated cheese and bread crumbs on top. Dot with the remaining 2 tablespoons of butter and place in the uppermost level of the preheated oven. Bake for 15 minutes, or until a light crust forms on top. Allow the "*turta*" time to cool until just lukewarm before serving.

AHEAD-OF-TIME NOTE: The entire dish may be assembled several hours before baking, but tastes best if not refrigerated. Dot with butter just before putting it in the oven.

SERVING SUGGESTIONS: See preceding recipe.

Zucchine Ripiene di Tonno

ZUCCHINI STUFFED WITH TUNA

WHEN I first came across this recipe, I had already started working on sauces in which tuna was not cooked: see the *fettuccine* on page 97 and the *penne* on page 130. I was reluctant to do anything with cooked tuna and decided to pass it up. As I thought about it longer, however, it seemed to me it might be good, my own rule notwithstanding, and so I tried it. The dish turned out to be both new and pleasing. For the stuffing, the tuna is mixed with parsley and Parmesan and, once the zucchini are browned, the pan

Zucchini Stuffed with Tuna (continued)

juices are used with fresh tomatoes to make a spirited, engagingly simple sauce. Although it is cooked, the tuna does not have the harsh taste I like to avoid, because it is insulated by the zucchini walls and does not dry out.

For 4 to 6 persons

1½ pounds fresh, firm zucchini, preferably young and small, soaked in cold water for 20 minutes
1 to 1¼ pounds fresh, ripe plum tomatoes
¼ cup tightly packed crumb (the soft, crustless part) from good-quality bread
2 tablespoons chopped parsley

⅓ cup freshly grated *parmigiano-reggiano* (Parmesan)
7 ounces Italian-style tuna packed in olive oil, drained
Black pepper in a grinder
⅓ cup extra virgin olive oil
Salt

1.   Wash the tomatoes, drop them into boiling water, and drain after 1 to 2 minutes. When cool enough to handle, peel them. Split them in half lengthwise, remove the seeds, and cut up the tomatoes into small pieces.

2.   When the zucchini have finished soaking, wash them in several changes of cold water, scrubbing their skin vigorously with your hands or with a stiff brush to dislodge all grit.

3.   Cut off and discard both ends from each zucchini. Cut the zucchini in half to obtain pieces no longer than 4 to 5 inches.

4.   Scoop out the zucchini flesh, leaving only the vegetable's thin outer wall, taking care not to puncture it. Keep ½ cup of the flesh and chop it fine.

5.   Soak the soft crumb in water, squeeze it tightly in your hand to force out as much liquid as possible, and put it in a bowl. Add the chopped parsley, grated cheese, tuna, chopped zucchini flesh, and several liberal grindings of pepper.

Mix thoroughly with a fork, combining all the ingredients into a homogeneous mixture. Stuff the mixture into the hollowed-out zucchini.

6.   Choose a sauté pan or skillet where the zucchini can subsequently fit without overlapping. Put in the olive oil and turn on the heat to high. When the oil is hot but not smoking, slip in the zucchini. Brown the zucchini all around, then transfer them with a slotted spoon to a platter. A little of the stuffing may drop out of the zucchini while you are browning them. Do not be concerned; just leave it in the pan.

7.   Add the cut-up tomatoes to the pan and turn down the heat to medium. Cook for 10 minutes, stirring occasionally.

8.   Return the zucchini to the pan, sprinkle with salt, and cook until they are tender but still a little firm. The time will vary depending on the freshness and age of the zucchini: If they are small and freshly picked, it may take no more than 6 to 8 minutes.

AHEAD-OF-TIME NOTE: The entire dish may be prepared in advance and reheated gently just before serving. To avoid loss and change of flavor, I suggest cooking the zucchini no earlier than the morning if they are to be served the evening of the same day.

SERVING SUGGESTIONS: A flavorful and one-dish meal. I'd follow it with a salad such as the *Finocchio* and Red Pepper on page 285.

Teglia di Cozze, Patate e Pomodori al Forno

MUSSELS BAKED WITH POTATOES AND FRESH TOMATOES

*I*T IS A COMMON thing to serve potatoes as an accompaniment to fish. I like to go further and cook them *with* fish, whose flavor they lengthen and underscore. In this baked mussel platter, potatoes are joined with another ingredient that is particularly compatible with seafood, and with mussels to an exceptional degree—tomatoes.

The mussel meat is coated with a mixture of olive oil, garlic, parsley, bread crumbs, and Parmesan; the potatoes are boiled and sliced; the tomatoes are raw. The three are layered in a baking dish, the tomatoes uppermost, barely disclosing the saffron-colored mussel meat beneath. Cheery looking, and cheering to eat.

For 4 to 6 persons

3 pounds fresh mussels
1 pound potatoes
6 tablespoons extra virgin olive oil
3 tablespoons chopped parsley
1 tablespoon chopped garlic
¼ cup toasted, unflavored bread crumbs

¼ cup freshly grated *parmigiano-reggiano* (Parmesan)
Black pepper in a grinder
10 ounces fresh, ripe plum tomatoes
Salt

1. Soak the mussels in a sink or basin of cold water. Pull away each mussel's protruding tuft of fibers, grasping it with your fingers. If the edge of the mussel shell is sharp and cutting, use a piece of thin cloth to grasp the tuft.

2. Wash the mussels in at least 5 changes of clean, cold water, rubbing one against the other or scrubbing them with a stiff brush.

3. Put the mussels in a tightly lidded pot without any water and turn on the heat to medium high. As soon as the shells open, which may happen very quickly, drain the mussels and set them aside to cool.

4. Wash the potatoes and boil them with their skins on.

5. Turn on the oven to 450°.

6. When the mussels have cooled enough to handle, detach the meat from the shell and put it in a bowl. Add 3 tablespoons of the olive oil, the chopped parsley, chopped garlic, 2 tablespoons of the bread crumbs, 2 tablespoons of the grated cheese, and several grindings of pepper and mix well.

7. Wash the tomatoes and skin them with a peeler. (Do not plunge them into boiling water— it would make them soggy.) Cut them in half

Mussels Baked with Potatoes and Fresh Tomatoes (continued)

lengthwise, remove the seeds, cut them lengthwise into 1/4-inch-wide strips, and place them in a colander to drain.

8.　When the potatoes are done, drain them, peel them, and cut them into 1/4-inch-thick slices. It doesn't matter if the slices break up a little.

9.　Choose a 13 by 9-inch oven-to-table baking dish (or its equivalent) and smear the bottom with 1 tablespoon of the olive oil. Cover the bottom with a layer of potatoes, preferably without too much overlapping, but use up all the potatoes. Sprinkle with salt. Cover the potatoes with a layer of mussels and all the seasoning in their bowl. Sprinkle lightly with salt. Top with the tomato strips. Do not add salt. Sprinkle with the rest of the bread crumbs and grated cheese and pour over it the remaining olive oil in a thin, uniformly distributed stream.

10.　Bake in the uppermost level of the preheated oven for 15 to 18 minutes, until the top begins to form a pale brown crust. Remove from the oven and allow to settle for at least 5 minutes before serving.

SERVING SUGGESTIONS: It can replace the first course of a seafood meal. It can be the only course for lunch or an informal dinner, followed by a salad of greens and then fresh fruit or ice cream. It would be a most attractive part of a warm buffet.

Sformato di Patate e Vongole

POTATO AND CLAM PUDDING

MY FONDNESS for cooking seafood and potatoes together has been disclosed elsewhere in this book (see pages 59 and 181). Here is another example.

Clam meat is chopped fine and quickly *insaporita*—flavor coated—with garlic and parsley sautéed in olive oil and its own boiled-down juices. Potatoes are boiled and mashed through a food mill or ricer. The two are mixed and baked, with bread crumbs, in an ovenproof serving dish.

For 4 to 6 persons

1 dozen littleneck clams
1/2 cup water
1 1/2 pounds boiling potatoes
1/2 cup extra virgin olive oil,
　　plus 1 1/2 tablespoons
2 teaspoons garlic chopped very fine

2 tablespoons chopped parsley
Black pepper in a grinder
Salt
1/2 cup fine, dry, unflavored bread crumbs,
　　toasted lightly in a pan as described on
　　page 21

1. Wash the clams in many changes of cold water, scrubbing every shell, one against the other or with a stiff brush.

2. Choose a broad, shallow pot with a lid. Put in the ½ cup of water and the clams, cover the pot, and turn on the heat to high. Turn the clams over from time to time. As soon as any clam unclenches its shell, transfer it to a bowl, using tongs or a slotted spoon.

3. When all the clams have opened up and have been put into a bowl, pour the juices from the pan into another bowl, pouring with care to leave as much sand as possible behind.

4. Detach the clam meat from the shells. Put it in the bowl containing the clam juice, swish it lightly to rinse it of any sand, then put it on a cutting board and chop all the clam meat rather fine.

5. Filter the clam juice through a strainer lined with a paper towel. Put the chopped clams into the filtered juice.

6. Turn on the oven to 450°.

7. Wash the potatoes and put them in a pot with enough water to cover amply. Turn on the heat to medium and bring to a boil.

8. While the potatoes are cooking, put the ½ cup of olive oil and the chopped garlic in a skillet or sauté pan. Turn on the heat to medium and cook until the garlic becomes colored a very pale nut brown. Add the parsley quickly, stir once or twice, then add the chopped clams with their juice. Raise the heat and cook, stirring frequently, until the clam juice has evaporated and the only liquid left is olive oil. Remove from the heat.

9. When the potatoes are done, drain them and peel them as soon as you are able to handle them. Pass them through a food mill fitted with a disk with small holes or through a potato ricer. Do not use a food processor or a blender because it would make the potato mash gluey.

10. Add to the potatoes the entire contents of the pan in which the clams were sautéed. Mix thoroughly to obtain a uniform blend of all the ingredients. Add several grindings of pepper and taste and correct for salt.

11. Coat the bottom of an oven-to-table baking dish with a thin film of olive oil, using a tablespoon or less. Sprinkle the bread crumbs over the oil. Turn the dish over onto a sheet of wax paper or foil and give it a sharp rap to shake off all loose crumbs.

12. Put the potato and clam mixture in the baking dish, distributing it evenly with a spatula. Over it sprinkle the leftover bread crumbs and pour on the remaining olive oil in a thin stream, making a crisscross pattern. Place in the uppermost level of the preheated oven and bake for 15 to 20 minutes. Allow to settle for a few minutes before serving.

AHEAD-OF-TIME NOTE: The entire dish may be assembled several hours in advance of baking and serving.

SERVING SUGGESTIONS: It would be a well-chosen part of a seafood buffet offering both warm and cold dishes. It also makes an appetizing light lunch.

Risotto Infornato con le Melanzane

BAKED RISOTTO WITH EGGPLANTS

SOME food scholars believe that, on its way to Italy from Asia, rice first stopped in Sicily. *Risotto* has since become more firmly established in the north, but Sicilian cooks have their own versions, such as this one.

The first stage of the dish consists of making a *risotto* with tomatoes and white wine. When done it is allowed to cool, then it is layered with fried eggplant, Parmesan, *romano,* and mozzarella and baked in the oven. It is a dense, richly savory dish, more like a country vegetable pie, a *torta rustica,* than a conventional *risotto.*

For 6 persons

2 to 2½ pounds eggplants,
     preferably the small, skinny ones
Salt
Vegetable oil for frying
3 to 4 tablespoons onion chopped fine
4 tablespoons butter, plus additional butter
     for dotting the completed dish
1½ cups canned Italian peeled plum
     tomatoes, cut up, with their juice
2 tablespoons chopped parsley
2 tablespoons chopped fresh basil

1½ cups Homemade Meat Broth (page 73),
     or ¾ cup canned beef broth diluted with
     ¾ cup water
1⅓ cups Italian Arborio rice
⅔ cup dry white wine
Black pepper in a grinder
⅓ cup freshly grated *pecorino romano*
⅔ cup freshly grated *parmigiano-reggiano*
     (Parmesan)
½ pound mozzarella, diced into ¼-inch cubes

1. Cut off the eggplants' green stem, peel them, and cut them lengthwise into ¼-inch-thick slices.

2. Stand the slices along the sides of a deep colander, sprinkle with salt, and place the colander over a bowl or basin. Allow the eggplant to rest for at least 30 minutes until most of its liquid runs off.

3. Pour enough vegetable oil in a frying pan to come ½ inch up the side of the pan. Turn on the heat to high.

4. Pat the eggplant slices thoroughly dry on both sides with a kitchen towel; when the oil is hot, slip them into the pan.

5. Turn the heat down slightly to medium high and cook the eggplant until it becomes colored a light golden brown.

6. With a slotted spoon or spatula transfer the eggplant to a platter lined with paper towels to drain. When the excess oil has been blotted by the paper, the eggplant can be stacked on a clean, dry plate.

7. Choose a heavy-bottomed pot suitable for making *risotto,* preferably an enameled cast-iron one, put in the chopped onion, 2 tablespoons of the butter, and 2 tablespoons of vegetable oil, and turn on the heat to medium high.

8. Sauté the onion until it becomes colored a pale gold.

9. Add the cut-up tomatoes with their juice

and turn down the heat to low. Cook for about 10 minutes, stirring from time to time.

10. Add the parsley and basil. Stir 2 or 3 times, then transfer a little more than two-thirds of the contents of the pot to a bowl.

11. Bring the broth to a simmer in a saucepan over medium-low heat.

12. Put the rice in the pot where you cooked the tomatoes and turn up the heat to medium high. Stir the rice for a few seconds until it is well coated, then put in the wine.

13. Cook, uncovered, stirring from time to time, until the wine has evaporated, then add a ladleful of simmering broth. Stir steadily until all the liquid of the broth has evaporated, then add another ladleful and continue stirring. Proceed in this manner, adding broth when necessary —if you run out of broth, continue with water— and stirring constantly to keep the rice from sticking to the pot, until the *risotto* is done. It should be tender, but firm: *al dente*. Altogether, it should take about 25 to 30 minutes. Add several grindings of pepper and a pinch of salt, taking into account that some saltiness will be contributed by the grated cheeses.

14. Spread the *risotto* on a platter to cool.

15. Turn on the oven to 400°.

16. Grease the bottom of a deep oven-to-table baking dish lightly with butter. Spread a 1-inch-high layer of rice on the bottom. Cover the rice with fried eggplant slices. Pour a little of the sauce from the bowl over the eggplant, then some grated *pecorino*, grated Parmesan, and diced mozzarella. Cover with another layer of rice and with the other ingredients in the sequence described above. The topmost layer may be either rice or eggplant, as works out best for you, but either way it should be sprinkled with grated Parmesan and dotted with the remaining 2 tablespoons of butter.

17. Bake for 10 to 12 minutes in the uppermost layer of the oven, until the cheese melts and forms a light, golden crust. Serve directly from the baking dish, after allowing it to settle for at least 5 minutes.

AHEAD-OF-TIME NOTE: The recipe may be prepared through step 6 as far as a day in advance and through step 16 as far in advance as the morning for the evening.

SERVING SUGGESTIONS: Serve as a single-course meal for lunch or an informal dinner. It is exceptionally suited to a hot buffet.

Tegame di Verza e Maiale al Forno

BAKED LAYERED SAVOY CABBAGE AND PORK

*T*HINK of this dish as a sort of *lasagne*, in which parboiled and flattened Savoy cabbage leaves replace the pasta, and sautéed ground pork takes the place of the meat sauce. As in *lasagne*, there is the aroma of nutmeg and, to bind the components, grated Parmesan and béchamel. Its season is late in the year, when outside it is cold and inside you want something warming.

For 6 persons

Baked Layered Savoy Cabbage and Pork (continued)

2 to 2½ pounds Savoy cabbage
Salt
2 tablespoons butter, plus additional butter
   for dotting the baking dish

1 tablespoon vegetable oil
1 pound ground pork containing at least
   25 percent fat
Black pepper in a grinder

For the béchamel:

1 cup milk
2 tablespoons butter

1½ tablespoons flour
⅛ teaspoon salt

⅛ teaspoon grated nutmeg
⅔ cup freshly grated *parmigiano-reggiano*
   (Parmesan)

1.   Detach from the cabbage head as many leaves as possible without tearing them or breaking them up. To do so, make a horizontal incision at the base of the leaves where they are joined to the root. Loosen the leaves, one by one, pulling them away gently from the bottom where you've made the incision. When you get to the heart of the head, the leaves may be too tightly curled into each other to separate; at that point, cut the heart into quarters from top to bottom.

2.   Soak all the leaves and heart in a basin of cold water while you bring a pot of 6 to 8 quarts of water to a boil. When the water comes to a boil, add 1 tablespoon salt. When the water resumes boiling, drop in the largest of the leaves. Boil for 5 minutes, then transfer the leaves to a colander, using a large slotted spoon. Drop the remaining, smaller leaves and heart into the pot. Since they are more tender, boil them for only about 3 minutes, then transfer them to the colander.

3.   Put the 2 tablespoons of butter and the vegetable oil in a medium-size sauté pan and turn on the heat to medium. When the fat is hot, add the ground pork. Crumble it with a fork,

sprinkle with salt and grindings of black pepper, and cook, turning it from time to time, until it is browned all over. Turn off the heat.

4.   Make the béchamel as described on page 112, put it in a bowl, and add the browned meat with all its pan juices. Add the nutmeg, all but 2 tablespoons of the grated cheese, and mix thoroughly. Taste and correct for salt and pepper.

5.   Turn on the oven to 400°.

6.   Smear the bottom of an oven-to-table baking dish with butter. Line the bottom with a layer of cabbage leaves. Spread enough of the pork and béchamel mixture over the cabbage to cover it thinly. Repeat the operation, alternating layers of cabbage leaves with coatings of pork until you have used up both ingredients. The heart of the cabbage can be spread open, flattened and used like the other leaves. You can end with a top layer of either cabbage or pork, but it is slightly better if it is the pork.

7.   Sprinkle the remaining 2 tablespoons of grated cheese over the top and dot with tiny dabs of butter. Bake in the uppermost level of the preheated oven for 20 minutes. Allow to settle for at least 5 minutes before serving.

SERVING SUGGESTIONS: Makes a hearty single-course lunch or simple dinner, followed by a salad of greens with possibly a little *rucola* (arugola), a nugget or two of *parmigiano-reggiano* (Parmesan), and accompanied by a slightly chilled, fruity, young red wine.

Pagnotta di Melanzane e Maiale

EGGPLANT AND PORK LOAF

*T*HE idea of doing a loaf of eggplant and pork came to me when, at a Sardinian dinner, we were served meatballs made of eggplant and lamb seasoned with *pecorino,* sheep's milk cheese. It may be that at the time I was fascinated more with meat loaves than with meatballs and that I was attracted by the thought of doing a new dish with pork and a vegetable. Whatever the reason, when I finished working on it, it had changed considerably from the original. I like the more finished look of the meat loaf, its compact consistency, and the fact that it is equally good served when just made, or lukewarm, or even at room temperature. Note that the eggplant is roasted directly over the flame of the burner to obtain a spicier, more penetrating flavor.

For 4 to 6 persons

3 medium eggplants, about 12 ounces
1 pound ground pork, preferably the
    shoulder
3 tablespoons chopped onion
1 teaspoon garlic chopped fine
2 tablespoons chopped parsley
1 egg

½ cup grated *pecorino sardo,* if available
    (see page 11), otherwise use *romano*
3 tablespoons extra virgin olive oil
½ cup fine, dry, unflavored bread crumbs,
    toasted lightly in a pan as described on
    page 21

1.   Wash the eggplants and place them whole over a burner or under the broiler, turning on the flame to high. When the skin is charred on one side, turn the eggplant, using flat, unserrated tongs or a pair of wooden spoons; take care not to pierce the skin, otherwise liquid from the eggplant will leak out. Continue turning them until the skin is charred on all sides and cook them until they feel soft. Remove them from the heat.

2.   Turn on the oven to 350°.

3.   When the eggplants are cool enough to handle, peel them and cut off the stems. If they contain an excessive amount of seeds, remove as many seeds as you can. You should end up with approximately 1½ cups of eggplant pulp.

4.   Drain the pulp of as much of its juice as possible and cut it up coarse. Place it in a bowl.

5.   To the bowl add the pork, onion, garlic, parsley, egg, *pecorino* cheese, and 1 tablespoon of the olive oil. Mix all the ingredients to a uniform consistency.

6.   Choose a loaf pan, gratin pan, or baking dish of any shape into which the mixture can be spread to a thickness of 1½ to 2 inches. Coat the pan with 1 tablespoon of the olive oil, then dust it with ¼ cup of the bread crumbs, distributing them evenly so they stick to the bottom and all the sides of the pan.

7.   Put the eggplant and pork mixture into the pan, leveling it and pressing it down slightly. Sprinkle it with the remaining bread crumbs

Eggplant and Pork Loaf (continued)

and olive oil. Place the pan in the uppermost level of the preheated oven and bake for about 45 minutes. The loaf is done when a toothpick pushed into it comes out nearly dry.

8. When the loaf has settled for a few minutes, loosen it from the sides of the pan with a knife and turn it over onto a board or a plate. When firm enough to cut, serve sliced or, if you used a round pan, cut into pie wedges.

AHEAD-OF-TIME NOTE: The dish may be prepared and cooked a day or two in advance and served at room temperature.

SERVING SUGGESTIONS: See preceding recipe.

Torta di Polenta Rossa e Verde col Trito di Maiale

RED AND GREEN POLENTA TORTA WITH GROUND PORK

POLENTA's familiar corn-gold color here becomes spinach-green and tomato-red. The *polenta* is divided into two batches, one mixed with sautéed chopped spinach, the other with a tomato sauce. Sandwiched between the red and green layers is ground pork cooked with wine and pine nuts. Twenty or so minutes in the oven meld all parts into an unusual *torta*, one of the best-looking things one can do with *polenta*.

For 8 to 10 persons

2 garlic cloves, peeled and cut into very thin slices

7 tablespoons extra virgin olive oil, plus additional oil for smearing the baking pan

1 cup canned Italian peeled plum tomatoes, cut up, with their juice

2 cups onion sliced very thin

Salt

Black pepper in a grinder

1 pound ground pork, not too lean

1/3 cup dry white wine

2 tablespoons pine nuts

1 pound fresh spinach

1/3 cup fine, dry, unflavored bread crumbs, toasted lightly in a pan as described on page 21

1 recipe *Polenta* (pages 167–8)

1/2 cup freshly grated *parmigiano-reggiano* (Parmesan)

1. Put half the sliced garlic and 2 tablespoons of the olive oil in a medium skillet and turn on the heat to medium.

2. When the garlic becomes colored a pale gold, add the tomatoes. Cook, stirring occasionally, for 20 minutes or so, until the oil floats free of the tomatoes. Remove from the heat.

3. In a lidded skillet or sauté pan put the onion and 3 tablespoons of the olive oil, turn on the heat to low, and cover the pan. Cook the onion until it is very soft, no less than 1 hour.

4. When the onion is soft, uncover the pan, turn up the heat, and sauté the onion until it becomes colored a pale nut brown.

5. Season with salt and pepper and add the meat. Cook the pork, stirring frequently, until it is well done. Add a little more salt and pepper, then add the wine. When the wine has bubbled away completely, add the pine nuts. Stir once or twice, then remove from the heat.

6. Trim and wash the spinach as described on pages 55-6, but do not chop it. Put it in a pot with just the water that clings to the leaves and 1 tablespoon of salt. Cover the pot and cook the spinach until it is tender but not too soft.

7. Drain the spinach and squeeze it to force out all the liquid possible. Chop the spinach very fine with a knife. Do not use a food processor or blender because they will liquefy it.

8. Put the remaining sliced garlic in a skillet together with 1 tablespoon of the olive oil and turn on the heat to medium.

9. When the garlic becomes colored a pale gold, add the chopped spinach. Sauté it for 1 to 2 minutes, stirring constantly, then remove from the heat.

10. Smear the bottom of a 10-inch springform pan lightly with olive oil and sprinkle over it all but 1 to 2 tablespoons of the toasted bread crumbs. Set aside.

11. Make the *polenta* as directed on pages 167-8. At any time while you are doing the *polenta*, turn on the oven to 450°.

12. When the *polenta* is done, divide it into 2 equal parts and put each in a separate bowl.

13. Add the spinach to one of the bowls and mix well.

14. Add the tomatoes to the other bowl and mix well.

15. Transfer the *polenta* and tomato mixture to the springform pan and level it. Sprinkle on it 1/4 cup of the grated cheese, then spread over it the ground pork and onions, and top with the remaining cheese.

16. Top with the *polenta* and spinach mixture. Over it sprinkle the remaining bread crumbs and dribble on the remaining tablespoon of olive oil. Work rapidly while the *polenta* is still warm, because when it cools and stiffens it becomes difficult to spread.

17. Place the pan in the uppermost level of the preheated oven and bake for 20 to 25 minutes. When done, remove from the pan and allow to settle for about 5 minutes before serving. Serve cut into wedges, like a cake.

AHEAD-OF-TIME NOTE: It may be prepared entirely in advance, through step 16, as far ahead as the morning for the evening. Do not refrigerate overnight because it would alter the spinach's flavor.

SERVING SUGGESTIONS: Suitable for a satisfyingly earthy single-course dinner as well as for a buffet.

Sopa Coada

SQUAB SOUP

IN ITS richness, in its monumentally robust flavor, squab soup makes me think of legendary feasts in some earlier, hardier century. It is, in fact, one of the oldest dishes in the cuisine of the Veneto, its roots perhaps too deep to establish its provenance exactly. Its origin is attributed, depending on the scholar, to Verona, to Treviso, to one or another of the Veneto's towns. The version I have liked the best was in Treviso, whose home cooking may be the most interesting in all Italy, and this recipe is based on that.

The squab are first pan-roasted in butter, with a *soffritto* of carrots and celery, until the meat is fully cooked. They are then boned, combined with sautéed bread slices, Parmesan, broth, and baked for 3 hours.

In my preceding books I shrank from putting in a dish so laborious to prepare. Then, one evening, I was surprised to be served excellent *sopa coada* made by Susan Lescher, the literary agent. If a busy woman and young mother like Susan could tackle it, I decided some of my readers might. To compensate for the long preparation, *sopa coada* can be done far in advance and it is so satisfying that you need cook little else to go with it.

For 6 persons

8 tablespoons butter, plus additional butter
    for smearing the baking dish
½ cup onion cut into very thin slices
½ cup carrot chopped very fine
½ cup celery chopped very fine
2 squab, washed inside and out and split
    lengthwise in two
Salt
Black pepper in a grinder
⅔ cup dry white wine

2 tablespoons vegetable oil
8 slices good country-style bread trimmed of
    its crust
A deep ceramic or earthenware oven-to-table
    baking dish with cover
1 cup freshly grated *parmigiano-reggiano*
    (Parmesan)
4 or more cups Homemade Meat Broth
    (page 73)

1. Choose a sauté pan that can subsequently accommodate the squab without overlapping. Put in 4 tablespoons of the butter and the onion and turn on the heat to medium high.

2. When the onion becomes very lightly colored, add the carrot and celery. Cook the vegetables, turning them from time to time, until they take on a little color.

3. Put in the squab skin side down. Brown them well on that side, then turn them and brown the other side. Add salt and several grindings of pepper.

4. Add the wine, let it bubble for about 1 minute, then turn the heat down to very low and cover the pan. Cook the squab, turning them occasionally, until the meat comes easily

off the bone and is cooked through and through.

5.   Remove the birds from the pan. Detach their skin and discard it. Remove all the bones and put the meat in a bowl. Add the vegetables from the pan, lifting them with a slotted spoon or spatula so as to leave all the fat in the pan.

6.   Put the remaining 4 tablespoons of butter and all the vegetable oil in a small skillet and turn on the heat to medium. When the fat is sizzling hot, slip in the bread, as many slices at a time as will fit without overlapping. When the side facing the bottom of the pan has formed a light brown crust, turn and brown the other side. Transfer them with a slotted spoon or spatula to blot on a platter lined with paper towels.

Repeat the procedure until all the bread is done.

7.   Turn on the oven to 300°.

8.   Smear a thin coating of butter on the bottom of the baking dish. Place 4 slices of bread in the dish to cover the bottom. Over the bread put the squab and the vegetables and any juice in the bowl. Sprinkle half the grated cheese on top. Cover with the remaining bread and top with the remaining grated cheese. Pour enough broth into the dish to cover the ingredients amply. Cover the dish and place in the middle level of the preheated oven. Bake for 3 hours. Check the broth level from time to time and add more if necessary. Serve directly from the dish in soup plates.

AHEAD-OF-TIME NOTE: The entire dish may be prepared several hours in advance and reheated in the oven.

SERVING SUGGESTIONS: It is a memorable meal, elegant and deeply satisfying, all by itself. To offset its weight, I would precede it with Tomatoes Stuffed with Goat Cheese and Chives (page 34), and before getting to dessert, follow it with Lemon, Cucumber, and Pepper Salad (page 286).

Tortino di Tartufi

WHITE TRUFFLES TORTINO WITH POTATOES
AND PARMESAN

*O*NE of my husband's never-wavering and absolute loves is white truffles. Fortunately for him, his birthday coincides with the height of the truffle season, and among my gifts to him there is always a *tortino di tartufi.* It can be very nice, on any ordinary day, to slice truffles on pasta, or a Parmesan *risotto,* or *scaloppine,* but in fulfilling a devotee's longings, nothing does the job so thoroughly as a *tortino.* It is composed of layers of thin potato slices, Parmesan, truffles, and butter baked in the oven until the topmost layer of cheese melts and forms a crust. What happens is not only that all the aroma of which the truffle is capable expands with overwhelming power but also that it saturates the other ingredients, transubstantiating them into redolent extensions of the truffle itself. A liberal supply of good bread must be available to make sure no precious drop or crumb of flavor is left on the dish.

White Truffles Tortino with Potatoes and Parmesan (continued)
NOTE: In Italy, the first white truffles appear in September, and the season
lasts through December. Canned white truffles are always available, but they
are a shadow of their fresh selves. I do not use them for a *tortino,* but if you'd like
to try them, be sure not to discard the liquid they are packed in: it contains
much of the aroma that is left.

For 2 persons (see Serving Suggestions)

10 to 12 ounces boiling potatoes
5 tablespoons butter
An oven-to-table gratin dish made of
    porcelain or earthenware, about 1½ to
    2 inches deep and 5 to 6 inches
    in diameter
Salt

Black pepper in a grinder
2 or more ounces fresh whole white truffle,
    brushed clean of all surface and
    embedded grit
3 ounces *parmigiano-reggiano* (Parmesan),
    shaved into thin strips with a peeler or
    vegetable slicing tool

1.   Wash the potatoes, cover, and boil them in their skins.

2.   Turn on the oven to 450°.

3.   When the potatoes are done, drain them and, as soon as you are able to handle them, peel them. Allow them to cool completely, then slice them into thin rounds.

4.   Smear the bottom of the gratin dish with 1 tablespoon of butter, then cover with a layer of potato slices sprinkled with salt and grindings of pepper. Using a truffle slicer or, if you don't have one, a peeler or other vegetable slicing tool, slice enough white truffle—very thin—to cover the potatoes. Top with a layer of Parmesan slivers, then dot with butter. Repeat the procedure, layering all ingredients in the same sequence, until you have used them all. Top with Parmesan and dots of butter.

5.   Bake in the uppermost level of the preheated oven for 10 to 15 minutes, until the Parmesan melts and forms a light crust. Allow the heat of the dish to subside before serving. Serve with slices of crusty, country-style bread.

SERVING SUGGESTIONS: If one precedes the *tortino* with a generous platter
of cold meats, this recipe could serve four people. A truffle *tortino,* however,
ought not to have to share main billing; our appreciation of it should be
favored by, not divided with, other dishes. My husband considers the amount
given here barely sufficient for one portion, which, except for a salad of small,
tender field greens to bring the event to a cool, clean close, would constitute
for him the entire meal. I prefer to begin with a light soup, such as *Zuppa
Imperiale* (page 74), Shredded Parsley *Frittata* Soup (page 76), or, from *The
Classic Italian Cook Book, Passatelli* (page 70); it soothes, but not smothers, one's
anticipation, and equips one's spirit and palate for serene enjoyment of the
truffle. Served thus, the quantity given in the recipe should be satisfactory for
a romantic dinner for two.

Soups

Il Brodo

HOMEMADE MEAT BROTH

ITALIAN broth is a light, thin, delicately savory liquid obtained from boiling vegetables, meat, and bones. It is not stock, nor a dark, reduced consommé, and neither of these can be substituted for it. Do not use lamb or pork, both of which give broth too strong a flavor. Do not make too liberal use of chicken giblets and carcasses; unless they are used sparingly, their sharp flavor will dominate the broth. Always include veal and beef in your assortment of meats.

1¹/2 to 2 quarts

1 teaspoon salt
1 carrot, peeled
1 medium onion, peeled
2 or 3 celery stalks
¼ red or yellow bell pepper, stripped of all
    its seeds

1 small boiling potato, peeled
1 ripe, fresh tomato, or 1 canned Italian
    plum tomato, drained of juice
5 pounds assorted pieces of meat and bones
    (see meat suggestions above), of which no
    less than 1¹/2 pounds is all meat

1.   Put all the ingredients into a stockpot, and add enough water to cover by 2 inches. Set the cover askew, turn on the heat to medium, and bring to a boil. As soon as the liquid starts to boil, turn down the heat so that it bubbles steadily at the gentlest of simmers.

2.   Skim off the scum that floats to the surface, fairly frequently at first, then only from time to time. Cook for 3 hours, at no time more rapidly than at a simmer.

3.   Strain the broth through a large wine strainer lined with paper towels, pouring it into a nonmetallic bowl. Allow to cool completely, uncovered.

4.   When cool, place in the refrigerator long enough for the fat to come to the surface and solidify. Remove the fat and pour the clear broth into ice-cube trays. Freeze.

5.   When the broth is frozen solid, unmold the cubes from the trays and divide them into 4 or 5 small plastic bags. Seal the bags tightly, and return to the freezer to keep until needed.

NOTE: Broth will keep in the freezer for up to 3 months. It will not keep in the refrigerator for any longer than 3 days.

Zuppa Imperiale

BOLOGNESE DUMPLING CUBES

IF YOU look into bakers' windows in Bologna, you may see trays of golden cubes that look like croutons. They are used mainly for soup, but they are not croutons: They are a much tastier, baked composition of flour, Parmesan, butter, eggs, and nutmeg. It is one of those specialties that have remained strictly local, like Romagna's spaetzlelike *passatelli,* and that no one elsewhere seems to know about.

As you will find in the serving suggestions below, *zuppa imperiale* not only makes a fine soup, when used with a good broth, but also a light pastalike dish, or even tidbits to munch with drinks.

For 4 persons

3 tablespoons butter, softened to room temperature, plus additional butter for smearing the cookie sheet

1/3 cup freshly grated *parmigiano-reggiano* (Parmesan), plus additional for the table

3 tablespoons coarse-ground semolina (granular hard-wheat flour)

1/4 cup all-purpose flour

1/2 teaspoon salt

3 eggs

1/8 teaspoon grated nutmeg

A cookie or other baking sheet

2 1/2 cups Homemade Meat Broth (preceding recipe)

1. Turn on the oven to 400°.
2. Put the softened butter, grated cheese, semolina, all-purpose flour, salt, eggs, and nutmeg in a bowl and mix all the ingredients thoroughly until they are evenly amalgamated.
3. Smear a cookie or baking sheet with butter and over it spread the mixture to a thickness of 1/2 inch or a little less.
4. Place in the uppermost level of the preheated oven. Bake for 5 to 6 minutes, until it begins to form bubbles and is easily loosened from the bottom of the sheet.
5. Remove from the oven and transfer from the cookie sheet to a cutting board or counter top to cool. When lukewarm, cut into 1/2-inch squares.
6. Bring the broth to a boil. Drop in the dumplings, cook them in boiling broth for 5 minutes, then turn off the heat and let rest for another 5 minutes before ladling into soup plates and serving. Serve with grated cheese on the side.

AHEAD-OF-TIME NOTE: The cubes can be prepared, baked, and cut into shapes 2 or 3 days before they are to be boiled and served.

ADDITIONAL SERVING SUGGESTIONS: The cubes alone can be used as one of an assortment of hors d'oeuvres served with apéritifs. After baking the batter and cutting it into cubes, put it back in a 300° oven to toast for 10 minutes or so. It can be served then, or later at room temperature.

To serve as a pasta course: Before baking, spread the mixture more thinly over the cookie sheet than you would when making it for soup. Bake only 4 minutes. Cut into strips ¼ inch wide and about 6 inches long. Prepare the following sauce: Put 2 or 3 peeled and mashed garlic cloves in a saucepan together with 3 to 4 tablespoons butter and 1 teaspoon dried rosemary leaves or a sprig of fresh rosemary. Sauté over medium heat until the garlic becomes colored a rich gold. Add half a bouillon cube, crushed. Stir until the bouillon cube has completely dissolved. Turn off the heat. Drop the cheese and egg strips into boiling salted water, cook for 15 to 20 seconds, drain, and toss immediately with the sauce. Serve with grated *parmigiano-reggiano.*

Palline in Brodo alla Mantovana

DUMPLING SOUP, MANTUA STYLE

*T*HERE is no end to the variety of dumplings Italians make for soup. In the northeast, Alto Adige and Trentino, there are *canederli* made with liver, ham, spleen, or even dried fruit. In Tuscany, there are ricotta and spinach *gnocchi.* There are the spaetzlelike *passatelli* from Romagna made of cheese and bread crumbs. There are Bologna's long, skinny *chenelle* of rice and chicken livers. The tiny dumplings in this recipe are native to Mantua. They are made of bread crumbs, cheese, and egg flavored with *pancetta,* nutmeg, and a muffled hint of garlic. They are lightning fast to do, especially if you use the food processor. Do take what little time is necessary to shape them into very small balls. They are light but savory, and small bitefuls convey no more or less than the most desirable load of flavor to the palate.

For 4 persons

Dumpling Soup, Mantua Style (continued)

½ garlic clove, peeled
1½ tablespoons chopped *pancetta*
½ tablespoon butter
½ cup toasted, unflavored bread crumbs
⅓ cup freshly grated *parmigiano-reggiano*
    (Parmesan), plus additional for the table

Tiny pinch grated nutmeg
1 egg
Black pepper in a grinder
2½ cups good homemade broth
    (beef, chicken, or a mixture)

1.   Combine the garlic, *pancetta,* and butter in the work bowl of a food processor fitted with a steel blade. Process until the mixture becomes creamy and finely homogenized.

2.   Mix the bread crumbs with the grated cheese and shape into a mound on a pastry board or other work surface. Make a hollow in the center of the mound. Put the garlic and *pancetta* mixture into the hollow and add the nutmeg, egg, and several grindings of pepper. Draw the sides of the mound together and knead until it is a well-amalgamated paste. Shape into tiny balls little more than ½ inch thick.

3.   Bring the broth to a boil in a soup pot. Put in the dumplings and cook for about 5 minutes. Serve with a sprinkling of Parmesan.

Frittatine di Prezzemolo in Brodo

SHREDDED PARSLEY FRITTATA SOUP

PARSLEY, Parmesan, and nutmeg flavor these crepelike *frittate*. Their principal use is for soup; for that purpose, they are cut into *fettuccine*-thin strands. If cut into wedges, they can be included in a cold *antipasto*. Or leave them whole and use them as wrappers for a filling of julienned ham, Parmesan, and béchamel, then pop them into a hot oven long enough to brown the edges and melt the cheese.

For 6 to 8 persons

3 large eggs
½ cup parsley chopped very fine
¾ cup freshly grated *parmigiano-reggiano*
    (Parmesan), plus additional for the table
⅛ teaspoon grated nutmeg
¾ cup flour

¾ cup milk
Salt
Black pepper in a grinder
3 tablespoons butter
4 to 5 cups Homemade Meat Broth (page 73)

1. Break the eggs into a small bowl and beat them well.

2. Add the parsley, grated cheese, nutmeg, and flour. Mix thoroughly.

3. Add the milk slowly in a thin stream, mixing constantly.

4. Add salt and liberal grindings of pepper.

5. Put 1 teaspoon of the butter in a 12-inch skillet and turn on the heat to medium low. When the butter has melted and its foam begins to subside, stir the *frittata* batter and put ⅓ cup of it into the pan. Tilt and rotate the pan to spread the batter evenly over the whole bottom.

6. When the batter has set and become firm, and the side facing the bottom of the pan becomes lightly colored, turn it over. Cook 1 minute longer, remove the pan from heat, and transfer the *frittata* to a platter.

7. Return the pan to the heat, add a little dollop of butter, and when it is hot pour in another ⅓ cup of batter, repeating the procedure described above. Continue in this fashion until you have cooked all the batter, which should give you about 8 thin *frittate*, stacked one above the other.

8. When the *frittate* are cool, roll them up loosely together like a jelly roll. Cut the roll crosswise into narrow strips. The strips should be as wide as *fettuccine*.

9. Unfold the *frittata "fettuccine"* and place them in a soup tureen.

10. Bring the broth to a boil, then pour it into the tureen. Sprinkle with grated cheese and serve with additional grated cheese available on the side.

Pasta Ripiena in Brodo

RICOTTA-COATED PASTA SQUARES IN BROTH

*T*HIS, and the recipe that follows, are soups I remember from my school days. When I was ready to begin work on my thesis, my professor switched from the University of Padua to that of Ferrara, where I followed him. With most of my fellow students I shared two basic problems, money and hunger: little of the former and consequently much of the latter. A family that was friendly with mine knew of my predicament and, from time to time, would ask me to join their Sunday dinner. Everything I had at their table seemed good, but the dish I recall with the greatest satisfaction is this stuffed pasta soup, typical of Sundays at home in Ferrara.

Although it does look like small ravioli, to describe it as stuffed pasta is somewhat misleading. It is actually two wafer-thin layers of pasta bound to one another by a scantily spread coating composed of ricotta, Parmesan, egg, and nutmeg. It is hearty and satiating, as pasta must be, yet extraordinarily fine and light.

For 6 to 8 persons

Ricotta-Coated Pasta Squares in Broth (continued)

¼ pound whole-milk ricotta

1 cup freshly grated *parmigiano-reggiano* (Parmesan), plus additional for the table

1 egg plus 1 yolk

⅛ teaspoon grated nutmeg

Black pepper in a grinder

Salt

Homemade pasta made with 2 large eggs and about 1½ cups flour, as described on pages 93–5

6 cups Homemade Meat Broth (page 73)

1. Place the ricotta in a bowl, discarding as much of its liquid as possible. Add the grated cheese, egg and extra yolk, nutmeg, and very liberal grindings of pepper. Mix thoroughly with a fork to amalgamate all the ingredients evenly. Taste and correct for salt.

2. Make the pasta, thinning it out to the narrowest setting on the machine. Lay each strip of pasta flat and, using a flexible rubber spatula, spread a thin coating of the ricotta mixture over the entire length, but only half the width, of the strip. Do not coat the pasta to the very edge of the strip, but stop about ½ inch short of it.

3. Fold the uncoated side of the strip over the other half, meeting it edge to edge, but not pressing down on it.

4. With a pastry cutting wheel cut the pasta into 1-inch squares. Place the squares on a towel laid out flat on a counter. Check to see that they are tightly sealed and make sure they do not overlap or touch each other. If you are going to use them several hours later, turn them over from time to time.

5. Bring the broth to a boil, then drop in the pasta. Do not let it boil too fast. As soon as the pasta is done—it should be a little firm to the bite—serve it along with the broth. Have grated cheese available on the side.

AHEAD-OF-TIME NOTE: The squares can be made in advance anytime the same day they are to be cooked, but they must be cooked only when ready to serve.

Riso in Brodo col Sedano

RICE IN BROTH SOUP WITH CELERY

*T*HERE was a period in my life when I had no other soup than this one. It was during my early university years, when I commuted to Padua from Venice, where I lived with my maternal aunt. We used to have *bollito misto* once a week, and my uncle—an engineer who had organized his life and ours by a few undebatable operating principles—had decreed that into the broth from the *bollito* it was pointless to put anything else but rice and, to give the soup fragrance and lightness, the celery.

It was a long time after I left that house that I had the soup again. When

I did, a substantial enough interval had elapsed for me to recognize that, single-minded though he had been, my uncle had not been entirely mistaken. With a rich meat broth this is a lovely, light soup to have, on occasion.

For 4 persons

3 cups celery diced into ½-inch cubes
2 tablespoons butter
Salt
5 cups Homemade Meat Broth (page 73), skimmed of its fat

¾ cup rice, preferably Italian Arborio rice
Freshly grated *parmigiano-reggiano* (Parmesan) for the table

1. Choose a pot that will be large enough to contain all the broth. Put in the diced celery and butter, cover, and turn on the heat to medium. Cook until the celery is tender but not mushy, approximately 15 minutes.
2. Add salt, stir, then add the broth.
3. When the broth comes to a boil add the rice. Stir frequently until the broth returns to a boil. Cover the pot and cook until the rice is tender, but firm—*al dente*. It should take about 15 minutes, but taste it from time to time to make sure it does not become overdone.
4. Serve immediately with freshly grated Parmesan cheese available for sprinkling to taste.

Zuppa di Carciofi e Topinambur

ARTICHOKE AND JERUSALEM ARTICHOKE SOUP

IN THIS, as in other preparations where artichokes are cut or sliced, it is essential that a substantial portion of the artichoke—the tough, inedible part—be trimmed away before cooking. It may seem wasteful, but it is far more wasteful to put good ingredients and precious effort in a dish that becomes unchewable.

Do not use a knife or scissors on the large outer leaves. They must be pulled back and down by hand so that they will automatically snap off at the base where the tough part meets the tender. The inner core of leaves should be truncated with a sharp knife where the dark green color fades away.

Here we have an unusual and happy combination: the keen, earthy taste of artichokes with the sweet, mild taste of *topinambur* (Jerusalem artichokes). It's not a soup where you look for crisp, undercooked morsels to crunch. The vegetables should be creamy and all but dissolve in your mouth. Therefore, be sure to give it sufficient cooking time and gentle heat.

For 4 persons

Artichoke and Jerusalem Artichoke Soup (continued)

3 medium artichokes

½ lemon

8 to 9 ounces Jerusalem artichokes or sun chokes, about 1½ cups

2 tablespoons butter

2 tablespoons extra virgin olive oil

2 tablespoons onion chopped fine

3 cups good homemade broth (beef, chicken, or any light broth)

1 egg yolk

3 tablespoons freshly grated *parmigiano-reggiano* (Parmesan)

Crostini (bread squares lightly browned in hot butter)

1. Detach the stems of the artichokes and pare away each stem's green outer layer until you reach the whitish core. Slice the core very thin and sprinkle a few drops of lemon juice over the slices.

2. Snap off the hard outer leaves of the artichokes with your fingers until you are left with a central cone of leaves pale at the base and green only at the tip. Cut off about 1½ inches from the top of the cone, taking care to eliminate all the dark green, inedible parts of the leaves. Rub all the cut edges with the half lemon.

3. Cut the trimmed artichokes into quarters. With a paring knife scrape away the inner choke and small, curled prickly leaves. Slice the quarters lengthwise as thin as you can. Sprinkle a little lemon juice over them.

4. Peel the Jerusalem artichokes and cut them into the thinnest possible slices.

5. Put the butter, olive oil, and chopped onion into a soup pot and turn on the heat to medium high. When the onion becomes colored a rich gold, add the sliced artichokes and Jerusalem artichokes, and turn down the heat a bit. Cook, stirring from time to time, for about 5 minutes.

6. Add the broth, turn the heat down to low, and cover the pot. Cook for 2 hours or more over very low heat, until the vegetables become pulpy soft. If more liquid is required during this time, add water not broth. When done, the consistency of the soup should be medium thin, somewhat runny.

7. Put the egg yolk in a soup tureen or other serving bowl and beat it lightly with a fork. Slowly pour the soup over the egg yolk, stirring all the while. Then mix in the grated cheese and serve with *crostini*.

Riso, Piselli e Fegatini in Brodo

RICE, PEAS, AND CHICKEN LIVER SOUP

*T*HE Italian word for liver is *fegato,* with the accent falling on the first syllable. In gastronomic usage, it usually refers to calf's liver. When you say *fegatelli,* you are talking about pork livers, so delicious when wrapped in caul and bay leaves and grilled over charcoal. Wherever you see the word *fegatini,* it means chicken livers, as in this light and delectable soup where small young peas play their sweet counterpoint to the more piquant flavors of the livers.

It is most important not to overcook the livers, either when sautéing them or finishing them in the soup. They must remain pink within and tender throughout.

For 4 persons

5 cups rich homemade broth
1/2 cup shelled fresh, young peas
1/3 cup rice, preferably Italian Arborio rice
1 tablespoon butter
1 tablespoon onion chopped very fine

3 chicken livers, rinsed, trimmed, and cut into 1/3-inch pieces
Salt
Freshly grated *parmigiano-reggiano* (Parmesan) for the table

1. Bring the broth to a boil in a soup pot. Add the peas and rice, stir, cover the pot, and turn the heat down to very low.

2. Put the butter and onion in a small sauté pan. Cook the onion over medium-low heat until it is tender and translucent, but not browned.

3. Add the chicken livers and salt and turn up the heat. Cook, stirring with a wooden spoon, for about 1½ minutes, or just until the livers have lost their raw red color. Turn off the heat and set aside.

4. When the rice is done—it should be tender, but firm to the bite, about 15 to 20 minutes' cooking time—put in the chicken livers. Let the broth bubble briskly for a few seconds. Taste and correct for salt. Serve promptly with grated cheese on the side.

Zuppa di Verza alla Valdostana

SAVOY CABBAGE SOUP, AOSTA STYLE

*T*HE Alpine valley of Aosta is just this side of the Alps of the French region of Savoie; and the cultural kinship of the two is apparent, not only in the language and in the many place names but in the most vital of all manifestations of cultures—cooking, as for example, in this superb soup that seems so much a dainty version of *soupe à l'oignon.*

The only time-consuming procedure in this recipe—the long, slow cooking of the cabbage until it is reduced to creamy softness—can be done several hours in advance. Once that is accomplished, the finishing steps, of which the most important is the "savoring"—*insaporire*—of the cooked cabbage in a *battuto* of onion and garlic, go very quickly, and the whole soup can be assembled in 20 to 25 minutes.

Savoy Cabbage Soup, Aosta Style (continued)
If you like, you can place the soup in ovenproof bowls and give it a gratin treatment in a very hot oven before serving it. It's a bit of fancy business that I don't find necessary, but it is up to you.

For 4 persons

About 1½ pounds Savoy cabbage
¼ cup extra virgin olive oil
3 tablespoons butter
1 tablespoon onion chopped very fine
½ teaspoon garlic chopped very fine
Salt
Black pepper in a grinder

2 tablespoons vegetable oil
4 slices good-quality white bread
¼ pound fontina cheese, sliced very thin
   (see Note)
6 tablespoons freshly grated *parmigiano-reggiano* (Parmesan)

1.   Remove any of the blemished outer leaves of the cabbage. Rinse the remainder in cold water and shred it into narrow strips. You should have about 5 cups.

2.   Put the strips in a soup pot, add sufficient water to cover by an inch or so, cover the pot, and bring the water to a boil. Turn down the heat so that the water bubbles slowly, and cook for at least 3 hours. When the cabbage has become very soft, drain it, but reserve the cooking liquid.

3.   Put the olive oil, 2 tablespoons of the butter, and the onion in a medium-size sauté pan and turn on the heat to medium. When the onion has become translucent, add the garlic, cooking it until it becomes just slightly colored.

4.   Add the drained, cooked cabbage and a liberal amount of salt and pepper; turn the heat up to high. Cook the cabbage for about 15 minutes, stirring frequently and mashing it

with a fork so that it becomes a creamy pulp.

5.   Transfer the cabbage and all the contents of the pan to a soup pot. Add enough of the cabbage's reserved cooking liquid to cover by 2 to 3 inches and bring it to a moderate boil.

6.   While the soup is bubbling, put the remaining tablespoon of butter and the vegetable oil in a small sauté pan or skillet and turn on the heat to medium. When the butter foam begins to subside, put in the bread slices, as many as will fit at one time without overlapping, and brown them on both sides. When browned, transfer to paper towels to drain.

7.   Put a slice of browned bread at the bottom of each of 4 individual soup plates; cover each with a slice of fontina and over each put the cabbage with just enough liquid to rise to the top of the cabbage. Sprinkle 1½ tablespoons grated Parmesan over each dish and serve at once.

NOTE: Genuine fontina from Val d'Aosta is a tender cheese that mingles savoriness with mildness in an inimitable manner and, in cooking, melts beautifully. The least acceptable substitutes for fontina are its American and Scandinavian imitations, which are totally lacking in character. If you cannot find authentic fontina, look for other semisoft cheeses that are creamy in texture and have a little spice to their aroma, such as Muenster or taleggio.

ABOVE A platter of tidbits we serve with our *aperitivo*. Next to the rim, walnuts with Parmesan butter; in the second row, canapés with whipped *mortadella* alternating with tomatoes stuffed with goat cheese and chives; in the third row, *tartine* of beaten tuna; in the center, *bruschetta* with tomatoes.

LEFT In my Venice kitchen. The *polenta* is done and I am checking to see if the lamb-stuffed veal rolls (see page 203) are ready to go with it.

ABOVE A pasta class in Venice. We are making *raviolini* stuffed with onion and beets, as described on page 107, and I am guiding the hand of a student who is sealing them. Another student is practicing on the machine's noodle cutter. Some of the other pasta we made: up front, green and yellow *pappardelle*, hand-cut broad noodles; behind them, bow ties and *garganelli*, the hand-turned tubular pasta from Romagna; in the background, *tortellini*, *ravioli*, *tonnarelli*, and *tagliolini*; a ball of spinach dough is waiting, sealed in plastic, to be thinned out for *lasagne*.

OPPOSITE The view from our east terrace takes in the Dominican church of SS Giovanni e Paolo, founded in the thirteenth century. To its left is the Renaissance façade of the Scuola di S. Marco, once a lay fraternity, now the municipal hospital of Venice. The two dishes on the terrace parapet are, on the left, pasta roses (see page 116) and, on the right, *fazzoletti della nonna* (see pages 144–7).

A BUFFET table is set in our living room. The room's ceiling beams were made in the early fifteenth century of larch taken from the once dense forests on the mainland, which supplied the wood for Venice's powerful fleets. On the table, starting counterclockwise at twelve o'clock: in the glass bowl, rice salad with shrimp; spinach with chick-peas; pasta roses; *fazzoletti della nonna*; scallops with rosemary; *polenta* with lamb-stuffed veal rolls; baked mussels and tomatoes; roast veal studded with pickles.

Zuppa di Zucchine all'Amalfitana

ZUCCHINI SOUP, AMALFI STYLE

*T*HIS recipe was given to me by my friend Pierino Jovene from Amalfi. Pierino is a cook of dazzling skill who owns a seafood restaurant in my hometown of Cesenatico. The restaurant is called Il Gambero Rosso, the red shrimp. Its fame is large enough to draw customers from all Italy.

Pierino is as gifted a storyteller as he is a cook; I wish I could reproduce in English syllables the melodious cadence of his Neapolitan speech. I shall be content if I have succeeded in duplicating the lyrical flavor of his ravishing soup.

The essential element that brings this soup to life is freshness. The zucchini must be young and firm; the tomatoes honestly ripened; the potatoes, if possible, new waxy boiling potatoes. And the basil! Although parsley is a tolerable substitute, what you really want is the crowning fragrance of young basil.

You will notice that half the potatoes are chopped very fine. This is so they will dissolve in the soup and thicken it. The zucchini must be cooked until very soft, but not mushy. In another extraordinary version of this dish, Pierino uses zucchini blossoms instead of zucchini. If you have a source for blossoms, by all means try it, following the same cooking procedure.

For 4 persons

3 tablespoons extra virgin olive oil
2 tablespoons *pancetta* chopped fine
1 tablespoon onion chopped fine
1/3 cup fresh, ripe tomatoes, peeled, seeded, and cut into 1/2-inch pieces
1/3 cup potato peeled and chopped very fine
1/3 cup potato peeled and diced into 1/2-inch pieces
Salt

Black pepper in a grinder
3/4 pound zucchini, thoroughly scrubbed and cut up into 1/2-inch pieces, about 2 cups
1 egg
2 tablespoons freshly grated *parmigiano-reggiano* (Parmesan)
4 or 5 basil leaves, or 1 tablespoon chopped parsley

1. Put the olive oil, *pancetta,* and onion in a soup pot and turn on the heat to medium. Cook, stirring with a wooden spoon, until the onion becomes colored a rich gold.

2. Add the tomatoes and cook for 2 to 3 minutes more.

3. Add both the chopped and diced potatoes and enough water to cover—about 1 cup. Add salt and grindings of pepper liberally, cover the pot, and continue cooking over medium heat until all the potatoes are tender.

4. Put in the zucchini, add more water to

Zucchini Soup, Amalfi Style (continued)

cover, and cook over low heat with the pot covered until the zucchini are very tender. When the zucchini are done, check the consistency of the soup. If it is extremely dense, add a little more water. But bear in mind that this is meant to be a thick soup.

5. Break open the egg into a soup plate or small bowl and beat it lightly with a fork. With the heat turned down very low, pour the egg in a thin stream into the pot, mixing thoroughly all the while with a wooden spoon.

6. Turn off the heat and mix the grated cheese into the soup. Tear the basil leaves into tiny pieces and add them (or the chopped parsley) to the soup. Mix once or twice, pour the soup into individual plates or bowls, and serve after a few minutes' rest when it has cooled off slightly.

TWO CHICK-PEA SOUPS WITH PORCINI MUSHROOMS

What is it about legumes that comforts men? When work or other afflictions bring down my husband, Victor, chick-peas will lift him from his depths. If I should add wild mushrooms, he soars. There are friends for whom I occasionally make these soups, but I associate them with more private celebrations, with winter evenings when Victor and I dine alone.

Although you'll find chick-peas and dried *porcini* mushrooms in both the soups that follow, they are distinctly different dishes. The first is a looser, slightly redder soup that features, in addition to the mushrooms, the fascinating combination of spinach and chick-peas. Both ingredients have an earthy quality, the spinach cooler, more mineral, the chick-peas denser and toastier.

The second soup is thickset and potent. In it the chick-peas and mushrooms sing out alone over the rich background of the *soffritto*—the sautéed carrot, celery, and *pancetta*.

You will find in both, as in all my recipes for chick-peas, instructions for skinning chick-peas. Don't be startled. It goes as easily and fast as snapping your fingers and does away with those bits of skin that look so messy in the dish and contribute nothing in the way of texture or taste.

Zuppa di Ceci, Spinaci e Porcini Secchi

CHICK-PEA, SPINACH, AND DRIED WILD MUSHROOM SOUP

For 4 persons

1½ ⅝-ounce packages dried *porcini*
   mushrooms, or 1 ounce if loose
3 cups lukewarm water
19-ounce can chick-peas
1 pound fresh spinach, or one 10-ounce
   package frozen whole-leaf spinach,
   thawed
Salt

2 tablespoons butter
3 tablespoons extra virgin olive oil
2 tablespoons onion chopped fine
¼ cup fresh, ripe tomatoes peeled, seeded,
   and chopped very fine
Black pepper in a grinder
3 tablespoons freshly grated *parmigiano-
   reggiano* (Parmesan)

1. Soak the dried mushrooms in the lukewarm water for at least 30 minutes. Lift out the mushrooms without stirring up the water and rinse them thoroughly in cold water. Chop them not too fine and set aside.

2. Filter the water in which the mushrooms soaked through a wire strainer lined with a paper towel. Set aside.

3. Empty the can of chick-peas with all its liquid into a bowl. Squeeze the peel off the chick-peas one by one, putting the peeled peas on a plate. When all the chick-peas have been peeled, put them back into the bowl with their own liquid. (Omit this step if you are not bothered by peels in the soup.)

4. If using fresh spinach, remove the stems and soak the spinach in a basinful of cold water, dunking it several times. Lift out the spinach and discard the water with the sand that has settled to the bottom. Refill the basin and repeat the operation again and again until the spinach is thoroughly free of sand. Cook it in a covered pan with a pinch of salt and just the water that clings to its leaves. When the spinach is tender,

after 10 minutes or so, drain it, squeeze it very lightly, and chop it rather coarse.

5. If using frozen spinach, cook the thawed spinach in a covered pan with a pinch of salt for a minute or two; then drain, squeeze, and chop it coarse.

6. Put the butter, olive oil, and onion in a soup pot and turn on the heat to medium. When the onion becomes colored a light gold, add the mushrooms. Cook, stirring, for a minute or so. Then add the tomatoes and cook and stir for another minute or so. Add the chopped spinach, salt, and grindings of pepper, and, after 1 or 2 minutes, the chick-peas drained of their juice. Stir for a little while, then add the filtered water from the mushrooms. Taste and correct for salt and pepper.

8. Turn down the heat to very low, cover the pot, and cook for 1 hour. The soup should end up being rather dense, but if necessary, while cooking, you can add a little warm water.

9. Off the heat, mix in the grated cheese. Allow the heat of the soup to subside for a few moments before serving.

Zuppa di Ceci Avantaggiata

CHICK-PEA SOUP WITH PANCETTA AND DRIED WILD MUSHROOMS

For 4 persons

1 ounce dried *porcini* mushrooms
3 cups lukewarm water
19-ounce can chick-peas
3 tablespoons extra virgin olive oil
2½ ounces *pancetta,* cut into the narrowest
  possible strips, about ½ cup
2 cups chopped onion
½ cup carrot chopped fine
½ cup celery chopped fine
2 teaspoons tomato paste dissolved in the

filtered water of the soaked mushrooms
  (see step 2 of the preceding recipe)
Salt
Black pepper in a grinder
3 cups Homemade Meat Broth (page 73), or
  3 bouillon cubes dissolved in 3 cups water
Toasted or grilled slices crusty, country-style
  bread
Freshly grated *parmigiano-reggiano* (Parmesan)
  for the table

1.   Soak the mushrooms in the water and rinse them, as described in step 1 of the preceding recipe.

2.   Empty the can of chick-peas with all its liquid into a bowl. Squeeze the peel off the chick-peas one by one, putting the peeled peas on a plate. When all the chick-peas have been peeled, put them back into the bowl with their own liquid.

3.   Put the olive oil, *pancetta,* and onion in a large saucepan or soup pot and turn on the heat to medium. When the onion becomes colored a medium gold, add the carrot and celery.

4.   Cook until the vegetables are not only nicely browned but tender. Add the soaked, rinsed mushrooms and the mushroom liquid with the dissolved tomato paste. Continue cooking in the uncovered pot until all the liquid has boiled away.

5.   Drain the chick-peas, add them to the pot, cover, and cook for about 10 minutes. Taste and correct for salt, adding a few grindings of pepper. Add the broth or dissolved bouillon cubes. When the soup has simmered for 2 minutes or so, serve in soup plates over the toasted bread, with grated cheese available on the side.

Pasta e Ceci

PASTA AND CHICK-PEA SOUP

OUR family does not ski, or ice skate, or bounce down hills on sleds, but we welcome winter because it is such a good time to make soup. Soup is no reason to give up pasta, however. Many shapes are made specifically for soup. The tiny, pretty ones shaped like stars, or little animals, or imitating rice, or the spindly noodles called angel hair are excellent with broth—a homemade meat broth, that is, extracted from beef, veal, and chicken simmered slowly with a few vegetables and a tomato or two. Chewier, stubby, tubular pasta known to Italians as *ditalini*, little thimbles, or *maltagliati*, lozenge-shaped short noodles cut from slightly thick homemade pasta, are better with beans. Any kind of beans. In the following version of the inexhaustible pasta and beans theme, I use chick-peas that are first sautéed with olive oil, garlic, rosemary, and sage, and then puréed to make a velvety-textured soup with powerfully satisfying chill-chasing properties.

For 4 to 6 persons

19-ounce can chick-peas
½ cup extra virgin olive oil
⅓ cup chopped onion
1 teaspoon chopped garlic
½ teaspoon chopped rosemary
½ teaspoon chopped sage
¾ cup canned Italian peeled plum tomatoes, drained of their juice
3 cups Homemade Meat Broth (page 73), or 1 cup canned broth diluted with 2 cups water
¼ pound stubby soup pasta
Salt
Black pepper in a grinder
3 tablespoons chopped parsley
Freshly grated *parmigiano-reggiano* (Parmesan) for the table

1. Use instructions in step 2 of the preceding recipe.

2. Put the olive oil and chopped onion in a large saucepan and turn on the heat to medium. When the onion becomes colored a pale gold, add the garlic, rosemary, and sage. Stir once or twice. When the garlic becomes colored a very pale gold, add the tomatoes. Cook, stirring occasionally, for 10 minutes.

3. Add the chick-peas drained of their liquid, and cook for another 5 to 6 minutes.

4. Pour the contents of the pot into a bowl, then purée them through a food mill back into the pot. Add the broth and turn on the heat to medium high.

5. When the liquid comes to a boil, add the pasta, cover the pot, and turn down the heat to medium. Cook until the pasta is *al dente*—tender but firm to the bite. Taste and correct for salt and add a few grindings of pepper. Turn off the heat, stir in the parsley, and serve with freshly grated cheese available on the side.

Zuppa di Fagioli e Biete

BEAN AND SWISS CHARD SOUP

*T*HIS is one of those masterful bean soups that are the glory of Central Italian cooking. From the point of view of technique, there are no intricate secrets to its success. The *battuto* of garlic and olive oil is enhanced by anchovies and rosemary. The remaining ingredients follow in the simple sequence described in the recipe. If you are making the soup in advance, do not put in the pasta to cook until you are ready to reheat the soup, or it will become soft and gluey.

For 4 persons

½ pound Swiss chard
Salt
2 flat anchovy fillets
¼ teaspoon dried rosemary leaves,
    or a 2- to 3-inch sprig fresh rosemary
⅓ cup extra virgin olive oil
2 whole garlic cloves, peeled
½ cup dried white kidney beans, soaked and

cooked as directed on page 294, or 2 cups canned *cannellini,* drained
Black pepper in a grinder
½ cup short, tubular pasta, about ½ inch long or less
¼ cup freshly grated *parmigiano-reggiano* (Parmesan)

1. Trim the ends of the Swiss chard stalks and discard any bruised or discolored leaves. Wash them, changing the water several times until it shows no trace of sand.

2. Put the chard in a pot with very little water and at least 1 teaspoon salt. Cover, bring to a boil, and cook over medium heat until tender. Drain the chard over a bowl, reserving all its cooking liquid. Chop the cooked chard coarse.

3. Chop the anchovy fillets very fine together with the rosemary. If using fresh rosemary, do not chop it.

4. Put the olive oil and garlic in a soup pot and turn on the heat to medium high. Cook, stirring frequently with a wooden spoon. When the garlic becomes colored a pale gold, add the anchovies and rosemary. Stir for a few seconds, then remove and discard the garlic. If using

fresh rosemary, discard the rosemary sprig.

5. Put the chard in the pot and cook for 2 to 3 minutes, stirring to coat well with oil.

6. Add the cooked beans or the drained canned *cannellini* and a liberal amount of salt and grindings of pepper. Cook for 2 to 3 minutes, stirring well.

7. Add the reserved cooking liquid from the chard and, if necessary, additional water, until the liquid comes up 3 inches from the top of the soup pot. When the liquid comes to a boil, put in the pasta and cook until it is done *al dente.* Taste, correcting for salt and pepper.

8. Turn off the heat and mix in the grated cheese. Spoon into individual plates or bowls. Wait a few minutes, allowing the heat of the soup to abate slightly, then serve with a few drops of raw olive oil trickled on top.

Pasta and Other First Courses

❧ PASTA ❧

In less than a decade, pasta has risen from the infamy of its *spaghetti* and meatballs days to become a favorite of cooks of all persuasions. Because it is such a simple compound—flour and eggs or flour and water—our attention is naturally drawn to what goes into the sauce or the stuffing and we tend to take for granted the essential component of the dish we are making, the pasta itself. This is regrettable. If we do not clearly perceive the differences in pasta character, if we cannot tell good pasta from bad, we can never master the vast range of expression of this most versatile and satisfying of all foods.

Pasta begins as a mass of dough. Whether or not it is made with eggs or with a particular kind of flour assumes importance only in relation to the method by which it is produced. What we need to distinguish, first of all, is how each method affects the properties of pasta that are most significant in terms of flavor: surface and body.

To become pasta, the original mass of dough must be thinned before it is cut or shaped. The thinning process can be accomplished by stretching, compressing, or extruding, the methods that, in turn, give us the three basic categories of pasta.

STRETCHED PASTA. To make stretched pasta, the mass of dough is gradually flattened and thinned out into a sheet by hand, using a long, perfectly cylindrical, narrow rolling pin over a counter made preferably of wood. What makes the stretching method unique is that no down-ward pressure is exerted to flatten the dough. Thus, it is fundamentally different from rolling out pastry dough, which, at first glance, it may seem to resemble.

As the rolling pin is rocked rhythmically forward and back, the cupped hands slide over the dough spreading it, rather than pushing it, from the center of the pin toward the ends. The dimensions of the pin are dictated by the technique. It is long so that the dough can be stretched over the longest manageable distance; it is narrow so that the hands can comfortably cup over it, exuding warmth to relax the dough and avoiding the pressure that comes naturally to palms opened flat.

When stretched rather than pressed, the pasta's hue is a deeper gold, its surface acquires a slightly irregular texture, etched by a fine, barely visible pattern of intersecting ridges and hollows. As it dries it resembles leather. When cooked, stretched pasta draws and holds sauce to its surface. The body is elastic and has "bounce." The capacity to absorb flavor deeply, combined with liveliness of texture and delicate consistency, makes pasta stretched by hand the paragon of homemade pastas.

The dough is composed of eggs and flour in the proportion of 1 large egg to approximately ¾ cup flour. The flour used in Italy is comparatively low gluten and known as "00," *doppio zero.* Its close American equivalent is unbleached all-purpose. In Bologna, where the standard for handmade pasta is set, no salt, oil, or water is added to the dough. For step-by-step directions on making pasta by hand, please consult *More Classic Italian Cooking*, pages 154–66.

COMPRESSED PASTA. Compressed pasta is made from dough that is flattened thin by pressure. The most familiar example is pasta made with either a hand-cranked or motor-driven machine equipped with two parallel rollers that take up the dough and squeeze it thin in gradual steps. It is pasta produced by this method that in Italian restaurants in the United States is called homemade and in pasta shops by that nearly meaningless term, fresh. (In connection with "fresh," please see Drying Pasta for Storage, page 96.)

Compressed pasta has a smoother surface, slicker texture, flabbier consistency than hand-stretched, and less flavor-absorption capacity. If one cannot make hand-rolled pasta, however, the machine with rollers, when employed as described on page 95, can produce an acceptable substitute. One advantage of the machine is that hard-wheat flour, which is nearly impossible to thin out by hand, can be substituted for all-purpose. Please see the discussion of hard-wheat flour on page 93.

Another example of compressed pasta is pasta rolled out as though it were pastry dough, with a conventional, two-handled pastry rolling pin. It is a method to avoid because, with greater exertion, it produces pasta less fine than the machine.

Also in the compressed pasta category are those shapes formed in the hand with bits of dough pinched from a kneaded mass. Examples are *orecchiette*, described in *The Classic Italian Cook Book*, pages 173–4, *cavatieddi* or *cavatelli*, and *trofie*, a spiral-shaped short pasta from the Riviera.

EXTRUDED PASTA. When a mass of dough is forced through a perforated die you have extruded pasta. After extrusion, the pasta must be dried slowly at carefully calibrated temperatures in special chambers. Extruded pasta requires machinery of industrial size, and it is therefore frequently referred to as factory-made. The most common examples are *spaghetti, rigatoni, ziti, fusilli, penne, conchiglie*, but there are dozens of other shapes.

The dough for dry, factory-made pasta is composed exclusively of selected hard-wheat flours and water. Since these are the only ingredients, the quality of each shows up in the finished product. Another important factor is the perforated die. Bronze dies produce a rough surface to which sauce can cling. Teflon-coated dies are easier to maintain and speed production, but they impart a slick, uninteresting texture.

High-quality factory pasta is as fine a product as the best homemade pasta. It is different as wool is from silk: neither better nor worse. Sadly, it has become fashionable to snub macaroni in favor of so-called fresh pasta. Anyone doing so is turning away from one of the most remarkable foods ever devised by any cuisine.

Factory pasta ought to have the pale gold color and flavor of good hard wheat, a faintly rough texture, and an exceptionally compact body that maintains its firmness in cooking while swelling considerably in size. To my knowledge, none that fulfills all these requirements is manufactured outside Italy.

Egg dough can be extruded, but it is better suited to the stretched or compressed methods. In recent years the market has seen the coming of extruding machines for home use. I am pained to think that, because of their enthusiasm for pasta, people have ended up buying these devices. Flour and eggs go in at one end, you push a button, and what comes out at the other end can be called pasta only in the loosest usage of the word. It is a gummy substance of no gastronomic interest whatever. No more damaging blow to good Italian cooking has ever been struck. Home extruders may have a place in the history of man's infatuation with gadgetry, but they have no place in a kitchen.

Making Pasta at Home by Machine

THE FLOUR

As Elizabeth David has demonstrated magnificently, one can write a volume about varieties of flour. When we focus on Italian cooking, however, and specifically on pasta, we limit our field to two basic kinds: soft-wheat, unbleached, all-purpose flour and durum or hard-wheat flour, also known as semolina or, in Italian, *semola*. The first is white, the second pale yellow.

Each of the two varieties has its virtues and drawbacks. For the classic pasta of Bologna, stretched by hand with a rolling pin, only soft-wheat flour is used. It is lower in gluten than semolina, hence it is easier to hand stretch. Soft wheat has a gentler, warmer fragrance than that of semolina's, which is faintly sharp. The sweet-smelling pasta it produces is plumper in body and of a fluffier consistency than any made with durum wheat flour. On the other hand, it requires utmost heedfulness in the cooking, because it can quickly pass that dangerous line from firm to overdone.

Semolina has so much tough gluten that it is next to impossible to stretch by hand in the Bolognese manner. It is more suitable for flat pasta compressed by a non-extruding home machine or for such industrially extruded shapes as *spaghetti* or *fusilli*. Pasta made with semolina flour is never as downy as the soft-wheat kind, but it makes up for it with a body tautly knit and admirably compact. It accepts an extraordinary variety of sauces and cooks to a perfect *al dente*, firm-to-the-bite consistency.

When buying semolina one must look out for flour that is ground too coarse. Unfortunately much of it is, including some brands that are sold as pasta flour. It should be talcum soft to the touch and impalpable, like other flour; otherwise it will be difficult to work with.

At home I use semolina when I want extra firmness, such as in *tonnarelli*. More frequently I use all-purpose, unbleached flour, which makes pasta closer to that made at home in Bologna. The choice, however, depends on one's preferences. Both flours make equally valid pasta.

THE DOUGH

INGREDIENTS. The dough for homemade pasta consists of flour and eggs, nothing else. The only exception is when spinach or Swiss chard leaves are added to the basic egg and flour dough to make green pasta. Olive oil, salt, colorings, seasonings have no gastronomic reason for being in pasta. Some, such as olive oil that makes pasta slicker, are wholly undesirable and a detriment to good pasta. If one respects the freshness and immediacy of the Italian approach to cooking, one puts all flavors and seasonings in the sauce.

PROPORTIONS. Use 1 cup of flour with 2 large eggs to produce approximately ¾ pound of pasta. The exact ratio, however, will vary depending on the size of the eggs, their flour absorption capacity, even on the humidity of the environment.

COMBINING THE EGGS AND FLOUR. Since you can never tell in advance exactly how much flour you will need, do not mix the flour and eggs in a bowl. You may find you want to use less flour than you thought. Pour the flour onto a work surface, shape it into a mound, scooping out a deep hollow in its center. Break the eggs into the hollow.

Beat the eggs lightly with a fork as though you were making an omelet. Draw some of the flour over the eggs, mixing it, a little at a time, until the eggs are no longer runny. Draw the sides of the mound together, pushing to one side any flour you think you may not use. Work the mixture of flour and eggs with your fingers and the palms of your hands until it is well amalgamated. If it is still too moist, work in more flour as needed.

Put the egg and flour mass to one side and scrape the work surface clean of all loose or caked bits of flour and of any crumbs of dough. Wash your hands and dry them. You are now ready to knead.

MAKING SPINACH DOUGH. For approximately 1 pound of green pasta, use 2 large eggs, approximately 1½ cups flour, and either ½ pound fresh spinach or half a 10-ounce package frozen leaf spinach.

If using fresh spinach, trim away all the stems and wash the leaves in several changes of cold water to remove every trace of soil. Cook it in a covered pan over medium heat with only the water that clings to the leaves and with ¼ teaspoon of salt to keep its color bright. Cook until tender, 15 minutes or more, drain, and let cool.

If using frozen leaf spinach, cook it in a covered pan with ¼ teaspoon of salt until tender. Drain and let cool.

Squeeze all the liquid out of the cooked spinach with your hands, then chop it very fine.

Follow the directions given for combining eggs and flour; beat the chopped spinach into the eggs in the well of flour before drawing any flour over them.

KNEADING THE DOUGH. Kneading dough may be the single most important step in making good pasta. It is best done by hand, which takes no more, and possibly less, time and effort than with a machine, if you include the work required to clean the machine.

Return to the egg and flour mass you had set aside. Push against it with the heel of your palm, keeping your fingers bent, fold it in half, give it a half turn, press hard again, and proceed thus for at least 8 minutes, pressing, folding, turning.

If you are not sure that you have put in enough flour, push a finger into the dough as far as its center. It should come out clean and dry. If it is moist or there are bits of dough stuck to the finger, work in what additional flour you judge the dough needs.

Unless you are ready to run the dough through the machine immediately, wrap it airtight in plastic wrap. Do not refrigerate it, but be ready to proceed with making the pasta within 2 or 3 hours at most.

THE MACHINE

THE TWO ADMISSIBLE KINDS. The basic pasta machine has paired steel rollers of two types: one is smooth and serves to compress and thin out the dough; the second set has parallel grooves that can cut the flattened dough into ribbons. Of this last set there are always two different pairs, a broad-grooved one that produces *fettuccine* and a narrower one that makes *tagliolini*. A movable handle can be inserted into different positions depending which of the rollers is to be turned.

Less common now than it was before the introduction of the wretched extruding machines is the electric machine made by Bialetti. It works on the same principle as the hand-cranked version, over which it has two major advantages: the rollers are of plastic material with a gritty surface that makes pasta with a livelier texture and better sauce-absorbing qualities; it is electrically driven and faster so that it is both easier to use and kinder to the dough, which wants to be worked as rapidly as possible.

No other kinds of machines than these two are suitable for making pasta at home.

Those who already own a hand-operated machine can now buy an ingenious little motor that replaces the crank, converting any hand-turned machine into an electrically driven one.

ROLLING OUT THE DOUGH WITH THE MACHINE. Flattening a ball of dough into a thin sheet is the pasta machine's primary function. To perform it, it has several settings that bring the thinning rollers gradually closer together.

Thinning the dough can be compared to reaching the sidewalk from a building's sixth story. The fastest way is to jump, but you will be a mass of shattered bones. One of the reasons that pasta made by shops is generally so mediocre is that the dough is flattened all at one time, rather than step by step: its body is smashed, its vital sinew broken, it is inert. Walking down the steps is one safe way: it corresponds to the heedful use of the machine's graduated thinning notches. Even less jarring would be to take the elevator: in making pasta, that would be the hand-stretched method.

If you are thinning a ball of dough made with 2 eggs, divide it into 4 equal parts, or proportionally more parts if it is a larger amount. Cover the counter beside the machine with clean, dry, cloth kitchen towels.

Set the thinning rollers at their maximum opening. Flatten 1 of the pieces of dough with your open hand and run it through the machine. Fold it in thirds, give it a quarter turn, and pass it through the machine again. Repeat the operation 2 or 3 times, then lay the flattened pasta strip on the towels. Take another piece of dough and flatten it as described above. Lay it next to the previously flattened strip on the towel, but do not let them overlap or touch. When all the dough has been flattened you can begin to thin it progressively.

Close the opening of the rollers one notch and run the first of the flattened strips through it once. Do not fold it, but lay it flat on the towel. Repeat the procedure with all the other flattened pasta strips. When all are done, close the opening down another notch and thin all the strips again as has just been described. Continue thinning the pasta one notch at a time until it reaches the desired thinness. (Note: If you are making stuffed pasta, and you work slowly, take each piece of dough all the way through the thinning process, stuff it, then do the next piece. Keep the dough waiting to be thinned wrapped in plastic wrap.)

CUTTING THE PASTA. If you are making *lasagne, cannelloni,* and any stuffed pasta, use the pasta immediately, as described in the appropriate recipe. For any pasta that encloses a stuffing, such as *tortelli, tortellini, raviolini,* the pasta must be cut and stuffed as soon as it is made, while it is still soft and sticky. Its softness makes it easier to shape and the stickiness is necessary to produce a tight seal, preventing the stuffing from spilling out during the cooking.

For any kind of noodle, however, allow the strips to dry on the towels for 10 minutes or more, depending on the temperature and air circulation of your kitchen. Turn the strips over from time to time. The pasta is ready when it is still soft and pliant enough that it won't crack when cut, but not so moist that the noodles will stick to each other.

Use the broad cutters on the machine to make *fettuccine,* and the narrower ones to make *tagliolini. Tagliatelle,* the classic Bolognese noodle, is slightly broader than *fettuccine.* If you are set on duplicating the Bolognese model, the pasta strips must be rolled up loosely and cut by hand into ¼-inch-wide ribbons.

The most interesting noodle cut of all is *tonnarelli.* It is as thick as it is broad, thus a cross section of it would be square. Its slightly greater thickness gives it the marvelous firmness and "bite" of *spaghetti,* while its surface has the texture and fine saucing qualities of all homemade pasta. The machine does a perfect job of making *ton-*

narelli, but you will have to think ahead when you are thinning out the dough. The thickness of the pasta strips that will subsequently be cut into *tonnarelli* must be equal to the width of the narrow grooves of the cutting roller. On many machines the corresponding thinning notch is the second before the last, but it is advisable that you measure and check for yourself.

As you cut the noodles, whatever their shape, separate them and spread them out on the cloth towels. To cook, pick them up with the towel itself, pulling its 4 corners together, and let them slide into the boiling water from the towel, releasing 2 of its corners.

DRYING PASTA FOR STORAGE

If it is not to be cooked shortly after it is made, noodle pasta can be dried completely and stored for weeks in a cupboard, just like *spaghetti.* While the noodles are still soft and pliant, take a few strands at a time and curl them into nest shapes. Allow them to dry totally, because if there is any moisture left when they are stored, mold will form. To be sure, let the nests dry on towels for at least 24 hours. When dry, place them in a large box or tin, interleaving each layer of nests with a sheet of paper towels. Handle the nests gently because they will be very brittle. Put the box away in a dry cupboard. Do not refrigerate. Pasta ought never to see the inside of a refrigerator.

Dry pasta will take longer to cook than the fresh, but when cooked there is no difference between them in taste or consistency. Thus the term "fresh," if it is used with implications of quality rather than as a description of the consistency of recently made raw pasta, has no significance whatever.

Fettuccine al Limone

FETTUCCINE WITH LEMON

OF ALL food fragrances none, to my mind, is more closely associated with Mediterranean life than lemon. Its refreshing pungency is as much a part of it as the spiced breezes of the sea itself. Lemon, both its rind and juice, is virtually the only ingredient in this sauce, yet it is a sly one: You do not see it, but oh, when the smell and taste reach you, do you know it's there! This is one of those lightning quick Italian triumphs; the sauce takes far less to make than for water to boil.

For 4 to 6 persons

4 tablespoons butter
1 cup heavy cream
2 tablespoons freshly squeezed lemon juice
The grated peel, but none of the white pith
    beneath, of 4 lemons

Fettuccine made with 3 large eggs and about
    2 cups flour, as described on pages 93–5
½ cup freshly grated *parmigiano-reggiano*
    (Parmesan), plus additional for the table

1.   Choose a skillet or sauté pan large enough to accommodate the cooked *fettuccine* later. Put in the butter and cream and turn on the heat to high. When the cream begins to boil, add the lemon juice and stir thoroughly. Add the grated lemon peel. Continue stirring while you reduce the cream to half its original volume. Do not reduce it completely because the *fettuccine* will be tossed with it later in the pan and absorb it all. Turn off the heat.

2.   Drop the pasta into a pot of abundant boiling salted water. When cooked, but still quite firm to the bite, drain, transfer to the pan with the lemon sauce, turn on the heat to medium, and toss the *fettuccine* thoroughly in the sauce for 15 to 20 seconds.

3.   Transfer all the pasta and sauce from the pan to a warm serving bowl. Add the grated cheese, toss two or three times, then serve at once with additional grated cheese on the side.

❧

Fettuccine col Sugo di Tonno con Aglio e Panna

FETTUCCINE WITH TUNA, GARLIC, AND CREAM SAUCE

CANNED tuna is a familiar ingredient in pasta sauces. Although I was once very fond of it, there was a harshness in the taste of tuna sauces, both other cooks' and my own, that began to trouble me. It took a long while, as my dissatisfaction grew, for me to identify its cause. At last I knew: Cooking altered tuna's taste. I looked for ways to make a sauce that did not require cooking the tuna. The one that pleased me most is derived from the buttery tuna spread described on page 38. To it I added garlic, egg, parsley, cream, and Parmesan, mixing everything by hand rather than in the processor to obtain a grainier, more interesting texture.

For another tuna sauce based on the same principle, please see Penne with Tuna and Roasted Peppers on page 130.

For 4 to 6 persons

Fettuccine with Tuna, Garlic, and Cream Sauce (continued)

A 7-ounce can of Italian-style tuna packed
    in olive oil
1/2 teaspoon garlic chopped very fine
2 tablespoons parsley
1 egg, lightly beaten
3 tablespoons butter, softened to
    room temperature

2/3 cup heavy cream
Salt
Black pepper in a grinder
1/2 cup freshly grated *parmigiano-reggiano*
    (Parmesan), plus additional for the table
Fettuccine made with 3 large eggs and about
    2 cups flour, as described on pages 93–5

1. Drain the tuna of all its oil and put it in a mixing bowl.

2. Add the garlic, parsley, egg, butter, cream, salt, liberal grindings of pepper, and the 1/2 cup of grated cheese. Mix well until all the ingredients are thoroughly amalgamated, using a fork to break up and mash the tuna.

Taste and correct for salt and pepper.

3. Drop the pasta into a pot of abundant boiling salted water and cook until it is done but firm to the bite, drain, and toss immediately with the tuna mixture. Serve at once, with additional grated cheese available on the side.

Fettuccine col Sugo di Vongole e Zucchine

FETTUCCINE WITH CLAMS AND ZUCCHINI

ELSEWHERE I have mentioned the happy affinity zucchini have for sea-food; please see Zucchini Boats Stuffed with Shrimp, page 43. It is a discovery that has also been made by Pierino, my chef friend from Amalfi, whose recipe this is. Clams have a pungency, a high flavor generally better suited to *spaghetti* than to homemade pasta. Once wedded to zucchini, however, they assume a gentle demeanor for which *fettuccine* are the perfect background.

The zucchini are cooked at first with a *soffritto* of olive oil, onion, and garlic, then finished with white wine. To complete the sauce they are combined with basil and with the clam meat briefly heated in its own reduced juices. The method is classic, the sauce new.

For 4 to 6 persons

2 dozen small littleneck clams
1 pound fresh, small, young zucchini, soaked
    in cold water for 20 minutes

1/2 cup extra virgin olive oil
1 cup chopped onion
1 tablespoon chopped garlic

Salt
Black pepper in a grinder
1/2 cup dry white wine

8 fresh basil leaves
Fettuccine made with 3 large eggs and about
   2 cups flour, as described on pages 93–5

1.   Wash the clams in several changes of cold water, rubbing the shells vigorously against one another, or with a stiff brush.

2.   Put the clams in a pot with 1/2 cup water, cover the pot, and turn on the heat to high. Stir from time to time with a long spoon. The clams are not likely to open all at the same time, so be prepared to remove them the moment they unclench their shells; otherwise they will overcook and become tough.

3.   When all the clams are open and out of the pot, transfer the liquid in the pot to a bowl, pouring it gently so that as much sand as possible will be left behind.

4.   Detach the clam meat from the shells and put it in the bowl to keep it moist until ready to use.

5.   When the zucchini have finished soaking, scrub them in several changes of cold water with your hands or with a stiff brush to dislodge all grit from their skins. Cut off both ends from each zucchini and dice the zucchini into 1/2-inch cubes.

6.   Choose a sauté pan that can subsequently accommodate all the zucchini without too much overlapping. Put in the oil and chopped onion and turn on the heat to medium. Cook for about 5 minutes, stirring occasionally, without letting the onion become more than lightly colored; then add the garlic.

7.   When the garlic becomes colored a very pale gold, add the diced zucchini and turn up the heat to medium high. Stir frequently, adding salt and liberal grindings of pepper. Add the wine, turning up the heat to high and scraping loose any cooking residues from the bottom of the pan. Cook the zucchini until tender, but firm and compact. Turn off the heat and transfer the cooked zucchini to a small bowl, using a slotted spoon or spatula.

8.   In the bowl containing the clam meat swish each clam gently in its juice to rinse it of any remaining sand, then place it on a cutting board. When there are no clams left in the bowl, filter the juice through a strainer lined with a paper towel or a fine cloth.

9.   Put the juice into the sauté pan and turn on the heat to high. While the juice is reducing, chop the clams into 4 or 5 pieces each and cut the basil leaves into fine strips. When the clam juice has almost completely evaporated, return the zucchini to the pan, add the chopped clams and the basil strips, stir 2 or 3 times, and turn off the heat.

10.   Drop the pasta into a pot of abundant boiling salted water. The moment it is tender but firm to the bite, drain, toss immediately in a warm bowl with the sauce, and serve at once.

AHEAD-OF-TIME NOTE: The sauce is best if used the moment it is done, but it can be reheated gently after a few hours.

Strette allo Zafferano col Trito di Vitello

NARROW NOODLES WITH SAFFRON AND VEAL

THIS recipe developed out of the desire to produce an alternative to Bolognese meat sauce that would be lighter, leaner, faster to make, and that would contain no tomato. I chose veal, which cooks rapidly and, unlike the beef in Bologna's *ragù*, does not need to be sweetened with slow-cooking vegetables like carrot. To give the flavor some spice, I added saffron dissolved in cream.

The sauce does everything I had looked for and, as a bonus, it endows the pasta with a lovely golden color similar to that of the pasta we used to make in the country, with eggs from chickens that had been fed only corn.

For 4 to 6 persons

2 tablespoons butter
1 tablespoon vegetable oil
4 tablespoons chopped onion
¾ pound ground veal, preferably from
    the shoulder
Salt
Black pepper in a grinder
¼ teaspoon powdered saffron*

¾ cup heavy cream
Tagliolini (or *strette* as they would be called
    in Bologna) made with 3 large eggs and
    about 2 cups unbleached flour,
    as described on pages 93–5
Freshly grated *parmigiano-reggiano* (Parmesan)
    for the table

*Powdered saffron is not as easy to find as saffron strands. However, it is worth making the effort to get because it dissolves better. If you must use the strands, chop them and increase the amount by at least ⅛ teaspoon to achieve comparable intensity of flavor.

1. Put the butter, vegetable oil, and chopped onion in a skillet or sauté pan and turn on the heat to medium high.

2. When the onion becomes colored a pale gold, add the ground veal. Cook the veal, crumbling it with a fork and turning it from time to time, until you have browned it all over. Sprinkle with salt and liberal grindings of pepper, turning the meat two or three times.

3. Add the saffron and cream, and reduce the heat to medium. Cook the cream down, stirring frequently, until it is no longer runny.

4. Drop the pasta into a pot of abundant boiling salted water. The moment it is tender but firm to the bite, drain, toss immediately in a warm bowl with the sauce, and serve at once with grated Parmesan on the side.

Tagliolini col Pesto al Caprino

THIN NOODLES WITH GOAT CHEESE PESTO

*T*HE fundamental cheeses that go into pesto are Parmesan and Sardinian *pecorino*. For a lighter taste impact, Genoese cooks sometimes thin the consistency by adding ricotta, as I have described on pages 190–1 in *More Classic Italian Cooking*. In the following recipe I have gone a little farther and substituted goat cheese for all other cheeses. It makes a more loosely knit pesto, one with notable freshness and tang. This, like all sauces derived from basic pesto (please see *The Classic Italian Cook Book*, pages 139–42), is a condiment that must be used raw, without undergoing any cooking, no matter how brief.

For 4 to 6 persons

1½ cups fresh basil
1½ teaspoons chopped garlic
3 tablespoons pine nuts
Salt
⅓ cup extra virgin olive oil

4 tablespoons creamy goat cheese
Black pepper in a grinder
Tagliolini, thin noodles made with 3 large eggs and about 2 cups flour, as described on pages 93–5

1. Wash the basil in cold water, then pat it as dry as possible with a kitchen towel.

2. Put the basil, garlic, pine nuts, and a pinch of salt in a food processor and chop briefly. If using a blender, add 3 tablespoons of oil.

3. Add all the oil—the remaining oil, if using a blender—and continue blending until the mixture becomes creamy.

4. Transfer to the bowl where you'll be serving the pasta. Add the goat cheese and a few grindings of pepper. Mash the cheese into the mixture with a fork until it is smoothly and evenly amalgamated. Taste and correct for salt.

5. Drop the pasta into a pot of abundant boiling salted water and cook until it is done but firm to the bite. Just before draining the pasta add a tablespoon or two of the water in which it is cooking to the sauce in the bowl. Drain the pasta and toss it immediately with the sauce. Do *not* serve with grated cheese.

Tagliatelle alla Romagnola con Sugo di Spinaci

NOODLES WITH SPINACH AND TOMATO

*T*HE birthplace of this spinach and tomato sauce is Romagna, that ancient enclave of the Byzantine Roman Empire on the Adriatic. It is my native region as well, and this recipe out of my childhood is the one my grandmother used. Chopped fresh raw spinach is first *insaporito*—coated—with sautéed garlic and olive oil, then fresh tomatoes are added. When the tomatoes are cooked, the sauce is done.

The traditional pasta for the sauce is *tagliatelle*, the noodles that so many families in Romagna still make by hand every day, and that is the one suggested here. For a change, we would occasionally make a *risotto* with this sauce. Or, in winter, we would dilute the sauce with meat broth and serve it as soup with small cuts of pasta. It is also excellent on its own as a vegetable dish to accompany a pork roast or a boiled brisket of beef.

For 4 to 6 persons

1 pound fresh spinach
1 pound ripe, fresh tomatoes
½ cup extra virgin olive oil
2½ teaspoons chopped garlic
Salt

Black pepper in a grinder
Tagliatelle or *fettuccine*, noodles made with
   3 large eggs and about 2 cups flour,
   as described on pages 93–5
Freshly grated *parmigiano-reggiano* (Parmesan)

1. Cut off and discard the root end of the spinach, separating all the leaves. Soak the spinach for at least 5 to 6 minutes in a large basin filled with cold water. (I use the kitchen sink, after washing it thoroughly clean.) Lift the spinach out of the basin or sink, taking care not to scoop up any soil that will have settled to the bottom. Rinse the spinach in several changes of cold water until you are satisfied that there is no more grit on the leaves. Drain well, using, if you have it, one of those salad spinners. Otherwise, wrapping the leaves in a large kitchen towel and shaking the water through it is just as effective. Chop the dried spinach not too fine and set aside.

2. In a large saucepan put enough water to cover the tomatoes later and bring it to a boil. Put in the tomatoes. After 2 to 3 minutes, drain and let the tomatoes cool just enough so that you can handle them. Peel them, split them, remove all the seeds that scrape away easily, and cut the flesh into narrow strips.

3. Choose a sauté pan large enough to accommodate all the chopped spinach. Put into it the olive oil and garlic and turn on the heat to medium. Cook until the garlic becomes colored a pale gold.

4. Add the spinach, salt, and a few gridings of pepper. Cook, stirring frequently, for a minute or two.

5.　Add the tomatoes and lower the heat so that the tomatoes can cook at a gentle simmer. Stir from time to time. When you see the oil separate from the sauce, in about 25 minutes or so, the sauce is done.

6.　Drop the noodles into a pot of abundant boiling salted water. When they are cooked but still firm to the bite, drain and toss immediately with the sauce. Serve with a liberal sprinkling of freshly grated Parmesan.

ADDITIONAL SERVING SUGGESTIONS: In farmhouses in Romagna, the sauce is diluted with homemade meat broth in which one then cooks small pasta squares, pasta barley, or other miniature soup pasta shapes.

Tonnarelli con la Belga e la Pancetta Affumicata

TONNARELLI WITH BELGIAN ENDIVE AND BACON

*A*MONG many other culinary treasures, Treviso is celebrated for its *radicchio.* It does not look like the round heads of red *radicchio* Americans have been becoming familiar with, although it is also a part of the same large chicory family. *Radicchio di Treviso* has the elongated shape of romaine but is considerably more slender, and its leaves are a purplish red with white striations. It comes into season very late in the fall, and it is used more in cooking than raw in salads. Combined with smoked *pancetta*—which in the Veneto is more prevalent than the unsmoked kind—it makes one of the great pasta sauces.

To duplicate the sauce, I looked for a substitute for *radicchio di Treviso,* which, at least at the moment I am writing this, is still too rare in America, and, when available, too costly to consider for a sauce wherein it goes in such quantity. Belgian endive, another member of the chicory family, turned out to be a perfect replacement for both its flavor and cooking qualities. As for smoked *pancetta,* good-quality bacon is a nearly exact equivalent.

You may find the amount of endive you have to cook startling. Do not be alarmed. It has to cook down to a fraction of its volume until it is so soft it almost dissolves so that later it will cling on the pasta.

I like the flavor of egg pasta in this dish, and I have chosen *tonnarelli* in particular because their extra firmness makes such an agreeable connection with the creamy endive sauce. But you needn't limit yourself to homemade pasta. *Spaghetti, fusilli,* or *rigatoni* will also work out well.

For 6 persons

Tonnarelli with Belgian Endive and Bacon (continued)

1½ to 2 pounds Belgian endive
2 tablespoons butter
½ pound prime-quality bacon, cut into
     ¼-inch-wide strips
Salt
Black pepper in a grinder

½ cup heavy cream
Tonnarelli made with 3 large eggs and 1¾ cups
     flour (preferably hard-wheat flour),
     as described on pages 93–5
½ cup freshly grated *parmigiano-reggiano*
     (Parmesan)

1.   Slice off just the bruised or discolored portion of the bottom of the endive root and discard it. Cut the endive lengthwise in strips ¼ to ½ inch wide, leaving them attached to the root end.

2.   Put the butter and bacon in a medium-size sauté pan and turn on the heat to medium. Cook the bacon until it becomes deeply colored, but not crisp.

3.   Add all the endive, turn it over once or twice, then cover the pan and turn the heat down to low. Cook, turning the endive over from time to time, for at least 15 minutes, or until the endive is tender, almost creamy in consistency.

4.   Uncover the pan and turn up the heat to medium high. If there is liquid in the pan, boil it away, stirring the endive steadily, making sure it does not brown. Add salt and liberal grindings of pepper, stir, and add the cream. Cook until the cream has been reduced by half, then remove from the heat.

5.   Drop the pasta into a pot of abundant boiling salted water. Cook until it is tender but still firm to the bite. Drain and toss at once with the sauce from the pan. Add the grated cheese, toss again, and serve immediately.

AHEAD-OF-TIME NOTE: The sauce may be prepared several hours in advance, but not the night before. Reheat gently while the pasta is cooking.

Tonnarelli al Melone

TONNARELLI WITH CANTALOUPE

*S*EVERAL years ago, an inventive young cook named Silvano surprised Venice by opening a restaurant serving neither of the city's great specialties, seafood and *risotto*. His first courses were all made with firm, factory pasta, each with an entirely original sauce. One day Silvano surprised everyone again: he sold his interest and disappeared, leaving behind only the memories of his dazzling cooking.

One of his dishes I most admired was *spaghetti* with melon. Cantaloupe is what he used and what works best. This version is based largely on the recipe he gave me, with minor adjustments of my own.

Tonnarelli are suggested for the same reasons given in the preceding recipe. Any good imported brand of *spaghetti*, however, will give excellent results.

For 4 to 6 persons

4 tablespoons butter
1 tablespoon vegetable oil
3 cups cantaloupe, rind and seeds removed, diced into ¼-inch cubes
1 cup heavy cream
1 tablespoon freshly squeezed lemon juice

½ teaspoon tomato paste
Salt
Black pepper in a grinder
Tonnarelli made with 3 large eggs and 1¾ cups flour (preferably hard-wheat flour), as described on pages 93–5

1. Put the butter and oil in a 10- to 12-inch sauté pan and turn on the heat to high. When the oil is hot but not smoking, add the melon. Cook the melon for about 2 minutes, stirring frequently. The melon must soften, but not dissolve completely; most of the pieces should still be separate.

2. Add the cream, lemon juice, and tomato paste. Stir and cook at high heat until the cream is reduced to half its original volume.

3. Add salt, very liberal grindings of pepper, stir once or twice, and remove from the heat.

4. Drop the pasta into a pot of abundant boiling salted water. The moment the pasta is tender but firm to the bite, drain it, toss immediately with the sauce in a warm serving bowl, and serve at once.

NOTE: If using eggless factory pasta such as *spaghetti*, which absorbs less sauce, reduce the heavy cream in cooking to one-quarter its volume.

Pappardelle Ripiene

GOAT CHEESE-STUFFED BROAD NOODLES

*T*HE soup *raviolini* with ricotta, whose recipe appears on page 77, moved me to devise this new shape for homemade stuffed pasta. A very thin strip of pasta is daubed with a mixture of goat cheese, Parmesan, egg, and nutmeg, doubled over, and trimmed into 6- to 7-inch-long narrow rectangles. Each rectangle looks like a short, broad, double noodle with a slightly plump center. I call them *pappardelle,* the broad noodles they resemble more closely than any other pasta cut.

The sauce I prefer for them is the nippy lemon sauce from the *fettuccine* recipe on page 96. Another good choice would be butter and sage, made by sizzling some butter for a few moments together with 3 or 4 whole sage leaves. Even more simply and no less good, toss with 2 to 3 tablespoons of fresh butter and a fistful of grated Parmesan.

For 4 to 6 persons

¼ pound creamy, mild goat cheese
1 cup freshly grated *parmigiano-reggiano*
    (Parmesan)
2 eggs
Black pepper in a grinder

⅛ teaspoon grated nutmeg
Salt
Homemade pasta dough made with 2 large eggs
    and about 1½ cups flour, as described on
    pages 93–5

1. Put the goat cheese, Parmesan, eggs, liberal grindings of pepper, and the nutmeg in a bowl and mix to an even consistency with a fork. Taste and correct for salt.

2. Make the pasta, thinning it out to the narrowest setting on the machine. Lay each strip of pasta flat and, using a rubber spatula, spread a thin coating of the cheese mixture over the entire length, but only half the width, of the strip. Do not coat the pasta to the very edge of the strip, but stop about ½ inch short of it.

3. Fold the uncoated side of the strip of pasta over the other half, meeting it edge to edge, but not pressing down on it.

4. With a pastry cutting wheel cut the pasta into long, narrow rectangles about 6 to 7 inches long and 1 inch wide. Make sure all edges are sealed tight. Spread the cut pasta on a towel laid flat on a counter. If you are not going to cook it immediately, turn it over from time to time. Make sure the stuffed strips do not overlap or touch each other.

5. To cook, drop into a pot of abundant boiling salted water. Drain when still firm to the bite. Toss with the lemon sauce from page 96 and serve at once.

AHEAD-OF-TIME NOTE: Although the noodles must be cooked only when ready to serve, they can be made several hours earlier the same day.

Raviolini di Rape e Cipolla col Burro e l'Erba Cipollina

MINIATURE BEET AND ONION RAVIOLI WITH BUTTER AND CHIVES

*I*N ITALY, except for the thousands of wives and mothers cooking in family *trattorie*, a professional female chef is next to unknown. One of the few was Anna Gennari, a slight, high-spirited, immensely talented blonde who has since retired as executive chef of the Carlton Hotel's Royal Grill in Bologna. The following recipe is of her devising.

Onions and pasta are a natural and—to those as fond of onion as I and most other Italians are—a delicious combination. The flavors of three members of the onion family supply the prevalent harmony in this recipe: in the stuffing onion itself dominates, joined by a few scallions; the beets add a surprising complementary flavor; the sauce is simply butter and fresh chives.

In this, as in any other Italian dish that requires a large quantity of onion, the onion's sharp bite must be removed by cooking it down slowly until it is very soft and sheds all its juice; that juice is boiled away, then the onion is sautéed briskly until it becomes colored a light brown. Only at that point is it both sweet and savory.

About 150 small ravioli, for 6 to 8 persons

For the stuffing:

1 large or 2 medium raw red beets, about 1½ ounces; or, less desirable, canned whole beets

Green tops of 6 scallions

1½ pounds onions, peeled and sliced as thin as possible

3 tablespoons butter

Salt

Black pepper in a grinder

1 cup freshly grated *parmigiano-reggiano* (Parmesan)

⅓ cup fine, dry, unflavored bread crumbs, toasted in a pan as described on page 21

1 egg yolk

For the pasta:

Homemade pasta dough made with 2 large eggs and about 1½ cups unbleached flour, as described on pages 93–5

For the condiment:

6 tablespoons butter

3 tablespoons chives chopped very fine

Freshly grated *parmigiano-reggiano* (Parmesan) to taste

Miniature Beet and Onion Ravioli with Butter and Chives (continued)

1. Discard the green tops of the beets and wash the bulbs thoroughly clean of all soil. Put them in a pot with ample water to cover and bring to a boil. Cook until pierced easily with a fork. Drain, peel, and chop extremely fine, using a food processor or any other method. If using canned whole beets, drain and chop fine.

2. Wash the green scallion tops and cut them into the thinnest possible rings.

3. In a skillet or sauté pan put the sliced onion, the scallion rings, and the 3 tablespoons of butter, cover the pan, and turn on the heat to very low. Cook until the onion is very soft, no less than 1 hour. If you check you will find that, at first, the onion will have thrown off considerable liquid. It will eventually vanish in the cooking.

4. When the onion is very soft, uncover the pan, add salt and liberal grindings of pepper, and turn up the heat to high. Cook, stirring frequently, until the onion becomes colored a pale nut brown. Transfer to a bowl with a slotted spoon or spatula, and let cool completely.

5. When the onion is cold, add the chopped beets, the 1 cup of grated cheese, the bread crumbs, and the egg yolk and mix thoroughly to amalgamate all the ingredients uniformly.

6. Knead the dough for the pasta as described on page 94. Cut off a piece, wrapping the rest in plastic wrap. Thin the dough in the pasta machine, step by step, as described on pages 94–5, until you reach the next to last setting of the machine. Trim the edges of the strips to make long rectangles about 3 inches wide or slightly less. Do not discard the trimmings. Knead them into the remaining ball of dough, rewrapping it after with plastic wrap.

7. Pinch off some stuffing, shaping it into little balls about the size of a hazelnut. Make sure that wisps of onion do not protrude or they may keep the *raviolini* from sealing tightly, causing them to open while cooking.

8. Dot the strip of pasta along one edge with stuffing, keeping the lumps about 1/2 inch apart and away from the edge. Fold the undotted side of the strip over the stuffing, forming a long, flat tube. Press the 3 cut edges of the tube firmly together. Use a pastry wheel to trim the edges, sealing them tightly, and to cut the tube into tiny squares of about 1 1/2 inches or less.

9. Separate the squares and spread them on a dry cloth towel spread on a counter, making sure they do not touch each other at any point because otherwise they will stick together.

10. Thin out another strip of pasta and repeat the entire stuffing and cutting operation.

11. When all the *raviolini* are done and spread out on towels, if you are not going to cook them immediately turn them from time to time so they will dry evenly and not stick to the towel.

12. When ready to serve, bring a large pot of water to a boil, add salt, gather the *raviolini* in a towel and, when the water resumes boiling, drop them into the pot. Drain them, retrieving them with a perforated scoop, when they are done but still firm to the bite. Shake them gently in a colander to throw off water. Transfer them immediately to a warm serving platter, toss at once with the 6 tablespoons of butter and the chopped chives, and serve piping hot with ample grated cheese available on the side.

AHEAD-OF-TIME NOTE: The *raviolini* may be made entirely in advance, up to the time they are ready to be cooked, several hours before dinner. Cook them only when ready to serve.

Tortelloni di Porri

TORTELLONI STUFFED WITH LEEK

*L*EEK makes a novel stuffing for pasta. The way it is handled in this recipe, however, illustrates a fundamental Italian approach. The leek is cooked down slowly, its liquid evaporated, then it is browned. Following that, it is chopped and mixed with egg, Parmesan, and nutmeg. Thus a new stuffing acquires a recognizably Italian taste.

Stuffing for pasta can be done with a variety of vegetables, cheeses, meats, or fish. It must not contain large pieces of anything; nor may it resemble the undifferentiated consistency of baby food. It should invariably contain at least one of the following elements of flavor: Parmesan or nutmeg and, in the case of cooked stuffing, that special savoriness that comes from *insaporire,* the sautéing and browning of ingredients.

The sauce for these *tortelloni* is a particularly rich one of tomatoes and cream in which the tomatoes are cooked over a *soffritto* of onion, carrot, and celery. It could be an excellent sauce for other stuffed pasta such as *tortelloni* with Swiss chard (see *The Classic Italian Cook Book,* page 164) or for tubular pasta such as *penne* or *rigatoni.*

About 115 tortelloni, *for 6 to 8 persons*

For the stuffing:

3 pounds leeks, about 8 cups when cut up
3 tablespoons butter
1 cup water
Salt
Black pepper in a grinder

1 egg
1/2 cup freshly grated *parmigiano-reggiano* (Parmesan)
1/8 teaspoon grated nutmeg

For the pasta:

Homemade pasta dough made with 3 large eggs and about 1⅔ cups unbleached flour, as described on pages 93–5

For the vegetable sauce:

3 tablespoons butter
2 tablespoons vegetable oil
1/2 cup chopped onion
1/2 cup chopped carrot
1/2 cup chopped celery
1 1/2 cups canned Italian peeled

plum tomatoes, cut up in large pieces, with their juice
1/2 cup heavy cream
Salt
Black pepper in a grinder

Tortelloni Stuffed with Leek (continued)

1 tablespoon extra virgin olive oil
1 to 2 tablespoons freshly grated *parmigiano-*

reggiano (Parmesan), plus additional for
the table

1. Cut off the roots from the leek and discard any discolored or blemished outer leaf. Trim a little bit from the green tips. Cut the leek crosswise into rounds about ¼ inch thick. Wash thoroughly under cold running water.

2. Put the leek in a skillet or sauté pan together with the 3 tablespoons of butter and the water, cover the pan, and turn on the heat to medium. Cook until the leek is reduced nearly to a pulp, then uncover the pan, turn up the heat, and brown the leek lightly, turning it 2 or 3 times. Should there be any liquid left in the pan, boil it away. Add salt.

3. Chop the leek with a knife or in the food processor, giving it just one quick spin of the blade. Put it in a bowl, adding a few grindings of pepper, the egg, the ½ cup of grated cheese, and the nutmeg. Mix thoroughly with a fork until all the ingredients are combined evenly. Press down with a spatula to eliminate any air pockets.

4. Knead the pasta dough as described on page 94. Cut off a piece, wrapping the rest in plastic wrap. Thin out the piece in the pasta machine, step by step, as described on pages 94–5, stopping at the next to last setting. Lay the pasta strip flat on a work counter.

5. Dot the pasta with ½-teaspoon lumps of leek stuffing, setting them down in a straight row along one side of the strip, and spacing them about 1½ inches apart and the same distance from the edge. Use one spoon to scoop up the stuffing from the bowl and another to push off the stuffing from the first spoon onto the pasta. Try not to get any stuffing on your fingers; otherwise you'll have to wash them each time you need to handle more pasta.

6. Fold the undotted side of the pasta over the stuffing. Use a *ravioli* cutter—a pastry wheel with a wavy edge—to trim the pasta edges where they meet or overlap, thus sealing them, and to cut the pasta into squares. Separate the squares and spread them on a clean, dry towel laid out flat on a counter.

7. Cut off another piece of the wrapped pasta dough, rewrapping the remainder. Press the pasta trimmings from the first batch of *tortelloni* into the dough and reknead it briefly, passing it 3 or 4 times through the pasta machine rollers at their widest setting. Thin it out as described above and repeat the entire operation, making a second batch of *tortelloni*. Continue making more *tortelloni* until you have used up all the pasta and/or all the stuffing. Make sure that the finished *tortelloni* do not touch each other or they will stick to one another.

8. Put the 3 tablespoons butter, the vegetable oil, and the chopped onion in a saucepan, turning on the heat to medium high. When the onion becomes colored a pale gold, add the carrot and celery. Cook until the vegetables are lightly browned, turning them from time to time.

9. Add the tomatoes with their juice. Cook for about 20 minutes, until the fat separates from the other juices.

10. Add the cream, salt, and a few grindings of pepper. Cook at high heat, stirring frequently, until the cream is reduced to a thick consistency.

11. Drop the *tortelloni* into a pot of abundant boiling salted water together with the olive oil. When they are done but slightly firm at the edges, drain them and toss immediately with the sauce. Sprinkle with the grated cheese, toss again, and serve with additional grated cheese available on the side.

Cannelloni con gli Asparagi

CANNELLONI WITH ASPARAGUS AND HAM

N*O STUFFED* pasta could be more elegant, none tastier, none more simple to assemble than *cannelloni.* Yet there is none whose execution is so consistently dreary. The error that most cooks make with *cannelloni* is that they take the stuffing, shape it like a sausage, and wrap layers of pasta around it. Thus *cannelloni* turn out to be dull, thick casings for a clumsy lump trapped in their center.

The correct method is not more difficult to carry out, but it yields incomparably finer results. The pasta is laid flat and the stuffing mixture, however it may be composed, is spread thinly over the entire surface. Then the pasta is rolled up loosely, like a jelly roll, so that each layer of pasta is filmily bound to the next by no more savory stuffing than is absolutely necessary.

Of the many stuffings for *cannelloni* I have experimented with, this one with asparagus and ham has never failed to please.

For 6 persons

2 pounds asparagus	Salt
6 tablespoons butter	6 ounces boiled unsmoked ham
1 cup water	

For the béchamel:

3 cups milk	4½ tablespoons flour
6 tablespoons butter	Pinch salt

1 cup freshly grated *parmigiano-reggiano* (Parmesan)	Homemade pasta dough made with 2 large eggs and about 1½ cups unbleached flour, as described on pages 93–5
⅛ teaspoon grated nutmeg	

1. Trim 1 inch or more off the butt ends of the asparagus, leaving only the moist, tender part of the stalk. Pare away the tough green skin from the base of the spear to the end of the stalk. Remove any tiny leaves sprouting below the base of the tip. Cut the trimmed asparagus into 2-inch lengths and wash in cold water.

2. Choose a lidded, shallow pan large enough to accommodate all the asparagus. Put in 4 tablespoons of the butter, the water, a little salt, and the asparagus. Cover and turn on the heat to medium. Cook until the asparagus is tender, but firm. If, when the asparagus is done, there is still liquid in the pan, uncover, raise the heat to high, and boil away the liquid while browning the asparagus lightly.

3. Cut up the ham and chop it in a food processor, but take care not to chop it too fine.

Cannelloni with Asparagus and Ham (continued)

Add the asparagus to the processor bowl and run the processor very briefly once or twice. The asparagus should be cut up into small pieces, but not blended to a creamy consistency.

4.   Make the béchamel: Heat the milk over low heat until it forms a ring of pearly bubbles, but do not let it break into a boil. While the milk is being heated, melt the butter in a separate pan over low heat. When the butter melts, add the flour, stirring constantly with a wooden spoon. When the flour has been wholly amalgamated with the butter, but before it becomes colored, remove from the heat. Add 2 tablespoons of milk at a time to the flour and butter mixture, stirring steadily and thoroughly. Add 2 more tablespoons of milk when the first 2 have been incorporated smoothly and evenly into the butter and flour. Stir and repeat the operation until you have put in 8 tablespoons of milk. At this point you can add the milk ½ cup at a time, always stirring steadily to obtain a homogeneous mixture. When all the milk has been worked in, place the pan over low heat, add the pinch of salt, and stir without interruption until the béchamel is as dense as a thick cream.

5.   Put the chopped asparagus and ham in a bowl, add half the béchamel, ⅔ cup of the grated cheese, and the nutmeg. Mix well.

6.   Knead the dough for the pasta and thin it out, stopping at the next to last setting on the machine, as described on pages 94–5.

7.   Cut the pasta strips into 5- to 6-inch-long rectangles, leaving them as wide as they come from the machine. Parboil them, rinse them, and spread on dry cloth towels, following the instructions in the recipe for *lasagne* (page 119).

8.   Turn on the oven to 450°.

9.   Choose a baking pan large enough (about 10 by 12 inches) to contain all the *cannelloni* snugly in a single layer. Smear the bottom generously with butter.

10.   Spread 1 tablespoon of béchamel on a plate. Place a rectangle of pasta over the béchamel, rotating it lightly so that its underside becomes coated. Over the pasta's top side spread about 1½ tablespoons of the asparagus mixture, thinning it evenly, but stopping just short of the edge of the pasta.

11.   Roll up the pasta softly, jelly-roll fashion, to form a *cannellone*.

12.   Place the *cannellone* in the pan, with the overlapping edge facing down. Repeat the operation, laying the *cannelloni* snugly side to side, until all the *cannelloni* are done. From time to time, smear more béchamel over the bottom of the plate, as necessary, but take care not to use up all the béchamel.

13.   When all the *cannelloni* are in the pan, spread the remaining béchamel over them, forcing some of the sauce into the spaces between the *cannelloni*.

14.   Sprinkle with the remaining ⅓ cup of grated cheese and dot with the leftover 2 tablespoons of butter. Place the pan in the uppermost level of the preheated oven and bake for 15 to 20 minutes, until a golden brown crust forms on top. Allow to settle for 5 to 8 minutes before serving. To serve, do not cut into the *cannelloni*, but loosen them, one from the other, with a spatula.

Cannelloni Ripieni di Coste di Biete

CANNELLONI WITH SWISS CHARD STALKS

AMONG leaf vegetables, Swiss chard is my favorite. The leaves, sweeter and more delicate than spinach, can be boiled and served as salad, dressed with olive oil and lemon juice; parboiled, then sautéed with butter and Parmesan or with olive oil and garlic; used in stuffing *tortelloni*; substituted for spinach to make green pasta. The stalks of mature chard are as meaty as celery without the strings, and considerably finer in texture. They can be braised, gratinéed, fried, stuffed, or made into filling for *cannelloni*.

Although this chard stuffing is derived from the preceding one with asparagus, its flavor has more force. One reason is that here I have used prosciutto instead of boiled ham; another is that the prosciutto, unlike the ham in the asparagus stuffing, is made even more savory by sautéing it with butter and shallots before combining it with the chard stalks. There is, moreover, a substantial difference in texture because, where the asparagus was chopped, the chard stalks are cut into long julienne strips.

For 6 to 8 persons

Enough Swiss chard to yield 1¾ pounds of
  stalks (the total amount depends on the
  size of the stalks)
5 tablespoons butter, plus additional butter
  for smearing the baking pan
6 ounces Italian prosciutto, cut into ¼-inch-
  wide strips (if prosciutto is absolutely
  unavailable, substitute 8 ounces cooked,
  unsmoked ham)

½ cup chopped shallots or onions
Salt
Black pepper in a grinder
Homemade pasta dough made with 2 large
  eggs and 1 to 1¼ cups unbleached flour,
  as described on pages 93–5

For the béchamel:

3 cups milk
5 tablespoons butter

4½ tablespoons flour
Pinch salt

⅛ teaspoon grated nutmeg
1 cup freshly grated *parmigiano-reggiano*
  (Parmesan)

3 tablespoons butter

1. Detach the Swiss chard stalks from the leaves. (The leaves should be set aside for other preparations; see introductory note.) Wash the stalks well and cut them into sticks about 3 inches long and ¼ inch wide.

2. Bring a pot of water to a boil. Drop in

Cannelloni with Swiss Chard Stalks (continued)

the stalks and cook no more than a minute or two. Drain when still a little crunchy and set aside.

3. Choose a skillet that can subsequently accommodate all the stalks with hardly any overlapping. Put in 2 tablespoons of the butter, the prosciutto strips, and the chopped shallots and turn on the heat to medium. When the shallots become colored a pale gold, add the chard stalks, salt, and a grinding or two of pepper and cook, turning the stalks frequently, for about 3 to 4 minutes.

4. Prepare the pasta dough as directed on pages 93–5, cut it into *cannelloni* strips, parboiling them, rinsing them, and laying them on a towel as described on page 119.

5. Make the béchamel as directed on page 112. When done, put aside ½ cup of it. Transfer the rest of the béchamel to a mixing bowl, adding to it the chard stalks, the grated nutmeg, and ⅔ cup of the grated cheese. Mix well.

6. Cover each of the pasta rectangles with the béchamel and chard mixture, arranging the stalks so that they are parallel to the longer side of the rectangle. Roll up each strip of pasta loosely, jelly-roll fashion.

7. Turn on the oven to 400°.

8. Choose an oven-to-table baking pan that can accommodate all the *cannelloni* in a single, snugly fitting layer. Smear the bottom of the pan with butter, then spread 1 tablespoon of béchamel over the butter.

9. Lay the *cannelloni* in the pan with the overlapping edge facing the bottom. They should overlap slightly. Squeeze a little béchamel between one *cannellone* and another, forcing them slightly apart.

10. Sprinkle the remaining ⅓ cup of grated cheese evenly over the *cannelloni* and dot with the remaining 3 tablespoons of butter.

11. Place the pan in the uppermost level of the preheated oven and bake for about 20 minutes, until a light golden crust forms on top. Allow to settle for at least 10 minutes before serving.

AHEAD-OF-TIME NOTE: Like *lasagne*, this dish can be completely assembled in advance and baked 1 day later.

Cannelloni Verdi Ripieni di Tonnarelli col Sugo di Belga

GREEN CANNELLONI STUFFED WITH TONNARELLI WITH ENDIVE SAUCE

*T*HE event that prompted the creation of this dish was a day in September when Craig Claiborne simultaneously celebrated his sixty-second birthday, his twenty-fifth year at the *Times,* and the publication of his autobiography. Thirty-five of Craig's friends from around the country and across the ocean came to East Hampton to cook for him and his guests. More than six hundred of the latter turned up. Under a vast tent, each cook had a table from which the dishes were served, except for Paul Prudhomme, who judiciously set up his flaming skillet of blackened redfish in the open air.

Craig had asked me to do a vegetable *lasagne.* I'd said I'd think about it. The people from Romagna are known for their obstinacy and independence and, since I am a *romagnola,* that may be the reason I find it difficult to accept directions. Whenever I am pushed to do one thing, I often end up doing something different. What I came up with in this case was to take my recipe for *tonnarelli* with endive sauce and wrap it in green *cannelloni.*

For Craig I had made the *tonnarelli* red, which together with the white of the sauce and the green of the wrappers provided an appropriately festive Italian national accent. When it comes to colored pasta, however, I strongly feel that the color must make gastronomic sense, that it must make a contribution to flavor, however subtle. There are only two ways to produce deeply colored red pasta that satisfies this criterion. One is to use commercially dried tomato powder, which, unfortunately, is usually unavailable to the general public. The second is to take tomato paste, dry it painstakingly in an oven, pulverize it, and mix it with the flour. The latter is too tedious for me to try it again, let alone propose it to others. For this book I have used *tonnarelli* made with basic egg pasta, which I find in no way diminishes the dish's appeal to the eye or the palate.

For 6 persons

1 recipe Belgian endive sauce (see page 104)
Tonnarelli made with 1 extra large egg and about ¾ cup flour (preferably hard-wheat flour), as described on pages 93–5
Spinach pasta made with 2 extra large eggs; one 10-ounce package frozen leaf spinach, thawed; ½ teaspoon salt; and about

1½ cups unbleached flour, as described on pages 93–5
Salt
½ cup freshly grated *parmigiano-reggiano* (Parmesan) for the *tonnarelli,* plus ¼ cup for the *cannelloni*

For the béchamel:

2 cups milk
4 tablespoons butter

3 tablespoons flour
Pinch salt

A 10- by 12-inch oven-to-table baking dish or its equivalent

2 tablespoons butter

1. Make the endive sauce.
2. Make the *tonnarelli* and spread out to dry.
3. Make the spinach pasta as described on

page 94, thinning it out to the next to last setting on the pasta machine. Spread the strips of dough, just as they come from the machine, on cloth towels.

Green Cannelloni Stuffed with Tonnarelli with Endive Sauce (continued)

4.   Drop the *tonnarelli* into a pot of abundant boiling salted water and cook until they are done but barely tender, very firm to the bite. Drain immediately, transfer to a platter, and toss at once with the endive sauce. Add ½ cup grated cheese and toss again. Set aside.

5.   Cut the green pasta strips into rectangles 5 to 6 inches long, leaving them as wide as they come from the machine. Drop 4 or 5 pieces at a time into boiling salted water. Cook them for no more than 10 seconds, retrieve them with a colander spoon, rinse them in a bowl of cold water, wringing them gently as though they were cloth, and spread flat, without overlapping, on cloth towels to dry.

6.   Turn on the oven to 450°.

7.   Make the béchamel as described on page 112.

8.   Use about ½ tablespoon of the butter to smear the bottom of the baking dish.

9.   Spread 1 to 2 tablespoons of béchamel on a plate. Place 1 of the green pasta rectangles over the béchamel, sliding it back and forth so that its underside becomes coated. Place just a few *tonnarelli*, but thickly sauced, over the green pasta. Roll up the green pasta strip loosely, jelly-roll fashion, forming a *cannellone*.

10.   Place the *cannellone* in the pan, the overlapping edge facing down. Repeat the operation, laying the *cannelloni* snugly side by side in the pan, until there are no more *cannelloni* left to be done. From time to time spread more béchamel over the plate, but make sure not to use up all the béchamel.

11.   Spread the remaining béchamel over the *cannelloni* in the pan, forcing some of it into the spaces between one *cannellone* and another. Sprinkle the top with ¼ cup of grated cheese and dot with the remaining butter.

12.   Bake in the uppermost level of the preheated oven for 5 to 7 minutes, until a golden brown crust forms on top. Allow to settle for at least 5 minutes after removing from the oven before serving.

AHEAD-OF-TIME NOTE: The entire dish, up to the time it is ready for baking, may be prepared up to 2 days in advance, refrigerated under plastic wrap, and baked when ready to serve.

Roselline di Pasta alla Romagnola

PASTA ROSES WITH HAM AND FONTINA

*I*F *I HAD* nine lifetimes in which to explore traditions of Italian cooking, I could use them up and still have dishes left to discover. The pasta "roses" in the recipe below are from my own native Romagna, yet the first time I came across them was only recently, in conversation. Margherita Simili, who has assisted me in Bologna for years, was talking about possible dishes to make for a new pasta shop she had been thinking of opening. She mentioned this and that, all familiar, and then she brought up *roselline*. "What is *roselline?*"

I asked. "Don't tell me you've never had them," said Margherita. But I did tell her; not only had I never had them but I had never even heard of them. It turned out that Margherita herself had had them only once, many years earlier, and had retained but a sketchy memory of the dish. After questioning all the old women I could talk to in my home territory, more than a score, I found one who remembered *roselline* and could tell me how they were made.

One begins as though one were making *lasagne,* with rectangles of pasta that, at first, are parboiled. The rectangles are layered with sliced ham and cheese, rolled up, placed in a baking dish, and covered with a pink butter and cream sauce. In the baking, each pasta roll spreads open slightly to resemble, poetic license permitting, a rose.

It is a strikingly attractive dish that I have been serving lately when people come to dinner for the first time. To suit my taste, I have lightened the original version, which had called for *mortadella* in addition to ham. Even so I have problems in America, where I must struggle to get ham sliced as thin as I would like for this dish. Do make the effort required to procure the thinnest possible slices so that you can obtain a finer, less assertive taste of ham.

For 6 to 8 persons

Pasta dough made with 1 large egg and about ¾ cup flour, as described on pages 93–5
Salt
4 tablespoons butter
1 cup heavy cream
1 tablespoon tomato paste
⅛ teaspoon grated nutmeg
An oven-to-table baking dish, 16 by 9 inches or its equivalent

1½ pounds boiled, unsmoked ham, cut into very thin slices
1 pound fontina, preferably genuine Italian fontina, cut into very thin slices
A pastry brush
2 to 3 tablespoons freshly grated *parmigiano-reggiano* (Parmesan)

1. Knead the pasta dough and thin it in a pasta machine, as described on pages 94–5. Thin it step by step, stopping at the next to last setting on the machine.

2. Trim the pasta strips into straight-sided rectangles. (The trimmings can be cut into lozenge-shaped *maltagliati,* described on page 87, dried, and saved to use on another occasion in soup.) Cut the rectangles into 10-inch lengths.

3. Bring a pot of water to a boil, add salt, and, as the water returns to a boil, drop in the pasta strips 2 or 3 at a time. Cook very briefly, for just seconds, retrieve the pasta with a perfo-

rated scoop or spatula, plunge it in a bowl of cold water, then rinse each strip under cold running water, wringing it delicately as though it were fine cloth. Gently squeeze as much moisture as possible out of each strip with your hands, then spread it flat to dry on a counter covered with clean cloth towels. Repeat the operation until all the pasta is done.

4. Put the butter and cream in a small sauté pan and turn on the heat to medium. Cook, stirring occasionally, until the cream becomes slightly reduced. Add the tomato paste, the nutmeg, and cook while stirring until the tomato

Pasta Roses with Ham and Fontina (continued)

paste has completely dissolved and the sauce is not much denser than buttermilk.

5. Spread just enough of the sauce into the baking dish to coat the bottom with a thin film, reserving the rest for later.

6. Turn on the oven to 450°.

7. On each strip of pasta place a single layer of sliced ham without overlapping and trimming the ham to fit where necessary. Cover the ham with a layer of sliced cheese. Roll up the pasta jelly-roll fashion. With a sharp knife slice the rolled-up strip into rings about ¾ to 1 inch wide. On one side of each ring make 4 equi- distant cuts, each about ½ inch deep, forming a cross pattern.

8. Place the rings in the baking dish, the side with the cross cuts facing up. Do not crowd them. Top with the remaining sauce, distributing it with the pastry brush and pressing on the tops of the rings to spread them slightly more open. Sprinkle with the grated Parmesan. Place the dish in the uppermost level of the preheated oven. Bake for about 15 minutes, until a very light crust forms on top. Allow to settle for a few minutes before serving.

AHEAD-OF-TIME NOTE: The entire dish may be assembled several hours in advance, ready for baking just before serving.

Lasagne Verdi con Pomodoro e Basilico

GREEN LASAGNE WITH TOMATOES AND BASIL

LASAGNE is one of the richest dishes in the Italian repertory, but it need not, indeed it ought not, ever be cumbersome. It is too often, in its transplanted versions, overloaded with an ill-matching combination of cheeses, vegetables, sausages, and meat. The key to successful *lasagne* is deftness, using the solid pasta strips as a base for a simple composition of ingredients that evoke the spirit of the season. In Italy, in the spring, one might use young, purple artichokes; in the fall, wild mushrooms; in the winter, a warmly nourishing Bolognese sauce. The recipe given here could be a parting salute to summer, a celebration of the ripeness of tomato and the poignancy of fresh basil.

Lasagne must be homemade to achieve the fine harmony of layer after delicate layer of pasta fused to its condiments. Of course one can make *lasagne*, as I am sure many will, utilizing packaged pasta from the supermarket. But those who do will have missed the point, as well as the pleasure.

For 6 to 8 persons

1 pound whole-milk mozzarella
1 cup extra virgin olive oil
4 pounds fresh, ripe plum tomatoes
Spinach pasta made with 2 large eggs;
    half a 10-ounce package frozen leaf
    spinach, thawed; and about 1¾ cups
    flour, as described on pages 93–5
Salt
1 cup fresh basil leaves

2 teaspoons garlic chopped very fine
1 cup freshly grated *parmigiano-reggiano*
    (Parmesan)
½ pound boiled, unsmoked ham,
    cut into strips about ⅛ inch wide
    and 2 inches long
A *lasagne* pan, 12 by 9 inches or its equivalent
¼ cup fine, dry, unflavored bread crumbs
    toasted to a nut brown in the oven

1.   Shred the mozzarella using either a hand grater with large holes or a food processor fitted with a shredding disk. Put it into a bowl with 2 tablespoons of the olive oil, mix thoroughly, and set aside to steep.

2.   Wash the tomatoes. Bring a pot of water to a boil, then put in the tomatoes. Drain after 1 minute. As soon as they are cool enough to handle, pull off their peel. Cut them in half lengthwise, remove the seeds, and slice the halves lengthwise into narrow fillets about ¼ inch wide. Spread the fillets on the inside of a colander, place the colander over a plate, and set aside to drain.

3.   Make the pasta as directed on pages 93–5. Do not roll it out too thin, but stop after you've passed it through the next to last setting on the pasta machine.

4.   Leave the strips as wide as they come from the machine, but shorten them to rectangles no more than 10 inches long.

5.   Place a bowl of cold water within easy reach of your burners and cover a section of your work counter with clean, dry cloth kitchen towels. The area should be large enough to accommodate later all the *lasagne* strips without overlapping.

6.   Bring 4 quarts of water to a rolling boil, add 1 tablespoon salt, and drop in 3 pasta strips. Cook for just seconds, until the water returns to a full boil. Retrieve the pasta with a slotted spoon or scoop and plunge it into the bowl of cold

water. Pick up the strips with your hands, one at a time, and rinse them under cold running water, rubbing them as though they were cloth. Squeeze each strip gently to drain off excess water and lay them flat on the cloth towels, without overlapping. Repeat the operation with the remaining pasta strips. When all the strips have been done, pat them dry from above with a fresh towel.

7.   Turn on the oven to 425°.

8.   Wash the basil leaves in cold water, then pat them dry with kitchen towels. Tear them into 3 or 4 small pieces and put them in a bowl. Add the tomatoes, mozzarella, garlic, ⅔ cup of the grated Parmesan, and the ham strips. Sprinkle with salt and mix well.

9.   Place 2 small bowls near the *lasagne* pan. In one bowl put the remaining olive oil and set a strainer over the other.

10.   Drop 2 or 3 pasta strips at a time into the bowl containing the olive oil. Make sure they are coated with oil on both sides, then transfer them to the strainer over the other bowl, to shed excess oil. Line the bottom of the *lasagne* pan with the coated pasta, leaving no gaps, and trimming where necessary so it fits neatly without overlaps.

11.   Spread enough of the tomato and mozzarella mixture over the pasta in the pan to cover lightly. Sprinkle with some of the bread crumbs.

12.   Cover with another layer of oil-coated

pasta, then some more of the tomato and mozzarella mixture, and sprinkle again with some bread crumbs. Repeat the operation, building up layers of pasta and tomato and mozzarella filling until you have used up all the pasta or all the filling. The top layer must be of pasta, over which you will sprinkle the remaining ⅓ cup of grated Parmesan, olive oil, and bread crumbs.

13.   Place the pan in the uppermost level of the preheated oven and bake for 15 to 20 minutes, until the top forms a golden brown crust. Allow to settle for 5 to 10 minutes before serving.

NOTE: If any of the tomato and mozzarella filling is left over, it makes a nice topping for slices of grilled crusty bread moistened lightly with olive oil.

Lasagne con le Verdure

VEGETABLE LASAGNE

N OWHERE better than in this recipe will you find an illustration of *insaporire,* making savory, the method that influences the taste of much good Italian cooking. (Please see the discussion of *insaporire* on page 16.) Each of the three vegetables in this *lasagne*—the carrot, the zucchini, the broccoli—is cooked separately in garlic-scented butter until it becomes impregnated with a flavor base that in turn stimulates release of the vegetable's own individual flavor.

With every biteful of the *lasagne* in which the rounded, vigorous, fully developed vegetable taste emerges, the purpose of the procedure becomes manifest.

For 6 to 8 persons

1 pound carrots, peeled, washed, and cut into
   ¼-inch disks
6 tablespoons butter, plus additional butter
   for greasing the *lasagne* pan
6 garlic cloves, peeled and cut in half
Salt
1 pound zucchini, soaked, washed,

and trimmed as described on page 42,
   and sliced into ¼-inch disks
1 pound broccoli
Homemade pasta dough made with 2 large eggs
   and 1 to 1¼ cups unbleached flour,
   as described on pages 93–5

For the béchamel:

3 cups milk
5 tablespoons butter

4½ tablespoons flour
Pinch salt

⅛ teaspoon grated nutmeg
1¾ cups freshly grated *parmigiano-reggiano*
  (Parmesan)

A *lasagne* pan, 12 by 9 inches or its
  equivalent

1. Choose a skillet that can subsequently accommodate the carrots loosely. Put in 1½ tablespoons of the butter, 2 of the garlic cloves, and turn on the heat to medium. When the garlic becomes colored a light brown, remove it from the pan.

2. Add the carrots and 3 tablespoons of water. Cook the carrots, stirring from time to time, until they are tender, but firm, somewhat shrunken, and a light brown in color. Do not let them break up. When done, add salt and transfer to a small mixing bowl.

3. In a clean skillet large enough to accommodate the zucchini loosely, put in 1½ tablespoons of the butter and 2 more garlic cloves. Turn on the heat to medium. When the garlic becomes colored a light brown, remove it from the pan. Add the sliced zucchini and cook them as you did the carrots. When they have shrunk, becoming colored a light brown, and are tender but firm, add salt, stir, then transfer them from the pan to a small mixing bowl.

4. Wash the broccoli in cold water, then peel away the hard green skin from the stems. Bring a pot of water to a boil, add salt, then drop in the broccoli. Cook until nearly tender, but still very firm. Drain; as soon as it is cool enough to handle, cut it into ½-inch pieces.

5. Put 2 tablespoons of the butter and the remaining 2 garlic cloves in a clean skillet and turn on the heat to medium. When the garlic becomes colored a light brown, remove it. Put in the broccoli pieces and cook, turning them frequently, until they are tender, but not mushy. Transfer them from the pan into a third mixing bowl.

6. Make the pasta dough and use it to make *lasagne* as described on page 119.

7. Make the béchamel sauce. When done, mix into it the grated nutmeg and 1 cup of the grated cheese. Set aside ½ cup of the béchamel and divide the rest into 3 equal parts.

8. Into each of the 3 bowls containing the cooked vegetables mix 1 of the 3 portions of béchamel. Taste and correct for salt.

9. Smear the bottom of a 12- by 9-inch *lasagne* pan (or its equivalent) generously with butter. Spread 1 tablespoon of béchamel over the buttered bottom. Line the bottom with a layer of pasta strips fitting them edge to edge, but making sure they do not overlap.

10. Turn on the oven to 400°.

11. Spread half of the zucchini and béchamel mixture over the pasta. It doesn't matter if there isn't sufficient to cover the pasta completely, as long as any gaps in the zucchini are filmed lightly with béchamel. Sprinkle some grated cheese evenly over this layer.

12. Cover the zucchini with another layer of pasta, always edge to edge and without overlaps.

13. Spread half the carrot and béchamel mixture over the pasta in the same manner you spread the zucchini, topping the layer with a sprinkling of grated cheese, and covering it with another layer of pasta.

14. Spread half the broccoli and béchamel mixture over this. Top again with pasta.

15. Repeat the above operations until you have used up all the vegetables. Top with a layer of pasta. Spread the remaining béchamel over the pasta, sprinkle the rest of the grated cheese

Vegetable Lasagne (continued)

over it, and dot with the remaining tablespoon of butter.

16. Place the pan in the uppermost level of the preheated oven. Bake for 15 to 20 minutes, until a light golden crust forms on top. Allow to settle for at least 10 minutes before serving.

AHEAD-OF-TIME NOTE: Like most *lasagne,* this one can be completely assembled a day before it is to be baked.

Sugo Fresco di Pomodoro

SIMPLE TOMATO SAUCE

*H*ERE is a recipe as sweet as it is short, a fresh-tasting tomato sauce with bright, summery flavor to use with many cuts of pasta: *Spaghetti, spaghettini, fusilli, penne, rigatoni, ziti* are some of the most suitable ones.

The special taste of the sauce depends largely on the way the garlic is handled. It must be sliced very thin, sautéed only until it becomes just faintly colored, and then allowed to simmer slowly in the tomato so that it can release all its sweetness. Raw basil at the end contributes a fragrant fillip. Make sure the basil does not undergo any cooking.

For 1 pound pasta

⅓ cup extra virgin olive oil
2 medium garlic cloves, peeled and sliced
    very thin
1½ cups canned Italian peeled
    plum tomatoes, cut into large pieces, with
    their juice

Salt
Black pepper in a grinder
10 fresh basil leaves, torn by hand into small
    pieces

1. Put the oil and garlic in a saucepan and turn on the heat to medium.

2. When the garlic becomes colored a pale gold, add the tomatoes and turn the heat down to very low. Cook, uncovered, until the oil floats free of the tomatoes, about 20 minutes.

3. Add salt and grindings of pepper and cook for another 2 to 3 minutes, stirring from time to time.

4. Off the heat, stir in the torn basil leaves.

AHEAD-OF-TIME NOTE: The sauce can be cooked several hours in advance. Add the basil after reheating, when ready to serve.

Conchiglie con Peperoni Verdi, Rossi e Gialli alla Panna

SHELLS WITH GREEN, RED, AND YELLOW PEPPERS AND CREAM

*M*Y *FAMILY* hums happily when I produce this dish. The different colors of peppers are immediately appealing to the eye, but they are not merely decorative. The pungently herbal green pepper neatly points up the riper sweetness of the red and the mellowness of the yellow. All the peppers are diced small and cooked over a flavor base of butter and onion. When done they are bound with thoroughly reduced cream. That is all there is to this sauce.

In the unlikely event there is sauce left over, or if you've made more than you intend to use on the pasta, try it the following day on veal *scaloppine* or sliced chicken breasts. Sauté the meat in butter and vegetable oil, when nearly done add the peppers sauce, and cook for a minute more while turning the veal or chicken in the sauce.

For 4 to 6 persons

3 tablespoons butter
1 tablespoon vegetable oil
1 cup onion chopped not too fine
1 cup green bell peppers
    diced into ½-inch cubes
1 cup red bell peppers
    diced into ½-inch cubes
1 cup yellow bell peppers, if available, diced
    into ½-inch cubes (if not available,
increase the red peppers by the same amount)
Salt
Black pepper in a grinder
⅔ cup heavy cream
1 pound *conchiglie* (pasta shells)
2 tablespoons chopped parsley
½ cup freshly grated *parmigiano-reggiano* (Parmesan)

1. In a 10- to 12-inch sauté pan put the butter, oil, and chopped onion and turn on the heat to medium. Sauté the onion until it becomes colored a pale gold.

2. Add all the diced peppers, turn up the heat to medium high, and cook until tender, turning them from time to time.

3. Add salt and generous grindings of pepper, stir well, add the cream, and turn up the heat to high. Cook until the cream is reduced by half.

4. Drop the pasta into a pot of abundant boiling salted water. Cook until it is barely tender but firm to the bite. Drain and toss immediately in a warm bowl with the peppers and cream and all their pan juices. Sprinkle with parsley and grated cheese, toss again, and serve at once.

Fusilli con le Zucchine a Scapece

FUSILLI WITH VINEGAR MARINATED ZUCCHINI

*L*OOKING into the origin of a dish is sometimes like looking into a telescope that contracts history rather than distance. The zucchini used here as sauce for *fusilli* are known as *a scapece,* an Italianization of the Spanish *escabeche.* It is a manner of pickling vegetables or small fish by first frying them in olive oil, then steeping them in vinegar and mint. Although the word comes from the Spanish, the dish comes from the ancient Romans and, before them, probably from the Greeks. The Spaniards found it when they became lords of Southern Italy, gave it a name of their own, which in turn was transformed and absorbed by the local dialect. Zucchini, carrots, or eggplant prepared this way can be put up in jars and served up to a month later as appetizers or condiments. To make zucchini *a scapece* one would usually slice them into rounds, but in the sauce they work better cut into julienne strips that curl around the whorls of the *fusilli.*

For 4 to 6 persons

3 pounds fresh, glossy zucchini
Salt
Vegetable oil for frying
3 tablespoons red-wine vinegar
1 teaspoon garlic chopped very fine

10 to 15 fresh mint leaves, torn by hand into
    small bits
1/3 cup extra virgin olive oil
Black pepper in a grinder
1 pound *fusilli*

1.   Soak the zucchini in a basin of cold water for at least 20 minutes, then scrub them vigorously under cold running water with a rough cloth or stiff brush to remove all embedded grit. Trim away the ends and cut the zucchini into sticks about 2 inches long and 1/4 inch thick.

2.   Set a large colander over a bowl or basin and place the zucchini in the colander. Sprinkle with 2 tablespoons of salt, turn them 2 or 3 times, and allow them to sit for at least 45 minutes to drain them of as much liquid as possible.

3.   If you have a deep-fat fryer, pour enough vegetable oil in to rise 4 inches up the side of the pan. If you are using a shallow frying pan, the oil should be 1 1/2 inches deep, if pos-

sible. Turn on the heat to medium high.

4.   When you are ready to begin frying, remove the zucchini sticks from the colander and blot them thoroughly dry in kitchen towels. As soon as the oil is hot, drop them into the pan, as many as will fit without being crowded. The moment they become colored a light brown, transfer them directly to the bowl where you will later toss the pasta.

5.   When you have finished frying the zucchini sticks and put them all in the bowl, pour the vinegar over them and turn them once or twice. Add the garlic, mint, olive oil, a few grindings of pepper, taste and correct for salt, and mix well.

6. Cook the pasta in a pot of abundant boiling salted water until it is barely tender but firm to the bite. Drain, toss immediately with the zucchini, and serve. No cheese is required or desirable with this dish.

AHEAD-OF-TIME NOTE: The zucchini may be prepared 2 or 3 days ahead of time. Refrigerate them with their marinade in a covered container. Turn them occasionally. Make sure to bring them back to room temperature before you cook the pasta.

Fusilli col Sugo dei Pomodori al Forno

FUSILLI WITH BAKED TOMATOES AND HOT PEPPER

*E*VERY family must have, among the dishes it cooks, some whose taste touches a chord of special satisfaction, some they never tire of making. In our family, one such dish is the tomatoes baked with garlic, olive oil, and parsley, whose recipe I first gave in *The Classic Italian Cook Book* (page 389). In summer we have them together with fried eggplant, at other times we eat them with breaded veal cutlets, with boiled beef, or we make a dish of them alone, with thick slices of crusty bread. When I make them, I make a lot.

Once, when I had some left over from the previous day, I was at a loss to satisfy my husband's and son's yearning for a different-tasting pasta. Then I remembered the tomatoes in the refrigerator. I mashed them through a food mill, added a trickle of olive oil and a little hot pepper, and I had a marvelous new tomato sauce that tasted unlike any other.

If you have never before had these tomatoes and would like to try them on their own, stop at the end of step 2 in this recipe. They can be served hot, but are tastiest at room temperature.

For 4 to 6 persons

Fusilli with Baked Tomatoes and Hot Pepper (continued)

2 pounds fresh, ripe tomatoes
3 tablespoons chopped parsley
2 tablespoons chopped garlic
Salt

Black pepper in a grinder
1/2 cup olive oil
1 pound *fusilli*
Hot red pepper to taste

1.   Turn on the oven to 400°.

2.   Wash the tomatoes and slice them in half across their width. Place them cut side up in a baking dish where they will fit snugly. Sprinkle with the chopped parsley and garlic, add salt and several grindings of pepper, and pour 1/4 cup of the olive oil over them. Place in the uppermost rack of the preheated oven. Bake for about 1 1/2 hours until they become shrunken and their skins are partly blackened.

3.   Fit the disk with medium-size holes in a food mill. Remove the tomatoes from the baking dish, leaving behind all the cooked oil, and purée them through the mill.

4.   Drop the pasta into a pot of abundant boiling salted water and cook until it is barely tender but firm to the bite. Drain and toss immediately with the puréed tomatoes. Add the remaining 1/4 cup of raw olive oil and crumbled hot red pepper to taste, toss again, and serve.

Fusilli alla Rustica

FUSILLI WITH VEGETABLES, HERBS, OLIVES, AND HOT PEPPER

IN SUMMER, when heat wilts appetite, spirited flavors can stir it up again. Pickled vegetables, garlicky salami, a spritzy white wine help cut the palate-obstructing torpor. It is with that objective in mind that I made this *fusilli* sauce. A host of lively components animate it: basil, oregano, olives, capers, hot pepper, *pecorino* cheese. But do not be daunted by the number of ingredients. Once you have set them up, it all goes very quickly because most of them cook briefly or hardly at all. That is part of the secret of the brisk flavor of the sauce. Please note that the tomatoes are fresh, raw tomatoes that are peeled, diced very small, and cooked only 5 minutes.

For 4 to 6 persons

1/2 cup extra virgin olive oil
3 cups onion sliced very thin
4 large or 6 small garlic cloves, peeled and
       sliced thin
3 ounces *pancetta,* cut into thin strips
2 tablespoons chopped parsley

1 large, meaty sweet bell pepper (preferably
       yellow, but if not available, red), cored,
       seeded, skinned raw with a peeler, and
       cut into strips about 2 inches long and
       1/2 inch wide
Salt

1 pound fresh, ripe plum tomatoes, skinned
  raw with a peeler and diced
  into ½-inch cubes
½ teaspoon oregano
½ cup green olives in brine, drained, pitted,
  and sliced into thin rings
2 tablespoons tiny capers
1 teaspoon hot red pepper, or more to taste

8 fresh basil leaves, torn by hand into
  small pieces
1 pound *fusilli*
Freshly grated cheese: ½ cup mellow *pecorino*,
  if available; otherwise, 3 tablespoons
  romano and 5 tablespoons *parmigiano-
  reggiano* (Parmesan)

1.   In a 10- to 12-inch sauté pan put the oil, onion, garlic, *pancetta*, and parsley. Turn on the heat to medium low and cook the onion, stirring from time to time, until it is tender but not brown.

2.   Add the pepper, stir occasionally, and cook slowly until tender. Add salt, stir, turn up the heat to high, and add the tomatoes. Cook for 5 minutes over high heat, stirring frequently, or until the tomatoes are no longer watery, then add the oregano, olives, capers, hot pepper, and basil. Stir once or twice, then remove from the heat.

3.   Drop the *fusilli* into a pot of abundant boiling salted water. Cook until tender but firm to the bite. Drain immediately, toss at once in a warm bowl with the vegetable sauce, add the grated cheese, toss again, and serve promptly.

I Maccheroni alla Moda di Victor

VICTOR'S PASTA WITH PARMESAN, BUTTER, AND CREAM

MANY Italians maintain no sauce can match the simple goodness of butter and freshly grated *parmigiano-reggiano* (Parmesan). This is my husband's own version, to which he has added a little cream.

Simple as the dish appears to be, it has its secrets. One is the sequence in which the ingredients are added to the pasta. Another is the manner in which the pasta is tossed. The basic principle of this sauce is that the cheese must melt in contact with the pasta and coat it. Thus it is added first, while the pasta is steaming hot. You begin to add butter when you see that cheese is coating every strand of *spaghetti* or every *rigatoni*. At the end, my husband, who allows no one else to prepare this dish, tosses the pasta with cream to bind all the components smoothly.

Cook the pasta to a firmer consistency than you would ordinarily, because it will continue to cook a little more as you toss it in the hot bowl. Make sure

Victor's Pasta with Parmesan, Butter, and Cream (continued)
you follow the recipe's directions for preheating the bowl. If it isn't hot, the pasta will cool too rapidly and the cheese won't melt satisfactorily.

For 4 to 6 persons

1 pound *spaghetti* or *rigatoni*
1¼ cups freshly grated *parmigiano-reggiano* (Parmesan)
3 tablespoons butter, partly softened to room temperature

2 tablespoons heavy cream
Black pepper in a grinder

1. Place a ceramic bowl in which you will later toss and serve the pasta in a 100° oven.

2. Drop the pasta into a pot of abundant boiling salted water.

3. When the pasta is done—barely tender and distinctly firm to the bite—remove the bowl from the oven (remember it's hot; use a towel or potholders), drain the pasta, and put it in the bowl.

4. Add ½ cup of the grated cheese, toss the pasta repeatedly, distributing the melting cheese evenly.

5. Add 1 tablespoon of the butter, toss again until the butter has melted, then add another ½ cup of grated cheese and another tablespoon of butter. Toss, turning the pasta over, 10 or 12 times, add the remaining tablespoon of butter and toss again, 4 or 5 times.

6. Add the cream, distributing it evenly in a thin stream. Toss the pasta again until it absorbs the cream.

7. Add the remaining ¼ cup of grated cheese, several grindings of pepper, toss 2 or 3 times, and serve at once.

Penne col Sugo di Pomodoro all'Aceto Balsamico

PENNE WITH TOMATOES AND BALSAMIC VINEGAR

ONE could spend a lifetime finding new tomato sauces to make and still have ideas left over for a reincarnation or two. Rosemary and balsamic vinegar account for the unusual, effusive fragrance of this sauce. Note that, in order not to disperse the vinegar's precious aroma, it is added off heat after the pasta has been tossed in the pan with the sauce.

For 4 to 6 persons

½ cup extra virgin olive oil
3 or 4 garlic cloves, sliced very thin
2 sprigs fresh rosemary, about 4 to 6 inches
   long, or 2½ teaspoons dried leaves,
   chopped
2 cups canned Italian peeled plum tomatoes,
   drained of their juice

Salt
Black pepper in a grinder
1 pound *penne* (quill-shaped pasta) or
   other short, tubular pasta
2 teaspoons *aceto balsamico* (balsamic vinegar,
   see page 6)

1. Put the olive oil and garlic into a sauté pan or skillet with, if it is fresh, the rosemary. Turn on the heat to medium.

2. As soon as the garlic begins to sizzle, add the tomatoes, salt, and liberal grindings of pepper; if you are using chopped, dried rosemary, put it in now. Cook for about 10 to 12 minutes, then turn off the heat.

3. Drop the pasta into a pot of abundant boiling salted water. When it is done but markedly *al dente*, very firm to the bite, drain and transfer immediately to the pan containing the sauce.

4. Turn on the heat to very low and toss the pasta with the sauce for about 1 minute.

5. Turn off the heat and make a well in the middle of the pasta. Pour the vinegar into the well, draw the pasta over it, toss thoroughly for a few seconds, and serve at once.

Penne col Sugo di Tonno e Peperoni

PENNE WITH TUNA AND ROASTED PEPPERS

*T*HE tuna and cream sauce for *fettuccine* on page 97 taught me that canned tuna makes a much finer sauce when you do not cook it. Here I follow the same principle in a sauce whose emphatic flavor forms a more congenial alliance with factory-made pasta than with homemade pasta.

Roasted peppers are *insaporiti*—made savory—over a lightly sautéed flavor base of olive oil and garlic. Parsley and capers are added, the heat turned off, and the crumbled tuna mixed in to complete the sauce.

For 4 to 6 persons

2 large or 3 medium sweet red or yellow bell peppers
6 tablespoons olive oil
1 tablespoon garlic chopped coarse
3 tablespoons chopped parsley
2 tablespoons capers
Salt

Black pepper in a grinder
6 to 7 ounces canned Italian-style tuna packed in olive oil
1 pound *penne* (quill-shaped pasta) or other short, tubular pasta
2 tablespoons fine, dry, unflavored bread crumbs, lightly toasted in the oven

1. Turn on the oven to 500°.
2. Wash the peppers, put them on a baking sheet, and place it in the uppermost level of the oven. (Peppers may also be roasted on a griddle or over charcoal, but for this recipe I prefer the oven because it makes them a little more tender.)
3. Turn the peppers from time to time until their skin is charred on all sides. Remove them from the oven and put them into a plastic bag. Tie the bag tightly and allow the peppers to cool.
4. When the peppers are cool, remove the skin, which will pull off easily. Cut the peppers open, remove the core and seeds, and cut the flesh lengthwise into strips 1/2 inch wide.
5. Put 3 tablespoons of the olive oil and the chopped garlic in a small saucepan, turning on the heat to medium. Cook the garlic for a minute

or two, stirring from time to time, until it becomes colored a light gold. Add the strips of red pepper, raise the heat, and cook, stirring frequently, for 2 to 3 minutes to let the peppers absorb flavor from the olive oil and garlic.
6. Add the parsley and capers, stir 2 or 3 times, then turn off the heat. Add salt, a liberal grinding of pepper, and the tuna. Break up the tuna into shreds with a fork or wooden spoon and mix thoroughly.
7. Cook the pasta in abundant boiling salted water. When it is barely tender but still firm to the bite, drain, transfer immediately to a serving bowl, and add the sauce from the saucepan. Toss well, adding the remaining 3 tablespoons of olive oil and the toasted bread crumbs. Serve at once.

Penne con il Rosmarino e la Pancetta Affumicata

PENNE WITH ROSEMARY AND BACON

*W*HEN we settled into our Venice apartment and I began marketing in the neighborhood, I was startled to find that the unsmoked *pancetta* that prevails nearly everywhere else in Italy was a scarce item, while there was an abundance of beautiful, fresh, smoked *pancetta*. Since it is virtually identical to good-quality lightly smoked American bacon, I was moved to work it into several new recipes.

In this one it has the commanding role, with a fragrant assist from garlic and rosemary. Please note that in this, as in all Italian recipes with *pancetta* or bacon, the bacon is cooked until it becomes colored, but not crisp.

For 4 to 6 persons

4 tablespoons butter
2 garlic cloves, peeled and lightly mashed
2 teaspoons fresh whole rosemary leaves,
    or 1 teaspoon dried leaves, chopped

¾ pound bacon, cut into narrow strips
1 pound *penne* (quill-shaped pasta)
½ cup freshly grated *parmigiano-reggiano*
    (Parmesan)

1. In an 8- to 10-inch sauté pan put 3 tablespoons of the butter and the mashed garlic and turn on the heat to medium. Sauté until the garlic becomes colored a deep gold.

2. Remove the garlic and add the rosemary. Stir once or twice, then put in the bacon. Sauté until the bacon becomes lightly colored, but not crisp.

3. Drop the pasta into a pot of abundant boiling salted water. Cook until it is barely tender, but firm to the bite, then drain and toss immediately with the sauce from the pan. Add the remaining tablespoon of butter, the grated cheese, toss again, and serve at once.

Penne col Sugo
di Funghi Coltivati

PENNE WITH MUSHROOM SAUCE

W*ITH* ingredients available in any supermarket, this sauce elicits from cultivated *champignons* mushrooms some of the muskiness, the depth of flavor one might associate with rare and expensive *porcini*.

The mushrooms undergo two cooking stages: the first one draws away and evaporates their bland, taste-diluting liquid; the second concentrates their flavor together with that of wine, anchovies, tomatoes, and parsley. An essential finishing touch is to drizzle the sauced pasta with a little raw olive oil.

For 4 to 6 persons

1 pound fresh mushrooms
1 tablespoon butter
1/3 cup extra virgin olive oil, plus additional for tossing the pasta
1 cup chopped onion
2 teaspoons chopped garlic
Salt
Black pepper in a grinder

1/3 cup dry white wine
4 flat anchovy fillets, chopped, or 2 teaspoons anchovy paste
1/2 cup canned Italian peeled plum tomatoes, drained and cut up
3 tablespoons chopped parsley
1 pound *penne* (quill-shaped pasta)

1. Wash the mushrooms under cold running water and pat dry immediately with a soft kitchen towel.

2. Cut the mushrooms into the thinnest possible lengthwise slices without detaching the caps from the stems. No slice should be any broader than 1 inch; if any of the mushrooms is particularly large, cut in half or quarters before slicing.

3. Choose a lidded skillet or sauté pan large enough to accommodate all the mushrooms later. Put in the butter, the 1/3 cup of oil, and the chopped onion and turn on the heat to medium high, leaving the pan uncovered.

4. When the onion becomes translucent, add the garlic.

5. When the garlic becomes colored a pale gold, add the mushrooms, salt, and a liberal grinding of pepper. Stir thoroughly and lower the heat to medium. Cook the mushrooms in the uncovered pan until all the liquid they will throw off has evaporated.

6. Add the wine. Stir thoroughly 2 or 3 times.

7. When the wine has evaporated, add the anchovies, tomatoes, and parsley. Stir thoroughly, cover the pan, and cook for another 10 minutes.

8. Cook the pasta in abundant boiling salted water. Drain when it is barely tender but still firm to the bite. Transfer immediately to a warm serving bowl and toss with the mushroom sauce. Pour a little bit of olive oil in a thin stream over the pasta, toss again, and serve at once.

Penne con Peperoni e Pancetta Affumicata

PENNE WITH PEPPERS AND BACON

HERE is another quick, tasty sauce inspired by Venice's baconlike *pancetta affumicata.* Peppers and bacon share the honors, both cooked in a flavor base of butter and onion. The peppers are diced small so that they cook in just minutes for this fast-paced sauce.

For 4 to 6 persons

2 or 3 sweet bell peppers, preferably red, but green are acceptable
1/3 cup onion chopped fine
3 tablespoons vegetable oil
4 tablespoons butter
6 ounces bacon, cut into 6 thin strips

Salt
Black pepper in a grinder
1 pound *penne* (quill-shaped pasta)
1/3 cup freshly grated *parmigiano-reggiano* (Parmesan)
3 tablespoons chopped parsley

1. Wash the peppers, split them in half lengthwise, remove the stems, core, and seeds, and cut them into 1/4-inch squares.

2. Put the onion, vegetable oil, and 3 tablespoons of the butter in a skillet and turn on the heat to medium high.

3. When the onion becomes translucent, add the bacon. Brown the bacon well, but not until it is crispy.

4. Add the peppers and cook, stirring frequently, for 6 to 8 minutes, until the peppers are tender, but not mushy. Add salt and liberal gridings of pepper, and turn off the heat.

5. Drop the pasta into a pot of abundant boiling salted water. Drain immediately when it is done but still firm to the bite. Toss at once with the sauce. Add the grated cheese and toss again. Add the remaining tablespoon of butter, toss briefly, sprinkle with the chopped parsley, and serve promptly.

Rigatoni al Forno con le Polpettine

BAKED RIGATONI WITH TINY MEATBALLS

IN THE early years of my career in cooking, the statement that seemed most to startle students and interviewers was that *spaghetti* and meatballs is not an Italian dish. To be exact: the concept is undoubtedly Italian; it is the execution—the colossal meatballs, overloaded with herbs, saturated with oil, buried in tomato sauce—that appears solely on the western side of the Atlantic. The diminutive meatballs in this festive *rigatoni* pie, produced with a minimum of seasoning, show how it is really done. Although I have used pork in the recipe because I like the flavor, one could as easily use beef or lamb or, as they call it in Abruzzi, the butcher's mixture: a combination of all three. *Rigatoni* is the shape to use when making any dish in which the pasta is cooked in two stages, first boiled alone, then baked with other ingredients. The shape's thick walls stand up to prolonged cooking without turning mushy, and the capacious hollow within them is an ideal receptacle for the béchamel that is nearly invariably used in such preparations to bind the other ingredients.

For 8 persons

For the meatballs:

¼ cup milk	⅓ cup freshly grated *parmigiano-reggiano*
1 slice good white bread trimmed of its crust	(Parmesan)
1 pound ground pork	1 egg
1 teaspoon chopped garlic	Salt
2 tablespoons chopped parsley	Black pepper in a grinder

1 cup flour, spread on a plate	Vegetable oil for frying

For the béchamel:

3 cups milk	1 pound *rigatoni*
6 tablespoons butter	⅓ cup freshly grated *parmigiano-reggiano*
4½ tablespoons flour	Pinch salt

⅛ teaspoon grated nutmeg	¼ cup milk
2 tablespoons butter	

1. Begin with the meatballs. Warm the milk in a small saucepan without letting it simmer. Turn off the heat and add the slice of white bread. Let it soak for a little while, then pick up the bread with your hand and squeeze it gently to force off excess milk. Put the bread in a mixing bowl.

2. Add the pork, garlic, parsley, grated

cheese, egg, salt, and a few grindings of pepper. Combine all the ingredients with a fork until they are evenly amalgamated.

3. Pinch off 2 small lumps of meat, each about the size of a raspberry. Place them about 2 inches apart on the palm of one hand. Bring the other palm over them and, keeping both palms flat, roll the lumps into little balls, using a circular movement while applying slight but steady pressure. If you are good with your hands, try making 3 balls at a time, so that the process will go that much faster.

4. When all the meatballs have been shaped, roll them in the flour, 15 to 20 at a time. Place the floured meatballs in a strainer and shake it smartly to dispose of excess flour.

5. Put enough vegetable oil in a skillet to rise ¼ inch up the sides of the pan and turn on the heat to medium high. When the oil is hot, put as many meatballs in the skillet as will fit without overcrowding. Brown them until they form a nice crust all around. When one batch is done, transfer it with a slotted spoon to a platter covered with paper towels to drain and do the next batch until all are done.

6. Prepare the béchamel as described in the recipe for *Cannelloni* with Asparagus and Ham (page 111), and add the nutmeg.

7. Cook the *rigatoni* in a pot of abundant boiling salted water. Drain when just barely done but still quite firm. Combine immediately in a bowl with two-thirds of the béchamel, half the grated cheese, and all the meatballs.

8. Turn on the oven to 400°.

9. Thickly smear the bottom and sides of a 12-inch springform pan with the butter. Put in the *rigatoni*, leveling them off with a spatula. Pour the milk over them, spread the rest of the béchamel on top, and sprinkle with the remaining grated cheese.

10. Place in the uppermost level of the preheated oven. Bake for 15 to 20 minutes until a golden brown crust forms on top.

11. Run a knife along the inside of the pan's ring to loosen the *rigatoni*. Remove the ring. Place the pasta, without removing it from the bottom of the pan, on a large round platter, allow to settle for about 5 minutes, bring to the table, and serve.

First

Rigatoni col Sugo Piccante di Salsiccia

RIGATONI WITH SPICY SAUSAGE SAUCE

*T*HIS is a sauce picked up, as it were, on a walk in the woods. It had been a good day for walking, and Victor and I wandered past our lunchtime into the early afternoon. Famished, we retreated to the nearest hamlet, a dozen houses, one of which had a sign: Bar Panini. *Panini*—sandwiches—are not what my husband considers food, but we had no other choice. Men were sitting at wooden tables, drinking *grappa*, talking about football. A pleasant, open-faced woman was behind the counter. My husband turned to her with his warmest gaze and pleaded, "Isn't there anything besides *panini* one can eat?"

Rigatoni with Spicy Sausage Sauce (continued)

"Yes, if you can wait twenty minutes," she smiled back. It was closer to thirty minutes, but we sat down to a plate of pasta that tasted like the best food on earth.

She had browned bits of spicy sausage in sweet homemade butter and garlic and added tomatoes she had sent a little boy to pick from the garden back of the house. It's a long story for a quick sauce, but it illustrates the impromptu nature of what to me is the best kind of Italian cooking.

In my version of the sauce there is no spicy sausage because I have never found any in America that wasn't loaded with odd, inappropriate flavors. For it I have substituted the combination of the plainest sausage one can buy with chopped hot pepper to taste.

For 4 to 6 persons

1½ pounds fresh, very ripe tomatoes
2 tablespoons butter
1 tablespoon chopped garlic
½ pound sweet breakfast sausages, skinned
Salt

1 teaspoon hot red pepper, or to taste
1 pound *rigatoni*
⅔ cup freshly grated *parmigiano-reggiano* (Parmesan)

1.   Skin the tomatoes with a peeler, split them in half, scoop out most of the seeds, and cut them up coarse.

2.   Put the butter and garlic in a sauté pan and turn on the heat to medium. When the garlic becomes colored a pale gold, add the skinned sausages, crumbling them fine in the pan with a fork. Cook, stirring from time to time, until the sausage is well browned.

3.   Add the tomatoes, turn up the heat to high, and cook, stirring occasionally, for 15 or more minutes, until the fat separates and floats free. Taste and correct for salt and mix in the hot pepper.

4.   Drop the pasta into a pot of abundant boiling salted water. When it is barely tender but firm to the bite, drain and toss immediately with the sauce and the grated cheese. Serve at once.

Ruote di Carro col Sugo di Salsicce, Panna e Pomodoro

CARTWHEELS WITH SAUSAGES, CREAM, AND TOMATO

*S*AUSAGES provide many quick and savory ways to make a delicious pasta sauce. They can be crumbled, sliced, cut up into pieces, used with tomato and cream, added to the stuffing of *tortellini,* or, in the center and south of Italy, combined with other ingredients in baked pasta dishes such as *lasagne* or *rigatoni.* In this light-handed version, both cream and tomatoes are used, just enough tomatoes to give the cream a deep pink blush. The sausages are sliced into thin disks before browning so that they maintain their shape, neither crumbling into the sauce nor weighing it down with thick chunks. Choose sweet sausages free of chile peppers, fennel, tomato, or other seasonings that are foreign to the sausages Italians commonly use. Cartwheels is an attractive and suitable pasta for the sauce, which nestles in the spaces this shape provides. Other appropriate shapes are *conchiglie,* shells, or *lumache,* snails.

For 4 to 6 persons

½ pound breakfast or other mild
    pork sausage
2 tablespoons extra virgin olive oil
1 teaspoon chopped garlic
⅔ cup canned Italian peeled plum tomatoes,
    cut coarse, with their juice
½ cup heavy cream

Salt
Black pepper in a grinder
2 tablespoons chopped parsley
1 pound *ruote di carro* (pasta cartwheels)
Freshly grated *parmigiano-reggiano* (Parmesan)
    for the table

1. Slice the sausages into disks ¼ inch thick.
2. Put the olive oil and chopped garlic in a skillet and turn on the heat to medium. When the garlic becomes colored a pale gold, add the sliced sausages. Turn them from time to time until they are nicely browned on all sides, about 15 minutes. Add the tomatoes, stir, and cook at a gentle simmer.
3. After about 20 minutes, when the fat separates from the other juices and floats free, add the cream and turn up the heat. Cook for 1 or 2 minutes, stirring frequently, until the cream is reduced. Add salt and a liberal grinding of pepper. Turn off the heat and stir in the chopped parsley.
4. Drop the pasta into a pot of abundant boiling salted water. When it is barely tender but firm to the bite, drain and toss immediately with the sauce. Serve at once with freshly grated cheese available on the side.

AHEAD-OF-TIME NOTE: The sauce may be prepared several hours in advance. It should be reheated gently when the pasta is almost cooked.

Spaghettini con le Cozze

THIN SPAGHETTI WITH MUSSELS

IN ITALY we call all shellfish *frutti di mare*: sea fruits. The term is both poetically descriptive and revealing of the pleasure Italians take in the fruit of their many seas. I remember my father going nearly every day to meet the fishing boats; the brightness in his eyes as he spread a mound of glossy black mussels or jumping live shrimp on the kitchen table was the same as when he brought home ripe, honeyed peaches from the farm or a basketful of berries from a walk in the woods. Shellfish is ideally suited to the temperament of the Italian cook, who thrives on fresh ingredients straightforwardly prepared. There is little you can do to shellfish to make it taste any better than it did when it came out of the sea. In this sauce very little cooking takes place, just enough to merge the flavors of the garlic, tomato, mussel juice, parsley, and hot pepper that punctuate the delectable mildness of the unmanipulated mussel meat. The mussels themselves go into the pan for that moment or two necessary to warm them. The ideal vehicle for this, as for most seafood sauces, is thin *spaghetti*, whose reduced surface does not obtrude yet whose firmness—when cooked *al dente*—is sufficient to carry the sauce.

For 4 to 6 persons

3 pounds live mussels
1/3 cup extra virgin olive oil
4 teaspoons chopped garlic
1 1/2 cups canned Italian peeled plum
     tomatoes, drained and cut up into
     large pieces

4 tablespoons chopped parsley
1/2 teaspoon chopped hot red pepper
Salt
1 pound *spaghettini*

1.   Place the mussels in a basin filled with cold water. With a paring knife cut away from each mussel the tuft of fibers protruding from the shell. Rub the mussel shells vigorously one against the other, or scrub with a stiff brush, to remove all the grime. Repeat the operation 3 or 4 times, each time with a fresh change of cold water.

2.   Put the mussels in a pot, cover, and turn on the heat to medium high. As soon as the shells open, transfer the mussels with a slotted spoon to a bowl, and pour the juices from the pot into another bowl. Detach the meat from each shell, swish it lightly in the juice in the other bowl, and put it in a small clean bowl. Line a strainer with a paper towel, set it over a bowl, and pour the mussel juice through it until it has all filtered through the paper.

3.   Put the olive oil and garlic in a saucepan and turn on the heat to medium high. When the garlic becomes colored a pale gold, add the tomatoes. Stir once or twice, then add the filtered

mussel juice, turning up the heat to high. When the juice has completely boiled away, add the parsley, hot pepper, and the mussels. Stir once or twice, taste and correct for salt, and turn off the heat.

4. Drop the *spaghettini* into a pot of abundant boiling salted water. When barely tender but firm to the bite, drain and toss immediately with the sauce.

AHEAD-OF-TIME NOTE: The sauce may be prepared several hours in advance and reheated gently a minute or two before the *spaghettini* are cooked.

Spaghettini col Sugo di Sogliola

THIN SPAGHETTI WITH FILLET OF SOLE

MANY people I meet ask me, "Why don't you give us recipes for sole?" My answer is that no flatfish from either the Atlantic or Pacific Coast resembles in consistency and flavor the sole of my native Adriatic. I test all the recipes I work with using American ingredients, and I have set down only those that, even if they do not duplicate exactly, at least strongly evoke recognizably Italian flavor.

Sole is one of the ingredients that satisfies me least. In this book I have included a recipe for marinated sole fillets—*Sfogi in Saor,* page 46—because at its origin it is a dish that could be prepared with fish of different kinds; it is valid, therefore, with gray sole, lemon sole, rex, petrale, flounder, whatever is available. The same is true of this sauce that, in Italy, we might do with several varieties of white-fleshed fish. You can experiment with your own substitute for sole, if you like.

The flavor base is a sauce of olive oil, onion, garlic, parsley, tomatoes, and hot pepper. Its taste should be as bright and fresh as possible; therefore the cooking times must be very brief. The sole, because it is cut into thin strips, needs very little cooking and should be put in only when the pasta is almost done.

For 4 to 6 persons

Thin Spaghetti with Fillet of Sole (continued)

1 pound fresh fillet of sole
½ cup extra virgin olive oil
½ cup onion chopped fine
2 teaspoons garlic chopped fine
3 tablespoons chopped parsley

¾ cup canned Italian peeled plum tomatoes,
  cut up, with their juice
Salt
Hot red pepper to taste, cut into thin rings
1 pound *spaghettini*

1. Wash the fish under cold running water and pat it thoroughly dry with kitchen towels. Cut it into strips about 3 inches long and 1½ inches wide and set aside.

2. Put the oil and onion in a medium-size skillet or sauté pan and turn on the heat to high.

3. When the onion becomes colored a pale gold, add the chopped garlic. Cook only until the garlic becomes translucent, then add the parsley.

4. Stir 2 or 3 times, then add the cut-up tomatoes with their juice, a liberal sprinkling of salt, and the hot pepper. Lower the heat to medium, cover the pan, and cook for 8 to 10 minutes, stirring from time to time. If after 10 minutes the tomatoes are still watery, uncover the pan, raise the heat, and evaporate excess liquid.

5. Drop the pasta into a pot of abundant boiling salted water.

6. Add the fish to the tomatoes and, leaving the pan uncovered, turn the strips of sole over frequently and gently, cooking them no more than 2 or 3 minutes, assuming the pasta is nearly done. The fish is done when its raw translucent color changes to dull white. If you are cooking the pasta later and the sauce will need to be reheated, either hold back the fish entirely until you reheat the sauce or cook it for just 1 minute the first time.

7. When the pasta is tender, but still firm to the bite, drain immediately and toss at once with the sauce. Serve promptly, without cheese.

Spaghettini col Sugo di Erbe e Pomodoro Crudo

THIN SPAGHETTI WITH HERBS AND RAW TOMATO

A POPULAR, nostalgic image of Italian cooking is that of a portly, grandmotherly woman stirring a simmering sauce for hours. Fortunately, it is only a fantasy. Of the thousands of pasta sauces, only a few take more than 15 to 20 minutes. This sauce for *maccheroncini* doesn't take even 1 minute.

The secret of its sprightly, fragrant flavor is that the herbs and tomatoes of which it is composed are virtually raw. They never see the inside of a saucepan but go directly into the serving bowl where they are splashed with hot olive oil. It is in that brief second or two, while the heat is at flash point, that the fruity scent of the sizzling olive oil is fused to the fresh aromas of the five herbs and the tomato. The texture of the tomato is practically unaltered, staying as juicy and firm as when it was cut up. The forthright style of the sauce agrees well with the sturdiness of macaroni pasta, either in tubular shapes or in the solid ones, like *spaghetti* or *spaghettini.*

For 4 to 6 persons

1½ pounds fresh, ripe tomatoes
3 tablespoons chopped fresh basil
1 tablespoon chopped fresh sage,
    or 3 to 4 dried leaves, crumbled
3 tablespoons chopped parsley
3 teaspoons fresh rosemary chopped fine

1 tablespoon chopped fresh mint
1 pound *spaghettini*
⅓ cup extra virgin olive oil
Salt
Black pepper in a grinder

1. Wash the tomatoes, split them in half, remove the seeds, and dice the halved tomatoes into ½-inch cubes.

2. Put the diced tomatoes, the basil, sage, parsley, rosemary, and mint in the bowl where you'll be tossing and serving the pasta.

3. Drop the *spaghettini* into a pot of abundant boiling salted water.

4. When the pasta is nearly done, put the olive oil in a small saucepan and turn on the heat to high. When the oil is smoking hot, pour it over the tomatoes and herbs in the serving bowl. It should be hot enough to sizzle as it hits the contents of the bowl. Add salt, a few grindings of pepper, and mix well.

5. When the pasta is done—it should be barely tender but firm to the bite—drain it well and transfer it immediately to the bowl, tossing it thoroughly with all the ingredients. Serve promptly.

Spaghettini con Pane, Acciughe e Olive

THIN SPAGHETTI WITH BREAD CRUMBS, ANCHOVIES, AND BLACK OLIVES

*N*O INGREDIENT is such an inexpensive source of concentrated flavor as are anchovies. When judiciously utilized, they bring to life a broad variety of dishes from appetizers, to pasta to roasts, to sauces for *scaloppine.*

Many of the most satisfying preparations using anchovies come from poor country kitchens, particularly the ones of the south, where cooks had nothing in abundance save for the genius of making things tasty. This pasta sauce is an example. In it, anchovies do it all, yet not many are required—

Thin Spaghetti with Bread Crumbs, Anchovies, and Black Olives (continued)
scarcely more than 1 fillet per portion. Bread crumbs take the place of more
expensive and, in this context, less appropriate cheese. Little heat is expended
because the cooking is held to a minimum, not much longer than is required
to brown the garlic and dissolve the anchovies. The olives, chopped to a pulp,
are put in at the end, off the heat: usually a good idea, I have found, whenever
any recipe calls for olives.

To obtain from this sauce the full measure of rich flavor of which it is
capable, prepare your own fillets from whole anchovies packed in salt. Please
see page 33 or, for detailed directions, *The Classic Italian Cook Book*, pages
35–6.

For 4 to 6 persons

½ cup extra virgin olive oil
3 garlic cloves, peeled
6 flat anchovy fillets, chopped very fine to a
    pulp
¼ cup fine, dry, unflavored bread crumbs,
    toasted in a pan as described on page 21

2 to 2½ dozen black Greek-style olives
    (not the purple Kalamata), pitted and
    processed or chopped by hand very fine
    to a pulp
1 pound *spaghettini*

1.   Put the oil and garlic in a small saucepan and turn on the heat to medium high. Cook
the garlic, turning it from time to time, until it
becomes colored a very light brown. Remove it
from the pan and turn the heat down to low.

2.   In about 20 to 30 seconds, when the heat
of the oil has partly subsided, add the chopped
anchovies. Cook, mixing steadily with a wooden
spoon, until the anchovies dissolve.

3.   Turn up the heat to medium, add the

toasted bread crumbs, and cook for 4 to 5 minutes,
stirring frequently.

4.   Remove the pan from the heat and stir in
the olives.

5.   Drop the pasta into a pot of abundant
boiling salted water. The moment it is barely
tender but firm to the bite, drain it and toss it
immediately with the sauce. Some like at this
point to add a thin trickle of raw olive oil, which
adds a fresh fragrance. Serve at once.

Spaghetti col Pomodoro Fresco e la Cipolla

SPAGHETTI WITH FRESH TOMATOES AND ONION

*O*NIONS and tomatoes do good things for each other, the sweetness of one merging into the tartness of the other to produce flavor that is at once mellow and fresh.

Only the onion in this sauce is cooked at length, simmered in a covered pan until it is tender and lightly colored. The fresh tomatoes are diced small so they can be cooked quickly at high heat. The heat must be turned off before they dissolve, when they still retain some body in their consistency.

For 4 to 6 persons

2 pounds fresh, ripe, firm plum tomatoes
6 tablespoons butter
3 cups onion chopped rather fine
Salt

Black pepper in a grinder
1 pound *spaghetti*
⅔ cup freshly grated *parmigiano-reggiano* (Parmesan)

1. Wash the tomatoes, skin them with a peeler, and split them in half. With the tip of a paring knife pick out as many of the seeds as possible. Dice the tomatoes into ¼-inch cubes.

2. Choose a 10- to 12-inch sauté pan with a lid. It is important that the pan be no smaller so that the tomatoes can be spread over a large surface and cooked quickly. Put in the butter and onion and turn on the heat to medium high. Cook, stirring well, for about 1 minute, then cover the pan and turn the heat down to low. The onion must cook until it is tender and colored a very pale gold, but it must not brown.

3. When the onion is done, uncover the pan, add the tomatoes, and turn up the heat to high. Cook, stirring frequently, for 6 to 8 minutes. Add salt and very generous grindings of pepper. There must be enough pepper to balance the sweetness of the onion. When done, the tomatoes should be soft, but not dissolved into sauce; the pieces should still be mostly separate.

4. Drop the pasta into a pot of abundant boiling salted water. The moment it is barely tender but still firm to the bite, drain it, toss it with the sauce in a warm serving bowl, add the grated cheese, toss again, and serve at once.

I Fazzoletti della Nonna

BAKED STUFFED CREPES

IN MY NATIVE Romagna, it is not uncommon, even now in the late 1980s, to find that older farm women keep their heads covered with a black kerchief folded into a triangle. That is likely to be the reason these triangularly folded stuffed crepes from Romagna are called *fazzoletti della nonna*, grandmother's kerchiefs. It is, regrettably, a dish that few remember and even fewer continue to make.

The proportions of flour, milk, and eggs give Italian crepes a firmer consistency than those of other cuisines, but they are made by the same universal method. If you have a special pan or a favorite technique for making crepes, by all means use it. It is not how you make them but what you do with them that matters.

You can develop a broad repertory of stuffings. The four recipes that follow the basic crepe recipe illustrate two ways of using vegetables and two ways of using meat. One vegetable stuffing is made of green beans, garlic, butter, and mozzarella; the other has tomatoes, zucchini, ham, olive oil, onion, garlic, and fontina cheese. The first of the meat stuffings has ground veal, ham, butter, cream, nutmeg, and parsley; the one that follows is composed of dried wild mushrooms, julienned ham, and béchamel. Please note how in all four instances the ingredients for the stuffing are thoroughly *insaporiti*—sautéed and coated with the basic flavor base.

When arranging the *fazzoletti* in the baking pan, make sure the plump, stuffed end faces down and the folded, pointed end up, as described in the recipe. The pointed end has four layers of crepe that will withstand baking without scorching better than the single layer enclosing the stuffing. Less important, but not entirely negligible, is that it also makes a more attractive presentation.

Although I have never tried it, seafood stuffing should work well in *fazzoletti*. If I were to do it, I would prefer olive oil to butter, and I would top with oil-drizzled bread crumbs instead of Parmesan.

On page 312 there is a dessert version of *fazzoletti* with a delicious apricot cream filling.

10 to 12 crepes

1½ cups flour	Salt
1⅓ cups milk	2 to 3 tablespoons butter
3 eggs	

1. Put the flour in a bowl and add the milk in a thin stream, a little at a time, mixing vigorously with a fork to avoid making lumps.

2. Add 1 egg at a time, beating it in rapidly with the fork. When all the eggs have been added, mix in a pinch or two of salt.

3. Smear the bottom of an 8-inch skillet with ½ teaspoon of the butter. Place the pan over a burner and turn on the heat to medium low.

4. Stir the batter and pour ⅓ cup of it into the pan. Tilt and rotate the pan to distrib- ute the batter evenly over the entire bottom.

5. As soon as the batter sets and becomes firm, turn it over with a spatula. When the other side is firm, remove the pan from the heat and transfer the wrapper to a platter.

6. Add ¼ teaspoon of the butter to the pan, return to the heat, stir the batter in the bowl, and put ⅓ cup of it in the pan. Cook as described above and repeat the operation until all the batter has been used up. Stack the wrappers as they are done, one on top of the other.

NOTE: Always stir the batter before putting it in the pan because its denser part tends to settle at the bottom of the bowl. Each time a crepe is done, remove the pan from the heat; otherwise the butter will become too hot and when you put more batter in, it will set too quickly before it can spread evenly over the entire bottom of the pan.

Fazzoletti della Nonna col Ripieno di Fagiolini e Mozzarella

BAKED CREPES WITH GREEN BEANS AND MOZZARELLA STUFFING

For 4 to 6 persons

¾ pound fresh, young green beans
Salt
5 tablespoons butter, plus additional butter
 for smearing the baking dish
2 medium garlic cloves chopped very fine
½ pound mozzarella, preferably buffalo-milk,
 if available, otherwise whole-milk

⅔ cup freshly grated *parmigiano-reggiano*
 (Parmesan)
A 9- by 12-inch oven-to-table baking dish
 or its equivalent
The crepes from the basic *fazzoletti* recipe
 (preceding recipe)

1. Snap off the ends of the green beans and wash the beans in cold water. Bring a pot of water to a boil, add 2 tablespoons of salt, and when the water resumes boiling, drop in the green beans. Cook until they are just tender but still firm to the bite. Drain and cut into ⅓-inch lengths.

2. Put 3 tablespoons of the butter and the chopped garlic in a sauté pan and turn on the heat to medium. When the garlic becomes col-

Baked Crepes with Green Beans and Mozzarella Stuffing (continued)

ored a pale gold, add the cut-up green beans. Cook, stirring frequently, for 2 to 3 minutes, then transfer the green beans to a bowl. Taste and correct for salt.

3. Grate the mozzarella on the large holes of a grater or chop very fine. When the beans are cool, toss them with the grated mozzarella and half the grated Parmesan.

4. Turn on the oven to 450°.

5. Butter the bottom and sides of the baking dish.

6. Lay a single crepe wrapper flat and spread over one-half of it about 2 to 2½ tablespoons of the green beans and cheese stuffing. Fold the bare half over the stuffing, making the edges meet. Fold again in half, creating a puffy triangle with 1 curved side. Stand the triangle in the baking dish with the curved side facing down. Proceed in this manner until all the *fazzoletti* have been stuffed and placed in the dish, with the curved sides all facing down.

7. Sprinkle the remaining grated Parmesan over the *fazzoletti*. Dot with tiny dabs of the remaining 2 tablespoons of butter, making sure that there is 1 dab on the peak of each of the *fazzoletti*.

8. Bake in the uppermost level of the preheated oven for 20 minutes, until the top is speckled with a golden brown crust. Remove from the oven and serve when the dish has settled for a few minutes.

Fazzoletti della Nonna col Ripieno di Zucchine, Pomodoro e Fontina

BAKED CREPES WITH ZUCCHINI, TOMATO, AND FONTINA STUFFING

For 4 to 6 persons

1½ pounds fresh, small, young zucchini, soaked in cold water for 20 minutes
1 pound fresh, ripe tomatoes
⅓ cup extra virgin olive oil
½ cup chopped onion
1 tablespoon chopped garlic
3 ounces boiled, unsmoked ham chopped fine
Salt
Black pepper in a grinder

¼ pound fontina, chopped
⅔ cup freshly grated *parmigiano-reggiano* (Parmesan)
Butter for smearing the baking dish and dotting
A 9- by 12-inch oven-to-table baking dish or its equivalent
The crepes from the basic *fazzoletti* recipe (page 144)

1. Drop the tomatoes in a pot of boiling water. Drain after 1 to 2 minutes and, when cool enough to handle, peel and cut up coarse.

2. When the zucchini have finished soaking, drain and rub their skin with your hands or a rough cloth to dislodge all embedded grit. Cut off both ends from each zucchini and dice the zucchini into ½-inch cubes.

ABOVE LEFT Fresh *porcini* mushrooms have just arrived at the Rialto produce market. They'll all be gone by mid-morning.

ABOVE RIGHT In the background, the double charcoal grill in a corner of our south terrace in Venice and, on the griddle, *porcini* mushrooms. The oil can is a souvenir from Spoleto.

LEFT The produce boat has just docked at the Rialto market. I am admiring the firm, slightly tart, under-ripe tomatoes we favor for salads in Northern Italy.

OPPOSITE Assembling the stuffed veal chop for grilling on the barbecue. Second row, left to right: the solid chop first, then the butterflied and pounded thin stage. First row, left to right: the stuffing of tomatoes, cheese, green beans, and basil, then the stuffed chop skewered shut. See the recipe on page 210.

ABOVE The pickle-studded veal roast glistening in the sun of our south terrace. See the recipe on page 206. Just behind it, my beloved and venerable rosemary plant.

LEFT Gianni, my pork butcher, passing me some smoked *pancetta*. Hanging above Gianni are some of his wonderful *luganeghe*, fresh, thick Venetian sausages. The stout, trussed salami above me is *soppressa*, a tender, garlicky specialty of the Veneto. In front, note the slabs of *pancetta*, the *coppa*, the *mortadella*.

ABOVE Boning sardines is so easy it can be done practically without looking. See the description of the similar procedure for fried butterflied smelts on page 180.

LEFT On the pier, in my hometown of Cesenatico, a fisherman has just unloaded a crate of sardines that, in less than fifteen minutes, will be in the market.

3. Choose a sauté pan that can subsequently accommodate all the zucchini without crowding, put in the oil and chopped onion, and turn on the heat to medium.

4. When the onion becomes colored a pale gold, add the garlic. When the garlic becomes colored a pale gold, add the chopped ham. Stir 2 or 3 times, then add the zucchini and turn up the heat to medium high. Cook the zucchini, stirring frequently, until they are nicely browned. Add salt and several grindings of pepper.

5. Add the tomatoes, turn up the heat to high, and cook, stirring frequently, until the oil separates and floats free, about 15 minutes or so.

6. Transfer the entire contents of the pan to a bowl, adding the fontina and half the grated cheese. Mix until all the ingredients are thoroughly combined.

7. Turn on the oven to 450°.

8. Butter the bottom and sides of the baking dish.

9. Stuff, fold, and bake the *fazzoletti* as described in steps 6, 7, and 8 of the preceding recipe.

Fazzoletti della Nonna col Ripieno di Vitello e Prosciutto Cotto

BAKED CREPES WITH VEAL AND HAM STUFFING

For 4 to 6 persons

4 tablespoons butter, plus additional butter
    for smearing the baking dish
3 tablespoons onion chopped very fine
½ pound ground veal from any inexpensive
    cut with a little fat in it
3 ounces boiled, unsmoked ham chopped fine
Salt
Black pepper in a grinder
½ cup heavy cream

⅛ teaspoon grated nutmeg
3 tablespoons chopped parsley
⅔ cup freshly grated *parmigiano-reggiano*
    (Parmesan)
A 9 by 12 oven-to-table baking dish
    or its equivalent
The crepes from the basic *fazzoletti* recipe
    (page 144)

1. Put 2 tablespoons of the butter and all the onion in a sauté pan and turn on the heat to medium. When the onion becomes colored a pale gold, add the ground veal. Crumble it with a fork and turn it over as it cooks, until it is evenly browned. Add the chopped ham and brown it as well. Add salt, liberal grindings of pepper, and stir. Add the cream and reduce it only partly, stirring frequently. The consistency of the stuffing should be fairly moist. Turn off the heat and add the nutmeg, parsley, and half the grated cheese. Mix well.

2. Turn on the oven to 450°.

3. Butter the bottom and sides of the baking dish.

4. Stuff, fold, and bake the *fazzoletti* as described in steps 6, 7, and 8 of the first recipe on the preceding page.

Fazzoletti della Nonna coi Funghi Secchi e il Prosciutto

BAKED CREPES WITH WILD MUSHROOMS AND HAM STUFFING

For 6 persons

2 ounces dried *porcini* mushrooms, soaked in
    1 quart lukewarm water for 30 minutes
5 tablespoons butter
⅔ cup chopped onion

For the béchamel:
2 cups milk
4 tablespoons butter

⅔ cup freshly grated *parmigiano-reggiano*
    (Parmesan)
Black pepper in a grinder
A 9- by 12-inch oven-to-table baking dish
    or its equivalent

Salt
10 ounces boiled, unsmoked ham, cut into
    thin strips

3 tablespoons flour
Pinch salt

½ cup fine, dry, unflavored bread crumbs,
    toasted lightly in a pan as described on
    page 21
The crepes from the basic *fazzoletti* recipe
    (page 144)

1. When the mushrooms have soaked the recommended amount of time, drain them, reserving the water from their soak. Squeeze the mushrooms in your hands, letting the liquid drip into the water where they had been soaking. Wash them in several changes of clean cold water. Cut them up into coarse pieces.

2. Filter the water from the mushroom soak through a strainer lined with a paper towel into a bowl and set aside.

3. Put 3 tablespoons of the butter and the chopped onion in a sauté pan and turn on the heat to medium. When the onion becomes colored a very pale gold, add the mushrooms, a little bit of salt, and cook for about 1 minute, stirring frequently.

4. Add the filtered water from the mushroom soak, turn the heat up to high, and bubble the liquid away, stirring occasionally, until it has evaporated completely.

5. Turn down the heat to medium, add the ham strips, and cook, stirring from time to time, until the ham is lightly browned.

6. Prepare the béchamel as described on page 112, add the mushroom and ham mixture, and combine thoroughly to amalgamate all the ingredients.

7. Add ½ cup of the grated cheese, several grindings of pepper, mix, taste, and correct for salt.

8. Turn on the oven to 450°.

9. Butter the bottom and sides of the baking dish. Sprinkle the toasted bread crumbs into the dish, then turn the dish upside down and rap it against the work counter to shake off excess bread crumbs. From the excess take 2 table-

spoons of bread crumbs and mix them with the remaining grated cheese.

10. Stuff, fold, and place the *fazzoletti* in the baking dish as described in step 6 of the recipe on page 145.

11. Sprinkle the grated cheese and bread crumb mixture over the *fazzoletti*. Dot with the remaining 2 tablespoons of butter, making sure there is a dab of butter on the peak of each of the *fazzoletti*. Bake in the uppermost level of the preheated oven for 20 minutes, or until a golden crust forms on top. Remove from the oven and allow the heat to subside a few minutes before serving.

Crespelle con gli Asparagi

CREPES WITH ASPARAGUS

*U*NLIKE the folded crepes in the preceding recipes for *fazzoletti*, here the wrappers are rolled up to resemble *cannelloni*. There is a family resemblance between these and the *cannelloni* with asparagus and ham on page 111. The technique of spreading the filling over the whole surface of the wrapper rather than bunching it in the center is the same. Similar also is the way the asparagus is prepared for the filling, a basic procedure equally applicable to other vegetable stuffings such as green bean or zucchini. A significant difference between this stuffing and that of the *cannelloni* is that this one is a wholly vegetarian composition.

For 6 persons

For the crepes:

1 cup milk
3/4 cup flour
2 eggs

1/8 teaspoon salt
About 1 1/2 tablespoons butter

---

1 1/2 pounds medium-size asparagus
Salt

For the béchamel:

2 cups milk
4 tablespoons butter

3 tablespoons flour
1/4 teaspoon salt

---

2 tablespoons butter, plus 2 to 3 tablespoons for dotting the finished dish
3 ounces Emmenthal cheese, cut into small pieces

1 cup freshly grated *parmigiano-reggiano* (Parmesan)
Black pepper in a grinder
A rectangular oven-to-table baking dish

Crepes with Asparagus (continued)

1. Make the crepes: Put the milk in a mixing bowl. Add the flour, shaking it through a strainer. Beat with a fork or whisk until the milk and flour are smoothly amalgamated.

2. Break both eggs into the bowl and add the salt. Beat with the fork or whisk until the eggs are thoroughly blended with the flour and milk mixture.

3. Put ½ teaspoon of the butter in the skillet and turn on the heat to medium low. Melt the butter without letting it become colored, tilting and rotating the pan to coat the bottom evenly.

4. The moment the butter is fully melted, stir the crepe batter and pour 2 tablespoons of it into the center of the pan. Immediately lift the pan above and away from the burner and tip it, in a seesaw motion, in several directions until the batter has spread evenly.

5. Return the pan to the burner and cook until the batter has set. Lift a corner of the crepe to see if its underside has become colored a light, creamy brown. When it has, turn it over with a spatula. When the other side becomes lightly colored, transfer the crepe to a platter.

6. Finish making the crepes, repeating the above operation and adding a small amount of butter, less than ½ teaspoon, to the pan each time before putting in the batter for the next crepe.

7. Trim and peel the asparagus as directed on page 111.

8. In a deep sauté pan that can later accommodate all the asparagus lying flat, bring water to a boil. Add a liberal quantity of salt and the asparagus. Cover the pan and, after the water returns to a boil, cook the asparagus for about 5 minutes, depending on their freshness and thickness. They should be somewhat underdone, because they will undergo additional cooking later. The stalks should be firm, not limp, yet not so hard that they are difficult to pierce with a fork.

9. Drain the asparagus and set aside to cool.

10. Prepare the béchamel sauce as directed on page 112, using the proportions listed above.

11. Pick out as many asparagus stalks as you have crepes. From these trim the bottoms so that the stalks are approximately as long or slightly longer than the diameter of the crepes.

12. Cut up the other asparagus, adding the pieces trimmed from the bottom of the stalks you've set aside.

13. Put 2 tablespoons of butter in a sauté pan, turn on the heat to medium high, and, when the butter foam begins to subside, put in the cut-up asparagus. Sauté for about 4 minutes, stirring occasionally.

14. Transfer the contents of the pan to the bowl of a food processor or blender and add the Emmenthal cheese. Chop briefly, just long enough to cut the ingredients very fine, but not so long that they are puréed.

15. Put the chopped asparagus and cheese in a bowl, adding 1⅓ cups of the béchamel sauce and the grated Parmesan. Mix all the ingredients thoroughly. Taste and correct for salt and add a few grindings of pepper.

16. Turn on the oven to 400°.

17. Take a platter larger than the crepes and spread 1 tablespoon of the béchamel sauce on the bottom. Place a crepe in the platter and slide it around lightly, using the palm of your hand, so that its underside is coated with béchamel.

18. Spread approximately 1½ tablespoons of the chopped asparagus and cheese mixture over the crepe.

19. At the center of the crepe place one of the whole asparagus stalks set aside earlier.

20. Fold the crepe very loosely, jelly-roll fashion, trapping the asparagus stalk in its folds.

21. Place the crepe in the baking dish. As

you roll up more crepes and put them in the dish, arrange them so that the asparagus tips all line up in the same direction and the end of the crepe with a tip rests on the bottom of the crepe ahead of it.

22.   Spread the remaining béchamel sauce over the crepes and dot with the 2 to 3 tablespoons of butter. Bake in the uppermost level of the oven for about 15 minutes, until a pale golden crust forms.

23.   Remove from the oven and allow to rest for at least 5 minutes before serving.

Tagliatelle di Frittata

FRITTATA NOODLES

*E*GGS are one of the foods that give me most comfort. At a restaurant, I rarely pass up the cold vegetable *frittate* that are often part of its *antipasti.* At home, a *frittata* with prosciutto, *pancetta,* or vegetables is one of the few dishes I will cook for myself, if I am alone.

This recipe grew out of curiosity about extending the repertory of egg batters. What developed was a kind of noodle with a taste and consistency conventional noodles can't duplicate. The idea could be taken further, incorporating herbs or other flavors in the batter, but I'd just as soon let others toy with that. With these noodles, just as with regular homemade pasta, I'd rather confine my experiments with flavor to the sauce and keep their composition as simple as possible.

For 4 persons

3 eggs
1 teaspoon salt
½ cup milk
5 tablespoons flour, plus 3 to 4 tablespoons
    for flouring the pan

1 tablespoon butter, plus about 1 tablespoon
    for greasing the pan
A 12- by 10-inch roasting or baking pan, or
    other pan of similar capacity

1.   Turn on the oven to 350°.
2.   Break the eggs into a mixing bowl, add the salt, and beat them lightly with a fork or whisk.
3.   Add the milk in a slow, thin stream, beating it into the eggs.

4.   Add the 5 tablespoons of flour a little bit at a time, passing it through a fine wire strainer, mixing thoroughly to prevent the formation of lumps.
5.   Grease the bottom of the pan thinly with butter. Sprinkle with a little flour, then turn the

Frittata Noodles (continued)

pan upside down on the work counter and give it a sharp rap to shake off excess flour.

6. Pour the mixture from the bowl into the pan, tilting the pan at different angles to spread the batter evenly.

7. Place the pan in the uppermost level of the oven and bake until the contents have set and become colored a light gold, about 10 to 12 minutes.

8. Using a spatula remove the *frittata* from the pan without breaking it and lay it on a cutting board.

9. When completely cool, roll it up loosely, jelly-roll fashion, and cut it into strips ¼ inch wide. Unroll the strips and spread them on a platter. If not using the same day, refrigerate for 3 to 4 days tightly covered with plastic wrap to keep them from drying.

HOW TO SERVE: Toss *frittata* noodles with a sauce and heat, together with that sauce, in a covered skillet or sauté pan over medium heat for 2 to 3 minutes.

With these noodles, I prefer a sauce that is not too shy of flavor, such as the one given below to which I have appended two slight variations that make it progressively more pungent.

Sugo di Aglio, Olio e Pomodoro per Tagliatelle di Frittata

GARLIC, OIL, AND TOMATO SAUCE FOR FRITTATA NOODLES

For 4 persons

¼ cup extra virgin olive oil
1 teaspoon garlic chopped fine
1 tablespoon parsley chopped fine
1 cup canned Italian peeled plum tomatoes, cut up, with their juice

Salt
Black pepper in a grinder
Frittata noodles from preceding recipe

1. Put the olive oil and garlic in a skillet or sauté pan that can later accommodate the noodles. Turn on the heat to medium and sauté the garlic until it becomes colored a very pale gold.

2. Add the parsley, stir once or twice, then add the cut-up tomatoes with their juice. Turn the heat down to very low and cook, uncovered, for about 20 minutes, or until the oil separates from the tomato and floats free.

3. Add salt and a liberal grinding of pepper.

4. Add the *frittata* noodles, toss well, cover the pan, turn up the heat to medium, and cook for 2 to 3 minutes, until the noodles are hot.

VARIATIONS: To make the sauce somewhat sharper, at step 2, above, after putting in the chopped parsley, add 2 tablespoons capers. Or, *in addition* to the capers, put in at the same time 3 flat anchovy fillets chopped fine.

❧ *RISOTTO* ❧

THE BASIC METHOD. To make *risotto*, medium-grain white rice (see varieties below) is added—raw and unwashed—to a flavor base of onion sautéed in butter or, much less frequently, in olive oil with or without garlic. After it is tossed and well coated with butter—or oil—it is cooked in the same uncovered pot by the gradual administration of small quantities of liquid. The rice must be stirred constantly so that it does not stew in the liquid and become mushy. What liquid it cannot absorb quickly must evaporate. When the grains are done to a firm, but not chalky, consistency, they must cling to each other as well as to any other ingredient that was incorporated into the *risotto*. There are no shortcuts or alternative procedures that achieve this result. Rice cooked by any other method, however good it may be, is not *risotto* nor should it be so described.

The fundamental technique is unalterable, but it permits the cook limitless freedom to introduce flavors derived from the flesh of any edible land, sea, or air creature and from any vegetable variety, singly or in any compatible combination. Save for a few rare instances when it is joined with independently prepared ingredients, *risotto* is not cooked separately from its flavor components, but it is fused with them. Everything that is to become part of a *risotto* ought to be cooked along with the rice.

On occasion, when one wishes to protect an ingredient from overcooking, as in the case of shellfish or some vegetables, that ingredient may be added late in the cooking. Steps must be taken, however, to introduce some of its flavor earlier. As an illustration, if making a clam *risotto*, put in the clams' meat at the end—otherwise it will become rubbery—but put in their juice at the beginning. Or, if you are making a zucchini *risotto* and you want firm bits of zucchini in the completed dish, hold back some of the zucchini, but not all; the rest should cook with the rice from the start. What you lose in consistency is amply compensated by the full release of zucchini flavor as it dissolves into the *risotto*.

THE CORRECT RICE VARIETIES. The characteristic clinging consistency of *risotto* is made possible when amylopectin, a starch with marked binding qualities present in rice, dissolves in cooking. The less of this starch rice grains contain, the more likely they are to separate; the higher its content, the more glutinous they become. A few Italian varieties possess just enough amylopectin to cling in cooking, but not so much to become gummy: The grain maintains sufficient firmness to provide the necessary *al dente* bite. The best of these varieties are Arborio, Vialone Nano, and Carnaroli.

Arborio

The most popular and, by a very large margin, the most plentifully produced premium rice in Italy, Arborio is classified as *superfino,* a term applied only to strains that produce the plumpest, largest grains. The thin outer layer of the grain disintegrates quickly in cooking, favoring a liberal contribution of the starch required for a well-bound *risotto*. It absorbs liquid generously and yields more in proportion to its original volume than most other varieties. Because of its size, it takes longer to cook, but it has to be closely watched in the final stages of cooking to keep it from becoming overcooked. It is the overwhelming choice of Piedmontese and Lombard cooks. Arborio's handsome size and superior clinging qualities make it the classic *risotto* rice for any careful cook.

Vialone Nano

A stubbier grain than Arborio, Vialone Nano is classified as *semifino*. Its production is only about one-quarter that of Arborio and nearly all of it goes to the Veneto, where its firmness and rapid cooking time make it the favorite of Venetian cooks.

Carnaroli

Carnaroli is the aristocrat of rice varieties for *risotto,* but like all true aristocrats, it is in short supply. A major rice grower of my acquaintance harvests so little Carnaroli that he packages his entire production as Christmas gifts for his friends. It does exist, however, and, if not abundant, is available for export, although at a substantially higher price than other varieties. Like Arborio, Carnaroli is a large, plump grain classified as *superfino*. It produces a *risotto* of lovely flavor with a consistency that has just the right "cling," while the grains cook to a perfect, chewy firmness.

For the record, other suitable, but less estimable *risotto* varieties are Roma, Razza 77, and Maratelli.

THE COOKING LIQUID. No liquid is so appropriate a cooking vehicle as homemade meat broth (except for a seafood *risotto*). It should be a pale amber broth in which veal and beef predominate, with minimal amounts of chicken and bones. Pure chicken broth generates distractingly sharp flavor. Stock in the French style is overrich and unacceptable. Canned broths are barely tolerable substitutes for the homemade product and must be diluted with water. I nearly always prefer bouillon cubes.

If there are dried wild mushrooms in the *risotto,* the water in which they were reconstituted should be added to the broth. If you are using a blanched vegetable, such as asparagus, save and add the blanching water to the cooking liquid. One may sometimes use wine, but as an addition to, not a replacement for, other liquid.

For a seafood *risotto* I don't like to use fish broth because it becomes too emphatic as it boils down. I prefer to use water to which I may add some white wine and, if I am using clams or mussels, the juices they released when they were opened.

THE PROPER POT. A *risotto* pot must transmit and retain consistent, even heat: lively enough so that the rice does not stew, yet not fierce enough to scorch it. Pure aluminum and other light ware is unsuitable. This is the kind of cooking that demands pots of substance. At home I always make *risotto* in enameled cast iron. Heavy-bottomed, stainless steel–jacketed alloys are also excellent. I have used them in my classes for over a decade. Heavy-gauge copper is fine, of course, but no better than other easier to care for and equally heat-retentive ware.

COOKING TIMES. In Italy, rice of *superfino* class such as Arborio and Carnaroli is expected to cook in 18 minutes. At the end of that time I find that the heart of the kernel is still chalky. I like firm rice, but don't like chalk, so I choose to cook the rice from 25 to 35 minutes. The figure is merely indicative, however. There are variations in the receptivity of rice to moisture: It is affected by the humidity of a given day or locality and by the pace at which it cooks—which depends on the intensity of heat employed as well as the amount of liquid used and the frequency with which it is added. The only way to know when a *risotto* is done is to taste it, which I begin to do after the 20-minute mark is passed.

STYLES OF RISOTTO. The kinds of *risotto* one can make are beyond counting, but the principal styles, in terms of finished consistency, are two: the compact, stickier style exemplified by *risotto alla milanese* and by the traditional *risotto* of Piedmont and Emilia-Romagna, and the looser, moister style characteristic of the Veneto. In the first, all the liquid that is not absorbed by the rice is allowed to evaporate so that the *risotto* becomes a more closely bound mass of grains. In the Venetian style one paces the addition of liquid so that a small quantity remains when the rice is done, resulting in a slightly runny consistency, *all'onda* as they call it in Venice, or "wavy." Each style has its merits. The substantial Milanese one is a satisfying vehicle for rich flavors such as those of sausages, game, wild mushrooms, truffles, saffron. The Venetian *risotto all'onda*, delicate and elegant, is eminently suited to seafood and vegetables.

Mantecare

Mantecare, which means to whip or beat to a creamy consistency, is an important finishing touch. When the *risotto* is nearly done, one puts in fresh butter and, if required by the recipe, grated Parmesan and beats them into the rice for one, two, or three minutes. Some styles of *risotto* are more *mantecati* than others. In Venice this is done off the heat to prevent all the liquid from drying out and so to keep the *risotto all'onda.*

AHEAD-OF-TIME NOTE. I would like to say nothing that might encourage making *risotto* in advance. A cold or reheated *risotto* fails totally to express the values of the dish. Nevertheless, if you are compelled by circumstances to interrupt the cooking, you can resume a few hours later, although not without some impairment of flavor. In such instances, stop the *risotto* when it is little more than 5 minutes' short of being done, taking care that all the liquid has either been absorbed or evaporated. Spread the rice in a thin layer on a previously refrigerated cookie sheet. When it has cooled, do not refrigerate it: You will want to have it at room temperature when, later that day, you will finish cooking it. To resume cooking, melt butter in a pot (or heat up olive oil if that was the original base), put in the rice, coat it thoroughly with hot butter or oil, add a ladleful of the same liquid you had used earlier, and proceed, following the basic technique, until the *risotto* is done.

Risotto coi Carciofi

RISOTTO WITH ARTICHOKES

VISITORS exploring Venice's small, good restaurants discover not only the remarkably tasty seafood of the Adriatic but a variety of extraordinary vegetables: miniature nutty salad greens, ravishingly fresh zucchini, green beans, peas. The best are grown on the farms of the surrounding islands under the savory ventilation of the briny sea air, picked in their infancy and landed in the market the same day. Perhaps the most remarkable of this produce are the tiny first artichokes called *castraure,* often used to make a surpassingly fine vegetable *risotto.*

Risotto with Artichokes (continued)

Castraure are so tender that they melt entirely in the *risotto,* their presence detectable only by a green tinge on the rice and the saturating, sweetly bitter artichoke taste. To achieve comparable, even if not identical, results with California artichokes is not impossible. The most important step, after having chosen the freshest, greenest artichokes you can, is to pare the vegetable down so that only the pale green, tender portion of the leaves remains attached to the heart. Then it is cut into the thinnest possible slices and cooked until very soft with a flavor base of garlic, olive oil, and parsley. At that point the rice is put in and the basic *risotto* procedure takes over.

For 4 to 6 persons

2 tablespoons extra virgin olive oil
1/4 cup chopped onion
2 teaspoons garlic chopped very fine
1/2 cup chopped parsley
4 large artichokes, cleaned as described on page 80, cut into 1-inch wedges then sliced very thin
1/2 cup water
Salt

5 cups Homemade Meat Broth (page 73), or 1 bouillon cube dissolved in 5 cups water, or 3/4 cup canned meat broth diluted with 4 1/4 cups water
1 1/2 cups Italian Arborio rice
Black pepper in a grinder
4 tablespoons butter
1/3 cup freshly grated *parmigiano-reggiano* (Parmesan)

1. Choose a heavy-bottomed pot large enough to accommodate the *risotto* later, put in the oil and onion, and turn on the heat to medium high.

2. When the onion becomes translucent, add the garlic. Cook until the garlic becomes colored a pale gold, then add half the chopped parsley. Stir, then add the sliced artichokes.

3. Cook the artichokes for about 3 minutes, turning them frequently, then add the water and a pinch of salt. Turn the artichokes once, cover the pot, turn down the heat to low, and cook for 20 to 30 minutes, depending on the freshness and youth of the artichokes, until they are very soft. Check the pot occasionally to make sure there is enough liquid for the artichokes to cook in without sticking and, if necessary, add a little water from time to time.

4. Bring the broth to a gentle simmer in a saucepan over medium-low heat.

5. Test the artichokes for tenderness by pricking them with a fork. When they are soft and all the water has evaporated, add the rice, turn up the heat to medium high, and keep the pan uncovered. Stir the rice thoroughly several times to coat the grains well with the contents of the pot.

6. Add a ladleful of broth and stir the rice constantly to wipe it away from the bottom and side of the pot. When all the broth in the pot has been absorbed, add another ladleful. Stir steadily to keep the rice from sticking, adding more broth, a ladleful at a time, as required. Repeat the procedure until the rice is done: It should be firm, but tender, without a chalky center. If you should run out of broth, add warm water instead.

7. Remove the pot from the heat, add salt and liberal grindings of pepper, the butter, grated cheese, the remaining half of the chopped parsley, and stir quickly and thoroughly to amalgamate all the ingredients. Serve at once.

Risotto con i Pomodori Freschi e il Basilico

RISOTTO WITH FRESH TOMATOES AND BASIL

*B*RIGHT tomato color and frank tomato taste are the reasons for this *risotto*'s simple, strong, summery appeal. Embark upon it only when you can get very ripe local tomatoes. Plum tomatoes are my choice because they are less watery. The tomatoes must be peeled, but I do not blanch them to pinch off the skin because I want them to be as firm as possible when I start them cooking with sautéed onion and butter. Therefore I peel them raw. (Please see page 21 for a description of this technique.)

When the tomatoes have simmered a few minutes, the rice is added and they finish cooking together. The *risotto* becomes colored a vivid red and exudes the effusively fresh, vibrant flavor of the tomatoes.

For 4 persons

1½ pounds firm, ripe plum tomatoes
5 cups Homemade Meat Broth (page 73), or
    1 bouillon cube dissolved in 5 cups water,
    or ¾ cup canned meat broth diluted with
    4¼ cups water
4 tablespoons butter
1 tablespoon vegetable oil

⅓ cup chopped onion
Salt
Black pepper in a grinder
1½ cups Italian Arborio rice
½ cup freshly grated *parmigiano-reggiano*
    (Parmesan)
10 fresh basil leaves, cut into very thin strips

1. Wash the tomatoes in cold water, skin them with a peeler, and cut them into ½-inch pieces. If there are very many seeds, pick out most of them with the tip of a paring knife.

2. Put the broth in a saucepan and bring it to a simmer.

3. In a heavy-bottomed pot put 2 tablespoons of the butter, the oil, and the chopped onion and turn on the heat to medium.

4. When the onion becomes colored a pale gold, add the tomatoes with a little bit of salt and grindings of pepper. Cook, stirring from time to time, for 10 minutes.

5. Add the rice and stir it a few times to coat it thoroughly.

6. Add a ladleful of broth and stir the rice constantly to wipe it away from the bottom and side of the pot. When there is no more broth in the pot, add another ladleful. Stir steadily to keep the rice from sticking at any point, adding more broth, a ladleful at a time, as required. Repeat the procedure, never ceasing stirring, until the rice is done. It should be firm but tender, without a chalky center.

7. Add the remaining 2 tablespoons of butter, the grated cheese, and the basil, stir for a minute or two, taste and correct for salt and pepper, and serve at once.

Risotto coi Fagioli Rossi

RISOTTO WITH RED KIDNEY BEANS

*E*ARTHY and comforting are words that come to mind in describing this *risotto*. The flavor base is cabbage, shredded fine and cooked with onion sautéed in butter. The rice is added then, and when it is more than half done, the cooked or drained canned beans are put in. At the end, the *risotto* is *mantecato*—beaten—with grated Parmesan and sage-scented melted butter.

For 4 persons

2/3 pound cabbage or Savoy cabbage
2 teaspoons salt
7 tablespoons butter
2½ to 3 tablespoons onion chopped very fine
6 or 7 fresh sage leaves
1½ cups Italian Arborio rice

10-ounce can red kidney beans, drained, or
    1 cup dried beans, soaked and cooked as
    described on page 294
Black pepper in a grinder
2/3 cup freshly grated *parmigiano-reggiano*
    (Parmesan), plus additional for the table

1. If using regular white cabbage, remove any bruised and discolored leaves, rinse the cabbage well in cold water, and cut it into quarters. Cook it in abundant boiling water with 1 tablespoon salt for 10 minutes. Drain well, but reserve the water in the pot.

2. If using Savoy cabbage, remove any discolored leaves and detach the other leaves from the head as described on page 64. Rinse the leaves in cold water. Cook the larger leaves first in abundant boiling water with the salt. Cook for 7 minutes, then remove from the pot with a large slotted spoon or spatula. Cook the smaller leaves in the same manner for 4 to 5 minutes. Reserve all the cooking liquid.

3. Cut the cooked, drained cabbage or Savoy cabbage into very fine shreds.

4. Choose a large, heavy-bottomed casserole and put into it 3 tablespoons of the butter and all the chopped onion. Turn the heat on to medium high and cook the onion, stirring occasionally, until it becomes colored a pale gold.

5. Meanwhile, in another pot, bring to a simmer the liquid in which the cabbage was cooked.

6. When the onion in the casserole has become pale gold, turn down the heat to medium, add the shredded cabbage, and cook, stirring from time to time, until the cabbage dissolves to a nearly creamy consistency.

7. While the cabbage is cooking, put the remaining 4 tablespoons of butter in a small saucepan together with the sage leaves and turn on the heat to medium. Cook, stirring occasionally, only until the butter becomes colored a pale gold; otherwise, it will become too pungent. Set aside.

8. When the cabbage has reached an almost creamy consistency, add the rice to it and turn on the heat to medium high. Stir until all the grains of rice are well coated, then add a ladleful of the simmering liquid previously used to cook the cabbage.

9. Stir steadily with a wooden spoon until all the liquid in the casserole has evaporated, then add another ladleful from the simmering

pot. Continue this procedure, adding liquid, stirring until the liquid evaporates, then adding more liquid, for about 15 minutes.

10. Add the beans, salt, and grindings of pepper. Stir thoroughly and steadily, as described above, adding a ladleful of liquid when necessary, until the rice is cooked *al dente*, tender but firm to the bite. When you see that the rice is nearly done, make sure you have

enough liquid in the casserole to achieve a slightly runny consistency. Taste for salt.

11. When the rice is done, turn off the heat and mix in the grated cheese. Put in the sage-flavored butter, pouring it through a strainer. If the butter has hardened too much to pour, melt it briefly first over medium-low heat. Stir the *risotto* thoroughly and serve immediately. Have additional grated cheese available at the table.

Risotto col Radicchio Rosso

RISOTTO WITH RADICCHIO

ONE of the best uses to which one can put *radicchio*, the intriguingly bitter red Italian lettuce, is to make a *risotto*. *Radicchio* dissolves almost totally to fuse creamily with the rice, and its original bitterness is rephrased by the cooking to emerge with a softer, gentler accent. Be prepared for a transformation in color: The raw red turns to a subdued, elegant black.

For 4 to 6 persons

1 pound *radicchio* (red Italian chicory)
1 tablespoon vegetable oil
5 tablespoons butter
½ cup chopped onion
5 cups Homemade Meat Broth (page 73), or 2 bouillon cubes dissolved in 5 cups water, or ¾ cup canned meat broth diluted with 4¼ cups water

1½ cups Italian Arborio rice
½ cup dry white wine
⅔ cup freshly grated *parmigiano-reggiano* (Parmesan)
Salt
Black pepper in a grinder

1. Detach the *radicchio* leaves from the stem and wash them well in cold water. Drain and pat thoroughly dry in a cloth or with paper towels. Bunch up 5 or 6 leaves at a time and cut them into skinny strips about ¼ inch wide.

2. Choose a heavy-bottomed pot and put in the vegetable oil, 3 tablespoons of the butter, and the chopped onion. Turn on the heat to medium.

3. While the onion is cooking, put the broth or bouillon in a saucepan and bring it to a low simmer.

4. When the onion becomes colored a pale gold, add the *radicchio*. Cook, turning from time to time, until the *radicchio* is tender.

5. Add the rice and turn it over 2 or 3 times until it is well coated. Add the wine, stir, and let the wine bubble away for 1 to 2 minutes.

Risotto with Radicchio (continued)

6.   Add 1 or 2 ladlefuls of simmering broth, turn up the heat to high, and stir constantly, wiping away the rice from the bottom and side of the pot. When the broth has evaporated, add another ladleful and stir constantly, never letting the rice stick to any part of the pot. Repeat the procedure, adding more broth as it evaporates and stirring steadily, until the rice is done: firm but cooked through, without a chalky center. At the end there should be just enough liquid left in the pot to give the *risotto* a slightly runny consistency. Should you run out of broth while cooking, continue with plain water.

7.   Off the heat, stir in the grated cheese and the remaining 2 tablespoons of butter, mixing for 1½ to 2 minutes. Add salt and liberal grindings of pepper, stir briefly, and serve at once.

Risotto coi Finocchi

RISOTTO WITH FENNEL

*W*HEN I discovered, long ago, that most people are acquainted with *finocchio* only in its raw stage, I regularly began to include a cooked version of it among the dishes I taught, frying it, sautéing it in butter, slow-cooking it in olive oil, or combining it with fish. It has consistently been one of the most warmly received of the vegetable dishes in my school's curriculum.

For this *risotto* the *finocchio* is first tossed with sautéed onion and butter, then cooked very slowly until it becomes a tender pulp. Its consistency is sacrificed to a distillation and refinement of its flavor. The vegetable's herbal piquancy that recalls its kinship with anise pervades the *risotto* mildly, endowing it with freshness and finesse.

For 4 persons

2 medium *finocchio* (fennel)
¼ cup chopped onion
4 tablespoons butter
1 tablespoon vegetable oil
⅓ cup water
Salt
1½ cups Italian Arborio rice
½ cup dry white wine

5 cups Homemade Meat Broth (page 73), or
     1 bouillon cube dissolved in 5 cups water,
     or ¾ cup canned meat broth diluted with
     4¼ cups water
2 tablespoons chopped parsley
⅔ cup freshly grated *parmigiano-reggiano*
     (Parmesan)
Black pepper in a grinder

1.   Cut off and discard the *finocchio* tops down to the bulbs. Remove any bruised or discolored outer leaf, then slice the bulbs very fine crosswise, producing thin rounds and half rings. Wash in several changes of cold water, drain, and set aside.

2. Put the chopped onion, 2 tablespoons of the butter, and the vegetable oil in the pot where you will subsequently cook the rice. Turn on the heat to medium.

3. When the onion becomes colored a pale gold, add the sliced *finocchio* and stir well. Add the water, cover the pot, and cook, stirring occasionally, until the *finocchio* becomes soft as pulp.

4. Uncover the pot, evaporate any remaining water, and, when the *finocchio* has become colored a creamy brown, add salt, stir 2 or 3 times, then add the rice. Stir well to coat the rice thoroughly, turn the heat up to medium high, and add the wine. In another pan, bring the broth to a simmer over medium heat.

5. While the wine bubbles, stir the rice constantly, wiping it away from the sides and bottom of the pot. When the wine has evaporated completely, add a ladleful of broth. Never stop stirring, always making sure that the side and bottom of the pot are wiped clean. When the first ladleful of broth has evaporated, add another, always continuing to stir. Continue the procedure, adding more broth as required, until the rice is done: It should be firm but tender, without a chalky center. At this point the consistency should be slightly runny. If you run out of broth before the rice is done, continue the cooking with water.

6. Off the heat add the remaining 2 tablespoons of butter, salt, the parsley, grated cheese, and liberal grindings of pepper. Stir for another minute or two until the consistency of the *risotto* is creamy smooth, then serve at once.

Risotto con la Verza e il Parmigiano

RISOTTO WITH SAVOY CABBAGE AND PARMESAN

*T*HE emphasis here is squarely on the sturdy virtues of Savoy cabbage. To prepare it for the *risotto*, the cabbage is shredded, tossed with sautéed onion and *pancetta*, and cooked to a dark brown color. When the full, rich flavor of the cabbage has been developed, the rice is added and the making of the *risotto* gets under way.

For 4 to 6 persons

3 tablespoons chopped onion
1/2 cup *pancetta* cut into very thin strips
1 tablespoon vegetable oil
4 tablespoons butter
1 pound Savoy cabbage, shredded very fine
Salt
5 cups Homemade Meat Broth (page 73), or

2 bouillon cubes dissolved in 5 cups water, or 1 cup canned beef broth diluted with 4 cups water
1½ cups Italian Arborio rice
½ cup freshly grated *parmigiano-reggiano* (Parmesan)
Black pepper in a grinder

Risotto with Savoy Cabbage and Parmesan (continued)

1. Choose a heavy-bottomed pot such as enameled cast iron or multilayered steel and put in the onion, *pancetta*, oil, and 3 tablespoons of the butter. Turn on the heat to medium high. Cook, stirring frequently, until the onion becomes colored a light gold.

2. Add the shredded Savoy cabbage, a little salt, turn with a wooden spoon 2 or 3 times, cover the pot, and turn down the heat to medium. Cook, stirring from time to time, until the cabbage has become colored a rich nut brown.

3. Bring the broth to a low simmer.

4. Add the rice to the pot containing the Savoy cabbage, uncover, and raise the heat to medium high. Stir the rice quickly and thoroughly with a wooden spoon, then add a ladleful of broth. Stir constantly, wiping away the rice from the bottom and side of the pot, until the broth has evaporated. Add another ladleful, and continue this procedure until the rice is done. When cooked, it should be firm to the bite, but cooked through, without a chalky center. When the rice is done, there should be sufficient broth left in the pot to give it a slightly runny consistency. If you run out of broth before the rice is done, continue with plain water.

5. Add the grated cheese, the remaining tablespoon of butter, stir well, taste and correct for salt, and sprinkle with liberal grindings of pepper. Transfer to a warm platter and serve at once.

~ THREE SEAFOOD RISOTTI ~

My aim in writing the following recipes was to set down a method that would yield seafood *risotti* with reasonably constant results nearly anywhere, irrespective of what fish might or might not be available locally. No ingredient is so susceptible to the environment that produces it as seafood, which varies dramatically even within relatively short stretches of water—all seafood, that is, except for squid. I have used it in Europe, in North America, in Asia, and I have found that its consistency, its sweet and spicy flavor changes little or not at all. More-over, it is found nearly everywhere, either fresh or, even in the most landlocked areas, frozen.

Squid is delectable in *risotto*, alone or as a flavor base for other ingredients. The first of the recipes below is for a basic *risotto* with squid. The second adds shrimp; the third, shrimp and clams. The simple procedure, once it is clearly grasped, can be applied to variations of one's own, with other crustaceans and bivalves such as lobster, crayfish, crab, scampi, mussels.

Risotto coi Calamari

RISOTTO WITH SQUID

For 6 persons

2 pounds whole squid to be cleaned, or 1½
   pounds already cleaned and sliced
½ cup extra virgin olive oil,
   plus 2 tablespoons
½ onion, chopped fine
1 tablespoon chopped garlic
3 tablespoons chopped parsley
½ cup dry white wine

1 cup canned Italian peeled plum tomatoes,
   drained of their juice; or peeled fresh
   plum tomatoes, if very ripe ones are
   available
2 cups imported Italian Arborio rice
Salt
Black pepper in a grinder

1.　If using whole uncleaned squid, clean it as directed on page 185, rinse it in cold water, and pat thoroughly dry. If using cleaned squid, wash it, dry it, and proceed to the next step.

2.　Chop all the squid and tentacles in a food processor or by hand, until no piece is larger than ½ inch.

3.　Choose a sturdy pot suitable for making *risotto,* put into it the ½ cup of olive oil and the chopped onion, and turn on the heat to medium.

4.　When the onion becomes translucent, add the garlic.

5.　When the garlic becomes very faintly colored, add 2 tablespoons of the chopped parsley, stir once or twice, then add the chopped squid. Cook for a minute or two, until the color of the squid turns from translucent to flat white. Stir 2 or 3 times, then add the white wine.

6.　When the wine has bubbled for 1 minute, add the tomatoes, turn down the heat to minimum, and cover the pot. Cook for at least 45 minutes, until the oil has floated free. Note:

Add no salt until later, when directed, because it would make the squid tough.

7.　In a separate pan, bring about 2 quarts of water to a simmer.

8.　Add the rice to the pot with the squid, turning up the heat to medium high and keeping the pot uncovered. Stir the rice several times, coating it thoroughly with the contents of the pot.

9.　Add a ladleful of the simmering water, stirring the rice constantly to wipe it away from the side and bottom of the pot. When the water has evaporated or been absorbed, add another ladleful and continue stirring. Add a ladleful of water whenever it is required, never ceasing to stir. After 10 to 15 minutes, add salt and liberal grindings of pepper. The rice is done when it is firm but tender, without a chalky center; the consistency of the finished *risotto* should be just slightly runny.

10.　Just before transferring the *risotto* to a serving platter, take the pot off the heat and stir in the 2 tablespoons of olive oil and the remaining tablespoon of chopped parsley.

AHEAD-OF-TIME NOTE: The squid may be cooked several hours in advance through step 6 and reheated gently when ready to proceed with the *risotto.*

Risotto coi Calamari e i Gamberi

RISOTTO WITH SQUID AND SHRIMP

For 6 persons

1¼ pounds shrimp in their shells
1½ pounds whole squid to be cleaned,
     or 1 pound already cleaned and sliced

All the other ingredients in the recipe for
     Risotto with Squid (preceding recipe)
Hot red pepper to taste (optional)

1. Shell the shrimp, devein them, wash them, drain them, and pat them dry.
2. Separate the cleaned shrimp into 2 equal parts. Chop 1 part into fine bits in a processor or by hand and set aside. Cut up the remaining shrimp into larger pieces—about 3 pieces to each shrimp, depending on its size—and set aside.
3. Follow steps 1 through 9 of the preceding recipe up to the point where the rice has cooked for about 15 minutes. Add the finely chopped portion of shrimp, salt, and liberal grindings of pepper. When the rice is about 5 minutes from being done, add the larger pieces of shrimp and hot pepper to taste. Finish the *risotto* as directed in the preceding recipe, stirring in the olive oil and parsley off the heat just before serving.

Risotto coi Calamari, i Gamberi, e le Vongole

RISOTTO WITH SQUID, SHRIMP, AND CLAMS

For 6 persons

12 littleneck clams
All the other ingredients in the recipe for

Risotto with Squid and Shrimp (preceding recipe)

1. Wash the clams in several changes of cold water, rubbing them vigorously one against the other or scrubbing them with a stiff brush.
2. Put the clams in a broad pot with 1 cup of water, cover the pot, and turn on the heat to high. When all the shells have opened, remove the clams from the pot, detach the meat from each shell, and swish it in the juices of the pot without plunging it in too deep, skimming the surface of the liquid. Place the clam meat on a cutting board and, when you have done all the clams, chop them into 2 or 3 pieces each.

3. Line a strainer with a paper towel and through it filter the clam juice from the pot, putting it into a bowl just large enough to contain the clam meat. Put the clam meat into the bowl and set aside.

4. Prepare the shrimp as described in steps 1 and 2 of the preceding recipe and set aside.

5. Follow the basic recipe on page 163 through step 8.

6. When the rice has been well coated with the squid base, add just the clam juice from the bowl, holding back the clam meat. Add a ladleful of simmering water and continue making the *risotto* as directed in the basic recipe.

7. When the rice has cooked for about 15 minutes, add the finely chopped portion of shrimp, salt, and liberal grindings of pepper. Stir the rice constantly, adding a ladleful of simmering water when needed. When the rice is about 5 minutes from being done, add the larger pieces of shrimp and hot pepper to taste. After stirring for another 2 or 3 minutes, add the clam meat. Continue stirring, cooking the rice until it is firm, but cooked all the way through. Its finished consistency should be faintly runny.

8. Remove the pot from the heat, stir in the olive oil and parsley, transfer to a serving platter, and bring to the table at once.

Gnocchi Verdi di Patate

GREEN POTATO GNOCCHI

ONE way to make green *gnocchi* is to combine spinach and ricotta, as described in *The Classic Italian Cook Book*, page 200. In that recipe the spinach is sautéed with onion, butter, and *mortadella*. Another method, popular in Venice and particularly light and fresh, simply combines chopped, cooked spinach with basic potato *gnocchi* dough.

The choice of potatoes for the dough is critically important, just as it is in making plain *gnocchi*. Mealy, baking potatoes or moist, new potatoes must be avoided: Use only old boiling potatoes. If the temptation to add eggs to the dough comes your way, resist it. It is the presence of eggs that makes potato *gnocchi* heavy, lumpish, excessively chewy. Proper *gnocchi* must be light and fluffy.

The best sauce to use is a simple, fragrant tomato sauce such as the one on page 122. Even more simply, toss the *gnocchi* with butter and a generous amount of choice freshly grated Parmesan. Or gratinate them thus: Cook and drain the *gnocchi* and put them in a flameproof serving dish; dot with butter, sprinkle liberally with Parmesan, and place them under a hot salamander or a grill for just the time it takes for the cheese to begin to melt. Don't keep them too long under the flame or the *gnocchi* will turn to mush.

For 6 to 8 persons

Green Potato Gnocchi (continued)

2 pounds fresh spinach
Salt

2 pounds boiling potatoes
2 cups flour

1.   Trim and wash the spinach as described on pages 55–6. Do not chop it.

2.   Put the spinach in a pot with just the water that clings to its leaves and 1 tablespoon of salt. Cover the pot and turn on the heat to medium. Cook the spinach until quite tender.

3.   When done, drain it and, as soon as it is cool, squeeze all the liquid you can out of it by twisting the leaves inside a dry towel. Chop the spinach very fine. Use a knife because a food processor would liquefy it.

4.   Wash the potatoes, put them in a pot with ample water to cover, put a lid on the pot, and turn on the heat to medium. Boil the potatoes until tender enough for a fork to pierce them easily.

5.   Drain the potatoes, peel them as soon as you are able to handle them, and mash them through a food mill using the disk with the narrowest holes.

6.   Knead the potatoes and spinach together with ⅔ cup of the flour and a pinch of salt. Knead just long enough to amalgamate all the ingredients uniformly, stopping when the mixture is smooth, but still soft and sticky.

7.   Dust your work surface with flour and shape the potato and spinach mixture into sausagelike rolls about 1 inch thick. Cut the rolls into ¾-inch lengths.

8.   At this point, the *gnocchi* are shaped exactly as directed in the recipe for basic potato gnocchi in *The Classic Italian Cook Book* (page 195). I find I cannot describe the procedure now more clearly than I did then, so I will repeat it here.

The technique is more complicated to explain than it is to execute. At first, just go through the motions of the step until you have understood them. Then start on the *gnocchi*, but without losing heart if the first few do not turn out quite right. You will soon acquire the knack and do a whole mess of *gnocchi* in 2 or 3 minutes. In working with *gnocchi*, remember that it will make your life much easier if you use flour to dust repeatedly the *gnocchi*, your hands, and any surface you are working on.

Take a fork with long, rounded, slim prongs. Working over a counter, hold the fork sideways—that is, with the prongs pointing either right to left or left to right—and with the concave side facing you. With the other hand, place a *gnocco* on the inside curve of the fork, resting it partly past the points of the prongs, pressing it against the prongs with the tip of your index finger, which should be pointing at and perpendicular to the fork. While pressing the *gnocco*, flip it away from the prong tips in the direction of the fork's handle. Don't drag it, roll it. As it rolls toward the base of the prongs, let it drop to the counter. Each *gnocco* should then be somewhat crescent shaped, with a ridge on one side formed by the prongs and a depression on the other side formed by your fingertip. This is not just a gratuitous decorative exercise. It serves to thin out the middle sections of the *gnocchi* so they can cook more evenly and to create little grooved traps on their surfaces for the sauce to sink into.

9.   To cook *gnocchi*, drop them, about 2 dozen at a time, into 5 quarts of boiling salted water. In a very short time they will float to the surface. Let them cook just 8 to 10 seconds more, then retrieve them with a slotted spoon or scoop and transfer to a warm platter. Season with some of the sauce you are using. Drop more *gnocchi* in the boiling water and repeat the procedure. For sauce suggestions, please refer to the introductory note on the preceding page.

AHEAD-OF-TIME NOTE: Gnocchi can be prepared in advance up to 2 or 3 hours before cooking. Cook them only when ready to serve. Do not reheat them after they have been cooked.

Polenta

Polenta consists of corn flour, water, and a well-lubricated elbow. The flour becomes *polenta* when, with constant stirring, it absorbs all the water and turns into a homogeneous, soft, yet compact mass that wipes cleanly away from the side of the pot.

In *The Classic Italian Cook Book* I gave a recipe for *polenta* with a high proportion of flour to water that required half the conventional time to stir. Although it has always worked well at home, I have found that some who have tried it for the first time have had difficulty in achieving a satisfactory consistency. I have therefore reduced the quantity of flour while increasing the water and the cooking time. Following this method I have seen students, although they grumble about all the stirring, turn out good *polenta* on their first attempt. It is vital to stir the flour and water uninterruptedly until it masses and not to let it cook faster than at a simmer.

HOW TO SERVE: Polenta can be used when just made, or it can be allowed to cool completely, then sliced and grilled or fried. Fresh *polenta*—warm, soft, and slightly quivering—is wonderful with meat stews and other casserole dishes, particularly when there are enough cooking juices for the *polenta* to absorb. Fricassees of birds—either game or domestic—pork ribs, or sausages with tomatoes are ideally matched with freshly made *polenta*.

When cold, *polenta* is firm and can be sliced like bread. The slices can be run quickly under a broiler or, even better, toasted on a charcoal grill. They are delicious just as they are, or as an accompaniment for sautéed liver (page 239), *sfogi in saor* (page 46), or with a roast bird or rabbit. In Venice, grilled *polenta* is always found with cuttlefish stewed in its ink and with any fried fish. Try spreading Gorgonzola or goat cheese on grilled *polenta* when still hot.

Sliced cold *polenta* can also be fried in vegetable oil and served very crisp in the same manner suggested for grilled *polenta*. When frying it, allow a transparent but not colored crust to form on both sides of the slices.

Also see the *lasagne*-like Baked *Polenta* with Meat Sauce in *The Classic Italian Cook Book*, page 208.

For 6 persons

Polenta (continued)

7 cups water   1²/3 cups (7 ounces) coarse-ground cornmeal
Salt

1.   Put the water in a broad, heavy-bottomed pot and bring it to a boil over high heat.

2.   Add the salt, then add the *polenta* flour in a thin trickle, letting it stream through the fingers of one hand and, with the other hand, beating it into the water with a whisk.

3.   When you have put in all the *polenta* flour, lower the heat to medium and begin to stir with a long wooden spoon. Cook, stirring constantly, for 40 minutes, or until the *polenta* comes easily away from the sides of the pot.

4.   Moisten the inside of a large bowl with water and turn the *polenta* into the bowl. Let rest for about 5 minutes, then turn the *polenta* upside down, out of the bowl, onto a wood board or a large, flat platter. See the introductory note above for serving suggestions.

Fish Courses

Filetti di Pesce al Vino Rosso

FISH FILLETS IN RED WINE

*W*HEN I used to travel professionally more than I like to do now, one of the dishes I frequently chose to demonstrate was this one. Any kind of fish that will yield firm fillets or steaks is suitable, which meant I could prepare this dish anywhere in the country where there was some fresh fish available. And, at the tastings, audiences were pleased to discover that not only is red wine acceptable with fish, it can be startlingly good.

The vegetables and the fish undergo separate preliminary cooking before they are combined. Onions, carrots, and celery are sautéed in butter and cooked until tender. The vegetables are removed from the pan, the fish browned quickly in the same butter, removed in turn from the pan to which one then returns the vegetables and adds the red wine. After the pan is deglazed with the wine, the fish goes back in again and finishes cooking with the vegetables.

The wine-colored fish will be tender and moist, unless you overcook it, and enveloped by the fine, fragrant vegetable bouquet.

For 4 persons

10 small white onions
3 tablespoons butter
3 tablespoons vegetable oil
1/2 cup diced carrots
1/2 cup diced celery
1/2 cup flour, spread on a platter or on a sheet of aluminum foil or wax paper
1 1/2 pounds filleted firm-fleshed fish such as red snapper, striped bass, sea bass, or monkfish; or halibut or tilefish steaks no more than 1 1/2 inches high
Salt
Black pepper in a grinder
1 cup robust red wine (Zinfandel, Barbera, Chianti Classico)

1. Cut a cross in the root end of the onions and put the onions, unskinned, in a small pot of boiling water. Cook for 5 minutes, drain, and skin when cool enough to handle.

2. Choose a lidded sauté pan large enough to accommodate the fish later without overlapping. Put in 2 tablespoons of the butter, the vegetable oil, and the onions. Turn on the heat to medium and brown the onions slowly for 5 to 7 minutes, turning them occasionally.

Fish Fillets in Red Wine (continued)

3.   Add the diced carrot and celery, cover the pan, and cook over medium heat until the vegetables are lightly browned and tender, about 10 minutes. Turn them from time to time.

4.   Turn off the heat and, using a slotted spoon or spatula, transfer the vegetables to a plate, leaving all the fat and cooking juices in the pan. Add the remaining tablespoon of butter to the pan.

5.   Turn on the heat to high. Pat the fish thoroughly dry with paper towels, turn it lightly in the flour, shaking off all excess flour. When the fat in the pan is hot (be careful not to let the butter turn brown), put in the fish in a single layer, without overlapping.

6.   Brown the fish on both sides, turning it delicately, using 2 spatulas, if necessary, so that it won't break up.

7.   Add salt and a liberal grinding of pepper, then transfer the fish carefully to a plate.

8.   Put the vegetables back in the pan and add the red wine.

9.   Cook the wine down to half its volume, at the same time scraping the bottom of the pan with a wooden spoon to loosen any cooking residues.

10.   Put the fish back in the pan, lower the heat to medium high, and cook for 5 to 7 minutes more, depending on the thickness of the fillets.

11.   Transfer the fish to a serving platter and serve immediately, covering the fish with all the vegetables and juices in the pan. If the juices are thin and runny, boil them down after transferring the fish and vegetables to the serving platter.

Filetti Farciti di Pesce Turchino

BAKED STUFFED BLUEFISH FILLETS

*T*HE most abundant fish in Italian water are the dark-fleshed ones we call *turchini*, or deep blue. They are the tastiest creatures that swim. When no other kind of food stirs my appetite, simply the odor of sardines grilling or the first bite of an anchovy cured in olive oil will arouse it violently. Of all my fish recipes, one of my favorites is the baked bluefish with potatoes, olive oil, garlic, and parsley that appears in *More Classic Italian Cooking*, page 208.

Here is another savory way to do bluefish. Like all dark-fleshed fish, it thrives on vigorous flavoring. It is exceptionally simple to do: Two layers of fillets sandwich a mixture of parsley, garlic, Parmesan, anchovies, and capers bound with olive oil and bread crumbs. Then they are baked, which I find is the way to keep bluefish most succulent.

For 4 to 6 persons

2 tablespoons chopped parsley
1 teaspoon chopped garlic
3 tablespoons freshly grated *parmigiano-reggiano* (Parmesan)
3 anchovy fillets, chopped
3 tablespoons chopped capers
5 tablespoons fine, dry, unflavored
    bread crumbs

5 tablespoons extra virgin olive oil
Salt
Black pepper in a grinder
2 bluefish fillets, skin removed, weighing 1¾ to
    2 pounds altogether

1. Turn on the oven to 400°.
2. Put the parsley, garlic, grated cheese, anchovies, capers, 4 tablespoons of the bread crumbs, and 3 tablespoons of the olive oil, salt, and pepper in a bowl. Mix thoroughly.
3. Wash the fish and pat it thoroughly dry with kitchen towels.
4. Choose a baking pan long enough to accommodate a whole fish fillet. Grease the bottom with 1 tablespoon of the olive oil.
5. Lay 1 of the fillets on the bottom of the pan. Spread over it two-thirds of the mixture from the bowl, then cover it with the other fillet, sandwich fashion.
6. Over the top fillet spread the remainder of the mixture, sprinkle the remaining tablespoon of bread crumbs, and trickle the remaining tablespoon of olive oil.
7. Bake in the uppermost level of the oven for 15 to 20 minutes, depending on the fish's thickness. If no more than 3 inches thick, 15 minutes may be sufficient.
8. Allow to rest for about 5 minutes before serving.

Coda di Rospo al Forno coi Funghi Secchi

DRIED WILD MUSHROOMS WITH BAKED MONKFISH OR OTHER FISH STEAKS OR LOBSTER

*I*TALIAN cooks generally prepare fish as simply as possible, grilling, steaming, or frying it, with hardly any other flavor used to assist the fish's own. To vary the routine, however, they may stew or bake it and introduce other ingredients, perhaps just garlic and parsley, or tomatoes, other vegetables, rosemary, wine. Whatever the combination, one must take care not to camouflage the delicate flesh or dull the freshness of the fish; it must not be a passive participant in any preparation. On the contrary, the stimulus of other flavorings must serve to prime it for an even livelier role.

Dried Wild Mushrooms with Monkfish or Fish Steaks or Lobster (continued)

In this recipe, such a stimulus is supplied by dried wild mushrooms. When reconstituted, they are sautéed in classic Italian fashion with olive oil, garlic, and parsley; then they are used as a marinade for the fish, which subsequently is baked together with the mushrooms.

Choose any fish with compact, somewhat fatty flesh. It ought not to flake easily, which rules out flounder and sole.

For 6 persons

1 ounce dried *porcini* mushrooms, soaked in 4 cups lukewarm water for 30 minutes

4 pounds monkfish, bone in; or sturgeon steaks, 2 inches thick (or other fish steaks—see introductory note); or 5 to 6 pounds live lobster or 4 pounds frozen lobster tails, thawed

6 tablespoons extra virgin olive oil

1½ tablespoons garlic chopped very fine

4 tablespoons chopped parsley

Salt

Black pepper in a grinder

5 tablespoons freshly squeezed lemon juice

2 tablespoons fine, dry, unflavored bread crumbs

1. *If using monkfish:* Unsheathe the fish from its skin, pulling it clean away and discarding it. With a sharp filleting knife loosen the fish from its center bone, but do not detach it completely; leave just enough flesh joined to the bone so that it remains in place. If the fish is more than 2 inches thick, make 1-inch-deep diagonal incisions in it, spaced about 2 inches apart. Wash the fish in cold water and pat thoroughly dry with kitchen towels.

If using sturgeon or other fish steaks: Wash in cold water and pat dry.

If using live lobster: Detach the tail from the head, or have the fishmonger do it for you. Detach the claws, set them aside, and discard the head, unless you want to cook it that day in a fish soup. Free the tail from its shell, cutting the shell away with poultry shears. Butterfly the tail.

If using frozen lobster tails: When the tails are thawed, free them from their shells and butterfly them.

2. When the mushrooms have finished soaking, remove them from the bowl with your hand. Squeeze them gently, letting the water trickle through your fingers back into the bowl. Wash the mushrooms in several changes of cold water, then cut them up into large pieces.

3. Filter the water in which the mushrooms soaked through a strainer lined with a paper towel. Set aside.

4. Put 3 tablespoons of the olive oil and all the chopped garlic in a skillet and turn on the heat to medium high. Sauté until the garlic becomes colored a pale gold.

5. Add the parsley, stir once or twice, add the cut-up mushrooms, stir once or twice again, then add the filtered soaking liquid, salt, and a few grindings of pepper and turn up the heat to high. When all the water has boiled away and the only liquid left in the pan is oil, turn off the heat.

6. Choose an oven-to-table baking dish that can accommodate all the fish. Smear the bottom lightly with olive oil. Put in the fish or the shelled lobster tail (if using live lobster, include the

uncracked claws) and pour over it the entire contents of the skillet. Add some salt and grindings of pepper and the lemon juice. Sprinkle the bread crumbs uniformly on top and over them pour the remaining oil in a thin stream, distributing it evenly.

7.   Place the dish in the refrigerator and let it marinate for a minimum of 1 hour, preferably for 5 to 6 hours.

8.   When ready to cook, turn on the oven to 400°. Remove the dish from the refrigerator and let it come to room temperature. Place in the uppermost level of the preheated oven and bake for 20 to 25 minutes if it is monkfish or fish steaks—depending on its thickness—or 12 to 15 minutes if it is lobster. Allow to settle for 5 to 8 minutes before serving.

Pesce da Taglio col Sugo di Vongole

BAKED HALIBUT OR OTHER FISH STEAKS
WITH CLAM SAUCE

*T*HE Italian dishes that most resist adaptation to another country's ingredients are those with seafood. The fish of the Atlantic or Pacific do not taste like those of the Adriatic, Tyrrhenian, or Ligurian Sea. In most of the recipes in this section, I have relied on the preparation to express Italian flavor, letting the fish taste as it must. This recipe is the result of a different approach.

I set out to produce, with what I could find in my neighborhood New York market, a dish wherein the fish itself developed a flavor that would somehow suggest Italy rather than the North Atlantic. I made a sauce of chopped clams sautéed in olive oil with garlic, parsley, shallots, and white wine. I used the sauce and bread crumbs to cover steaks of mild-flavored fish, which I then baked.

Flavor perceived is impossible to draw a picture of or measure out. It is an emotion stirred up by memory and the senses. This recipe is like that of no other Italian dish I know. Yet, if I were to taste it unwarned, somewhere in Italy, I could not give a name to it, but it would not taste foreign.

For 6 persons

Baked Halibut or Other Fish Steaks with Clam Sauce (continued)

2 dozen live littleneck clams
⅓ cup extra virgin olive oil
¼ cup shallots chopped very fine
1 tablespoon garlic chopped very fine
¼ cup chopped parsley
⅓ cup dry white wine
3 to 3½ pounds halibut, red snapper, tilefish,
   or similar fish steaks, sliced ¾ inch thick

Salt
Black pepper in a grinder
3 tablespoons fine, dry, unflavored bread
   crumbs, toasted lightly in the oven or in
   a skillet

1. Soak the clams in a basin or sink filled with cold water for 5 minutes. Drain and refill the basin with fresh cold water. Scrub the clams one by one with a stiff brush or rub them vigorously one against the other. Drain, refill the basin with fresh cold water, and scrub the clams again. Repeat the operation 2 or 3 times, scrubbing the clams in fresh changes of cold water until you see little or no sand settling to the bottom of the basin.

2. Discard any open clams that do not clamp shut when touched. Put the rest in a large pot with ⅓ cup of water, cover tightly, and turn on the heat to high. After 1 minute transfer any open clams to a bowl, using a slotted spoon or a pair of tongs. They needn't open more than a crack, although some may open wide. Move the clams remaining in the pot around, bringing to the top some of those resting on the bottom, and vice versa. Cover, and after another minute remove more opened clams. If some are still shut, move them around and cover the pan again, but check them after 15 seconds or so to avoid overcooking them.

3. When you have removed all the clams from the pot, pour the liquid in the pot into a bowl.

4. The moment the clams are cool enough to handle, detach the meat from the shells and put it into the bowl containing the clam juices from the pot. Try not to waste any of the juice still in the shells, adding it to the bowl.

5. Gently swish the clams, one by one, in their juice with your fingers, to rinse them of any sand, and place them on a cutting board. When you have rinsed them all, chop them very fine.

6. Line a strainer with a sheet of paper towel, place it over a bowl, and pour the clam liquid into the strainer. As you lift the paper towel to squeeze the last of the juice through it, be careful not to tear it or the sand will get through and you will have to start all over again.

7. Put the olive oil and shallots in a skillet and turn on the heat to medium. When the shallots become colored a pale gold, add the garlic. When the garlic as well becomes colored a pale gold, add the parsley, stir once or twice, then add the wine. When all the wine has evaporated, add the filtered clam juice. When the clam juice has evaporated, turn off the heat, add the chopped clams, and stir thoroughly.

8. Turn on the oven to 450°.

9. Place the fish steaks in a baking pan where they will fit snugly, but without overlapping. Sprinkle the fish lightly with salt and pepper, then cover with the clam sauce from the skillet. Sprinkle the toasted bread crumbs over the sauce. The crumbs should absorb some of the juices of the sauce. If you find that there are dry patches of crumbs, spoon up the sauce that has collected at the bottom of the pan and trickle it over the crumb topping.

10. Place the pan in the uppermost level of the preheated oven and bake for 10 to 12 minutes. Let settle for 4 to 5 minutes before serving.

AHEAD-OF-TIME NOTE: If served hot, the dish should be served just after baking, and not reheated. Its consistency will be tender and flaky and its taste mild. It is excellent, however, as a cold dish, prepared a day or two in advance and brought to room temperature before serving. When cold, its consistency is firm and the sauce acquires a tangy, spicier flavor.

Spiedini di Pesce Spada con Peperoni, Pomodoro e Limone

SWORDFISH SKEWERS WITH PEPPERS, TOMATO, AND LEMON

W*HAT* gives these skewers liveliness is the faintly gamy taste of swordfish contrasted with the soft tomato, the pungently vegetal pepper, and the tart Sicilian scent of grilled lemon. It is an ideal fish for an outdoor barbecue, but it is also completely satisfactory cooked in an indoor broiler.

For 4 to 6 persons

1¾ to 2 pounds swordfish, sliced at least 1½ inches thick
2 sweet bell peppers, preferably yellow but if unavailable, red
1 large or 2 smaller ripe, firm tomatoes
1 large lemon

⅓ cup extra virgin olive oil
Salt
Black pepper in a grinder
Freshly squeezed juice of ½ lemon
1 tablespoon fine, dry, unflavored bread crumbs, toasted as described on page 21

1. Remove the skin from the swordfish and cut the fish into cubes of about 1½ to 2 inches.

2. Rinse the peppers in cold water, cut them in half, and remove all the seeds and the core. Cut them into squares of about 2 inches.

3. Rinse the tomato and cut into ½-inch-thick sections, discarding the seeds and letting any juice run off.

4. Slice the lemon into disks about ¼ inch thick, then cut the disks in half into a half-moon shape.

5. Put the swordfish and peppers into a bowl, add the olive oil, salt, pepper, lemon juice, and bread crumbs. Mix well and let marinate at room temperature for 20 to 30 minutes.

6. Turn on the broiler.

7. Using 1 pair of skewers at a time, held parallel, insert the ingredients in the following sequence: pepper, tomato, lemon, swordfish; then again lemon, tomato, pepper. Try always to end with a piece of pepper, if you can, and to bracket each chunk of fish between 2 slices of lemon.

8. When the broiler is hot, put in the skewers, basting the upper part with half the marinade from the bowl. Cook for about 4 minutes, then turn over the skewers and baste the other half with the remainder of the marinade. Cook for 3 to 4 minutes more, then serve immediately.

Pesce Lesso

BOILING FISH IN THE ITALIAN MANNER

*T*HIS recipe appears here at the insistence of my husband, who claims the boiled or steamed fish he eats in restaurants has either little taste or too much that is not of itself. Here is how it is done in Italian homes, with a little bit of vinegar in the water, no herbs except for parsley, and a restrained use of vegetable odors.

For 4 or more persons, depending on the fish

1 medium carrot
2 celery stalks
1 medium onion
1 or 2 thick parsley stalks
3 tablespoons wine vinegar

3 tablespoons salt
A whole fish, 2 or more pounds, head and
    tail on, scaled, gutted, and washed; or the
    equivalent in fish steaks
Extra virgin olive oil

1. Wash, peel, and cut the carrot in half lengthwise.
2. Wash the celery and cut it into 2 or 3 short pieces.
3. Peel the onion and cut it in half.
4. If using a whole fish, choose a fish poacher or other long, narrow, shallow pan. If using fish steaks, choose a lidded sauté pan large enough to accommodate them. Put enough water in the pan to cover the fish later, put in the carrot, celery, onion, and parsley and turn on the heat to medium, covering the pan.

5. Five minutes after the water has come to a boil, add the vinegar and salt. When the water returns to a boil, put in the fish and cover the pan. Cook for about 10 minutes per inch of the thickest portion of the fish, calculating the time from the moment the water has resumed boiling. The fish is done when it is moistly tender all the way through and has lost its pinkness next to the bone.
6. Drain the fish. If using a whole fish, lift off and discard its skin while it is still warm and moist. Brush its flesh all over with olive oil.

SERVING NOTE: The fish tastes best when served slightly warm or at room temperature soon enough after cooking so that it doesn't need to be refrigerated. Serve with olive oil, freshly squeezed lemon juice, chopped parsley, and salt to taste, or with *Bagnet,* the Piedmontese sauce on page 295, or with the green sauce from the recipe that follows.

Salsa Verde
coi Cetriolini sott'Aceto

GREEN SAUCE WITH PICKLED CUCUMBERS

Green sauce for 4 to 6 portions of boiled fish, boiled meats, or grilled meat

¹⁄₃ cup *cornichons* or other fine cucumbers
   pickled in vinegar
6 green olives in brine
¹⁄₂ tablespoon onion chopped very fine
¹⁄₈ teaspoon garlic chopped very fine

¹⁄₄ cup chopped parsley
1¹⁄₂ tablespoons freshly squeezed lemon juice
¹⁄₂ cup extra virgin olive oil
Salt
Black pepper in a grinder

1.   Drain the pickles and chop them into pieces not smaller than ¹⁄₄ inch.
2.   Drain and pit the olives and chop them like the pickles.
3.   Combine the pickles and olives with the remaining ingredients in a small bowl, beating them lightly with a fork to amalgamate them evenly. Serve directly from the bowl or transfer to a sauceboat.

AHEAD-OF-TIME NOTE: The sauce should be used the day it is made and not refrigerated. If prepared a few hours in advance, stir well before serving.

"Smelts" Fritti alla Moda
delle Sarde

FRIED BUTTERFLIED SMELTS

*O*NE of the fish varieties I find it hard to do without when I am in America is fresh sardines. (The ones sold as such are actually a variety of small, strong-tasting herring.) Often, in Italy, I fry sardines, and they are so irresistible that I rarely manage to get them out of the kitchen. When I prepare them, family and friends crowd around me in the kitchen; by the time they have finished "tasting," there is nothing left to bring to the table.

The closest I could come in looking for an equivalent was smelts. The taste is very much leaner, but the size and textural quality is not too distant from that of sardines, so that they fry to very nearly the same captivating

Fried Butterflied Smelts (continued)

crispness. Frying them is easy and fast. What takes a little time, until you acquire the knack, is boning and butterflying them, a necessary procedure described in detail below.

For 4 persons

20 smelts, about 10 to 12 inches long
Vegetable oil for frying
1 cup flour, spread on a plate

Salt
Lemon wedges

1. Cut off and discard the heads of the smelts. With a scissor cut the belly open from the head end to the tail. With your fingers scoop out the intestines and all other loose matter. Beginning at the tail end of the fish, slip your thumbnail under the bone and slide it toward the head end, loosening the bone from the flesh. Repeat the procedure under the other side of the bone. The central bone together with the belly bones should now be completely detached from the flesh and attached only to the tail. Snap it loose from the tail and discard it. The bone-free fish can now be opened flat.

2. When you have boned and butterflied all the fish, rinse them thoroughly under cold running water and dry well with paper towels.

3. Pour enough vegetable oil in a frying pan to come 1/2 to 3/4 inch up the side of the pan. Turn on the heat to high.

4. When the oil is hot, dredge each fish, one by one, in the flour, holding it by the tail. Shake it vigorously to throw off all excess flour. Slip it into the pan skin side up. Do not put in any more fish than the pan can accommodate without crowding.

5. Fry the fish until 1 side becomes colored a light nut brown, which takes less than 1 minute, then turn them and fry them on the other side for about 40 to 60 seconds. Using a slotted spoon or spatula, transfer them to drain on paper towels over a platter or, even better, over a cooling grill set on a tray. Repeat the procedure until all the smelts are done. Sprinkle with salt and serve at once with lemon wedges on the side.

AHEAD-OF-TIME NOTE: The smelts can be cleaned and boned several hours before you are ready to fry and serve. Refrigerate them covered with plastic wrap or foil.

Gamberi al Forno con gli Asparagi

BAKED SHRIMP WITH ASPARAGUS

*D*URING the early 1980s one of the best places to eat in Venice was (and still is at this writing) Fiore, a former *osteria*, a wine pub, taken over by a handsome, tireless young couple, Maurizio and Mara Martin. Mara does all the cooking, some firmly traditional, some of her own devising. One of her dishes I have admired is a creamy *risotto* with shrimp and asparagus; it led me, in turn, to derive from it a baked dish with all the same ingredients except for the rice. The rice I replaced with boiled potatoes mashed through a food mill.

Among the ingredients of this recipe are butter, cream, and Parmesan, apparently violating one of the most frequently repeated axioms of Italian cooks, that one does not use dairy products with fish. Some people do, however, who are indisputably Italian.

In Italy, olive oil is without question the traditionally preferred ingredient to cook fish with. It is the one that I, along with every other Italian cook, would automatically turn to, for there can be no more apt combination of flavors. When I am not cooking automatically, however, when I am reaching for a less obvious statement of flavor, I find that butter and cheese—natural and historic products of the Northern Italian plain—can extend, rather than distort, the expressiveness of my native seafood cuisine.

For 6 persons

2 pounds asparagus
Salt
2 pounds medium shrimp, in their shells
½ pound potatoes
⅔ cup chopped onion
5 tablespoons butter

1 tablespoon vegetable oil
¼ cup heavy cream
½ cup freshly grated *parmigiano-reggiano*
    (Parmesan), plus 2 tablespoons
    for topping
Black pepper in a grinder

1.   Trim the asparagus, cutting off 1 inch or more of the hard root end and peeling away the tough green skin from the lower half of the stalk. Wash thoroughly in 1 or 2 changes of cold water.

2.   Choose a shallow pan that can accommodate all the asparagus lying flat. Pour in about 2 inches of water and bring it to a boil over medium-high heat. Add 1 tablespoon of salt and, when the water resumes boiling, slip in the asparagus and cover the pan. Cook for just a few minutes—depending on the freshness and thickness of the vegetable—until the asparagus is barely tender, but still firm to the bite. Drain and set aside to cool.

3.   When the asparagus has cooled, cut it into pieces 1½ inches long.

Baked Shrimp with Asparagus (continued)

4.   Shell the shrimp, remove the dark vein just below the surface of their backs, and wash them in cold water. Pat thoroughly dry with kitchen towels.

5.   Wash the potatoes and boil them, un-peeled, in abundant water. When they are done, drain them, peel them, and pass them through a food mill or potato ricer into a bowl large enough to accommodate later all the other ingredients.

6.   Turn on the oven to 450°.

7.   In a medium saucepan put the chopped onion, 3 tablespoons of the butter, and the vegetable oil and turn on the heat to medium. Sauté the onion until it becomes colored a deep gold or even very light brown. Add the asparagus, turn up the heat to high, and sauté the asparagus, turning them constantly, for 3 to 4 minutes.

8.   Transfer the asparagus with all the pan juices to the bowl containing the potatoes. Add the cream, ½ cup of grated cheese, salt, liberal grindings of pepper, and the shrimp. Toss thoroughly.

9.   Choose a 12- by 9-inch oven-to-table baking dish (or its equivalent). Smear the bottom with a little butter. Pour into it all the contents of the bowl, leveling with a spatula. Sprinkle the top with 2 tablespoons of grated cheese, and dot with the remaining 2 tablespoons of butter.

10.   Bake in the uppermost level of the preheated oven for 15 to 20 minutes, depending on the thickness of the shrimp. After removing the dish from the oven, allow it to settle for 5 minutes before serving.

AHEAD-OF-TIME NOTE: All the components of the dish can be prepared 2 to 3 hours in advance through step 7. Resume with step 8 only when ready to bake the dish. In the interval, if the asparagus has thrown off any liquid, pour off the liquid before combining it with the other ingredients.

❧ *TWO RECIPES FOR SCALLOPS* ❧

Two kinds of scallops are common in Italy. *Cappe sante,* or more succinctly, *cappe,* are the larger and sweeter of the two. The smaller variety, *canestrelli,* is somewhat spicier.

American scallops, particularly the less stringy bay scallops, accommodate themselves most gracefully to the Italian style of cooking. The first of the two recipes that follow is based on one for *canestrelli.* In it scallops are combined with mushrooms that were cooked in olive oil, garlic, shallots, and white wine. To duplicate the special tangy accent of *canestrelli* is not feasible, but to evoke it, even if in a sharper key, I have added some hot pepper.

The second recipe is derived from one I like to do with the sweeter *cappe sante.* It is simple and very fragrant. Scallops and rosemary are added to garlic sautéed in olive oil. When the scallops are nearly done, they are drizzled with lemon juice and cooked just another moment or two at very high heat.

Canestrelli Saltati con i Funghi

SAUTÉED SCALLOPS AND MUSHROOMS

For 4 persons

1 pound firm, fresh mushrooms
½ cup extra virgin olive oil
2 tablespoons chopped shallots
1 tablespoon chopped garlic
Salt

½ cup dry white wine
1 pound scallops, preferably fresh bay scallops
1 teaspoon chopped dried hot pepper,
   or 2 teaspoons fresh
3 tablespoons chopped parsley

1.   Rinse the mushrooms rapidly in cold running water, pat them dry with a cloth or paper towel, then slice them wafer thin.

2.   Choose a lidded sauté pan that can later accommodate the mushrooms and scallops comfortably, put in 5 tablespoons of the olive oil and all the shallots, and turn on the heat to high.

3.   Sauté the shallots, uncovered, until they become colored a pale gold, then add the garlic.

4.   When the garlic also becomes colored a pale gold, put in the mushrooms, turn down the heat to medium, add salt, and cover the pan.

5.   As you stir from time to time, you will find that the mushrooms throw off some liquid. After 15 minutes, uncover the pan and turn up the heat to medium high to evaporate the liquid.

6.   When the mushroom liquid has evaporated, add the white wine. Cook, stirring, until the wine has also evaporated and the only liquid left in the pan is the olive oil.

7.   Rinse the scallops in cold water and pat dry very thoroughly. Put them in the pan together with the hot pepper and the parsley. Add a little more salt. Turn up the heat to high and cook for 3 to 4 minutes, stirring frequently. Serve piping hot.

Cappe Saltate al Rosmarino e Limone

SAUTÉED SCALLOPS WITH ROSEMARY AND LEMON

For 4 persons

1½ pounds scallops, preferably tiny
   bay scallops
¼ cup extra virgin olive oil
2 medium garlic cloves, peeled and sliced
   very thin

1½ teaspoons whole fresh or chopped dried
   rosemary leaves
Salt
Black pepper in a grinder
2 tablespoons freshly squeezed lemon juice

Sautéed Scallops with Rosemary and Lemon (continued)

1. Wash the scallops and pat them thoroughly dry with a towel. If using large sea scallops, cut them into 2 or 3 pieces.

2. Choose a skillet that can accommodate the scallops in a single layer later. Put in the oil and garlic and turn on the heat to medium.

3. When the garlic becomes colored a pale gold, add the rosemary, stir quickly, add the scallops, salt, and grindings of pepper and turn up the heat to high. Cook, stirring frequently, for about 2 minutes, until the scallops change from translucent to a flat white.

4. Add the lemon juice, turn up the heat as high as possible, stir once or twice, then transfer to a warm platter and serve at once.

❧ TWO WAYS OF STUFFING SQUID ❧

Whatever other thoughts the squid may have about its role in the scenario of life, my conviction is that it was created to be an incomparable container of good things to eat. Consider its sac: a ready-made, leakproof receptacle; firm enough not to tear, buckle, or sag, yet more tender, when cooked properly, than any meat; forthright in its own delivery of flavor, yet respectful of the other flavors it may carry, however delicate. The tentacles, moreover, add to the tastiness of the stuffing or to the juices in which the sac is cooked.

In the first of the following recipes, the stuffing is raw shrimp, while the tentacles are cooked alongside the sac. In the other recipe, the stuffing consists of strips of red pepper and the chopped tentacles.

Squid is born tender, as anyone who has had it raw in Japanese restaurants knows. To remain tender, it must be cooked either briefly at high heat, as when it is fried, or a long time over slow heat. Any variance from this procedure will make it rubbery. Cook stuffed squid over low heat for at least 1 hour, as directed in these recipes.

Calamari Ripieni di Gamberi

SQUID STUFFED WITH SHRIMP

For 6 to 8 persons

8 to 10 squid, with sacs 6 to 7 inches long
    measured from the base of the tentacles
⅔ cup extra virgin olive oil

1 pound (unshelled weight) shrimp, in their
    shells
1 tablespoon chopped garlic

3 tablespoons chopped parsley
⅓ cup fine, dry, unflavored bread crumbs, toasted lightly in a pan as described on page 21

Salt
Black pepper in a grinder
1¼ cups dry white wine

1. Place the squid in a large bowl of cold water and let soak for at least 20 minutes.

2. While the squid are soaking, shell and devein the shrimp, wash them in cold water, and place them in a colander to drain.

3. Pull off the tentacles from each squid with one hand, holding the sac with the other. The tentacles come away with the inside pulp of the squid to which they are attached. Cut the tentacles straight across just above the eyes. Discard all the pulpy matter from the eyes down. Squeeze off the tiny beak at the base of the tentacles. Wash the tentacles in several changes of cold water, drain well, and pat dry with paper towels. Set aside.

4. Remove the floppy, cellophanelike bone from the sac. Peel off the sac's outer mottled skin. Cut a tiny—no more than ¼ inch—opening at the bottom of the sac. Hold the sac under running water with the large opening facing the faucet and wash it thoroughly. Drain and pat dry.

5. Put the shrimp in a bowl and toss with half the olive oil. Add the garlic, parsley, bread crumbs, salt, and several grindings of pepper and toss repeatedly to coat the shrimp well.

6. Stuff the squid sacs no more than three-quarters full with the shrimp. Sew up the large opening with needle and thread. When all the sacs have been stuffed and sewn, put the needle away safely.

7. Choose a sauté pan that can subsequently accommodate all the squid without overlapping. Put in the remaining olive oil and turn on the heat to medium high. As soon as the oil begins to be hot, slip in the squid sacs and all the tentacles. Let the sacs brown on one side, then turn them until they have browned all over.

8. Add the wine, let it bubble for a few moments, then turn the heat down to very low and cover the pan. Cook for at least 1 hour, turning the squid from time to time.

9. To serve, first slice off a thin strip from the sewn top to dispose of the thread, then cut the sac into 3 rounds. Place the rounds in the center of a platter, pour all the pan juices over them, and surround them with the tentacles. Serve at once.

AHEAD-OF-TIME NOTE: The entire dish can be cooked, up to the point the squid is ready to be sliced, several hours in advance. It should be reheated gently in the pan with its own juices, then sliced and served immediately.

Calamari Ripieni di Peperoni Rossi

SQUID STUFFED WITH RED PEPPERS

For 4 to 6 persons

3 or 4 sweet red bell peppers
2½ pounds fresh or thawed frozen
   large squid, preferably with sacs at least
   8 inches long, cleaned as directed on
   page 185
2 teaspoons garlic chopped very fine
4 tablespoons chopped parsley

6 tablespoons extra virgin olive oil
3 tablespoons fine, dry, unflavored
   bread crumbs, pan-toasted as described on
   page 21
Salt
Black pepper in a grinder
½ cup dry white wine

1.   Remove the raw peppers' skin with a peeler, cut them in half lengthwise to remove the seeds and whitish core, then cut the halves into lengthwise strips about 1 inch wide. Divide the total number of strips into as many parts as you have squid to stuff and set aside.

2.   Chop the tentacles from the cleaned squid very fine. It can be done in a food processor.

3.   Put the chopped tentacles in a bowl and mix them with the chopped garlic and parsley, 3 tablespoons of the olive oil, the bread crumbs, salt, and grindings of pepper.

4.   Begin stuffing the squid by first putting into each sac 2 long strips of red pepper, making sure they reach the bottom of the sac.

5.   Finish stuffing the sacs using the chopped tentacles mixture and the remaining strips of red pepper. Make sure to leave the sac about one-quarter empty, because it will shrink while it cooks and, if packed too full, will burst.

6.   Sew up the open end of the sacs with needle and thread, remembering, when finished,

and before doing anything else, to put the needle safely away.

7.   Choose a sauté pan that can accommodate all the squid in a single layer without overlapping. Put in the remaining 3 tablespoons of olive oil and place over medium-high heat.

8.   When the oil is hot, put in the squid and brown them well on all sides.

9.   Add the wine, cooking briskly for a minute or two until it evaporates. Cover the pan and turn down the heat as low as possible.

10.   Cook for about 1 hour, turning the squid from time to time. If you find that there is not enough juice in the pan as the squid cook, add up to ¼ cup lukewarm water.

11.   Transfer the cooked squid to a cutting board and slice them into rings about 1½ to 2 inches thick. Cut off and discard a thin strip from the end that was sewn up, to dispose of the thread. Place the slices on a serving platter, pouring over them the juices from the pan.

AHEAD-OF-TIME PREPARATION: See preceding recipe.

Meat Courses

Pollo Arrosto con la Pancetta e gli Odori

ROAST CHICKEN WITH PANCETTA AND HERBS

*T*HERE is not a way of preparing chicken I don't like, even simply boiling it, but there are times I have a yen for a particular consistency, a special fragrance. This recipe is one I use when I want a savory roast chicken that is not just tender but moist, with marked aromatic character. The key flavor ingredients, which go into the cavity, are rosemary and sage, chopped lemon peel, and *pancetta*. In the first stage of cooking, the bird is baked, wrapped in foil, in a medium oven, favoring the secretion and accumulation of tasty juices. In the second stage, the foil is removed, the oven temperature raised, and the chicken finishes roasting basted in its juices. One practical aspect of the recipe is that it requires only occasional attention, leaving one free to put together the rest of the dinner.

For 4 to 6 persons

A roasting chicken, about 2½ pounds
2 teaspoons fresh rosemary, or 1 teaspoon dried, chopped; together with 3 or 4 fresh sage leaves, or 1 teaspoon dried leaves
2 or 3 strips lemon peel (outer skin with none of the white pith beneath), chopped fine

Salt
Black pepper in a grinder
2 ounces *pancetta*, cut into narrow strips
3 tablespoons extra virgin olive oil
¼ cup freshly squeezed lemon juice

1. Turn on the oven to 350°.
2. Wash the chicken under cold running water and pat thoroughly dry with kitchen towels. Rub its cavity with the mixed chopped rosemary and sage, the chopped lemon peel, salt, and several grindings of pepper. Place the strips of *pancetta* in the cavity.
3. Line a baking pan with a sheet of heavy-duty aluminum foil or parchment paper large enough to fold over the chicken subsequently and enclose it completely. Place the chicken breast side up over the foil. Moisten the chicken with the olive oil, distributing it evenly in a thin stream. Do likewise with the lemon juice. Fold the ends of the foil over the chicken, crimping them to make an airtight seal.

Roast Chicken with Pancetta and Herbs (continued)

4.   Place the pan with the chicken in the uppermost level of the preheated oven and bake for 35 minutes.

5.   Remove the chicken from the oven, turning up the temperature to 425°. Unwrap the bird, discarding the foil but taking care to pour all the cooking juices back into the pan. Place the chicken in the pan breast side down and return it to the oven. After 20 minutes, turn the bird on one side, bake for 10 minutes more, then turn it on its other side and bake for another 10 minutes. At this point, turn it with its breast facing down and bake for a final 10 to 15 minutes.

6.   Remove the chicken from the oven and, after it has rested for about 5 to 8 minutes, cut it into several pieces, detaching the wings and legs and cutting the breast and back into 2 pieces each. Transfer to a warm serving platter. Pour over the chicken all the cooking juices collected in the pan and spread over it the strips of *pancetta.* Serve at once.

Pollo Spaccato agli Odori e Vino Bianco

SPLIT CHICKEN WITH HERBS AND WHITE WINE

*T*HE crusty texture of the skin in this split chicken makes me think of some of the wonderful roast birds one orders in Chinese restaurants just for the sake of their skin. The method, ingredients, and flavor, however, are unequivocally Italian. The chicken is first cooked in a pan with wine, garlic, bay leaf, and basil. Then its skin, saturated with cooking juices, is caked with grated Parmesan and the bird goes into a very hot oven, or under a salamander or broiler.

For 4 persons

A 1¾- to 2¼-pound chicken
1 tablespoon butter
1 tablespoon vegetable oil
Salt
Black pepper in a grinder
1 cup dry white wine
1 tablespoon chopped parsley

½ teaspoon chopped garlic
1 bay leaf
4 or 5 fresh basil leaves, torn into pieces
2 cloves
1 teaspoon chopped rosemary
¼ cup freshly grated *parmigiano-reggiano* (Parmesan)

1.   Split the chicken in half lengthwise from the back.

2.   Place the chicken breast side down on a counter or cutting board. Pound it as flat as possible with a meat pounder. If in doing so you splinter some of the small bones, work them

loose and remove them. Wash the chicken in cold water and pat thoroughly dry with kitchen towels.

3.   Choose a lidded sauté pan that can subsequently accommodate the chicken lying completely flat. Put in the butter and oil and turn on the heat to high. Do not cover the pan. When the fat is hot, slip in the chicken skin side down. Brown the skin side well first, then turn it and brown the other side.

4.   Add salt, several grindings of pepper, and all the other ingredients except for the grated cheese. Turn the heat down to medium and cover the pan, setting the lid slightly askew. Turn the chicken from time to time while it cooks. Cook until the meat is tender enough that it comes easily off the bone.

5.   Turn on the oven to 450°.

6.   Using tongs or a large slotted spatula, transfer the chicken to a shallow baking dish, placing it skin side up. Tilt the pan and spoon off all the clear fat. Pour the remaining cooking juices over the chicken. Sprinkle the grated cheese uniformly over the chicken, patting it down with your hand to make it stick. Place the baking dish in the uppermost level of the oven and bake for about 10 minutes, until the cheese melts and forms a slight crust. Serve at once.

AHEAD-OF-TIME NOTE: The entire dish may be prepared in advance up to the time the chicken is ready to be placed in the oven.

Pollo con l'Aceto

FRICASSEED CHICKEN WITH VINEGAR

*T*HE acids in lemon, vinegar, or wine all add sprightliness to the taste of chicken. In this recipe I use vinegar. But I also use another stimulating ingredient: anchovies. When used as directed below, anchovies do not call attention to themselves; they dissolve, sinking into and deepening the other flavors. You are not aware of them, but if you were to try the dish without them, you'd miss them.

For 4 persons

Fricasseed Chicken with Vinegar (continued)

A 2½-pound chicken, cut into 8 pieces, washed and thoroughly patted dry
3 tablespoons vegetable oil
½ cup flour, spread on a plate
Salt
Black pepper in a grinder

1 teaspoon chopped rosemary
1 teaspoon chopped garlic
4 flat anchovy fillets chopped very fine
2 tablespoons extra virgin olive oil
⅓ cup wine vinegar

1.   Choose a lidded sauté pan that can subsequently accommodate all the chicken pieces without overlapping. Put in the vegetable oil and turn on the heat to high, leaving the pan uncovered.

2.   When the oil is hot but not smoking, dredge the chicken pieces in the flour on all sides and slip them into the pan. Turn the heat down to medium and cook the chicken, turning the pieces from time to time, until a golden crust forms on all sides. Turn off the heat and transfer the chicken to a plate. Sprinkle with salt and several grindings of pepper.

3.   Discard the oil from the pan and wipe the pan clean, making sure you remove every trace of flour.

4.   Combine the rosemary, garlic, and chopped anchovies in a small bowl.

5.   Put the olive oil into the pan and turn on the heat to medium. Add the rosemary, garlic, and anchovy mixture. Cook, stirring frequently, until the garlic exudes its characteristic scent.

6.   Return the chicken to the pan, turn the pieces 2 or 3 times, then add the vinegar. Cook for 1 to 2 minutes, letting the vinegar fumes dissipate, then turn the heat down to low and cover the pan. Cook, turning the chicken pieces from time to time, until the chicken feels tender through and through when pricked with a fork. It should take about 1 hour. If, before the chicken is done, you find that there is no more cooking liquid left in the pan, add 2 or 3 tablespoons of water. Serve promptly when done.

AHEAD-OF-TIME NOTE: The dish can be prepared in advance several hours ahead of time through step 5.

Pollo con le Cipolle

FRICASSEED CHICKEN WITH ONIONS

*T*HE quality of creaminess does not belong to cream alone; onions have it too. The creaminess of cooked-down onions acquires a piquant sweetness that in this recipe envelops the fricasseed chicken. To make onions clingingly creamy and tasty, it is worth repeating here what has been said elsewhere: They must first be cooked in a covered pan a long time over low heat, then uncovered and browned lightly.

For 4 persons

6 cups onion sliced very thin
3 tablespoons extra virgin olive oil
Salt
Black pepper in a grinder
A 2½- to 3-pound chicken, cut into 8 pieces

¼ cup vegetable oil
½ cup flour, spread on a plate
2 tablespoons Cognac or other grape brandy
2 tablespoons chopped parsley

1.　Choose a skillet or sauté pan that can subsequently accommodate all the chicken pieces loosely. Put in the onion and olive oil, cover the pan, and turn on the heat to low. Cook the onion slowly, until very soft, for no less than 1 hour.

2.　When the onion is soft, uncover the pan, add salt and generous grindings of pepper, turn up the heat, and sauté the onion until it becomes colored a pale nut brown. Remove from the heat.

3.　Wash the chicken pieces in cold water and pat them thoroughly dry with kitchen towels.

4.　Put the vegetable oil in a smaller skillet and turn on the heat to medium high.

5.　When the oil is hot but not smoking, turn the chicken pieces in the flour, one at a time, shake loose excess flour, and slip the chicken into the pan, as many pieces as will fit comfortably without being crowded.

6.　Cook until a fine golden crust forms on one side, then turn the pieces over and do the other side. When the chicken has formed a crust all over, transfer it with a slotted spoon or spatula to a platter, sprinkle with salt and pepper, and do another batch.

7.　When all the chicken is done, return the pan with the onion to the fire, turning on the heat to medium high and keeping the pan uncovered. Add the chicken, turning it in the onions 2 or 3 times. Add the brandy, turn the heat down to very low, and cover the pan. Cook for about 45 minutes, turning the chicken occasionally. It is done when the meat feels tender all the way through when pricked with a fork. Sprinkle with chopped parsley and serve.

AHEAD-OF-TIME NOTE: The dish may be prepared a day in advance and reheated just before serving, with no loss, and perhaps an improvement, in taste. Add the parsley only when ready to serve.

Pollo con le Olive Nere

FRICASSEED CHICKEN WITH BLACK OLIVES

*H*ERE is a recipe my son, Giuliano, improvised on one of his visits home. The first dish he had ever cooked was at age eleven, when he decided to produce *lasagne* for twenty of his classmates. After that startling but successful debut, as he grew older I would let him tinker in the kitchen on those not rare occasions when he felt like cooking and I did not. The will to eat well and, necessarily, cheaply during college and the succeeding bachelor years served only to spur his culinary inclinations.

On this particular occasion, I had told Giuliano I would make pasta if he

Fricasseed Chicken with Black Olives (continued)

looked after the rest of the dinner. He inspected the fridge, poked through the cupboards, checked the basil in the window box, and said, "It's simple; all I need now is a chicken." And, while it revealed a young man's partiality for vigorous flavor (note the use of wine, vinegar, *and* lemon juice), simple it was and good. Incidentally, it demonstrates that if your kitchen—and your mind— are organized for Italian cooking, with just a quick trip to the market, you can produce a meal on short notice.

For 4 to 6 persons

A 3-pound chicken
½ pound black Greek-style olives
⅓ cup vegetable oil
4 garlic cloves, lightly mashed
Salt
Black pepper in a grinder

½ cup dry white wine
3 tablespoons wine vinegar, preferably white
5 small flat anchovy fillets chopped fine
2 tablespoons chopped parsley
1½ tablespoons torn-up fresh basil leaves
3 tablespoons freshly squeezed lemon juice

1.   Cut the chicken into 10 pieces, as in step 4 of the next recipe for chicken with eggplant. Wash it in cold water and put it in a colander to drain. After 15 to 20 minutes, pat it thoroughly dry with kitchen towels.

2.   Pit the olives, cutting the flesh away from the pits in pieces as large as possible. Set aside half the pitted olives, choosing the largest pieces; chop the other half very fine to a pulp and set aside separately.

3.   Choose a lidded sauté pan that can accommodate later all the chicken pieces without overlapping. Put in the oil and the garlic and turn on the heat to medium. Sauté the garlic in the uncovered pan until it becomes colored a pale gold.

4.   Add the chicken pieces and turn up the heat to high. Brown the chicken well on all sides, starting with the skin side facing the bottom of the pan to melt its fat. Sprinkle with a little salt and generous grindings of pepper. When you have browned the chicken well all

over, turn down the heat to medium, remove the garlic, add the white wine and the vinegar, and cover the pan.

5.   When the liquid in the pan has evaporated by half, put in the chopped anchovies and the chopped half of the olives, turn the chicken pieces over, cover the pan, and continue cooking. Cook until the chicken is done through and through and feels very tender when pricked with a fork.

6.   Tilt the pan, pushing the chicken to one side to let the juices collect at the other end. Spoon off and discard most of the clear fat, but none of the brown cooking juices. Add the olive pieces, the parsley, and the basil and cook for 1 or 2 minutes longer, turning the chicken over once or twice.

7.   Add the lemon juice, turn the chicken pieces over, and transfer at once to a warm serving platter together with all the cooking juices in the pan.

AHEAD-OF-TIME NOTE: The chicken can be cooked several hours in advance through to the end of step 5. When ready to serve, reheat gently for a few minutes in the covered pan, then proceed with step 6.

Pollo con le Melanzane e i Pomodori Freschi

FRICASSEED CHICKEN WITH EGGPLANT AND FRESH TOMATOES

*A*UGUST in Italy brings the ripest eggplants and tomatoes and, as a natural consequence, this flavorful way of fricasseeing chicken. When I need fried eggplant, as I do for this recipe, I fry a lot: The quantity of oil required is the same whether you are doing a small amount or a large, and you clean up but once. Fried eggplants keep well in the refrigerator for two or three days and, once they are available, you have a good start on another day's menu that might include eggplant *parmigiana*, or an eggplant sauce for *fusilli*, or even just to enrich a cold meat sandwich.

For 4 persons

1½ pounds eggplant
Salt
½ pound fresh, ripe tomatoes
A 2½-pound chicken
¼ pound *pancetta*
2 tablespoons extra virgin olive oil

2 garlic cloves, lightly mashed
½ cup dry white wine
Black pepper in a grinder
1 tablespoon parsley chopped fine
Vegetable oil for frying

1.   Wash the eggplant in cold water, cut off the green tops, and slice it into strips about 3 inches long, 1 inch wide, and 1 inch thick.

2.   Place a pasta colander over a bowl and spread the eggplant strips along the sides of the colander. Sprinkle liberally with salt and let stand for about 1 hour to allow the bitter eggplant juice to drain away.

3.   Bring water to a boil in a medium-size saucepan. Wash the tomatoes in cold water and put them into the boiling water. A minute or two after the water returns to a boil, drain the tomatoes. As soon as they are cool enough to handle, peel them and cut them up.

4.   Cut up the chicken into 10 pieces: 2 wings, 2 drumsticks, 2 haunches, and 2 pieces each the breast and the back. Wash all the pieces in cold

water, including all the giblets, and pat thoroughly dry with kitchen towels.

5.   Chop the *pancetta* very fine. (A food processor does the job best.)

6.   Choose a lidded sauté pan large enough to accommodate later all the chicken pieces without overlapping. Put in the olive oil, *pancetta*, and garlic and turn on the heat to medium high, keeping the pan uncovered.

7.   When the garlic becomes colored a pale gold, add the chicken pieces. Brown them well, skin side down first to melt the fat, then on their other side.

8.   Add the wine and sprinkle with salt and several grindings of black pepper. When the wine has evaporated, add the parsley and the cut-up peeled tomatoes, turn the contents of

the pan over once or twice with a wooden spoon, then cover the pan and turn down the heat to medium. Turn the chicken pieces over from time to time.

9. While the chicken cooks, take a frying pan and pour in enough vegetable oil to come ½ inch up the side of the pan. Turn the heat on to high.

10. Dry the eggplant strips thoroughly with kitchen towels. When the oil is hot enough to make the eggplant sizzle, slip as much of it into the pan at one time as will fit without overlapping or crowding. Fry the eggplant on both sides until it becomes colored a rich gold, then transfer with a slotted spoon or spatula to a platter covered with paper towels to blot.

11. When the chicken is done—it should be cooked through and through and feel very tender when pricked with a fork—turn off the heat and tilt the pan to spoon off nearly all the clear fat.

12. Add the fried eggplant, turn on the heat to medium, and cook for 3 to 5 minutes, stirring from time to time. Some of the eggplant may dissolve, helping to make the sauce creamier. Transfer to a warm platter with all the pan juices and serve immediately.

AHEAD-OF-TIME NOTES: The eggplant may be fried and set aside several hours before cooking the chicken. The entire completed dish may be made a day ahead of time and reheated gently just before serving.

Ali di Pollo in Fricassea

FRICASSEED CHICKEN WINGS

*T*HERE may not be too much meat on a chicken wing, but no part of the bird is more tender or tasty. The wings are subjected here to the basic Italian fricassee treatment: They are floured, browned, then cooked with other ingredients in liquid, and when done, they are stirred with a dash of lemon juice. The liquid in this case is a mixture of broth and milk; the other ingredients are pearl onions and mushrooms, which help the humble wings cut a genteel figure.

For 4 to 6 persons

½ pound pearl or other tiny onions
½ pound fresh mushrooms
12 chicken wings
3 tablespoons butter
1 tablespoon vegetable oil
1 cup flour, spread on a plate

Salt
Black pepper in a grinder
2 tablespoons meat broth
1 cup milk
¼ cup freshly squeezed lemon juice

1. Peel the onions, drop in a pot of boiling salted water, cook for 5 minutes, then drain.

2. Clean the mushrooms rapidly under cold running water, pat dry with kitchen towels, and cut into very thin slices.

3. Trim away the tips from the chicken wings and cut the wings in two at the joint.

4. Choose a lidded sauté pan that can subsequently accommodate all the wings without crowding. Put in the butter and oil and turn on the heat to high, keeping the pan uncovered.

5. When the fat is hot, dredge the wings in flour on both sides and slip them into the pan. Cook on one side and then the other until they become colored a rich gold all over.

6. Add the onions, mushrooms, salt, and liberal grindings of pepper. Cook for 2 to 3 minutes, always at high heat, turning all the ingredients over frequently.

7. Add the broth and milk, turn down the heat to medium, cover the pan, and cook until the liquid in the pan has become reduced to a small amount of dense juice and the wings feel very tender when pricked with a fork. Turn the wings over occasionally while cooking. If, when the chicken is done, there is still too much liquid in the pan, uncover, turn up the heat, and boil it away, while stirring constantly.

8. As soon as the chicken is done, stir in the lemon juice off the heat, and serve at once.

AHEAD-OF-TIME NOTE: The entire dish may be prepared several hours in advance up to the time the lemon juice is added, then reheated and completed just before serving.

Gambe di Pollo Farcite

CHICKEN DRUMSTICKS STUFFED WITH HAM AND CHEESE

WORKING the bone loose from chicken legs takes no particular skill, as you will see from the directions, but it takes patience and care to make sure the skin, which holds the leg together, is not torn. When the bone is gone, it leaves room for a stuffing of ham, Parmesan, garlic, and sage. The legs are then browned and cooked in white wine. It is a lovely dish to present and, with this treatment, the dark meat becomes even more interesting and delectable.

For 4 to 6 persons

Chicken Drumsticks Stuffed with Ham and Cheese (continued)

12 large chicken drumsticks

3½ tablespoons chopped boiled,
    unsmoked ham

2 tablespoons freshly grated *parmigiano-
    reggiano* (Parmesan)

1 teaspoon chopped garlic

10 small sage leaves chopped fine

Salt

Black pepper in a grinder

2 tablespoons butter

1 tablespoon vegetable oil

1 cup flour, spread on a plate

⅔ cup dry white wine

1. With a cleaver or other heavy chopping knife hack off the knuckle at the narrow end of the drumsticks.

2. Use a sharp paring or other narrow-bladed knife to detach the meat from the bone. Begin working at the broad end of the chicken leg, severing all the tendons that fasten the meat to the bone. Do not cut or pierce the skin. As the meat begins to come loose, push it down with your fingers, working it toward the narrow end of the leg. Occasionally, it may turn inside out like a glove; turn it right side in again and continue working it down as you detach it from the bone. As soon as it comes away easily, pull off and discard the bone.

3. Put the ham, grated cheese, garlic, sage leaves, salt, and a few grindings of pepper in a bowl. Mix with a fork until all the ingredients are smoothly combined.

4. Use the ham and cheese mixture to stuff the cavities of the boned drumsticks. Close the open end of the legs with a toothpick or truss it with a light thread. If you choose to truss, make sure to put the needle safely away the moment you are finished.

5. Choose a lidded sauté pan or skillet that can later accommodate all the drumsticks without crowding. Put in the butter and oil and turn on the heat to medium. Do not cover.

6. Dredge the drumsticks in the flour. When the fat is hot, slide them into the pan. Brown them well all over, taking care when turning them not to break the skin or let it stick to the pan.

7. Add the wine. When it has bubbled for a minute or two, lower the heat to very low and cover the pan. Cook for 30 minutes or so, until the chicken is tender. Turn the legs from time to time while cooking, handling them gently so as not to tear the skin.

Quaglie in Tegame

PAN-ROASTED QUAIL

*W*HEN I was asked by Hong Kong's Mandarin Hotel to supervise an Italian fortnight to be held in one of their restaurants, my principal task, once we had agreed on the menu, was to instruct the staff in the preparation of the dishes. They were so professional that it all went rather smoothly, except for a slight collision with the French *sous chef* over these quail. When I informed him they had to cook for close to 1 hour, he gasped, *"Ce n'est pas possible!"* But not only was it *possible,* it was *nécessaire.*

One of the joys of birds, particularly small birds, cooked in the Italian manner is eating them with your fingers, each tender bite coming effortlessly off the bone, all but dissolving in the mouth.

Here the quail are roasted in a pan—a procedure described below and discussed on page 18—together with wine, *pancetta*, and sage, the classic Italian flavorings for game.

For 6 persons

12 quail, preferably fresh
12 thin slices *pancetta*
12 fresh or dried sage leaves
3 tablespoons butter
2 tablespoons vegetable oil
Salt
Black pepper in a grinder
½ cup dry white wine

1. Wash the quail thoroughly inside and out under cold running water, then place them in a large colander to drain for at least 20 minutes.

2. Pat the quail dry with cloth or paper towels. Stuff the cavity of each bird with 1 slice of *pancetta* and 1 sage leaf.

3. Choose a lidded sauté pan that can subsequently accommodate all the quail without overlapping. Put in the butter and oil and turn on the heat to high. Do not cover the pan.

4. When the fat is hot, slip in the quail. Brown one side, then gradually turn them until they have been browned all around. Sprinkle with salt and grindings of pepper, and add the white wine, turning the birds once.

5. Allow the wine to bubble for about 1 min-
ute, then lower the heat to medium and cover the pan, setting the lid slightly askew. Cook for 45 minutes to 1 hour, or until the birds feel tender when probed with a fork and the meat comes easily away from the bone. Check from time to time to see that there is sufficient juice in the pan to keep the quail from sticking. If there is not, add 1 or 2 tablespoons of water.

6. Remove the birds from the pan and put them on a serving platter. Add ¼ cup water to the pan, raise the heat to high, and, scraping with a wooden spoon, loosen all cooking residues from the bottom of the pan while allowing all the water to boil away. Pour the pan juices over the quail and serve at once.

Scaloppine di Vitello al Sedano e all'Arancia

VEAL SCALOPPINE WITH CELERY AND ORANGE

*L*EMON and veal *scaloppine* are a classic coupling. In looking for similar quickening flavor but different aromas, I found this combination of orange and celery, which I first tested on one of the small classes I give at home in Venice. It was so kindly received that I felt encouraged to include it here. The orange is used in two forms, as juice, for its fragrance, and as peel together with celery as a source both of flavor and of textural interest.

For 4 persons

4 tablespoons butter
1 tablespoon vegetable oil
1 pound veal *scaloppine,* pounded very thin
1 cup flour, spread on a plate
1 cup celery stalks, stripped of their strings and cut into strips about ¼ inch thick and 1½ inches long

Salt
1 tablespoon orange peel cut into very fine strips
¼ cup freshly squeezed orange juice
Black pepper in a grinder

1.   Put 3 tablespoons of the butter and all the vegetable oil in a skillet and turn on the heat to high.

2.   When the fat is very hot, dredge the *scaloppine,* one by one, in the flour on both sides, shake them to shed excess flour, and slip them into the pan. Do not put any more *scaloppine* into the pan at one time than will fit loosely without overlapping.

3.   Brown the *scaloppine* quickly on both sides and transfer them to a platter.

4.   Put the celery in the pan, turning the heat down to very low. Add the remaining tablespoon of butter, a little salt, and all the juice the *scaloppine* will have thrown off in the platter.

Stir once or twice, cover the pan, and cook until the celery is tender but slightly crunchy, about 10 minutes.

5.   When the celery is done, uncover the pan, add the orange peel and orange juice, turn up the heat to medium, and stir with a wooden spoon, loosening the cooking residues from the bottom of the pan.

6.   Sprinkle the *scaloppine* with salt and grindings of pepper.

7.   Return the *scaloppine* to the pan and turn them 2 or 3 times, just long enough to warm them through. Transfer to a warm serving platter, pour all the contents of the pan over the *scaloppine,* and serve at once.

AHEAD-OF-TIME NOTE: The dish may be prepared several hours in advance, stopping at the end of step 5, when the celery and orange sauce is done.

Listarelle di Vitello con Cetriolini e Peperoni Rossi

VEAL SCALOPPINE STRIPS WITH CUCUMBER PICKLES AND RED PEPPERS

*T*HIS is a dish I discovered unexpectedly near Siena at the end of a long, hard business day. My husband and I had been in meetings for hours, working on a project that, as we had feared, never came to life, and we couldn't have been more dispirited. We had accepted our host's invitation to dine at a country restaurant he warmly recommended, although I was so tired I didn't think I could eat. We were in Tuscany, so we declined the cook's offer of homemade pasta, settling instead for a platter of home-cured prosciutto and salami, to be followed by a veal dish we were urged not to miss. I did not record the name of the cook, and the place I cannot remember either, but I do still remember the sparkling, immediately uplifting flavor of the veal, cut into narrow strips thin as *scaloppine*, sautéed and sauced with pickles, young onions, peppers, and cream. As I revived and shrugged away the frustrations of the day, I reflected on the magic power of good cooking to restore hope and on the benevolence of a Providence that has put such magic into the hands of so many plain people.

For 4 persons

2 large or 3 medium sweet red bell peppers
½ pound scallions
⅓ cup extra virgin olive oil
1 pound veal *scaloppine,* cut into rectangular strips about 2 by 4 inches
1 cup flour, spread on a plate

¼ cup *cornichons* or similar cucumber pickles, cut lengthwise into slices less than ¼ inch thick
⅓ cup heavy cream
Salt
Black pepper in a grinder

1. Peel the peppers using a swivel-action peeler (see technique, page 21). Split them, remove the core and seeds, and cut them lengthwise into strips about ½ inch wide.

2. Cut the scallions in half lengthwise and then into pieces about 2 inches long. Wash in cold water and drain.

3. Choose a lidded sauté pan large enough to accommodate later all the peppers and the meat. Put into it 2 tablespoons of the olive oil, the scallions, turn on the heat to medium low, and cover. Stir from time to time.

4. Add the strips of pepper to the scallions in the pan. Continue to cook in the covered pan, stirring occasionally, until the peppers are tender.

5. Uncover the pan, turn up the heat to high, and cook for a few moments longer while quickly stirring the contents of the pan.

Veal Scaloppine Strips with Cucumber Pickles and Red Peppers (continued)

6. Transfer the scallions and peppers to a dish, using a slotted spoon or spatula, and add the remaining olive oil to the pan, keeping the heat at high.

7. Dredge the veal strips in flour on both sides and, when the oil is hot, put as much of the meat in the pan as will fit without overlapping.

8. Cook the meat for a few seconds on each side, without letting it brown too much because it will become overcooked. Transfer to a dish and do the next batch of meat, repeat-ing the operation until all the meat is done.

9. Put the scallions and peppers back in the pan, reduce the heat to medium high, and add the pickles. Stir once or twice, then add the cream. Cook the cream down, stirring frequently, until it is no longer runny.

10. Return the meat to the pan, add salt and a few grindings of pepper, and cook for about 1 minute, stirring all the contents of the pan thoroughly. Transfer to a warm serving platter and serve at once.

Scaloppine di Vitello con le Nocciole e l'Aceto Balsamico

VEAL SCALOPPINE WITH HAZELNUTS AND BALSAMIC VINEGAR

*H*AZELNUTS are exceptionally popular with Italians. *Gelato di Nocciola,* hazelnut ice cream, stands out among all the extraordinary Italian ice creams, and puréed, chopped, or whole hazelnuts will be found in cakes, nougats, and chocolates. Their toasty flavor is also particularly compatible with veal. The hazelnut sauce for these *scaloppine* is made by cooking chopped toasted hazelnuts in wine until the wine evaporates, at which point the sauce is combined with the previously sautéed *scaloppine*. A keen expression of flavor is achieved at the end when, to the faintly bitter nuttiness of the hazelnuts, one adds the sweet-and-sour accent of balsamic vinegar.

For 6 persons

½ cup hazelnuts
4 tablespoons butter
1 tablespoon vegetable oil
1½ pounds veal *scaloppine,* pounded very thin
1 cup flour, spread on a plate

⅔ cup dry white wine
Salt
Black pepper in a grinder
1 tablespoon *aceto balsamico* (balsamic vinegar, see page 6)

1. Put the hazelnuts in a skillet, turn on the heat to high, and toast them, turning them frequently. Remove from the pan and, if you are using unpeeled hazelnuts, squeeze most of their skin off with your fingertips as soon as you are able to handle them.

2. While the hazelnuts are still warm, chop them not too fine: The largest piece should be the size of a rice kernel.

3. Put 3 tablespoons of the butter and all the oil in a sauté pan and turn on the heat to high. As soon as the fat is hot, dredge the *scaloppine* on both sides in the flour, shake off excess flour, and slip the *scaloppine* into the pan. Do not put more *scaloppine* into the pan at one time than will fit very loosely. Cook the *scaloppine* very briefly on both sides, no longer than it takes to brown them lightly. Transfer them to a platter and do another batch.

4. When all the *scaloppine* are done, put the wine in the pan, scraping loose any cooking residues from the bottom. Add the hazelnuts, letting the wine bubble away until it has evaporated completely. Stir in the remaining tablespoon of butter.

5. Sprinkle the *scaloppine* with salt and grindings of pepper. If they have thrown off any juice in the platter, pour it into the pan. Return the *scaloppine* to the pan, turning them 2 or 3 times.

6. Turn off the heat. Pour the balsamic vinegar over the *scaloppine*. Turn them once or twice, then transfer them to a warm serving dish with all the pan juices. Serve at once.

AHEAD-OF-TIME NOTE: The dish can be prepared a few hours in advance to the end of step 3.

Bracioline di Vitello con l'Agnello

VEAL ROLLS STUFFED WITH LAMB

*E*VERY successful veal preparation must solve two problems: how to enrich the flavor of veal without masking its delicacy and how to keep the lean flesh tender and moist. When veal is sliced thin, as in *scaloppine,* it must cook briefly over high heat, but the sauces with which it will subsequently be joined require slower cooking and must be prepared separately. This recipe is an interesting illustration of both principles at work.

Here the veal rolls are stuffed with a creamy mixture of fine-ground lamb and flavorings. The more unctuous tasty lamb supplies just those qualities veal is short of, without overwhelming it, the properties of the two meats fusing as though a new kind of meat were created. Do make sure the lamb you buy has a little fat on it.

After the veal is browned and removed from the pan, a simple sauce of tomatoes and wine is made. When it is done, the rolls are turned in the sauce over heat, but for the shortest possible time.

For 4 to 6 persons

Veal Rolls Stuffed with Lamb (continued)

6 ounces boned lamb (any cut that is not
   too lean)
3 tablespoons onion chopped fine
3 tablespoons chopped parsley
2 tablespoons extra virgin olive oil
Salt
Black pepper in a grinder
1½ pounds veal *scaloppine*, cut from the top
   round and pounded very thin

Toothpicks, preferably the strong, round kind
2 tablespoons butter
2 tablespoons vegetable oil
⅔ cup dry white wine
⅔ cup canned Italian peeled plum tomatoes,
   drained and puréed through a food mill

1.   Cut the lamb into cubes of about 1 inch and put them in a food processor together with the onion, parsley, and olive oil. Process to a creamy consistency. (If you do not have a food processor, have the butcher grind the lamb fine, passing it through the meat grinder 2 or more times, and mix it later at home with the other ingredients.)

2.   Add salt and liberal grindings of pepper, mixing thoroughly.

3.   Lay the *scaloppine* flat on a counter and, over each, spread the lamb mixture evenly.

4.   Roll up the *scaloppine* loosely and fasten with a toothpick. Insert the toothpick in the same direction as the long side of the veal roll so that it will turn easily when cooking.

5.   Choose a sauté pan that can subsequently accommodate all the rolls without overlapping. Put in the butter and vegetable oil and turn on the heat to high. When the fat is hot, slip in the meat rolls. First brown the side resting on the bottom of the pan, then turn them and gradually brown them all over. When done, transfer them to a platter, using a slotted spoon or spatula.

6.   Add the wine and the tomatoes. Simmer the tomatoes, stirring from time to time, for about 15 minutes, or until the tomatoes and fat separate and the fat floats.

7.   Return the veal rolls to the pan, turn them in the tomato sauce, lower the heat to very low, cover the pan, and cook for no more than 1 minute. Transfer the entire contents of the pan to a warm platter and serve at once.

AHEAD-OF-TIME NOTE: Although the entire dish can be made in advance and reheated, the meat will become drier and won't taste as good as when freshly made.

Vitello Stracciato con le Verdure

SAUTÉED VEAL STRIPS WITH VEGETABLES

W*HILE* I was working on the recipe on page 201, I was moved to develop another, more exuberant version, adding olives, other vegetables, *pancetta affumicata*—bacon—and omitting the cream. It is curiously suggestive of a Chinese dish, yet it is accomplished through procedures that are unmistakably Italian. It further confirms my long-held belief that, of all other cuisines, the one the spirit of Italian cooking has most in common with is the Chinese.

For 4 persons

3 tablespoons butter
2 tablespoons vegetable oil
1½ cups onion sliced not too thin
  (about ¼ inch)
2 ounces bacon, cut into ¼-inch strips,
  about ½ cup
1 medium garlic clove, sliced very thin
3 medium carrots, washed, peeled, and cut
  into sticks 2 inches long and ¼ inch thick,
  about 1½ cups
2 cups altogether of mixed green, red, and

yellow bell peppers, peeled and cut into
  ¼-inch strips (if yellow peppers are
  unobtainable, use the green and red alone
  for a total of 2 cups)
10 ounces fresh mushrooms, wiped clean with
  a moist cloth and sliced as thin as possible
Salt
Black pepper in a grinder
1 pound veal *scaloppine,* cut into strips
  3 inches long and 1 inch wide
10 black Greek-style olives, pitted

1. Choose a sauté pan that can later accommodate all the ingredients. Put in 2 tablespoons of the butter, the vegetable oil, onion, bacon, and garlic and turn on the heat to medium. Cook, turning the onion over from time to time, until it is tender and becomes colored a medium gold.

2. Add the carrot sticks and cook for 5 minutes, turning them over occasionally.

3. Add the peeled pepper strips and turn up the heat to medium high. Cook the pepper until it is tender, stirring 3 or 4 times. When the pepper is tender, transfer all the vegetables from the pan to a platter, using a slotted spoon.

4. Add the mushrooms to the pan with a little salt and cook them, stirring frequently,

over high heat so that all the liquid they throw off will evaporate quickly.

5. Return the cooked vegetables in the platter to the pan, add salt and several grindings of pepper, and cook over high heat for 1 minute, turning and mixing all the vegetables to favor an exchange of flavors. Do not add the vegetables to the mushrooms until all the mushroom liquid has evaporated; otherwise they will become mushy, and their flavor will be diluted.

6. Transfer the contents of the pan to a bowl, using a slotted spoon or spatula so that as much of the cooking fat as possible remains in the pan. When, after a minute or two, the fat clinging to the vegetables has dripped to the

Sautéed Veal Strips with Vegetables (continued)

bottom of the bowl, pour it back into the pan.

7. When ready to serve, turn on the heat under the pan to high and add the remaining tablespoon of butter. When the fat is hot, add the veal strips. Cook over highest heat for little more than 1 minute, turning the meat over constantly. Add salt and pepper, return the vegetables to the pan, add the olives, turn everything over 3 or 4 times, then serve at once.

AHEAD-OF-TIME NOTE: The dish may be prepared several hours in advance through step 6.

Arrosto di Vitello Lardellato con Pancetta e Cetriolini sott'Aceto

ROAST VEAL STUDDED WITH PANCETTA AND PICKLED CUCUMBERS

A ROAST of veal is here prepared for cooking by larding it with *pancetta* and cucumber pickles and then marinating it in lemon juice. The *pancetta* not only radiates flavor but bastes the veal internally as it cooks and keeps it moist. The pickles and the lemon juice contribute vivacity and aromatic qualities to the taste. The meat is first browned in butter over a burner, then roasted in the oven with cream, a procedure that helps the veal stay juicy and tender. Cross sections of pickle and *pancetta* will show up in the slices; the attractive appearance together with the lively delicacy of flavor make this a most distinctive roast.

For 6 persons

A 2½-pound boneless veal roast, such as top
   round, rump, sirloin, or shoulder
A larding needle
3 ounces *pancetta*, prosciutto, or salt pork, cut
   into 2½- to 3-inch-long strips from
   a ¼-inch-thick slice
8 to 10 *cornichons* or other small cucumbers
   pickled in vinegar, cut in half lengthwise

¼ cup freshly squeezed lemon juice
3 tablespoons butter
2 tablespoons vegetable oil
Salt
Black pepper in a grinder
⅓ cup heavy cream

1. Place one strip of *pancetta* at a time on a larding needle and insert it into the roast, pushing the needle in along the same direction as the grain of the meat. Distribute the *pancetta* strips as broadly as possible within the roast so they don't all collect in one spot.

2. Repeat the larding procedure with the cucumber pickles.

3. Place the larded meat on a platter and pour over it the lemon juice, moistening it well on all sides. Let it marinate in the juice for 30 minutes at room temperature, turning it and basting it from time to time.

4. Turn on the oven to 350°.

5. Choose a casserole with a tight-fitting lid suitable for cooking both over a burner and in the oven. Put it on the burner, put in the butter and oil, and turn on the heat to high.

6. Pat the meat thoroughly dry with paper towels and, when the fat is hot enough so that the butter's foam begins to subside, put the meat in the pot. Brown it thoroughly on all sides, then add salt and a few grindings of pepper.

7. Add the cream and, as soon as it comes to a boil, cover the pot and put it in the oven. Cook for 1½ to 2 hours, turning the roast from time to time. The meat is done the moment it feels tender when pierced with a fork.

8. Allow the roast to rest for a few minutes, then slice it and serve it with its cooking juices. If, by chance, the juices are too watery, after removing the roast from the pot place the pot over a burner turned on to high and reduce the juices quickly, stirring constantly and loosening any residues stuck to the bottom of the pot.

Arrosto di Vitello Incrostato

ENCRUSTED ROAST SHOULDER OF VEAL

*U*NCOMMON appearance and texture set this roast aside from all others. At first, it is cooked in traditional fashion over a burner, in a roasting pot with onion, herbs, white wine, and Marsala, whose aromas and flavors it makes its own. When done it is coated with a mixture of bread crumbs and Parmesan and placed in a hot oven just long enough to form a crust marvelous for the crispness of the bread crumbs and the savor of the cheese.

For 6 persons

Encrusted Roast Shoulder of Veal (continued)

3 tablespoons extra virgin olive oil

2½ tablespoons butter

2½ pounds boneless veal shoulder,
    tied tightly into a roll

3 tablespoons chopped onion

1 teaspoon chopped fresh or dried rosemary

½ teaspoon chopped dried sage leaves,
    or 4 or 5 fresh sage leaves

Salt

Black pepper in a grinder

⅔ cup dry white wine

½ cup dry Marsala

¼ cup freshly grated *parmigiano-reggiano*
    (Parmesan)

2 tablespoons fine, dry, unflavored, toasted
    bread crumbs

1. Choose a heavy-bottomed, lidded pot where the meat can fit snugly. Put in the olive oil and 2 tablespoons of the butter and turn on the heat to medium high, leaving the pot uncovered. When the oil is hot, put in the meat, brown it on all sides, then transfer it to a plate.

2. Turn down the heat to medium and put the onion, rosemary, and sage into the pot. When the onion becomes colored a deep gold, return the meat to the pot, adding salt and several grindings of pepper. Cook for 4 to 5 minutes, turning the meat from time to time.

3. Add the wine and the Marsala. When they have begun to bubble for a few moments, turn down the heat to very low and cover the pot, setting the lid slightly askew. Cook for about 1½ hours, turning the roast from time to time. If before that time you find the cooking liquid has dried out, replenish it with ¼ cup of water.

4. Turn on the oven to 550°.

5. Choose a small roasting pan or heavy baking sheet just large enough for the veal and

smear the bottom with the remaining ½ tablespoon of butter.

6. Combine the grated cheese and bread crumbs and spread on a plate. Transfer the meat to the plate and turn the meat on all sides, pressing it hard against the plate, to coat it as thoroughly as possible. Place the meat in the roasting pan and put it in the preheated oven for 5 to 6 minutes, until it forms a dark crust.

7. While the meat is in the oven, warm up the juices in the pot, scraping loose any residues stuck to the bottom. If necessary to loosen the residues, add 1 to 2 tablespoons of water.

8. When the roast has formed a nice dark crust, remove it from the oven, allow it to settle for a few minutes, then cut it into thin slices, arranging them on a warm serving platter. Pour the juices from the pot over the slices and serve at once. If you prefer not to let the juices soften the roast's crust, serve them in a warm sauceboat on the side.

AHEAD-OF-TIME NOTE: The entire dish may be made several hours in advance through step 3. Before readying the roast for the oven, reheat it gently in the pot, adding, if necessary, 3 to 4 tablespoons of water.

Nodini di Vitello coi Funghi e il Vino Bianco

SAUTÉED VEAL CHOPS WITH MUSHROOMS AND WHITE WINE

*B*ORROWED flavors come together to produce the rich, elegant taste of these chops. Some of the aromatic quality of fine game is bestowed on the veal by cooking it in sage and butter, sage being the traditional herb for game in Italy. The fresh mushrooms are cooked with the reconstituted dried wild mushrooms, benefiting thus from the woodsy *porcini* taste that they appropriate. The chops and mushrooms are then combined and bound with reduced cream. The recipe can also be done with *scaloppine* should one prefer them to the more substantial chops.

For 4 persons

½ ounce dried *porcini* mushrooms, soaked in 1 cup lukewarm water for at least 30 minutes
¾ pound fresh mushrooms
4 tablespoons butter
4 or 5 dried sage leaves, chopped fine

4 veal chops, about 1 inch thick
½ cup dry white wine
2 tablespoons chopped parsley
Salt
Black pepper in a grinder
½ cup heavy cream

1. Wash the fresh mushrooms rapidly under cold running water, then cut them into very thin slices.

2. When the dried mushrooms have finished soaking, lift them out of the water with your hand or a slotted spoon. Line a strainer with a paper towel and filter the water the mushrooms soaked in by pouring it through the strainer into a bowl or beaker. Set it aside.

3. Wash the *porcini* mushrooms in several changes of cold water until they are free of all grit, then cut them up into large pieces. Set aside.

4. Put the butter and sage in a sauté pan and turn on the heat to medium high. When the butter is hot, slip in as many chops at one time as will fit without overlapping. Brown them well on one side, then turn them and brown the other side. Continue to cook them, turning them once or twice more, for 3 to 4 minutes, until the meat is done. It should be pink and moist, but not raw.

5. Add the wine, let it bubble for about half a minute, then transfer the chops to a platter, using a slotted spoon or spatula. Continue to let the wine bubble until it has evaporated completely, scraping the bottom of the pan meantime with a wooden spoon to loosen any browning residues.

6. When the wine has evaporated, add the reconstituted dried mushrooms and their filtered

Sautéed Veal Chops with Mushrooms and White Wine (continued)

liquid to the pan. Stir from time to time as the liquid evaporates.

7.   When all the liquid has boiled away, add the sliced fresh mushrooms and the chopped parsley. Stir well, add salt and several grindings of pepper, stir again, then lower the heat to medium and cover the pan. As the fresh mushrooms cook they will shed liquid. Continue to cook, stirring occasionally, until all the liquid has evaporated.

8.   Add the heavy cream, leave the pan uncovered, and cook the cream down until it is more creamy than runny.

9.   Sprinkle the chops on both sides with a little salt and ground pepper and return them to the pan. Keep them in the pan just long enough to heat them through and through, turning them once or twice. Serve promptly when they are done.

AHEAD-OF-TIME NOTE: The dish may be prepared in advance through step 8.

Costolette di Vitello alla Guido Reni

GRILLED VEAL CHOPS STUFFED WITH VEGETABLES AND CHEESE

GUIDO RENI was the glory of seventeenth-century Bolognese painting, and the veal chop that borrows his name is, appropriately, one of the glories of Bolognese cooking art today. Grilled veal chops can be so good, but they can also be so dry. This recipe is a masterly solution to the problem. The chop is divided in half to obtain two slices of meat joined at one side only, where they meet the bone. The slices are flattened to the thinness of *scaloppine*. It is not difficult to prepare the chops yourself, following the directions in the recipe, but if you have an accommodating butcher, he can do it for you. Parboiled green beans, tomatoes, cheese, and basil are placed between the two flaps of the chop, which are then stitched together with toothpicks. They grill in no time, because the meat is so thin, and the fragrant, soft, moist stuffing does wonderful things for the veal.

Although they are best grilled—and most of all over a charcoal or wood fire—the chops can also be sautéed in a pan with butter and vegetable oil.

For 4 persons

ABOVE It looks like a scene from a Fellini film, but it is the port of my native Cesenatico. The canal, which brings the waters of the Adriatic and the fishing boats into the heart of town, was laid out by Leonardo da Vinci. On the table is my pick of the day's catch, which includes *rombo*, the local baby turbot; scampi and small soles from the Adriatic, the finest of all flatfish; *mazzancolle*—tasty gray shrimp; *cannocchie*—a very sweet crustacean native to the northern Adriatic; and fresh anchovies and tiny mullets.

LEFT The women from the farms just outside Cesenatico have their own little market in town where, each morning, they sell the produce picked that day. I have already bought the zucchini blossoms to fry in flour and water batter. The farm woman is weighing out eggplants of the shell-like white color that originally gave the vegetable its English name.

LEFT The lemon and cucumber salad from page 286, which I love to serve with seafood.

RIGHT Fennel and black olives salad, one of my favorites in this book (see page 285).

ABOVE Fruit grilled as described on page 316. Note pears, peaches, plums, figs, and the bottle of rum.

LEFT In the Cesenatico kitchen Elisa, my pickles specialist, is slicing eggplant. See pages 50-2 for Elisa's pickled eggplants and peppers. Note the cherry tomatoes on the cupboard that will be hung in the cellar to use for sauce during the winter.

OVERLEAF Assorted desserts are laid out on our main Venice terrace. In the background, from left to right: braised pears, strawberries with balsamic vinegar, a bowl of *croccante*—Italian praline candy—with *zalett*—Bolognese *polenta* cookies; on the platter: cream ice cream, the Cipriani's dark chocolate ice cream, fig sorbet, and pomegranate sorbet.

12 fresh, young green beans
Salt
2 fresh, ripe, firm plum tomatoes
4 veal rib chops, at least 1 inch thick
¼ pound fontina or mozzarella,
    cut into ¼-inch slices

4 fresh basil leaves
Black pepper in a grinder
12 round toothpicks
1 tablespoon extra virgin olive oil
A hot broiler, preferably charcoal

1. Trim both ends away from all the green beans and wash them in cold water. Bring a small saucepan of water to a boil, add 1 tablespoon salt, and, when the water resumes boiling, drop in the green beans. Cook for just a few minutes and drain while the beans are still rather firm to the bite.

2. Skin the tomatoes with a peeler, cut them lengthwise into ¼-inch-wide slices, and remove the seeds with the tip of a paring knife. Toss them in a strainer 2 or 3 times to shake off any juice.

3. Cut the veal chops in half horizontally, stopping at the bone, obtaining from each 2 parallel slices of meat attached to 1 bone. Fold back one of the slices and pound the other one as thin as possible, moving the pounder outward from the bone. Turn the chop over, fold back the flattened slice, and pound the other one.

Take care not to pound a hole through the meat. Repeat the operation with the other chops.

4. Divide the tomatoes and cheese into 4 equal parts. Place 1 part of each in between the 2 halves of each chop together with a basil leaf, liberal grindings of pepper, and 3 green beans. No part of the stuffing must protrude beyond the edge of the chop, so cut the green beans and trim the cheese slices to fit if necessary.

5. Seal the borders of the chops, skewering each chop with 3 round toothpicks.

6. Brush olive oil on both sides of each chop.

7. Place the chops on the hot grill. Cook for about 2 minutes on one side, sprinkle with salt, turn over, sprinkle the other side with salt, and cook for about 1 minute longer. Do not overcook because the thin slices of veal will dry out if overdone.

AHEAD-OF-TIME NOTE: The chops can be prepared several hours ahead of
time up to the point where they are ready for grilling.

Spiedini di Vitello e Verdure al Marsala

SAUTÉED SKEWERS OF VEAL AND VEGETABLES
WITH MARSALA

*T*HIS is an economical and very pretty way to serve veal, taking the cut you would use for stewing, skewering it with vegetables, and sautéing it, as you might do with *scaloppine,* in olive oil and Marsala.

For 4 persons

1 red or yellow sweet bell pepper
1 medium onion
½ pound eggplant, peeled and
    cut into 1-inch cubes
¾ pound veal shoulder,
    cut into 1½-inch cubes

⅓ cup extra virgin olive oil, plus
    1 tablespoon
Salt
Black pepper in a grinder
⅓ cup dry Marsala

1. Cut the pepper open along its creases, discard the seeds and core, skin it with a peeler, and cut it into squares of about 1½ inches.

2. Peel the onion, quarter it, and divide each quarter into 3 nearly equal pieces by separating the layers.

3. Place the pepper, onion, eggplant, and veal on skewers, arranging them in any order as long as you begin and end with eggplant and avoid placing the eggplant next to the meat.

4. Put the olive oil in a sauté pan large enough to accommodate all the skewers without overlapping and turn on the heat to medium. When the oil is hot, put in the skewers. Brown them well on all sides, add salt, grindings of pepper, turn them over once or twice, then add the Marsala. Let the Marsala evaporate for a minute or two, then cover the pan. Turn the heat down to medium low and cook for 15 to 20 minutes, until the meat feels tender when pricked with a fork. Turn the skewers from time to time as they cook.

5. When the meat is done, serve at once together with the little bit of sauce in the pan. If the sauce appears to be exceptionally liquid, after transferring the skewers to a warm serving platter, turn the heat under the pan up to high and reduce the juices somewhat. Do not over-reduce them, however; the sauces of Italian meat courses are simply the cooking juices and rarely very dense.

AHEAD-OF-TIME NOTE: The skewers may be assembled several hours in advance, but the meat will be juicier and the vegetables taste sweeter if they are cooked just before serving.

Spezzatino di Vitello alle Olive Verdi

VEAL STEW WITH GREEN OLIVES

A STEW may not be your dainty best-silver-and-crystal sort of fare, but I wonder if one with good olive oil, garlic, and some pork fat isn't the most happy thing that can be done with meat, veal included. Everyone must supply his or her answer, but this is, in any case, what I mean by a good stew, forthright and basic as it can be. Everything in it is fundamental. The onion and *pancetta affumicata* (bacon) sautéed in olive oil. The garlic sliced thin so it will release sufficient but not obtrusive flavor. The white wine. The only modest flight of fancy are the olives, but they do no damage.

For 4 persons

3 tablespoons extra virgin olive oil
½ cup chopped onion
¼ pound slab bacon, cut into julienne strips
1 large garlic clove, peeled and sliced into thin disks
1 pound veal shoulder, cut into 1½-inch cubes

½ cup dry white wine
Salt
Black pepper in a grinder
10 green olives in brine, drained, rinsed, pitted, and cut up into rough pieces

1. Choose a lidded sauté pan large enough to accommodate all the veal with little or no overlapping. Put in the olive oil, onion, and bacon and turn on the heat to medium.

2. When the onion becomes translucent, add the garlic and the veal. Turn up the heat to medium high and brown the veal pieces well on all sides.

3. Put in about 2 tablespoons of the wine, add salt and freshly ground pepper, turn the heat down to medium low, and cover the pan.

4. Stir from time to time and, as the wine evaporates, add more, 2 tablespoons at a time. If, when you have used up all the wine, the meat is still not fully cooked, continue cooking adding 2 tablespoons of water as needed to keep the stew from drying out.

5. When the meat is fork tender, put in the olives, mix thoroughly, and serve.

NOTE: If preparing the stew ahead of time—it can be cooked even 2 or 3 days in advance—put in the olives only after you've reheated it.

❧ TWO VEAL LOAVES ❧

A *polpettone,* or Italian meat loaf, is not baked in a loaf pan. It is patted into a cylindrical shape that somewhat recalls an especially stout salami —or a small torpedo—and it is cooked in a pot in the basic Italian top-of-the-burner roasting method discussed on page 18. The entire surface of a *polpettone* is exposed and forms a crisp, savory crust that no unmolded, pan-shaped loaf can possess. The one difficulty is that until it is browned all over, a *polpettone* is subject to crumbling and therefore needs a steady pair of hands when turning it to keep it together. Once browned, there are no further problems.

The first of the *polpettoni* that follow is rolled up with a layer of skinned and flattened roasted peppers. The alternation of peppers and veal looks beautiful in the slicing, but it is no less good to eat than to look at.

The second *polpettone* is one whose key flavor ingredient, celery, gave me a great deal of trouble. In Italy I had made it with chopped celery stalks, a small quantity of which produced an intense, refreshing fragrance. When I retested it in New York, I had a series of disasters. I never could get the persistence and clarity of fragrance I wanted, and I kept increasing the amount of celery. But American celery is inordinately watery: The more I put in, the more the *polpettone* became soggy and infuriatingly difficult to work with. My husband suggested I move on to something else, but my Romagna stubbornness kept me on it. The solution came eventually. It was to use celery leaves instead of stalks. It may not be an exact duplicate of my Italian *polpettone,* but it has an aromatic character of its own that makes this meat loaf uncommonly fine.

Polpettone di Vitello Farcito di Peperone Rosso

VEAL MEAT LOAF STUFFED WITH RED PEPPER

For 4 to 6 persons

1 large or 2 smaller sweet red bell peppers
1½ pounds ground veal shoulder
1½ teaspoons chopped garlic
2 tablespoons chopped parsley
½ cup freshly grated *parmigiano-reggiano*
    (Parmesan)
1 egg

Salt
Black pepper in a grinder
1 cup toasted, unflavored bread crumbs
3 tablespoons butter
2 tablespoons vegetable oil
⅔ cup dry white wine

1. Wash the pepper and roast it over the flame of a burner, if you have a gas stove, or in the oven, turning it from time to time, until its skin is charred all over. Put it in a plastic bag, twist the bag tightly shut, and set aside until the pepper is cool enough to handle.

2. While waiting for the pepper to cool, put the meat, garlic, parsley, grated cheese, egg, salt, and generous grindings of pepper in a bowl. Mix thoroughly with a fork until all the ingredients are combined uniformly.

3. Pull off all the peel from the pepper, then split the pepper in half, lengthwise, to remove the stem, core, and all seeds. Cut the pepper lengthwise into strips about ½ inch wide.

4. Unroll about 10 to 12 inches of wax paper, lay it flat on a work counter, and moisten its surface with a towel soaked in water.

5. Spread the meat mixture over the paper to a thickness of 1 inch, pressing it down flat.

6. Place the strips of pepper over the meat, arranging them so that they lie in the same direction as the meat's longer side. Begin laying them down at one end, but stop at about 2 inches short of the opposite end.

7. Make a jelly roll of the meat, starting at the end topped with pepper. Use the wax paper to help you lift and roll the meat, but do not roll up the paper inside the loaf. Press gently to make a compact round loaf and pinch both ends to seal them.

8. Sprinkle the bread crumbs over the wax paper and roll the meat over the crumbs, exerting a little pressure until the loaf is thoroughly and firmly coated.

9. Choose a lidded pan that can subsequently accommodate the meat loaf lying flat. Put in the butter and oil and turn on the heat to medium high. Do not cover the pan. When the fat is hot, slip in the meat. Let it form a brown-gold crust on the side resting on the bottom of the pan before turning it, then turn it gently, using 2 spatulas, taking care not to allow the loaf to break up.

10. When the meat has a nice crust all around, add the wine. Let it bubble for about 1 minute, then turn the heat down to very low and cover the pan. Cook for 50 minutes, turning the roll from time to time. If, at some point, you find the juices in the pan are drying up, add up to 2 tablespoons of water.

11. Transfer the loaf to a cutting board and cut it into serving slices. Transfer them to a platter, pour all pan juices over them, and serve.

AHEAD-OF-TIME NOTE: If it is to be served warm, the veal loaf tastes best the moment it has been cooked. It can be made in advance, however, as its flavor is excellent when served at room temperature.

Polpettone di Vitello al Sedano

VEAL LOAF WITH CELERY

For 4 to 6 persons

2 ounces *pancetta* or bacon
½ cup leaves from the tops of the
    celery heart
2 bay leaves
1 pound ground veal shoulder
1 egg
Salt

Black pepper in a grinder
1 cup fine, dry, unflavored bread crumbs,
    toasted lightly in a pan as described on
    page 21
4 tablespoons butter
1 tablespoon vegetable oil
½ cup dry white wine

1. In a food processor, or by any other method, chop the *pancetta* or bacon together with the celery leaves and bay leaves. Chop to a very fine consistency, making sure no long, sharp bits of bay leaf remain.

2. Combine the chopped *pancetta* or bacon mixture with the ground meat, adding an egg, about 1 teaspoon of salt, and several grindings of pepper.

3. Knead the meat with your hands to amalgamate all the ingredients thoroughly. Shape the meat into a roll about 6 to 7 inches long and 4 inches thick.

4. Spread the bread crumbs on a length of wax paper or aluminum foil. Roll the meat over the bread crumbs so that the crumbs will cover it and adhere to it all over.

5. Choose a lidded pot that can subsequently accommodate the veal roll with enough room for it to be turned. Put in the butter and oil and turn on the heat to medium high.

6. When the butter foam subsides, put in the meat, keeping the pot uncovered. Brown it well on one side, then turn it over. Turning it requires care to avoid breaking up the roll. Try using a spatula in either hand and handle it very gently.

7. When the meat has been browned all over, add the wine. Let the wine bubble for about 1 minute, then turn the heat down to minimum and cover the pan, leaving the lid slightly askew. Cook for about 1 hour, turning the meat gently from time to time.

8. Transfer to a serving platter. Let the meat rest for a few minutes, then slice it. Pour the pan juices over it and serve. It is equally good hot, lukewarm, or at room temperature.

AHEAD-OF-TIME NOTE: The dish may be cooked through to the end entirely in advance, but do not slice it before reheating. To reheat, if the pan juices are insufficient, add up to ¼ cup water.

Polpettine di Vitello alla Panna Rosa

VEAL PATTIES WITH PINK CREAM

*F*OR these patties, ground veal is mixed with parsley, a small amount of garlic, Parmesan, an egg, and soft bread crumb soaked in milk. They are sautéed in butter and tossed with a light, quick tomato and cream sauce. It is a dish originally prepared for children, but there must be something of the child in grown-up palates, for I have found it equally appealing to adults.

For 4 persons

½ cup milk
½ cup crumb (the soft, crustless part) from
    good-quality white bread
1 pound ground veal, preferably the shoulder
1 teaspoon garlic chopped very fine
2 tablespoons chopped parsley
Salt
Black pepper in a grinder
2 tablespoons freshly grated *parmigiano-reggiano* (Parmesan)

1 egg
⅔ cup fine, dry, unflavored bread crumbs,
    toasted in an oven or pan as described on
    page 21
2 tablespoons butter
2 tablespoons vegetable oil
¾ cup canned Italian peeled plum tomatoes,
    cut up, with their juice
½ cup heavy cream

1. Warm the milk in a small saucepan without letting it come to a boil. Turn off the heat and add the soft bread crumb, allowing it to soak until it becomes thoroughly saturated.

2. Pick up the crumb with your hand, squeeze it to drain away excess milk, and put it in a mixing bowl. Add the ground veal, garlic, parsley, salt, pepper, the grated cheese, and the egg. Mix well with a fork, amalgamating all the ingredients into a uniform mixture.

3. Spread the dry bread crumbs on a plate. Make flat patties from the veal mixture about 2½ to 3 inches in diameter and 1 inch thick. Dredge them in the bread crumbs, coating them well on both sides.

4. Choose a lidded sauté pan that can later accommodate all the patties without overlapping. Put in the butter and oil and turn on the heat to medium high. When the butter and oil are hot, put in the patties, keeping the pan uncovered. When the patties have formed a nice brown crust on one side, turn them over. When the other side has formed a crust, add the cut-up tomatoes with their juice.

5. Turn the patties once or twice with the tomatoes, then turn down the heat to medium low, cover the pan, and cook for 10 minutes.

6. Uncover the pan and put in the cream. Stir once or twice and cook until the cream becomes reduced, turning into a deep pink sauce.

AHEAD-OF-TIME NOTE: The dish can be prepared through to the end a day in advance and reheated. When reheating, if there is not enough juice in the pan, add ¼ cup water and heat until it evaporates completely.

❧ TWO RECIPES FOR FILLET STEAKS ❧

It would be hard to claim for beef fillets a historic place in Italian cooking. True beef has always been scarce, and the fillet of *vitellone*—young beef—although more plentiful, was not so large or tasty to warrant separating it from the loin. Cooks began paying serious attention to beef fillets in the early years of Italy's post–World War II affluence. On its own, as just meat, tenderloin is cloyingly bland and flabby. It is what you do with it that makes it interesting.

The first of the recipes that follow produces a spicy, vibrantly savory fillet with remarkably simple means. The flavoring agents are Parmesan in wafer-thin slivers, chopped hot red pepper, and parsley. One tops the fillets with them off the heat, but while they are still hot and in the pan. The heat of the meat and of the pan juices fuses the flavorings and partly melts the cheese.

The second recipe was formulated by Alessandro Stanziani, who was for many years the master of the kitchen at the Colomba, when that restaurant was Venice's best. A trio of assertively flavored vegetables—peppers, eggplant, celery—are sautéed together with shredded romaine lettuce. The vegetables are replaced in the pan by the fillets, which are cooked in their juices and butter. All the cooking juices are then deglazed with white wine and Marsala, whereupon the vegetables and the meat are brought together and tossed briefly.

Filetto col Parmigiano

TENDERLOIN FILLETS WITH PARMESAN CHEESE, HOT RED PEPPER, AND PARSLEY

For 4 persons

4 tablespoons butter
1 tablespoon vegetable oil
4 tenderloin fillets, sliced 1½ inches thick
⅓ cup dry white wine
Salt

Black pepper in a grinder
Parmigiano-reggiano (Parmesan), shaved into
    4 tablespoons of fine slivers
½ teaspoon hot red pepper chopped fine
3 tablespoons chopped parsley

1. Choose a skillet that will accommodate the tenderloin fillets without overlapping or crowding. Put into it the butter and oil and turn on the heat to high.
2. When the oil is hot, put in the meat. Brown the meat well on both sides, then transfer to a platter, using a slotted spoon or spatula.

3. Add the white wine to the pan and evaporate it over medium-high heat, while scraping loose with a wooden spoon any of the browning residues from the bottom of the pan. Pour into the pan any liquid thrown off by the meat in the platter.
4. When all the wine and liquid have evap-

orated, return the fillets to the pan. Sprinkle with salt and a few grindings of pepper and turn them quickly once or twice.

5. Top each fillet with cheese slivers, hot red pepper, and parsley and turn off the heat.

While the meat is still in the pan, spoon up the juices in the pan and pour them over the meat, repeating the operation 2 or 3 times. The cheese topping will absorb some of the juices and melt slightly. Serve at once.

Filetto di Bue alla Moda di Sandro

TENDERLOIN FILLETS WITH VEGETABLES, WHITE WINE, AND MARSALA

For 4 persons

⅓ cup vegetable oil
⅔ cup celery, sliced into half rounds
⅛ inch thin
1½ cups sweet red bell pepper cored, seeded, and cut into strips ¼ inch wide and about 1½ inches long
1½ cups eggplant peeled and cut into sticks ½ inch thick and about 2 inches long

1 cup romaine lettuce shredded very fine
3 tablespoons butter
1 pound beef tenderloin, cut into slices about ⅔ inch thick
½ cup dry white wine
½ cup dry Marsala
Salt
Black pepper in a grinder

1. Choose a skillet large enough to accommodate later all the beef fillets without overlapping. Put in the oil, celery, red pepper, and eggplant and turn on the heat to medium high.

2. Cook the vegetables, stirring from time to time, until they are tender but not dissolved.

3. Add the shredded lettuce and cook for 2 to 3 minutes, stirring frequently.

4. Transfer the vegetables from the pan to a dish, using a slotted spoon or spatula. Add the butter to the pan, turn up the heat a little, and when the butter is hot put in the meat in a single layer, without overlapping it. Brown the meat quickly, about a minute or

two for each side, then transfer it to a dish.

5. Add the white wine and Marsala to the pan and let them evaporate. Add any liquid the fillets may have thrown off in the dish. Scrape the bottom of the pan with a wooden spoon to loosen any cooking residues.

6. When all the liquid in the pan, except for the fat, has evaporated, return the vegetables and meat to the pan. Add salt and a few grindings of pepper and cook just long enough to reheat the meat and vegetables, no more than about 1 minute, turning the meat 2 or 3 times. Serve at once, pouring all the juices from the pan over the meat.

AHEAD-OF-TIME NOTE: You can stop the cooking at the end of step 4 and resume it several hours later.

Filetto di Manzo in Tegame

PAN–ROASTED BEEF TENDERLOIN

UNLIKE the two preceding recipes, here the tenderloin is handled like a roast, cooked in the Italian over-the-burner method. To compensate for the meat's intrinsic blandness, it is prepared for çooking by studding it with a mixture of garlic and rosemary, each studding slit sealed by prosciutto fat or salt pork. It is cooked with onions and wine over low heat for a time that may seem long but is required for the development of more flavor than is usually associated with tenderloin.

For 6 persons

3 teaspoons garlic chopped very fine
6 teaspoons fresh rosemary leaves, or 3 teaspoons dried leaves chopped very fine
Black pepper in a grinder
About 3½ pounds beef tenderloin, 3 to 3½ inches thick, trussed tightly with kitchen string

¼ cup prosciutto fat or salt pork, cut into thick strips
2 tablespoons butter
1 tablespoon vegetable oil
1 medium onion, peeled and quartered
½ cup dry white wine
Salt

1.   Combine the garlic, rosemary, and generous grindings of pepper in a bowl.

2.   With a paring, filleting, or other narrow-bladed knife make numerous incisions all around the meat, spaced about 2 inches apart. Press a little of the garlic and rosemary mixture into the cuts, forcing it with a finger as deeply as possible into the meat. Seal each cut with the prosciutto fat or salt pork. Do not discard any leftover strips of fat.

3.   Choose a lidded, heavy-bottomed pot large enough to accommodate the meat later. Put in the butter, oil, and any leftover strips of fat and turn on the heat to medium. Do not cover the pan yet. When the fat is hot, put in the meat and the quartered onion.

Brown the meat well on all sides.

4.   Pour in the wine and sprinkle adequately with salt. When the wine has bubbled away for a minute or so, cover the pan and turn the heat down slightly. Cook for 45 minutes.

5.   When the meat is cooked, check the juices in the pan to see if they are too liquid. If this is so, remove the meat, turn up the heat to high, and reduce the pan juices until they separate from the fat. Reheat the meat briefly in the pot over medium heat.

6.   Transfer the roast to a cutting board, cut it into thin slices, place them in a warm serving platter together with any juices collected on the board, pour the pan juices over them, and serve immediately.

Rotolo di Manzo Farcito con Frittatine e Prosciutto Cotto

BEEF ROLL STUFFED WITH CHEESE FRITTATA AND BOILED HAM

ONE of the best-known inventions of Southern Italian cooking is the *braciola* or *braciolone,* a slice of beef rolled up with a variety of ingredients and often served with a dense tomato sauce. This is a refined variation on that classic theme. The stuffing is composed of cheese *frittate*—very thin, flat Italian omelets—parsley, bacon, and boiled ham. It is layered over the *scaloppine*-thin slice of beef, which is then rolled up and trussed firmly. The beef roll is cooked with onion and white wine and served, sliced, with no other sauce than its own elegantly restrained cooking juices.

For 6 persons

For the frittate:

2 tablespoons flour	2 tablespoons freshly grated *parmigiano-reggiano* (Parmesan)
¼ cup milk	
2 eggs	1 tablespoon butter
Salt	

For the beef roll:

1 pound beef bottom or top round, cut into 3 very thin slices	Black pepper in a grinder
Sewing needle and white cotton thread	6 slices bacon, cut into ¼-inch-wide strips, about 1 cup
2 tablespoons chopped parsley	½ pound boiled, unsmoked ham sliced thin
Salt	Needle and white cotton thread

2 tablespoons butter	½ cup dry white wine
2 tablespoons vegetable oil	
1 medium onion sliced very thin, about ⅔ cup	

1. Put the flour in a small bowl and pour the milk into it in a thin stream, mixing steadily with a fork to avoid lumps.

2. In another bowl, beat the eggs with a pinch or two of salt.

3. Slowly pour the beaten eggs into the milk and flour mixture, beating constantly with a fork. Add the grated cheese, beating until all the ingredients are combined uniformly.

4. Put the tablespoon of butter in a 10-inch

Beef Roll Stuffed with Cheese Frittata and Boiled Ham (continued)

skillet and turn on the heat to low. When the butter has melted, pour one-third of the *frittata* batter into the pan. Tilt and rotate the pan to spread the batter evenly over its whole surface. When the *frittata* becomes firm but before it browns, turn it over and cook for a few seconds on its other side. Transfer to a platter and repeat the procedure with the remaining batter, making altogether 3 thin *frittate,* which you will set aside for later.

5.   If the beef slices are thicker than 1/4 inch, pound them thinner. Trim their sides to straighten them. Bring 2 slices together, edge to edge, along their longer side. Sew them together with needle and white cotton thread. Repeat the procedure, fastening the remaining slice to the preceding 2, obtaining 1 large sheet of meat. Immediately put the needle out of harm's way, preferably outside the kitchen.

6.   Place the *frittate* over the meat, covering it as much as possible in a single layer. Sprinkle the chopped parsley over the *frittate,* add salt, grindings of pepper, and the bacon strips, distributing them evenly. Top with the boiled, sliced ham.

7.   Roll up the meat tightly, jelly-roll fashion, and bind it securely with kitchen trussing string.

8.   Put the butter, vegetable oil, and the sliced onion in a heavy-bottomed pot and turn on the heat to medium high. Do not cover the pot. When the onion becomes translucent, add the beef roll. Brown it well all over, then add the wine. When the wine has bubbled for 2 or 3 seconds, cover the pot, setting the lid slightly askew, and turn down the heat to low. Cook, turning the roll over from time to time, for 45 minutes or more, until the meat feels tender all the way through when pricked with a long fork. During the cooking, if you should find that there is insufficient juice in the pan to keep the meat from drying out, add 2 tablespoons of water as needed.

9.   When the meat is done, if the pot juices are still rather liquid, transfer the meat to a cutting board, uncover the pot, turn up the heat to high, and reduce the cooking juices. To serve, remove the trussing string, pull out the cotton thread gently without unraveling the roll, and cut the roll into 1/2-inch slices. Place on a serving dish, pour the pot juices over the meat, and serve piping hot.

AHEAD-OF-TIME NOTE: The beef roll can be cooked entirely in advance, up to the time it is ready for slicing. When ready to serve, reheat in the covered pot in a 250° oven for 15 to 20 minutes. Slice and serve as directed above.

Stracotto di Manzo al Latte

BEEF BRAISED IN MILK

A FIXTURE of my cooking courses is a dish that consistently surprises and gladdens my students: pork braised in milk, a masterpiece of Bolognese cooking. (The recipe is given in *The Classic Italian Cook Book* on page 284.) It is the model on which I based this recipe for beef. In working with the beef, I have had to deviate slightly from the astonishing simplicity of the original, which contains, aside from the shortening, only pork and milk. Beef being less tasty than pork, I have studded it with *pancetta* and added the flavor foundation of a basic *soffritto*—sautéed chopped onion, carrot, celery, and *pancetta*. Aside from those additions, the procedure is the same: The meat braises slowly to a tender end in the milk, which is eventually transformed into delicious, nut-colored clusters of sauce.

For 4 to 6 persons

2 pounds bottom round of beef
1/4 pound *pancetta,* or salt pork,
    or prosciutto fat
A larding needle or a meat probe or other
    narrow, long, cylindrical tool
2 tablespoons butter
1/2 cup diced carrot

1/2 cup diced celery
1/2 cup onion cut up coarse
Salt
Black pepper in a grinder
3 cups milk
1 tablespoon freshly squeezed lemon juice
3 tablespoons chopped parsley

1.   Lard the meat in several places with 1 ounce of *pancetta,* or other pork fat, using a larding needle or any satisfactory substitute.

2.   Choose a solid, heavy-bottomed pot with a close-fitting lid. Put in the butter, carrot, celery, and onion. Chop the remaining *pancetta* fine and put that in. Turn on the heat to medium, leaving the pot uncovered, and sauté the vegetables, turning them from time to time, until they are browned lightly.

3.   Add the beef and brown it on all sides. When well browned, add salt and pepper, turn the meat once or twice, then add the milk. Turn down the heat to medium low, cover the pot, and slowly bring the milk to a low simmer. Cook for 2 hours, turning the meat from time to time. If the liquid in the pot is boiling too fast, turn down the heat a little.

4.   After 2 hours, set the pot's cover slightly askew and raise the heat a little. Cook for 15 minutes longer, letting some of the liquid evaporate.

5.   Remove the meat to a cutting board, uncover the pot, turn up the heat, and further reduce the liquid, stirring steadily. Then strain all the cooking juices through a food mill fitted with a small-holed disk. Into this strained sauce stir the lemon juice.

6.   Slice the meat very thin and return it to the pot, spreading some of the sauce over each slice. Pour any remaining sauce over the meat, cover the pot, and turn on the heat to low.

7.   Reheat gently for 3 to 4 minutes, taking care that the sauce does not simmer.

8.   Transfer the meat with all its sauce to a warm serving platter, sprinkle the parsley over it, and serve at once.

AHEAD-OF-TIME NOTE: The entire dish may be prepared in advance through step 6. It can then be reheated just before serving. It is also very tasty served at room temperature.

Il Tapūlon di Borgomanero

PIEDMONTESE HASHED BEEF WITH RED WINE

*T*HE earthy, solid satisfaction delivered by this Piedmontese hashed beef with cabbage, herbs, and red wine comes straight from the most abundant source of good Italian cooking, the peasant kitchen. The ingredients are the modest ones available to country families (the meat originally used for the dish was donkey), the technique necessarily simple, the paramount objective: supremely comforting flavor. It is best served with *polenta* (page 167) or, as a speedier alternative, boiled rice.

For 6 to 8 persons

¼ pound *pancetta* or salt pork, chopped very fine to a creamy consistency
4 tablespoons extra virgin olive oil
4 tablespoons butter
2 tablespoons garlic chopped very fine or mashed
2 pounds beef round, ground coarse
2 pounds Savoy cabbage, shredded into thin strips

2 bay leaves, chopped
3 cloves
½ teaspoon fennel seeds
1½ cups Ghemme, Barbera, or other stout, fruity red wine such as Zinfandel or Côtes du Rhône
Salt
Black pepper in a grinder

1. Choose a large, lidded sauté pan. Put in the *pancetta*, oil, butter, and garlic. Turn on the heat to medium high and, leaving the pan uncovered, sauté the garlic until it becomes colored a pale brown.

2. Add the meat, breaking it up with a fork, and brown it well over high heat.

3. Add the shredded Savoy cabbage, bay leaves, cloves, and fennel seeds. Continue cooking over high heat, stirring frequently, for 2 to 3 minutes.

4. Add the wine, stir, cover the pan, and reduce the heat to medium low. Cook for 35 to 40 minutes, stirring occasionally.

5. Season with salt and grindings of pepper and serve.

Involtini di Verza Ripieni di Manzo

SAVOY CABBAGE ROLLS WITH BEEF STUFFING

NEARLY every cuisine with which I have some acquaintance—Central European, French, Spanish, Turkish, Mexican, Chinese—makes use of the universally appealing quality of a vegetable wrapper containing meat with cheese or other ingredients. These cabbage rolls clearly give away their Italian provenance. In addition to ground beef, the stuffing contains *pancetta* or ham, garlic, parsley, Parmesan, and egg. Once stuffed, the rolls are browned in butter and vegetable oil and cooked in white wine.

For 4 to 6 persons

1 head Savoy cabbage
Salt
3/4 pound ground beef
6 ounces *pancetta*, prosciutto, or boiled, unsmoked ham, chopped very fine
1 teaspoon garlic chopped very fine
3 tablespoons chopped parsley
1/3 cup fine, dry, unflavored bread crumbs

2/3 cup freshly grated *parmigiano-reggiano* (Parmesan)
1 egg
Black pepper in a grinder
4 tablespoons butter
2 tablespoons vegetable oil
1 cup dry white wine

1.   With a paring knife cut the cabbage leaves at their base where they meet the stem. Pull them gently away from the head, loosening them first at the base where you cut them. Pull off 14 leaves if it is a large head of cabbage, or double the amount if it is a small, young head. Take care not to tear any of the leaves. Save the rest of the head for a vegetable soup or other dish.

2.   Bring 4 quarts of water to a boil. Add salt and, as soon as the water resumes boiling, drop in the cabbage leaves. Cook for no more than 2 minutes from the time the water boils again, or less if the leaves are from a very young cabbage. They must not cook any longer than it takes for them to become limp enough to be used later as wrappers for the meat stuffing. When the leaves

are done, retrieve them with a slotted spoon and set aside to cool in a large colander.

3.   Put the ground meat, *pancetta*, garlic, parsley, bread crumbs, grated cheese, egg, salt, and several grindings of pepper in a bowl and mix thoroughly until all the ingredients are amalgamated into a homogeneous mixture.

4.   Place a cabbage leaf flat on a work surface. If the leaf is as large as about 8 by 8 inches, cut it in half lengthwise, removing the central rib. If it is a small leaf, place it face down with the hump of the rib facing up, and carefully slice away the protruding hump without cutting into the leaf itself. Prepare all the leaves in this manner.

5.   Divide the beef mixture into as many portions as you have leaves and shape them

into oval balls, twice as long as they are thick.

6.   Place a ball of stuffing at the edge of a leaf and roll up the leaf. As you roll it, tuck the ends of the leaf under to leave no openings.

7.   When all the leaves have been stuffed and rolled up, take them, one by one, in your hand and squeeze them gently but firmly. This will cause them to shed any excess liquid and to stick more tightly closed.

8.   Choose a lidded sauté pan that can subsequently accommodate all the cabbage rolls in a single layer, but fitting snugly together. Put in the butter and oil and turn on the heat to high, keeping the pan uncovered. When the fat is hot but not smoking, slip in the rolls and turn them to brown them all over. When they have been browned, add ½ cup of the wine, turn down the heat to medium, and cover the pan, setting the lid slightly askew. When the wine has bubbled away completely, add the remaining ½ cup. When all the wine has evaporated, the rolls are done. Allow their heat to subside a few minutes before serving.

AHEAD-OF-TIME NOTE: The dish can be completed several hours in advance and reheated gently, adding a little water if necessary. Do not keep overnight, however, because the flavor of the cabbage declines after a day.

Costolette di Agnello Saltate all'Aglio e Rosmarino

SAUTÉED LAMB CHOPS WITH GARLIC AND ROSEMARY

THE ingredients in this recipe are essentially those of lamb done in the Roman style: olive oil, garlic, rosemary, and white wine. The variant is the lamb, which is not a roasting cut but consists instead of single rib chops. Their thinness reduces cooking time considerably and, since each morsel has had more surface exposed to browning and to contact with the flavorings, the meat is much tastier. Chops served this way are, you may find, more graceful and interesting than the massive, wearying two- or three-rib broiled ones.

For 4 persons

12 single-rib lamb chops
A meat pounder
4 tablespoons extra virgin olive oil
6 garlic cloves, peeled
5 or 6 sprigs fresh rosemary, 5 inches long,
    or 2 tablespoons dried leaves, chopped

⅔ cup dry white wine
Salt
Black pepper in a grinder

1. Trim the chops of skin and excess fat. Flatten them from the bone outward with a meat pounder until they are no more than ½ inch thick.

2. Choose a skillet or sauté pan that can subsequently accommodate at least 6 of the chops at one time without overlapping. Put in the olive oil, garlic, and the fresh rosemary, if you are using it. If using dried rosemary, hold it back for later. Turn on the heat to medium high.

3. When the garlic becomes colored a pale gold, remove it, turn up the heat as high as possible, and slip in as many of the chops as will fit without overlapping. Brown the chops on one side, turn them, and do the other side. Do not overcook them. Two minutes for the first side and 1 minute for the other should be more or less sufficient. Then transfer them with a slotted spoon or spatula to a platter. Add the remaining chops to the pan and brown these on both sides.

4. When all the chops have been browned and removed from the pan, add the dried rosemary, if you are using it, stir once or twice, then pour in the wine. Let the wine bubble away until only about 3 to 4 tablespoons of it are left.

5. Sprinkle the chops with salt and grindings of pepper and return them to the pan, 2 or 3 at a time. Turn them once or twice quickly in the pan juices, always over high heat, then push them to the far side of the pan, piling them one over the other, and add more chops to the pan. When all the chops are done, transfer them with all the pan juices to a warm platter and serve at once.

Spezzato di Agnello coi Fagioli

LAMB STEW WITH WHITE KIDNEY BEANS

*T*HERE are dishes in which the ingredients, when brought together, transcend the familiar extent of their single ability to please and generate flavor so powerfully thrilling that before it all reflective appraisal gives way, surrendering the palate to abandoned delectation. In this dish it happens with lamb, beans, and garlic.

There are several stages to the cooking. First the lamb is browned. Then it is cooked with a *soffritto*—a sautéed flavor base—of onion, olive oil, and sage. After it cooks some more with white wine, the meat is transferred to the oven. Drained canned *cannellini* beans are added after 1½ hours' stewing. When the lamb and beans have cooked together a while longer and are ready to serve, chopped garlic and parsley are mixed in. This last potent fillip completes the stirring character of the dish.

For 6 persons

Lamb Stew with White Kidney Beans (continued)

Vegetable oil

3 pounds lamb shoulder, bone in, cut into
    about 3-inch pieces

2/3 cup flour, spread on a plate

3 tablespoons extra virgin olive oil

2½ cups onion sliced thin

1 teaspoon dried sage leaves, crumbled,
    or 6 or 7 small fresh leaves, torn by
    hand into small pieces

Salt

Black pepper in a grinder

1 cup dry white wine

2 teaspoons tomato paste

1 cup Homemade Meat Broth (page 73), or
    1 bouillon cube dissolved in 1 cup water

Two 19-ounce cans *cannellini*

2 teaspoons garlic chopped fine

3 tablespoons chopped parsley

1. Pour enough vegetable oil into a skillet to cover the bottom completely and turn on the heat to medium high.

2. When the oil is hot, dredge the lamb pieces, one by one, in the flour and slip them into the pan. Fill, but do not crowd, the pan. Brown the meat well on all sides, then transfer it to a plate, using a slotted spoon or spatula. As you remove a piece from the pan, replace it with one freshly dredged in flour, continuing thus until all the lamb has been browned.

3. Turn on the oven to 350°.

4. Choose a lidded pot that can later accommodate all the meat and beans. (If you have one that can go from the burner to the oven and subsequently to the table it would be most convenient.) Put in the olive oil, sliced onion, and sage and turn on the heat to medium. Cook the onion, uncovered, stirring occasionally, until it becomes colored a light brown.

5. Add the meat, turning it 2 or 3 times. When the meat begins to sizzle, add salt, several grindings of pepper, and the wine.

6. Dissolve the tomato paste in the meat broth. When the wine in the pot has boiled away, add the broth, mix well, cover the pot, and place it in the uppermost level of the preheated oven. Cook for 1½ hours, turning the meat once every 30 minutes.

7. Drain the beans and add them to the pot. Cook for another 15 minutes.

8. Before serving, mix in the chopped garlic and parsley. Serve piping hot.

AHEAD-OF-TIME NOTE: The entire dish may be prepared several days in advance, refrigerated when cool, and reheated before serving. When preparing it in advance, it would be preferable to stop short of adding the garlic and parsley until it is reheated so as not to muffle the fresh, vigorous accent of the raw ingredients. If there are leftovers, however, you can reheat them without concern; the dish will still taste good even if slightly muted in flavor.

Spezzato di Agnello coi Carciofi

LAMB STEW WITH ARTICHOKES

*A*RTICHOKES and lamb are an apt association of flavors. The palate-coating succulence of the lamb benefits from the mordant freshness of the artichokes. Should the artichokes be not quite as young and tender as they ought to, do not hesitate to extend the cooking time; it will do the dish no harm.

For 6 persons

4 or 5 artichokes
Freshly squeezed juice of 1 lemon
3 tablespoons vegetable oil
3 tablespoons chopped onion
1 teaspoon chopped rosemary
2½ pounds lamb shoulder,
    cut into 2- to 3-inch pieces

2 teaspoons chopped garlic
Salt
Black pepper in a grinder
½ cup dry red wine
3 tablespoons tomato paste
½ cup lukewarm water

1. Clean the artichokes as described on page 80, making sure to cut the tops down to the tender, edible part. Slice the artichokes into wedges ¾ inch thick and put them in a bowl of cold water together with the lemon juice.

2. Choose a lidded sauté pan that can later accommodate all the lamb pieces without overlapping. Put in the oil, onion, and rosemary and turn on the heat to medium high. Do not cover the pan.

3. When the onion becomes colored a pale gold, add the meat, browning it on all sides. Do not be concerned if you see the onion become colored very dark brown. Add the garlic.

4. Sprinkle with salt and several grindings of pepper and add the wine. Let the wine bubble for about 1 minute, then turn down the heat to low and cover the pan. Cook for about 1 hour, until the meat feels tender when pricked with a fork.

5. Dissolve the tomato paste in the water.

6. Drain the artichokes and add them to the pan. Stir thoroughly once or twice, then add the dissolved tomato paste, stir again, cover the pan, raise the heat to medium low, and cook until the artichoke wedges are tender, testing them with a fork. Depending on the youth and freshness of the artichokes, it should take about 15 minutes. At the end, there should be no watery liquid left. If there is still some remaining by the time the artichokes are done, uncover the pan, raise the heat, and boil the liquid away.

AHEAD-OF-TIME NOTE: The entire dish can be made up to 1 day in advance. Reheat gently in a covered pan over the burner just before serving.

Stufato di Agnello alla Marchigiana

SLOW-COOKED LAMB CUBES, MARCHES STYLE, WITH TOMATOES AND WHITE WINE

*T*HERE is much good lamb raised on the sea-facing slopes of the region where this recipe originates, the Marches on the central Adriatic. The lamb cubes should be cut with some bones in. They are cooked with garlic, rosemary, and white wine, the last possibly the Marches' own Verdicchio. The long, slow cooking makes the meat very tender and loosens it from the bones that, by that time, will have contributed their valuable portion of flavor.

For 4 persons

1 tablespoon extra virgin olive oil
3 pounds lamb shoulder, bone in, cut into
    2-inch cubes
1 teaspoon chopped garlic
2 teaspoons fresh rosemary leaves,
    or 1 teaspoon dried leaves, chopped

Salt
Black pepper in a grinder
1/2 cup Verdicchio or other dry white wine
1 cup canned Italian peeled plum tomatoes,
    with their juice

1. Put the oil in a medium-size sauté pan and turn on the heat to high. When the oil is very hot, put in as many pieces of lamb as will fit without crowding. Brown the meat well on all sides, transfer it with a slotted spoon or spatula to a platter, and put in more pieces. Proceed in this manner until all the meat has been browned and removed from the pan.

2. Turn down the heat to medium and put in the garlic. When the garlic becomes colored a pale gold, add the rosemary. Stir once or twice, then return the meat to the pan. Turn the lamb pieces over 2 or 3 times and season with salt and several grindings of pepper. Turn them over again and add the wine. When the wine has bubbled away for a minute or two, add the tomatoes. Stir the meat and tomatoes, cover the pan, and turn down the heat to low.

3. Cook for about 1 1/2 hours, stirring from time to time. When the lamb feels tender when pricked with a fork, it is done. It should be cooked through and through and come easily off the bone. There should be no runny liquid left in the pan, but only dense, lovely, dark cooking juices. Should you find that the juices are still too thin and liquid, transfer the meat to a warm platter, raise the heat to high, and reduce the sauce while scraping loose any cooking residues from the bottom of the pan. Pour immediately over the lamb and serve at once. Just before serving, I like to remove any of the bones that come away easily.

AHEAD-OF-TIME NOTE: The entire dish may be prepared several hours to a day in advance and reheated gently just before serving.

Spiedini di Agnello con la Pancetta Affumicata

GRILLED LAMB SKEWERS WITH BACON

P ANCETTA AFFUMICATA—bacon—plays a tasty, juicy role here: While basting the lamb as it grills, it laces it with some of its tangy flavor. The bread, moreover, absorbs some of the savory bacon fat as it melts in the cooking. The quantity of garlic in the mixture with which the lamb is coated should be calibrated carefully to keep its presence from being too intrusive. If it is particularly dry and pungent, you may use even less than the small amount indicated in the recipe.

For 4 persons

½ teaspoon garlic chopped very fine
1 tablespoon rosemary chopped fine
3 tablespoons vegetable oil
Salt
Black pepper in a grinder

1¾ to 2 pounds boned lamb shoulder, cut into
 1½-inch cubes
10 slices slab bacon, cut ¼ inch thick
Stale country-style bread trimmed of its crust
 and cut into 1½-inch squares

1. If using a charcoal grill, light the charcoal early enough so the coals are well lit and have formed a coating of white ash when you are ready to cook. If using a gas or electric grill, turn it on in time for it to be hot when you are going to use it.

2. Put the garlic, rosemary, oil, salt, and liberal grindings of pepper in a bowl and mix thoroughly with a fork.

3. Add the lamb cubes and toss until the meat is well coated with seasoning all over.

4. Cut the bacon into ¼-inch squares.

5. On each skewer alternate the ingredients in the following order: a piece of bacon, bread, bacon, lamb, bacon, bread, bacon, and so on, ending with bacon.

6. If grilling over charcoal, place the skewers not too close to the heat to avoid scorching. If grilling in a gas or electric broiler, which cooks with less intense heat, place the skewers in the level closest to the source of heat. Grill for 2 minutes on one side and 1 minute on the other, if you like your lamb pink.

Fettine di Maiale in Saor con Aceto Balsamico

SLICED PORK TENDERLOIN WITH RAISINS, PINE NUTS, AND BALSAMIC VINEGAR

SFOGI IN SAOR (see page 46) inspired me to apply the same method to thin slices of pork. Venetians I have sprung this on have confirmed what I had hoped, that although it is an improvisation, it tastes as though it had always been part of their city's cooking. To the basic *saor* marinade I have added a little balsamic vinegar, whose sweet-and-sour taste goes so well with pork.

Unlike the *sfogi*, the pork is ready to eat the moment it is done, while it is still warm, and thus takes its place in the repertory of pork second courses. Like the *sfogi*, however, it develops deeper flavor the longer it steeps in the marinade, thus becoming a perfect dish to prepare long in advance and to serve, without reheating, at room temperature.

For 4 persons

1/3 cup seedless raisins
1/2 cup red-wine vinegar
1 pound pork tenderloin, cut into thin slices
1/2 cup extra virgin olive oil
6 cups white onions sliced very thin
Salt

1 cup flour, spread on a dish
Black pepper in a grinder
1/3 cup pine nuts
1/4 cup *aceto balsamico* (balsamic vinegar, see page 6)

1. Soak the raisins in 1/4 cup of the red-wine vinegar and 1/4 cup of water for at least 30 minutes. Then drain, forcing off additional liquid by squeezing the raisins in your hand.

2. Flatten the tenderloin slices with a meat pounder to make them as thin as possible.

3. Put 1/4 cup of the olive oil and all the sliced onion in a large sauté pan, turn on the heat to very low, and cover the pan. Cook the onion slowly, turning it occasionally, until it is very tender. All the liquid must evaporate and the onion should become a blond gold color without browning. Using a slotted spoon or spatula, transfer the cooked onion to a dish,

leaving as much of the oil as possible in the pan. Sprinkle with salt and set aside.

4. Add the remaining 1/4 cup of olive oil to the pan and turn on the heat to medium high.

5. When the oil is hot, turn the pork slices in the flour, shake off excess flour, and put them in the pan. Do not put in more meat than will fit without overlapping. If the pan cannot accommodate all the slices at one time, do them in batches.

6. Brown the meat well on both sides; if it has been pounded very thin, do not cook altogether for more than 5 to 6 minutes.

7. Transfer to a serving platter where it can

fit without too many overlaps and season with salt and grindings of pepper.

8. Return the onion to the pan, turning on the heat to medium low. Add 2 tablespoons of water, the remaining ¼ cup of red-wine vinegar, the drained raisins, and the pine nuts. Cook, stirring, for a minute or two. Turn off the heat and stir in the balsamic vinegar. Pour the contents of the pan over the meat, spreading them evenly.

NOTE: You can serve the dish immediately or several hours later, at room temperature. Or you can refrigerate it when the meat has cooled and serve the following day after bringing it to room temperature.

Portafoglio di Maiale con Fegato di Vitello

PORK CHOPS STUFFED WITH CALF'S LIVER

I WOULD be unable to say, in this recipe, which profits more from being cooked next to the other, the pork or the calf's liver. The liver, enclosed within the chop, cooks to that perfect degree of tenderness and sweetness that sometimes eludes us in other preparations. And the pork acquires unexpected delicacy and succulence.

The lovely taste is matched by an equally lovely appearance when, in cutting into the pork, you find the liver, a moist, pink center for the chop. The chops are made ready for stuffing by the same method used on the veal chops on page 211, a not difficult procedure described again here. Should you find it daunting, however, ask your butcher to do it for you.

For 4 persons

4 pork rib chops cut from the loin, bone in but without the tenderloin eye, about 1 inch thick
Salt
Black pepper in a grinder
½ pound calf's liver, sliced very thin

4 fresh bay leaves, or 2 dried leaves
Toothpicks, preferably round
4 tablespoons butter
1½ tablespoons vegetable oil
⅓ cup flour, spread on a platter
¼ cup freshly squeezed lemon juice

1. Cut the meat of the chops in half lengthwise, as though they were to be butterflied, but do not detach from the bone. Make sure to cut all the way to the bone and remove any skin attached to the meat.

2. Pound each half of the chop separately with a meat pounder, using one hand to lift the other half and hold the chop. Pound from the bone, sliding the pounder outward, toward and past the edge of the meat.

Pork Chops Stuffed with Calf's Liver (continued)

3.   When both halves of each chop have been flattened, sprinkle the inner sides with salt and grindings of pepper. Trim the liver slices to fit the chops and place 1 slice inside the chop together with a whole bay leaf.

4.   Stitch the open end of each chop shut with 3 or 4 round toothpicks.

5.   Choose a lidded sauté pan that can accommodate all the chops lying flat, without overlapping. (If you have no such pan, you will have to cook the chops in separate batches.) Put in 3 tablespoons of the butter and the vegetable oil and turn on the heat to medium high.

6.   When the butter foam begins to subside, dredge the chops lightly in flour on both sides and put them in the pan.

7.   Cook over medium-high heat until the bottom side of the chops becomes colored a light brown, then turn them and continue cooking until the other side is also light brown. At that point, turn the heat down to medium low and cover the pan. Cook for 5 to 7 minutes longer. The liver inside the chops should become no darker than a faded pink.

8.   Uncover, add the lemon juice, and raise the heat to high. Add the remaining tablespoon of butter and scrape the bottom of the pan with a wooden spoon to loosen all cooking residues.

9.   Transfer the chops to a warm serving platter, remove the toothpicks and the bay leaves, pour over the meat all the juices from the pan, and serve immediately.

Arista di Maiale in Tegame con i Porri

PAN-ROASTED PORK LOIN WITH LEEKS

SWEET, pungent things are good complements for pork, and the mildly savory leek is one of the best of these. The leek is first cooked in butter until tender. The pork loin roasts, over the burner, with part of the leek. The remaining portion is puréed, forming a creamy sauce that is added to the pork for the last 10 minutes' cooking. The pork develops flavor so gentle that it could be mistaken for veal.

For 4 persons

3 thick or 4 or 5 thinner leeks
3 tablespoons butter
2½ pounds pork loin roast with rib bone
Salt

1 tablespoon vegetable oil
½ cup flour, spread on a platter
Black pepper in a grinder
½ cup dry white wine

1. Cut the roots away from the leeks and discard any portion of the tops that is wilted, bruised, or yellowed. Cut the leeks in half lengthwise. If the resulting halves are 1 inch thick or more, cut them in half again, always lengthwise. Next, cut them crosswise in ½-inch-wide sections to produce approximately square slices. Rinse in cold water and drain well.

2. Choose a lidded casserole or deep sauté pan that can later accommodate the meat. Put in 2 tablespoons of the butter and all the cut-up leeks. Cover the pan, turn the heat on to low, and cook until the leeks are thoroughly wilted and tender, but not browned.

3. Detach the rib bone from the roast, then tie it back in place with a string.

4. When the leeks are tender, add salt, stir, then remove two-thirds of the leeks from the pan and set aside.

5. Put the remaining tablespoon of butter and the vegetable oil in the pan and turn on the heat to medium high. Do not cover.

6. Turn the meat over lightly in the flour and put it in the pan. Brown it well on all sides.

7. Add salt and liberal grindings of pepper. Add the wine and turn up the heat to high for 10 to 15 seconds. Cover the pan, turn the heat down to low, and cook for about 2 hours, or until the meat is tender when pricked with a fork. Transfer the meat to a warm platter.

8. Purée the remaining leeks from the pan together with their juices through a food mill or in a food processor or blender.

9. Return the puréed leeks to the pan together with the previously reserved cooked leeks and the meat. Cover the pan, turn on the heat to medium, and cook for 10 minutes, turning the meat and leeks from time to time.

10. Transfer the meat to a cutting board. Remove the string and the rib bone. Cut the pork into serving slices and place them on a platter.

11. Taste and correct the leeks in the pan for salt and pepper, then pour them, together with all cooking juices, over the sliced pork.

Lombata di Maiale al Forno

ROAST PORK LOIN WITH JUNIPER AND ROSEMARY

*T*WO roasting methods are used to get the most out of this pork loin in terms of texture, tenderness, and taste. The first phase—in which the meat, coated with a rosemary and juniper berry mixture, roasts in an open pan in the oven—produces a good, crusty surface permeated by the mingled seasonings. The second phase takes place over the burner with tomatoes and butter added: The roast completes its cooking in a moist environment that keeps it as juicy as pork can be and surrounds it with the purest of tomato sauces.

For 6 to 8 persons

Roast Pork Loin with Juniper and Rosemary (continued)

3 pounds boned pork loin
1 teaspoon rosemary chopped very fine
14 juniper berries, mashed in a mortar or ground very fine
Salt

Black pepper in a grinder
5 tablespoons butter
1 cup canned Italian peeled plum tomatoes, passed through a food mill, with their juice

1.   Turn on the oven to 475°.

2.   Rub the meat all over with the chopped rosemary, the mashed juniper, salt, and several grindings of pepper.

3.   Smear the bottom of a baking pan with ½ tablespoon of the butter. Put in the meat, dotting it on top with 2½ tablespoons of the butter. Do not cover the pan. Place in the middle level of the preheated oven.

4.   Turn the meat after 45 minutes. Bake for another 15 minutes, then remove it from the oven.

5.   Choose a heavy, lidded casserole that can contain the pork snugly. Transfer the meat to the casserole, leaving in the baking pan all the melted fat. Add the remaining 2 tablespoons of butter and the puréed tomato. Cover, place the pot over a burner of the range, turn on the heat to low, and cook for 1½ hours. Turn the meat from time to time. If you find during the cooking that the juices in the pan are drying up, add up to ¼ cup of water. Serve promptly when done.

AHEAD-OF-TIME NOTE: It tastes best the moment it is done but, if necessary, it can be prepared 1 or 2 hours in advance, kept out of the refrigerator, and reheated gently on the burner, in a covered pan, over low heat.

Salsiccie e Patate alla Paesana

SAUSAGES AND POTATOES, COUNTRY STYLE, WITH TOMATO, GARLIC, AND BAY LEAVES

W*HEN* I was a young girl in Romagna, my father had a farm, run, like nearly every farm then in Italy, on a crop-sharing basis. The owner supplied a house to live in, the peasants the labor, and they divided the proceeds more or less equally, depending on the watchfulness of the former and the craftiness of the latter. My father often took me along on his tours of inspection. I loved the outing, which included, if we timed it well, an invitation to eat at the farmhouse. It was wonderful food in a setting that had me spellbound.

The house was a rough, stout, brick structure. In the low-ceilinged upper story, the family had its sleeping quarters; the floor below it consisted of a single, large, dusky room. Into it, a tiny window strained dusty daylight. At one end there was a hearth and, beside it, blackened, thickly encrusted grills and trivets, battered pans, piles of dried vine canes and other firewood; in front of it, a crude table and chairs. Against a wall there were hoes, spades, picks, and other paraphernalia scattered where they had been dropped. The farmer butchered his own pig, and hams and sausages were hung in the corner farthest from the hearth. Also hanging were tomatoes and bunched garlic; save for the fire, they were the only sources of color and brightness in the room, their cheeriness, in that cavernous, mysterious place, seeming almost frivolous. Baskets on the floor held potatoes and onions. A streaked cupboard contained flour, and to one side of it hung the long, narrow pasta pin. In that smoky, primitive room I had some of the best meals of my life.

I used particularly to hope for this dish of sausages. Over the open fire, the peasant woman would start them going with olive oil, garlic, and onion; while the sausages were cooking, she skinned the tomatoes, cut up the potatoes, and, whenever she was ready to, dropped them in. The making of the dish, its ingredients pulled literally out of the shadows, was like ritual magic. But what may be even more magical is that, when I make it today, its good flavor and the flavor of those days come through neat, as one.

For 4 to 6 persons

1 pound sweet breakfast sausages
2 tablespoons extra virgin olive oil
3 large garlic cloves, peeled and sliced very thin
1 pound onions sliced very thin
1 pound fresh, ripe plum tomatoes

6 bay leaves, cut in half
1½ pounds new potatoes, peeled and cut into wedges 1½ inches thick
Salt
Black pepper in a grinder

1. Pierce the sausages in various places with a toothpick or trussing needle or any similar, pointed, narrow tool. Put the sausages in a saucepan with the oil, garlic, and sliced onion. Cover and turn on the heat to medium low.

2. While the sausages and onion are cooking, wash the tomatoes and drop them in a pot of boiling water. Drain after 1 or 2 minutes, and as soon as they are cool enough to handle, peel them, chop them, and set aside.

3. When the onion is tender, uncover the pan, raise the heat to high, and cook, stirring frequently, until the onion becomes colored a light golden brown. Add the tomatoes.

4. Add the bay leaves, cover the pan, and turn down the heat to medium. Cook for another 10 to 12 minutes, stirring from time to time, then add the potato wedges, salt, and liberal grindings of pepper. Pick out and remove all the bay leaves. Cover the pan again and continue to cook until the potatoes feel tender when pricked with a fork. Serve at once.

AHEAD-OF-TIME NOTE: The entire dish may be prepared in advance and reheated, covered, over medium heat just before serving.

Salsiccie con Cime di Rapa

SAUSAGES WITH BROCCOLETTI DI RAPE

IT IS IN THE south of Italy that the mildly bitter, peppery taste of *broccoletti di rape*, known there as *cime di rapa*, is most popular. Their earthy quality agrees so well with sausages. After browning the sausages, one uses their browning residues, along with olive oil and garlic, to finish cooking the already parboiled greens, a savory procedure. For the last few minutes of cooking, the sausages and the *broccoletti di rape* are then brought together.

For 4 persons

1 pound *broccoletti di rape*
Salt
1 pound sweet breakfast sausages containing
    no herbs or spices except for salt and
    pepper

¼ to ⅓ cup extra virgin olive oil
    (depending on how fatty the sausages are)
2 teaspoons chopped garlic
Black pepper in a grinder

1. Wash the *broccoletti di rape* in several changes of cold water and peel away the green skin from the thick part of the stalks.

2. Bring a pot of water to a boil, add 2 tablespoons of salt, and drop in the *broccoletti di rape*. Cook until tender but still quite firm, then drain and set aside.

3. Choose a skillet or sauté pan large enough to accommodate both the sausages and, subsequently, the greens. Put in ¼ cup of water, the sausages, and turn on the heat to medium high. Prick the sausages in several places with a fork.

4. When the water evaporates, allow the sausages to brown thoroughly on one side, then add another ¼ cup of water. When this evaporates, brown the sausages on the other side. Transfer the sausages to a dish, using a slotted spoon or spatula, leaving the dark browning residues in the pan.

5. If the pan juices, including the melted fat from the sausages, amount to 1 tablespoon or less, put ⅓ cup olive oil in the pan. If the fat and juices are more abundant, reduce the amount of olive oil to ¼ cup. Add the garlic and turn down the heat to medium.

6. When the garlic becomes colored a pale gold, add the cooked *broccoletti di rape*. Cook them for 2 to 3 minutes, turning them several times to coat them thoroughly with the pan juices.

7. Add the sausages and cook for 4 to 5 minutes, turning them over with the greens from time to time. Taste for salt and sprinkle with a grinding or two of pepper. Serve piping hot.

Il Fegato del Salumaio

SAUTÉED CALF'S LIVER WITH BACON, ONION, AND WHITE WINE

*I*N VENETIAN *ciacolare* means to chat; in Venice, a city of narrow streets without cars where people are constantly meeting, *ciacolare* is everyone's favorite activity. The daylong exchange of soft, consonant-dropping Venetian patter on the footbridges, by the newsstand, at the café, in the shops is the shuttle that weaves the city's singular social fabric. Unless you are a stranger, you do not just buy a pound of butter, a loaf of bread, a dozen slices of prosciutto: You have a conversation.

The morning I stopped in at Gianni's pork store, I had just been to the butcher. After a 10-minute survey of major topics, partly shared with the other customers, Gianni asked me what I'd be cooking for lunch. "Liver *alla veneziana*," I replied. "If I give you the *pancetta*, Mrs. Hazan, and my recipe, will you try it my way?" *"Pancetta?"* My curiosity was roused. "Sure," I said. Later, with the *pancetta*—which in Venice is smoked, like bacon—and Gianni's instructions, we were at table with a version of *fegato alla veneziana* that we all liked even more than the familiar one.

The basic ingredients, calf's liver and smothered onions, are those of the traditional recipe, but in this one the onions are cooked first with bacon and later with white wine. The final touch of parsley is also new to the dish. With this, as with any sautéed liver, it is vital to cook the liver briefly at very high heat so that it doesn't acquire that flaccid consistency and vapid, steamed taste characteristic of slow-cooked liver.

For 6 persons

5 tablespoons extra virgin olive oil
3 cups onion sliced very fine
¼ pound bacon, sliced somewhat thick,
    if possible, and cut into narrow strips
1½ pounds calf's liver, sliced thin
    (about ¼ inch thick)

½ cup dry white wine
Salt
Black pepper in a grinder
2 tablespoons parsley chopped fine

1.   Choose a 10- to 12-inch lidded sauté pan or skillet and put into it 2 tablespoons of the olive oil, the sliced onion, and the bacon strips. Cover and turn on the heat to medium low.

2.   Let the onion cook down slowly, stirring it from time to time, until it becomes colored a pale brown and is considerably reduced in volume. At the beginning the onion may throw off some liquid, but when done the only liquid left in the pan should be the oil and some of the

Sautéed Calf's Liver with Bacon, Onion, and White Wine (continued)

bacon's dissolved fat. The bacon should be well cooked, but not crispy.

3.   When the onion and the bacon are done, transfer them to a bowl, using a slotted spoon or spatula.

4.   Remove all the thin, tough skin that may still be attached to the liver, but take care not to break up the slices.

5.   Put the remaining 3 tablespoons of olive oil in the pan, raise the heat to high, and put in as many of the liver slices as will fit flat, without overlapping.

6.   Cook the liver at very high heat in the uncovered pan. When one side of the slice has lost its raw red color, turn it, and when the other side has done the same, transfer the meat to a platter.

7.   When all the liver slices are done and out of the pan, return the previously cooked onion and bacon to the pan, add the white wine, sprinkle with salt and a few grindings of pepper, stir, and cook at medium-high heat until all the wine has evaporated. As the wine evaporates, stir with a wooden spoon, scraping loose any cooking residues from the bottom of the pan. If the liver on the platter has thrown off some juice, add this juice to the pan.

8.   When all the liquid in the pan save for the fat has evaporated, put the liver slices back in the pan. Add the chopped parsley, turn the liver over quickly 2 or 3 times, then transfer the liver with all the contents of the pan to a warm platter and serve at once.

Animelle al Marsala coi Carciofi

SWEETBREADS WITH MARSALA AND ARTICHOKES

*T*HE elegantly mild flavor of sweetbreads is set off in this recipe by a judicious dose of the earthier tastes of artichokes and ham. The artichokes are cooked separately, in olive oil. The ham, sautéed in butter, serves as a flavor base for browning the sweetbreads. The sweetbreads are diced to reduce the browning time and to create more surfaces that absorb flavor. Marsala is used at the end to temper, with its sweetness, the artichokes' astringency and promote a smooth conjunction with the sweetbreads.

For 4 persons

4 large artichokes
Freshly squeezed juice of ½ lemon
1 pound fresh sweetbreads, preferably from
    the thymus rather than the pancreas
2 tablespoons wine vinegar
Salt
3 tablespoons extra virgin olive oil

3 tablespoons butter
2 tablespoons onion chopped fine
¼ pound boiled, unsmoked ham,
    cut into narrow strips
Black pepper in a grinder
½ cup dry Marsala

1. Clean the artichokes as described on page 80, then cut them into 1-inch wedges and keep them in water acidulated with the lemon juice.

2. Place the sweetbreads in a bowl with enough water to cover amply and let soak for 10 to 15 minutes. Drain, add fresh water, and strip the sweetbreads of as much of their enveloping membrane as possible.

3. In a pot put sufficient water to cover the sweetbreads later. Bring the water to a boil. Add the vinegar and 1 tablespoon of salt. When the water returns to a boil, put in the sweetbreads. Cook the sweetbreads for 10 minutes after the water returns to a boil, then drain.

4. When the sweetbreads are cool enough to handle, remove any of the remaining outer membrane.

5. Drain the artichoke wedges and rinse them in fresh water.

6. Put the artichokes and the olive oil in a saucepan and turn on the heat to medium. Brown the artichokes very lightly for 1 to 2 minutes, then add ¼ cup of water and cover the pan. Cook for 20 minutes or more, depending on the youth and freshness of the artichokes, until they are tender all the way through when pricked with a fork. If, while they are cooking, they need additional liquid, add 2 tablespoons of water. When they are done, however, there should be no liquid left in the pan except for the oil. When cooked, sprinkle with salt, turn them, and remove from the heat.

7. Dice the sweetbreads into 1-inch cubes.

8. In a large skillet or sauté pan put the butter and onion and turn on the heat to medium.

9. When the onion becomes translucent, add the ham strips. Brown them lightly for 1 to 2 minutes, stirring frequently.

10. Add the diced sweetbreads and turn up the heat to high. Turn the sweetbreads over frequently and, as soon as they are browned evenly, add salt and grindings of pepper, turn them once or twice, then add the Marsala.

11. When the Marsala has boiled away, add the artichokes. Turn several times to mix the artichokes with the contents of the pan, lower the heat to medium, cover the pan, and cook for 30 minutes. Serve piping hot.

AHEAD-OF-TIME NOTES: The sweetbreads may be prepared a day in advance through step 4; when cool, store in the refrigerator. Bring to room temperature when resuming cooking. The entire dish may be cooked in advance and reheated gently just before serving.

Rognoncini d'Agnello coi Funghi

LAMB KIDNEYS WITH MUSHROOMS

*T*HE most tender kidneys come from lamb, and, when I find them, they are what I use. An acceptable second choice is calf kidneys. For Italian dishes, kidneys are sliced very thin before they are soaked. There are three advantages: Once sliced, their cleansing soak is more thorough, so their taste is milder; two, they can be cooked more rapidly; three, more of their surface is exposed during cooking to the flavoring used.

When sliced, kidneys look remarkably like sliced mushroom caps, a fact that was taken into account when pairing the two in this recipe. It is a coupling both congenial and interesting, congenial in the flavor, interesting in having two ingredients whose looks and consistency are similar, but whose taste differs. Note that the fresh mushrooms are cooked with reconstituted dried *porcini*, whose flavor they appropriate.

For 4 persons

10 to 12 fresh lamb kidneys
½ cup wine vinegar
1 ounce dried *porcini* mushrooms, soaked
   in 2 cups lukewarm water for at least
   30 minutes
1 pound fresh mushrooms

3 tablespoons extra virgin olive oil
3 teaspoons chopped garlic
3 tablespoons chopped parsley
Salt
Black pepper in a grinder
⅓ cup dry white wine

1. Cut the kidneys across their long side to produce narrow slices ¼ inch thin. When you reach the center of the kidneys as you slice, remove any bits of white matter.

2. Put the kidney slices in a bowl, cover completely with water, and add ¼ cup of the wine vinegar. After the kidneys have soaked for about 30 minutes, you will find that they have released blood into the water. Drain them and rinse them in several changes of water until you see little or no blood. Return the sliced kidneys to the bowl, add enough water to cover well and the remaining ¼ cup of vinegar. Let soak another 30 minutes or more, then drain, rinse once more

in several changes of water, and place in the bowl again with enough fresh water to cover. Let soak until ready to cook.

3. Wash the fresh mushrooms rapidly under cold running water, then pat thoroughly dry. Cut into ¼-inch slices.

4. Scoop the *porcini* mushrooms from their soak, using a slotted spoon or spatula. Do not discard the water in which they have soaked. Squeeze the mushrooms with your hands, letting the liquid run into the bowl where they had soaked. Rinse the mushrooms in many changes of fresh water.

5. Line a strainer with paper towels, place

over a bowl, and filter the liquid from the mushroom soak through the paper.

6.   Put 1 tablespoon of the olive oil and 1 teaspoon of the chopped garlic in a small to medium-size skillet or sauté pan and turn on the heat to medium.

7.   When the garlic becomes colored a pale gold, add 1 tablespoon of the chopped parsley. Stir once or twice, then put in the *porcini* mushrooms. Stir 2 or 3 times, then add the filtered water from the mushroom soak. Turn up the heat to high.

8.   Stir from time to time until all the liquid in the pan, except for the oil, has boiled away. Add the sliced fresh mushrooms, salt, a liberal grinding of pepper, and turn the mushrooms a few times to coat them well. When the mushrooms begin to release liquid, cover the pan and turn down the heat to medium low. Cook, stirring occasionally, until all the liquid has evaporated or been absorbed. Remove the pan from the heat.

9.   Drain the kidney slices, rinse them in fresh water, then pat them thoroughly dry with kitchen towels.

10.   Choose a pan larger than the one containing the mushrooms, put in the remaining olive oil and chopped garlic, and turn on the heat to medium.

11.   When the garlic becomes colored a pale, pale gold, add the remaining chopped parsley, stir once or twice, then put in the sliced kidneys. Add salt and grindings of pepper and turn up the heat to very high. Turn the kidneys over as they cook for 1½ to 2 minutes, then transfer them to a bowl, using a slotted spoon or spatula.

12.   Boil away from the pan all the liquid thrown off by the kidneys, scraping loose from the bottom any cooking residues. Then add the wine and cook it down until it has evaporated completely.

13.   Transfer all the mushrooms from the smaller pan to the larger. Add the kidneys from the bowl, lifting them with a slotted spoon or spatula. Cook, stirring constantly, for another 1½ to 2 minutes, always over high heat. Transfer the entire contents of the pan to a warm platter and serve at once.

AHEAD-OF-TIME NOTE: The dish may be prepared almost entirely in advance, in the morning for the evening. Stop at the end of step 12, when you have cooked the kidneys and removed them from the pan. Resume cooking from the beginning of step 13 only when you are ready to serve.

Vegetables

Asparagi e Biete Gratinati col Parmigiano

GRATINÉED ASPARAGUS AND SWISS CHARD

*I*T IS A RARE vegetable that cannot profit from this classic treatment: parboiling it, placing it in a baking dish with butter and Parmesan, and baking it until the cheese forms a crust. In this instance it is a combination of two vegetables, Swiss chard and asparagus. Since their spearlike shape is similar, the contrast in appearance is the subdued one of Swiss chard white against asparagus green. In taste the differences are equally fine, but nonetheless perceptible: the gentle flavor of Swiss chard, the more explicit one of asparagus, a mutually helpful association.

Only the stalks of the chard are employed here. Do not discard the leaves, however; use them in one of the ways suggested in the introduction to the recipe for *cannelloni* on page 113.

For 4 persons

2 pounds Swiss chard
Salt
1 pound asparagus
An oven-to-table baking dish

5 tablespoons butter
1 cup freshly grated *parmigiano-reggiano* (Parmesan)

1.   Trim the Swiss chard stalks of all leaves. Cut off any discolored portion of the bottom of the stalks but shorten them no farther. Wash them in several changes of cold water.

2.   Bring a pot of water to a boil. Drop in the stalks and cook them until they feel tender when probed with a fork. Scoop them out with a colander or slotted spoon and set aside.

3.   Clean the asparagus as described on page 111.

4.   Bring the water to a boil once again, add 2 tablespoons of salt, and, as the water returns to a boil, drop in the asparagus. Cook until tender but not limp. Drain.

5.   Turn on the oven to 400°.

6.   Smear the baking dish with ½ tablespoon of the butter. Line the bottom with a layer of chard stalks. Sprinkle with salt, then top with a layer of asparagus. Repeat the procedure until you have used up both vegetables. Sprinkle the

Gratinéed Asparagus and Swiss Chard (continued)

grated cheese on top, distributing it evenly. Dot with the remaining butter. Place the dish in the uppermost level of the preheated oven for 15 to 20 minutes, or until a light brown crust forms on top. Serve a few minutes after removing from the oven to allow the heat to subside and the flavors to emerge.

AHEAD-OF-TIME NOTE: The dish can be prepared several hours in advance the same day it is to be served, up to the point where it is ready to be placed in the oven.

Coste di Biete Farcite e Fritte

FRIED STUFFED SWISS CHARD STALKS

*T*HERE is very little one can't coax Swiss chard into doing. Here pairs of stalks trimmed to size are used to sandwich a mixture of béchamel, ham, egg, and Parmesan, then they are breaded and fried. What gives this novel vegetable sandwich elegant interest is the alternation of textures: the coating crisp over the juicy stalk, which encloses, in turn, the melting spread of béchamel and ham.

For 4 to 6 persons

1½ pounds Swiss chard with broad,
    thick stalks

For the béchamel:

1 cup milk   1½ tablespoons flour
2 tablespoons butter   ⅛ teaspoon salt

¼ pound boiled, unsmoked ham, chopped   1 cup fine, dry, unflavored bread crumbs,
    fine   spread on a dish
½ cup freshly grated *parmigiano-reggiano*   Vegetable oil for frying
    (Parmesan)   Salt
2 eggs   Black pepper in a grinder

1. Detach the green tops from the Swiss chard stalks. Set them aside to use for any recipe calling for Swiss chard greens (see page 113, or *The Classic Italian Cook Book*, pages 164 and 414, or *More Classic Italian Cooking*, page 390).

    2. Trim the stalks into rectangles. Wash in

cold water and boil in unsalted water until they are barely tender but still firm. Drain and set aside to cool.

3. Make the béchamel as described on page 112. In a bowl, combine the béchamel with the ham, grated cheese, and 1 egg. Stir, mixing the ingredients into a homogeneous mass, and set aside to let the béchamel cool completely.

4. Pair off the stalks that are most nearly equal in width, then trim them so that they coincide in length. If an odd stalk is left over, cut it in half and trim it to make a pair.

5. On one of each of the paired stalks spread a little of the béchamel mixture, a bit less than ¼ inch thick. Top with the matching half of the pair, making a sandwich.

6. Beat the remaining egg lightly in a deep dish. Dip each stuffed pair of stalks in the egg, first on one side then the other. After dipping in the egg, place in the bread crumbs, turn the pair of stalks over, and press it into the bread crumbs with the palm of your hand to make the coating adhere tightly. As each pair of stalks is dipped and breaded, transfer it to a clean platter.

7. In a skillet put enough vegetable oil to come at least ½ inch up the side of the pan and turn on the heat to high. When the oil is very hot, slip the stalks into the pan, no more at one time than will fit without crowding. Fry them on one side until it becomes colored a golden brown, then turn them over and do the other side. Transfer them to a draining rack or to a platter covered with paper towels. Sprinkle with salt and pepper. Serve while piping hot.

Belga alla Moda del Radicchio di Treviso

GRILLED BELGIAN ENDIVE

*E*LSEWHERE in this book (see *Tonnarelli* with Belgian Endive and Bacon, page 103), I have mentioned the uses in cooking of the winter *radicchio* of Treviso, the romaine-shaped red and white member of the chicory family. The best-known way to cook *radicchio di Treviso* is over a slow wood or charcoal fire, basting the lettuce with olive oil as it wilts gradually to a pliant, tender consistency; the flame must not be allowed to char it. It can also be done successfully on an indoor grill, as described here.

In America, I have only rarely seen *radicchio di Treviso*, and then at frightfully high prices. The round *radicchio* that looks like a little red cabbage is more available, but it too is quite expensive, and it is perhaps better raw than cooked. In my opinion, the most satisfactory substitute for the skinny

Grilled Belgian Endive (continued)

Treviso *radicchio* is that far more abundant member of the same chicory family, Belgian endive.

The one ingredient for which there is no acceptable alternative in this dish is good olive oil, whose irreplaceable flavor must seep into the endive as it softens slowly over, or under, the fire.

For 6 persons

5 thick heads endive, about 1½ pounds
Salt

Black pepper in a grinder
¼ cup extra virgin olive oil

1. Turn on the broiler.
2. Discard any of the endive's bruised or wilted outer leaves. Cut away a thin slice from the root end to remove the usually discolored surface portion of the stem. Wash the endive under cold running water, then shake off the moisture.
3. Cut each head of endive in half lengthwise. Make a cut in the root end, cutting half as deep as the root is thick and running the cut from the bottom to where the leaves join the root.
4. Place the endive cut side up on a broiling pan. Sprinkle liberally with salt and grindings of pepper and pour the olive oil over it in a thin stream. Insert the pan in the broiler at the level farthest away from the heat.
5. After 10 minutes, turn the endive over and baste with the oil in the pan.
6. After 7 or 8 minutes, turn the endive over once more so the cut side will again be facing up. Baste again with the oil from the pan, directing it, as much as possible, between one leaf and another, and adding fresh, raw oil if necessary.
7. Bake for about 5 minutes, depending on the thickness of the endive. It is done when you can easily pierce the root end with a fork. Expect the tips of the leaves to be somewhat blackened. It is not only acceptable, but desirable. Serve hot or even lukewarm.

Purea di Borlotti agli Odori

PURÉED BEANS WITH HERBS

*I*N *THE* pursuit of certain lusty gratifications for the palate, no ingredient can take you further than beans. I have never known any beans I didn't like, but cranberry beans are among my favorites. Raw, they are marbled purple and white, but cooked, the color and, surprisingly, the taste are those of chestnuts. The purée from this recipe can be thought of as an earthier, tastier alternative to mashed potatoes. The beans cook, at first, with bay leaves, sage, and whole garlic to become deeply fragrant. They are mashed together with a potato for a lighter consistency. Béchamel gives their texture smoothness and polish, the grated cheese rich Parmesan flavor, and the parsley a cheery splash of color and a touch of freshness.

For 6 persons

2 to 2½ pounds fresh cranberry beans, or 1 to 1¼ cups dried, soaked overnight in water
2 bay leaves
2 garlic cloves, peeled

4 fresh or 3 dried sage leaves
1 medium potato, peeled and cut into 1-inch pieces
Salt

For the béchamel:

1 cup milk
2 tablespoons butter

1½ tablespoons flour
Pinch salt

⅓ cup extra virgin olive oil
½ cup freshly grated *parmigiano-reggiano* (Parmesan)

Black pepper in a grinder
2 tablespoons chopped parsley

1. Shell the beans and wash them, if using the fresh; drain them of their overnight soak, if using the dried. Put them in a pot with the bay leaves, garlic, sage, and enough water to cover by 3 inches. Cover and turn on the heat to medium low. Cook at a very slow simmer.

2. When the beans are almost tender, wash the cut-up potato and add it to the pot. When both beans and potato are tender, turn off the heat and stir in a little salt.

3. Drain the beans and potato, picking out and discarding the bay leaves, sage, and, if you can, the garlic. Pass them through a food mill fitted with a small-holed disk and into a bowl.

4. Make the béchamel as described on page 112. Add to the beans and potato along with the olive oil, grated cheese, and generous grindings of pepper. Taste and correct for salt.

5. Transfer to a serving bowl and sprinkle with the chopped parsley. Serve while still warm.

AHEAD-OF-TIME NOTE: The entire dish may be made in advance by several hours and reheated gently in a double boiler. Add the parsley just before serving.

Carciofi col Burro e il Parmigiano

ARTICHOKES WITH BUTTER AND PARMESAN

A *PART* of the artichoke most people discard, to their loss, is the stem. Once trimmed of its tough, green outer layer, the stem is all tender pulp, similar to the heart, with concentrated artichoke flavor. In this recipe the artichokes are stuffed with a mixture composed of their own chopped stems, plus garlic, parsley, and Parmesan. They are cooked entirely in butter. The taste is essence of artichoke, faintly aromatized by the garlic and parsley — delicate enough, in its savoriness, to accompany a broad variety of meat dishes.

For 4 persons

4 medium to large artichokes
1 lemon, cut in half
¼ teaspoon garlic chopped fine
2 tablespoons chopped parsley
3 tablespoons freshly grated *parmigiano-reggiano* (Parmesan)

Salt
Black pepper in a grinder
5 tablespoons butter

1. Detach the stems from the artichokes. With a paring knife trim away the entire green outer layer of the stems, leaving only the pale, tender core. Chop the core very fine and set it aside.

2. Clean the artichokes as described on page 80, snapping off all the dark green outer leaves at the base and slicing off 2 inches or more from the top of the exposed cone of leaves. Leave attached only the edible, tender, pale portion of the leaves that is close to the bottom of the artichoke. With the tip of a paring knife remove the small, prickly, purple-tipped leaves in the artichoke's hollow and scrape away the fuzzy choke beneath them. Rub all cut edges of the artichoke with lemon, squeezing the lemon all the while, to keep them from turning black.

3. In a small bowl combine the chopped artichoke stems, garlic, parsley, grated cheese, salt, and a few grindings of pepper. Mix thoroughly and divide the contents of the bowl into 4 equal parts.

4. Stuff each artichoke's cavity with 1 of the parts of the mixture.

5. Choose a lidded saucepan or sauté pan that can accommodate all the artichokes snugly. Put 1 tablespoon of the butter in the pan, put in the artichokes top side up, and put 1 tablespoon of butter over each artichoke. Pour in enough water to come ½ inch up the sides of the pan. Cover the pan and turn on the heat to medium.

6. After 10 minutes, check to see if there is still liquid in the pan and if the artichokes are done. If they are very fresh, they may already be tender, which you can determine by pricking them with a fork. If it enters easily, they are cooked. At this point, if there is still liquid left in the pan, uncover, turn up the heat, and boil

the liquid away, scraping loose any cooking residues from the bottom of the pan. On the other hand, if the artichokes are still tough and there is not sufficient liquid to continue cooking, add 2 to 3 tablespoons of water and cover the pan again. Continue checking every 8 to 10 minutes until the artichokes are tender. Depending on their freshness, it may take as long as 30 minutes to cook them.

7. When they are done, transfer the artichokes to a serving platter, pouring over them the little bit of juice left in the pan, if it is not too runny. If it is, reduce it over high heat. Serve the artichokes when lukewarm.

Spicchi di Carciofi in Tegame con la Pancetta

SLOW-COOKED ARTICHOKE WEDGES WITH PANCETTA

*N*EXT to steaming them, this may be the simplest way to do artichokes. There are no herbs, onion, or garlic, only some *pancetta*—the unsmoked kind—and white wine. To keep cooking time brief, and to expose as much of the vegetable as possible to the wine and *pancetta*, the artichoke is cut into bite-size wedges.

For 4 to 6 persons

4 large or 6 medium artichokes
Freshly squeezed juice of ½ lemon
3 tablespoons extra virgin olive oil
¼ pound *pancetta*, cut into thin strips,
    about 1 cup

Salt
Black pepper in a grinder
½ cup dry white wine

1. Trim the artichokes of the tough outer leaves and tops as described on page 80. Cut them into wedges about 1 inch broad at their thickest point. Place them in a bowl with cold water and the lemon juice.

2. Put the oil and *pancetta* in a sauté pan and turn on the heat to medium high.

3. Drain the artichokes and pat them thoroughly dry with a kitchen towel.

4. When the *pancetta* is well browned—but not crackling crisp—add the artichokes, salt, and several grindings of pepper. Stir, turning the artichokes over 2 or 3 times, then add the wine. When the wine has bubbled for about 1 minute, turn down the heat to medium and cover the pan. Cook until the artichokes are tender when pricked with a fork, about 30 minutes, depending on the freshness and youth of the vegetable. When the artichokes are done, if there are watery juices in the pan, uncover, turn up the heat, and evaporate the excess liquid.

Carote in Scapece

SAUTÉED CARROTS WITH VINEGAR AND OREGANO

*T*HE *scapece* method of frying vegetables, then steeping them in vinegar and herbs—described in the introduction to the recipe for *fusilli* with zucchini in *scapece,* on page 124—is triumphantly successful with carrots. The carrot's natural sweetness, reinforced with sugar, is in lively contrast to a chorus of sour and spicy seasonings.

For 4 to 6 persons

2 pounds carrots
3 tablespoons extra virgin olive oil
3 or 4 garlic cloves, peeled and cut in half
½ cup wine vinegar

½ teaspoon granulated sugar
1 teaspoon oregano
¼ teaspoon chopped hot red pepper
Salt

1. Peel and wash the carrots and slice them into rounds ¼ inch thick.
2. Bring a pot of water to a boil and drop in the carrots. Cook them just until they are slightly tender but still crunchy, not fully cooked. Drain and set aside.
3. Choose a skillet large enough to accommodate the carrots later, put in the oil and the garlic, and turn on the heat to medium high.
4. When the garlic becomes colored a light nut brown, remove it, put in the carrots, and turn up the heat to high. Cook the carrots for a minute or two, stirring them frequently.
5. Add the vinegar, sugar, oregano, hot pepper, and salt. Continue cooking, stirring from time to time, until all the liquid has evaporated. Transfer the carrots to a serving platter and serve either lukewarm or at room temperature. They taste best the day they are made, but they can be served a day or two later if you don't mind an accentuated sharpness in flavor.

Carote e Belga in Padella

SLOW-BROWNED CARROTS AND ENDIVE

IN THIS combination with carrots, endive substitutes for the long *radicchio di Treviso* I would use in Italy. (Also see *Tonnarelli* with Belgian Endive and Bacon on page 103.) Its appeal is based on the racy contrast of flavors and consistencies: the carrot sweet, the endive slightly bitter; the former firm, the latter creamily soft. The carrot must first be cooked slowly and at length, with butter and no liquid, to evaporate all the moisture that dilutes its flavor, and to keep the carrot rounds firm. Since the endive throws off much liquid, it is also, at first, cooked separately from the carrots; otherwise it would steam them. It takes only a few minutes' additional cooking together, after the preliminary separate procedures, to link the two vegetables' flavors.

For 4 to 6 persons

1 pound carrots, peeled and sliced
    into ¼-inch rounds
4 tablespoons butter
Salt

¾ to 1 pound Belgian endive,
    shredded lengthwise into strips
    ¼ inch wide

1. Choose a sauté pan or skillet that can accommodate all the carrots without crowding them. Put in the carrots and butter, and turn on the heat to medium low. Cook, stirring from time to time, until the carrots have greatly diminished in bulk, becoming withered and colored a light nut brown. It should take about 1 to 1½ hours. Sprinkle with salt, stir, and turn off the heat.

2. Transfer the carrots to a platter, using a slotted spoon or spatula in order to leave as much butter as possible in the pan.

3. Put the endive in the pan and turn on the heat to medium low. Cook, turning it over from time to time, until the endive becomes very soft, about 30 minutes. Add salt.

4. Return the carrots to the pan and cook for 5 minutes longer, together with the endive.

Variante con la Pancetta Affumicata

VARIATION WITH BACON

After step 2 of the preceding recipe, add to the pan ½ cup of bacon shredded very fine. Turn on the heat to medium and cook until the bacon becomes lightly browned but not crisp. Add the endive, cook until very soft, add salt, return the carrots to the pan, cook for 5 minutes longer, then serve promptly.

Cavolfiore con l'Uvetta e i Pignoli

CAULIFLOWER WITH RAISINS AND PINE NUTS

RAISINS and pine nuts disclose the southern origin of this dish. They do good work on the cauliflower. Those who are already fond of the vegetable will find new stimulus for their affection; those who are usually indifferent to cauliflower's aloof personality may be pleased to discover what reserves of flavor were waiting to be released by sautéing in olive oil with garlic, raisins, and pine nuts.

For 4 to 6 persons

1 ounce seedless raisins
1 young head cauliflower, about 1½ pounds
⅓ cup extra virgin olive oil
2 teaspoons garlic chopped fine

1 ounce pine nuts
Salt
Black pepper in a grinder
2 tablespoons chopped parsley

1. Soak the raisins in water for 15 to 20 minutes.

2. Trim the cauliflower of all its outer leaves except for the tender, almost totally white ones. Drop it into 4 quarts of boiling water. After the water returns to a boil, cook for 6 to 7 minutes until it is halfway done, that is, until you feel resistance when pricking it with a fork. Drain it and cut it into 1½-inch pieces.

3. When the raisins have finished soaking, drain them and squeeze them gently in your hands to force off excess liquid.

4. Choose a lidded sauté pan that can sub-sequently accommodate all the cauliflower pieces without overlapping. Put in the oil and the garlic and turn on the heat to medium without covering the pan.

5. When the garlic becomes colored a pale gold, add the cauliflower, raisins, pine nuts, salt, generous grindings of pepper, cover the pan, and turn down the heat to low. Cook for 8 to 10 minutes or more, stirring from time to time, until the cauliflower feels tender when tested with a fork. Sprinkle on the chopped parsley and serve hot.

PANCETTA AND ONIONS: TWO DIFFERENT WAYS

Onions and *pancetta*—the unsmoked Italian bacon—make one of Italian cooking's steadiest pairings. The two, chopped and sautéed, are a good flavor base for pasta sauces, roasts, stews, and some vegetable dishes. In the following two recipes, the *pancetta* and onions come together solely for their own delicious sake.

In the first of the two dishes, *pancetta* is the

principal ingredient in a stuffing that includes garlic, parsley, anchovies, and capers, with which large halved onions are baked.

The second recipe calls for very small onions. *Pancetta* forms the flavor base when it is browned in olive oil with rosemary. The onions are then browned whole in the *pancetta* until thoroughly *insaporite*—coated with its flavor. Next they are cooked with a solution of water and vinegar until they are tender.

Cipolle Ripiene al Forno

BAKED STUFFED ONIONS

For 4 to 6 persons

8 yellow onions, 3 to 3½ inches in diameter, about 1½ pounds
2½ ounces *pancetta,* chopped fine
2 tablespoons chopped parsley
1 teaspoon chopped garlic
8 flat anchovy fillets, chopped fine

2 tablespoons tiny capers
5 tablespoons extra virgin olive oil
2 tablespoons fine, dry, unflavored bread crumbs, toasted in a pan as described on page 21

1. Turn on the oven to 400°.
2. Peel the onions and drop them into a pot of boiling water. Cook for 10 to 12 minutes, depending on their thickness, then drain them.
3. Combine the *pancetta,* parsley, garlic, anchovy fillets, and capers. (If the capers are not the tiny variety, chop them a little first.)
4. Cut the onions in half across their width. Remove their centers, gutting the onions of half their rings. Chop the gutted rings very fine and add to the *pancetta,* parsley, and mixture. Add 1 tablespoon of the olive oil and mix thoroughly.
5. Choose a baking dish in which all the onion halves can fit comfortably and smear the bottom with 1 tablespoon of the olive oil. Place the onions cut side up in the dish and fill their center hollows with the chopped onion and *pancetta* mixture. Sprinkle the bread crumbs uniformly over the onions and trickle over them the remaining 3 tablespoons of olive oil. Bake in the uppermost level of the preheated oven for 45 minutes. Serve when lukewarm.

AHEAD-OF-TIME NOTE: When cooked, the onions may be kept for several hours at room temperature and reheated gently before serving.

Cipolline in Tegame con la Pancetta

PEARL ONIONS WITH PANCETTA, ROSEMARY, AND VINEGAR

For 6 persons

1 pound pearl onions (tiny white onions)
2 tablespoons extra virgin olive oil
1 tablespoon butter
6 ounces *pancetta,* cut into very narrow strips
1 teaspoon whole fresh or chopped dried
    rosemary leaves

2 tablespoons wine vinegar
Salt
Black pepper in a grinder

1.   In a saucepan bring enough water to a boil to cover the onions. When the water reaches a rolling boil, put in the onions. Cook for 5 minutes after the water returns to a boil, then drain. As soon as the onions are cool enough to handle, peel them and cut a cross into the root end.

2.   Choose a lidded skillet or sauté pan that can subsequently accommodate all the onions without crowding them. Put in the olive oil, butter, *pancetta,* and rosemary and turn on the heat to medium high. Cook the *pancetta* in the uncovered pan until it is lightly browned but not crisp.

3.   Add the onions and cook these until they are also lightly browned, turning them from time to time.

4.   Add the vinegar, salt, grindings of pepper, and ⅓ cup of water. Turn the onions once or twice, then cover the pan and turn down the heat to low. Cook until the onions are tender, turning them occasionally. If the onions are not truly tiny, it will take a little longer for them to cook and you may need to add water from time to time; do not, however, add any more than ¼ cup of water at one time, or the onions will cook with too much moisture, becoming soggy and losing intensity of flavor. Serve at once.

AHEAD-OF-TIME NOTE: The entire dish may be prepared an hour or two in advance and reheated gently over the burner just before serving.

Fagiolini con Pomodoro,
Aglio e Basilico

GREEN BEANS WITH TOMATO, GARLIC, AND BASIL

*E*ARLY in the summer, when basil's aroma is at its freshest, green beans are young and tender, and the first ripe tomatoes make scarlet pyramids at the vegetable stand, this is the kind of dish one's thoughts turn to. The beans are cooked entirely in the tomatoes' juices so their cool, vegetal flavor does not boil away in water, and, while they become tender, they retain a satisfying degree of firmness. I have had this as a vegetable dish and as a pasta sauce, and I was equally happy with both. When using it to sauce pasta, choose a firm-bodied tubular factory pasta such as *penne* or *rigatoni*.

For 4 to 6 persons

1 pound very ripe fresh tomatoes, or 1 cup
    canned Italian peeled plum tomatoes, cut
    up, with their juice (1½ pounds fresh or
    1½ cups canned if using as a pasta sauce)
1½ pounds green beans
½ cup extra virgin olive oil (plus
    2 tablespoons if using as a pasta sauce)

2 teaspoons garlic chopped not too fine
    (1 tablespoon if using as a pasta sauce)
Salt
Black pepper in a grinder
1 cup fresh basil leaves

1.   If using fresh tomatoes, rinse them in cold running water and drop them into a pot of boiling water. When the water returns to a boil, cook for about a minute, then drain and allow to cool. When cool enough to handle, peel them and cut them up in large pieces.

2.   Snap off the ends of the green beans and rinse the beans in cold water.

3.   Choose a sauté pan with a lid that can later accommodate all the green beans. Put in the olive oil and garlic. Turn on the heat to medium and sauté the garlic until it be-comes colored a pale gold.

4.   Add the tomatoes, turn up the heat, and cook for about 5 to 6 minutes.

5.   Add the green beans, turn down the heat to medium, sprinkle with salt and pepper, and cover the pan. Cook, stirring occasionally, until the green beans are tender but firm. If, when the beans are done, the juices in the pan are watery, remove the beans with a slotted spoon or spatula, turn up the heat, and boil away excess liquid. Then return the beans to the pan, mix in the basil leaves, and serve.

NOTE: If using this as a pasta sauce, do not add the basil to the pan. When the pasta is cooked and drained, toss with the beans and all the contents of the pan, add the basil leaves, toss again, sprinkle with the extra 2 tablespoons of olive oil, and serve immediately.

Purea di Fave con Cime di Rapa

PURÉED FAVA BEANS WITH BROCCOLETTI DI RAPE

*M*Y *FIRST* experience of *purea di fave* was in a villa near Perugia, midway through a long weekend celebrating the wines and country food of Umbria. As long as I shall have a working memory, the bliss that flooded my senses on that day in Umbria will endure as one of the best moments of my life at table.

Reconstituted dried fava beans are cooked and puréed with milk-soaked bread and olive oil. The parboiled greens are sautéed in olive oil scented with garlic. The two are put on a platter, the puréed fava below, the *broccoletti* above, and drizzled with a little raw olive oil. The flavor I find so affecting is monastically simple. It comes from the exchange between the creamy, mellow, nutty beans and the slightly bitter, garlicky strands of *broccoletti di rape,* and from the good olive oil that connects them both. Reverently is how I eat it, as slowly and as wordlessly as I can manage.

For 4 to 6 persons

1 pound dried fava beans
Salt
¼ cup milk
1½ slices good-quality, firm white bread
    trimmed of its crust

⅔ cup extra virgin olive oil, preferably
    Italian
1½ pounds *broccoletti di rape*
3 or 4 garlic cloves

1. Soak the dried beans overnight in a bowl of cold water.

2. The following day, drain the beans, put them in a pot with enough cold water to cover amply, and turn on the heat to medium high. Cover and cook for 5 minutes after the water comes to a boil.

3. Drain the beans, put them in a bowl of cold water, and peel them.

4. Put the peeled beans in a saucepan with enough cold water to cover amply and 2 teaspoons of salt. Cover, turn on the heat to medium, and cook at a steady simmer for about 30 minutes, until they are reduced to a pulp. If, during the cooking, you find there is not enough liquid in the pan, replenish with fresh water. Make sure, however, that by the time the beans have finished cooking, all the water has evaporated, leaving them moist but not soggy.

5. Put the milk in a saucepan and heat it until lukewarm but not simmering.

6. Put the white bread in a small bowl and pour the warm milk over it. Let soak for 5 minutes, then drain excess milk from the bread by squeezing it gently in your hands. Set aside.

7. Purée the cooked beans through a food mill into a bowl, using the disk with the smallest holes. Use a potato ricer if a food mill is not available.

8. Add ⅓ cup of the olive oil and the milk-

soaked bread and beat the mixture with a whisk or wooden spoon until it is blended smoothly. At this point, if you find that the consistency is too runny—it should be nearly as dense as mashed potatoes—return the fava to the pot and cook it down further, stirring frequently. Set aside.

9. Remove any very hard wooden stalks from the *broccoletti di rape* and peel the larger, more tender stalks. Rinse the greens thoroughly in cold water.

10. Choose a lidded saucepan that will accommodate all the greens. Put in 3 to 4 cups of cold water, cover, and turn on the heat to medium high. When the water boils, add 2 tablespoons of salt and the greens. Cover and cook, stirring occasionally, until the greens have become thoroughly tender but not mushy. Drain and set aside. Both the greens and the beans can now wait several hours at room temperature until you are ready to complete the dish and serve it.

11. Warm the puréed beans in a double boiler, stirring them frequently.

12. Peel and crush the garlic cloves. Put them in a sauté pan together with 3 tablespoons of the olive oil and turn on the heat to medium. Sauté the garlic until it becomes colored a pale gold, then remove it from the pan with a slotted spoon.

13. Add the cooked greens and sauté for 5 to 6 minutes, stirring them from time to time.

14. Taste both the beans and the *broccoletti di rape* and correct for salt.

15. Spread the puréed fava on a serving platter and over it distribute the *broccoletti*. Pour over both, in a thin stream, the remaining raw olive oil.

Lattuga al Forno con la Pancetta Affumicata

BAKED BOSTON LETTUCE WRAPPED IN BACON

*A*LONG with many other Italian cooks, I have always been intrigued by the fascinating role that plain salad greens can play in cooking. In this book, for example, see the *tonnarelli* on page 103 and the grilled endive on page 249; in *More Classic Italian Cooking*, see the stuffed lettuce soup on page 115. Boston lettuce is very similar to *cappuccina*, a tender Italian lettuce; in this recipe it gets its chance to show the remarkably expressive flavor it has once it is let out of the salad bowl.

The parboiled lettuce is wrapped with the butcher's best bacon, baked for a time, then topped with slices of milk-soaked bread, with beaten egg, nutmeg, and Parmesan, and baked some more until a crust forms on top. The rich taste makes this not only a strikingly interesting side dish but also a worthy course on its own.

For 4 to 6 persons

Baked Boston Lettuce Wrapped in Bacon (continued)

4 plump, full heads Boston lettuce
Salt
4 tablespoons butter
¼ pound bacon, sliced thin
⅔ cup freshly grated *parmigiano-reggiano*
    (Parmesan)

½ cup milk
6 thin slices good-quality, firm white bread
    trimmed of its crust
1 extra large egg or 2 smaller ones
Black pepper in a grinder
⅛ teaspoon grated nutmeg

1.   Cut the lettuce heads in half lengthwise and make a cut halfway into the root ends so they will cook more evenly.

2.   Soak the lettuce in several changes of clean cold water.

3.   Bring 4 to 5 quarts of water to a boil. Put in 3 tablespoons of salt. When the water resumes boiling, put in 2 lettuce halves. Boil for 7 to 8 minutes, then transfer to a colander, using a large slotted spoon. Repeat the procedure with the remaining lettuce halves, boiling them 2 at a time.

4.   Turn on the oven to 450°.

5.   When the lettuce is cool enough to handle, fold each half inward and squeeze it gently with your hand, forcing out as much water as possible. Leave the lettuce folded after squeezing.

6.   Choose an oven-to-table baking dish large enough to accommodate all the lettuce without overlapping. Smear the bottom of the dish with ½ tablespoon of the butter.

7.   Divide the bacon slices into 8 portions and use each to wrap a lettuce half. Lay the wrapped lettuce side by side in the baking dish. Place in the uppermost level of the oven and bake for 20 minutes.

8.   At the end of 20 minutes remove the baking dish, but do not turn off the oven. Sprinkle the top with half the grated cheese and a little bit of salt.

9.   Put the milk in a deep dish and soak the bread slices in it. When the bread has been well steeped, use it to cover the top of the lettuce in the baking dish.

10.   There should be a little milk left in the soaking dish, but if there is none put in 1 tablespoon of milk. Break the egg into the dish and beat it well together with a pinch of salt and liberal grindings of pepper. Pour the beaten egg over the bread in the baking dish. Combine the rest of the grated Parmesan with the nutmeg and sprinkle on top. Dot with the remaining butter and return the dish to the hot oven. Bake for another 15 minutes, or until the top has formed a golden brown crust. Serve when lukewarm.

Finocchi e Patate al Forno

BAKED FINOCCHIO AND POTATOES

*W*HEN, from a vegetable dish, one asks substance and discreet but interesting flavor, these unusual baked potato slices graced with the aroma of *finocchio* may be the simple answer.

For 4 persons

1 large or 2 small *finocchio* (fennel)
A baking pan, 14 by 10 inches or
    its equivalent
4 tablespoons butter
2 tablespoons vegetable oil

Salt
1½ pounds boiling potatoes, peeled,
    sliced into thin disks, and washed
Black pepper in a grinder

1.   Turn on the oven to 425°.
2.   Trim away the *finocchio* tops down to the bulb. Pull off and discard any bruised, discolored outer leaf. Cut the *finocchio* lengthwise into ¼-inch-thick slices. If parts of the *finocchio* separate from the slice do not worry, it is still usable.
3.   Wash the *finocchio* in 2 or 3 changes of cold water, shake dry, and place flat in the baking pan. Add the butter and oil and sprinkle with salt. Put the pan in the uppermost level of the preheated oven.
4.   Turn the *finocchio* over after about 10 minutes. Continue baking until halfway done.

Depending on the freshness of the *finocchio,* it may take another 5 to 10 minutes: When pricked with a fork it should feel firm and somewhat resistant.
5.   Add the potatoes, tossing them well with the *finocchio* to separate all the potato slices. Sprinkle with salt and add a few grindings of pepper. Return to the oven. Bake until the potatoes are tender, about 25 to 30 minutes, and the *finocchio* has become colored a light nut brown. Turn and baste the *finocchio* and potatoes every 8 to 10 minutes. Serve after allowing the dish to settle briefly out of the oven.

❧ *A PAIR OF EGGPLANT RECIPES* ❧

The following recipes differ in only two ways: The first is baked, the second grilled; parsley is the herb used for the first eggplant, rosemary for the second. The preparatory procedure is otherwise identical, and both are equally easy to execute. The baked eggplant with parsley is milder than the grilled, which develops piquancy because of both the grill and the rosemary.

Both eggplants can be served in a gratifying variety of ways: as a vegetable, hot off the fire, lukewarm, or at room temperature; as sauce for pasta; as a spread or dip. See the recipes that follow for specific instructions.

Melanzane al Forno

BAKED EGGPLANT WITH GARLIC AND PARSLEY

For 6 persons

1½ pounds small, skinny eggplants,
    or their equivalent in 1 or
      2 large eggplants
Salt

½ cup extra virgin olive oil
2 teaspoons chopped garlic
2 tablespoons chopped parsley
Black pepper in a grinder

1. *If using small eggplants:* Trim away the green tops and slice them in half lengthwise. Make small incisions in the flesh in a crisscross pattern, taking care not to cut so deeply as to puncture the skin.

If using large eggplants: Trim away the green tops and slice across their width into disks 1½ inches thick. On one side of each disk make crisscross incisions spaced 1 inch apart, taking care not to cut through to the other side.

2. Spread the eggplant slices on the inside wall of a large colander set over a bowl and sprinkle liberally with salt. Let stand for about 30 to 45 minutes, allowing as much as possible of their bitter juice to drain away.

3. Turn on the oven to 450°.

4. Choose a baking pan large enough to accommodate all the eggplant slices without overlapping. Smear the bottom lightly with a little bit of the olive oil. Place the eggplant in the pan; if using halved small eggplants, lay them skin side down; the slices of large eggplant, crosshatched side up.

5. Sprinkle the garlic and parsley over the eggplant, distributing it as uniformly as possible and pressing it into the cuts. Add a pinch of salt and several grindings of pepper. Pour half the olive oil over the eggplant, guiding it as much as possible into the cuts.

6. Place the pan in the uppermost level of the preheated oven. After 15 minutes, remove the pan, pour the rest of the olive oil over the eggplant, and return it to the oven. Bake for 15 or more minutes, until the eggplant feels as tender as dense cream when tested with a fork. Serve hot, lukewarm, or at room temperature. Do not refrigerate and reheat.

LEFTOVER NOTE: If enough eggplant is left over, it can be chopped fine, added to chopped garlic and parsley lightly browned in olive oil, and used as a sauce for *spaghettini.*

Melanzane in Graticola

GRILLED EGGPLANT

For 4 to 6 persons

2 pounds eggplant, preferably skinny ones,
    but at most no thicker than 3 inches
Salt
1 teaspoon chopped garlic

1 teaspoon chopped rosemary
Black pepper in a grinder
½ cup extra virgin olive oil,
    or more as needed

1.   Rinse the eggplants in cold water, trim away the green stem, and cut them in half lengthwise.

2.   Cut the exposed eggplant flesh in a crisscross diamond pattern, but do not cut through the skin. Sprinkle the cut sides liberally with salt and stand them along the side of a deep colander. Place the colander in a bowl or basin and let the eggplants rest for 30 to 45 minutes to allow their bitter juices to drain away.

3.   When the eggplants go into the broiler later, they should not be much closer than 12 inches to the heat. If the lowest grooves on which the broiler pan rests do not permit you to grill at that distance from the heat, place the pan directly on the bottom of the broiler. Turn on the broiler.

4.   Squeeze the eggplant halves gently, forcing any remaining liquid to run off.

5.   Spread the crisscross cuts slightly open and force into them a little garlic, rosemary, and a grinding of pepper. Pour part of the olive oil in a thin stream, guiding it into the cuts so that it seeps into the eggplant. Place the eggplants cut side up on the griddle of the broiler pan.

6.   After 7 to 8 minutes, baste the eggplants with a little more olive oil, particularly those that may be drier than others. Repeat the operation after another 7 minutes. After 2 to 3 minutes, test for doneness with a fork. The eggplants are done when their flesh becomes creamy tender. They may be served piping hot, lukewarm, or at room temperature.

ALTERNATIVE COOKING METHOD: I have discovered lately that if you have very skinny Italian or Chinese eggplants, they cook faster and to an equally flavorful conclusion in a skillet. Prepare the eggplants as described in steps 2 and 5, and place them skin side down in a pan with just enough oil to coat the bottom. Cover the pan and cook at medium high heat for about 6 minutes. Turn the eggplants over and cook, always keeping the pan covered for 1 to 2 minutes, then turn them over and cook until tender, about 2 more minutes, depending on the eggplants.

ADDITIONAL SERVING SUGGESTION: When cold, the eggplant flesh, scooped out and mixed with onion chopped very fine, makes a delicious spread on a grilled or toasted slice of good, crusty bread. Top with a few drops of raw extra virgin Italian olive oil.

Patate Maritate

BAKED SLICED POTATOES WITH MOZZARELLA
AND PARMESAN

*E*LISA, the woman from Benevento who gave me the recipes for pickled eggplant that appear on pages 50-2, is my mother's cleaning woman. When she arrives for work, the mutual good mornings are followed by a ritual exchange. I ask Elisa what she cooked the previous evening and, exultingly, she recites the specialties she prepared for her Giuseppe, trumpeting the names as though she were a general asked to cite the battles won.

Occasionally, a dish is new to me. One morning, to the usual question, Elisa exclaimed, *"Patate maritate!"* "Married potatoes? Married to whom?" I asked, not without the feeling that I was being led into a trap. But Elisa was serious: "Married to mozzarella, *signora*!"

Explanations followed, and so did the making of the dish. Sliced raw potatoes are layered in a pan with mozzarella and a mixture of Parmesan, garlic, and parsley, and they are baked for about 1 hour. There is nothing more to it than that, except that if you have available imported buffalo-milk mozzarella, use it. It will make a much happier marriage for the potatoes.

For 4 persons

1 pound boiling potatoes
¼ cup extra virgin olive oil
3 teaspoons chopped garlic
4 tablespoons chopped parsley
Black pepper in a grinder
¾ cup freshly grated *parmigiano-reggiano* (Parmesan)

Salt
5 tablespoons fine, dry, unflavored bread crumbs, toasted lightly in a pan as described on page 21
10 ounces whole-milk mozzarella, chopped fine or grated on a grater's largest holes

1. Turn on the oven to 400°.
2. Wash the potatoes in cold water, peel them, and cut them into very thin slices. Put the slices in a bowl and toss them with 2 tablespoons of the olive oil.
3. In a small bowl mix the garlic, parsley, liberal grindings of pepper, and the grated Parmesan.
4. Sprinkle the potatoes with salt and toss to season them uniformly.

5. Choose an oven-to-table baking dish where one-third of the potatoes will fit without too much overlapping. Grease the bottom and sides of the pan lightly with olive oil, then over it sprinkle 3 tablespoons of the bread crumbs.
6. Cover the bottom of the dish with a layer of potato slices, using one-third of the total amount, overlapping them only slightly if necessary. Over the potatoes spread half the Parmesan mixture from the small bowl, and over this sprin-

kle half the chopped or grated mozzarella. Cover with another one-third of the potatoes, then the remaining half of the Parmesan mixture, and over it the rest of the mozzarella. Top with the remaining one-third of the potatoes. Over them sprinkle the remaining 2 table-spoons of bread crumbs and pour the remain-

ing olive oil, distributing it in a thin stream.

7.   Place the dish in the uppermost level of the preheated oven. Bake for 50 to 60 minutes, until the potatoes feel tender when pricked with a fork. Allow to settle for a few minutes before serving.

Le Patate di Campagna

COUNTRY-STYLE POTATOES WITH GARLIC AND ROSEMARY

*L*ITTLE more than ten miles southwest of Bologna, a group of hills, covered with vines and cherry trees, forms a territory known as Monte San Pietro. My husband escorts our classes there for a visit to a wine estate. After the visit, we all meet for dinner in a *trattoria* in the nearby hamlet of Stiore. Known as Perla, the *trattoria* is restaurant, billiard parlor, *grappa* bar all at the same time, a gathering place for the local farmhands, other workers, and sometimes their employers. Four old men on mandolins and guitars play polkas, waltzes, tangos. Perla is run by a family of three, each performing a vital function: The mother cooks; Perla, the daughter, waits on table; the father plays cards and drinks with the customers.

Stiore is so small it is not on any map, but the people, the music, the food have registered it securely in the memories of hundreds of my students. One of the dishes that many of them have asked the recipe for is Perla's mother's potatoes, pan-fried in lard with garlic and rosemary. What makes them memorable is a thin, crackling crust that encloses a tender, almost creamy center. It is not at all difficult to do, as you will find from the instructions in this recipe.

For 6 persons

Country-Style Potatoes with Garlic and Rosemary (continued)

2 pounds boiling potatoes
½ cup lard
3 or 4 garlic cloves, peeled but not crushed
1 short sprig fresh rosemary, about 3 inches
    long, or 1 teaspoon dried leaves
Salt

1. Peel the potatoes, dice them into 1-inch cubes, wash them in 2 or 3 changes of cold water, and pat them dry with a kitchen towel.

2. Choose a lidded heavy frying pan, preferably iron, where the potatoes will fit without overlapping. Put in the lard and turn on the heat to medium high.

3. When the lard is wholly melted and hot (but take care not to let it reach the burning point), put in the potatoes, the garlic, and the rosemary. Turn the potatoes until all the pieces are coated with lard. Cover the pan and turn down the heat to medium.

4. Cook without stirring until the sides of the potatoes in contact with the bottom of the pan have formed a well-colored crust. Loosen the potatoes from the pan and turn them. Add salt.

5. Cover the pan and cook for 5 or more minutes, until the sides of the potatoes next to the bottom of the pan have formed a crust. Test the potatoes for doneness with a fork. If tender, raise the heat and cook, uncovered, for 1 minute more, stirring frequently.

6. Transfer the potatoes to paper towels to drain, using a slotted spoon or spatula. Do not let them sit on the paper towel longer than a moment, however, or they will lose crispness.

NOTE: You can, if you must, substitute vegetable oil for the lard, but the crust will not turn out so thin and crisp and the potatoes will be slightly less savory.

Patate e Cipolle alla Pizzaiola

BAKED POTATOES AND ONIONS WITH TOMATOES AND OREGANO

*W*HEN we say a dish is *alla pizzaiola* — pizza style — we don't have mozzarella in mind; we mean with tomatoes and oregano. In this instance, potatoes and onions are sliced into rounds, coated with olive oil and oregano, topped with diced fresh tomatoes, and baked. The oregano-spiked aroma may recall pizza, but the honest taste of fresh tomatoes and good olive oil is, alas, one it shares with no corner-store pizza I know.

For 6 persons

1½ pounds boiling potatoes
½ cup extra virgin olive oil, plus 1 table-
    spoon for greasing the baking pan
Salt
Black pepper in a grinder
1½ teaspoons dried oregano, or
    2½ teaspoons fresh
1 pound yellow onions
5 or 6 ripe, fresh plum tomatoes,
    or equivalent quantity of other tomatoes

1. Peel the potatoes, slice them into ¼-inch-thick disks, soak them in cold water, and then dry them thoroughly with kitchen towels.

2. Turn on the oven to 400°.

3. Put the sliced potatoes in a bowl together with ¼ cup of the olive oil, salt, a liberal grinding of pepper, and half the oregano. Toss well to coat the potato slices evenly.

4. Peel the onions and slice them into rounds ¼ inch thick.

5. Peel the tomatoes, discard the seeds, and cut the tomatoes into ½-inch squares. The yield should be 1 to 1½ cups.

6. Choose a baking pan made of oven-to-table ware and grease the bottom with 1 tablespoon of olive oil.

7. Place the sliced potatoes and onions in the pan making parallel rows of each, overlapping each slice roof-tile fashion. If at first there does not seem to be space for all the slices, bunch them a little closer together at a straighter angle.

8. Spread the cut-up tomatoes over the potatoes and onions, adding some more salt and pepper and the remaining oregano.

9. Pour the rest of the olive oil over the vegetables, spreading it evenly in a thin stream.

10. Bake in the uppermost level of the oven for about 45 minutes, or until the potatoes and onions are tender when pricked with a fork. Serve directly from the baking dish.

PEPPERS OUTSIDE, PEPPERS INSIDE:
❖ TWO RECIPES ❖

The colors that summer brings to Italy's vegetable stalls are, no doubt, enchanting, but, month after month, the never-diminishing mounds of peppers, tomatoes, and zucchini can be an exasperating challenge to a cook's imagination. Volunteering a new recipe for peppers can be the warmest demonstration of neighborliness. Here are two that have already earned me some goodwill.

The first recipe uses red peppers as containers for a zucchini stuffing. The peppers are peeled while raw and cut into gondola-shaped sections. These are heaped with zucchini sliced into disks and coated with a mixture of olive oil, garlic, parsley, cheese, bread crumbs, and thyme. They differ from other stuffed peppers because,

being sectioned, the stuffing is uncovered and forms a lovely crust. Moreover, the peppers have been skinned before cooking so one can bite into them without having to deal with the pesky peel.

In the other recipe it is the peppers that are the stuffing and tomatoes the containers. For the stuffing, the peppers are marinated in a blend of basil, garlic, capers, olive oil, and bread crumbs. I prefer yellow peppers, if I have a choice. If they are not available, it doesn't trouble me too much to use red peppers, even if they repeat the tomatoes' color. Green peppers are not as desirable because of their tart, unripe taste.

In addition to serving as vegetable dishes, both of these make excellent appetizers or handsome additions to a buffet.

Peperoni al Forno Ripieni di Zucchine

BAKED RED PEPPERS STUFFED WITH ZUCCHINI

For 6 persons

4 large sweet red bell peppers
½ cup extra virgin olive oil, plus 1
    tablespoon for greasing the baking pan
1 teaspoon garlic chopped fine
3 tablespoons chopped parsley
¼ pound fontina or Emmenthal cheese,
    grated to yield about 1 cup

⅓ cup fine, dry, unflavored bread crumbs,
    plus 2 tablespoons
½ teaspoon thyme
Salt
Black pepper in a grinder
5 small zucchini, scrubbed thoroughly clean
    and sliced into the thinnest possible rounds

1. Turn on the oven to 400°.

2. Peel the peppers with a swivel-action peeler, using a side-to-side sawing motion and a light touch (see page 21). Cut the peppers into sections at least 2½ inches broad or in halves. Following the peppers' creases when you cut will help you obtain boat-shaped sections. Remove the seeds and core.

3. Choose a bowl ample enough to accommodate all the sliced zucchini later. Put in ¼ cup of the olive oil, the chopped garlic, parsley, grated cheese, the ⅓ cup of bread crumbs, the thyme, salt, and grindings of pepper. Mix well, then add the sliced zucchini. Stir thoroughly to coat all the zucchini surfaces with the mixture.

4. Stuff the sectioned peppers with the zucchini, filling them generously to make a nicely rounded mound.

5. Choose an oven-to-table dish in which the peppers will fit in a single layer, grease the bottom with 1 tablespoon of the olive oil, then put in the peppers, stuffing facing up. Over the peppers sprinkle the 2 tablespoons of bread crumbs and pour the remaining ¼ cup of olive oil, in a thin stream.

6. Bake in the upper third of the oven, until the peppers are tender and the surface of the zucchini stuffing has formed a nice brown crust, about 45 minutes.

7. Serve when no longer piping hot, or even at room temperature.

Pomodori Gratinati Ripieni di Peperoni

GRATINÉED TOMATOES STUFFED WITH PEPPERS

For 4 persons

2 pounds ripe, but firm tomatoes
1 sweet bell pepper, preferably yellow,
    but if unavailable, red
8 to 10 fresh basil leaves, chopped to yield
    2 tablespoons
1 teaspoon chopped garlic
¼ cup capers

5 tablespoons fine, dry, unflavored bread
    crumbs, toasted lightly in a pan as
    described on page 21
⅓ cup extra virgin olive oil
Salt
Black pepper in a grinder

1.   Cut the tomatoes in half horizontally and scoop out all the seeds.

2.   Cut open the pepper and remove the stem, the whitish core, and all the seeds. Cut it into ½-inch squares and put these in a bowl.

3.   Add the basil, garlic, capers, 3 tablespoons of the toasted bread crumbs, 2 tablespoons of the olive oil, salt, and grindings of pepper. Mix well and let steep for at least 30 minutes or up to 1½ hours.

4.   Turn on the oven to 400°.

5.   Choose a shallow baking pan large enough to hold the tomatoes in a single layer. Grease the bottom of the pan lightly with olive oil and place the tomatoes on it cut side up.

6.   Stuff the tomatoes with the marinated pepper mixture from the bowl, heaping it high enough to form a little mound. Over them sprinkle the remaining bread crumbs and olive oil.

7.   Place the pan in the uppermost level of the oven. Bake for 45 to 60 minutes, depending on the size of the tomatoes. They must lose most of their moisture, and the tops should become a golden brown color. It is perfectly all right if the skin becomes partly blackened, because when you eat them you will scrape off the flesh that is easily loosened from the skin. Serve at room temperature or slightly warm.

Porcini ai Ferri

GRILLED FRESH PORCINI MUSHROOMS

O*F THE* extraordinary variety of fresh ingredients that have begun to appear on American markets, none is more wonderful than *boletus edulis,* the wild mushrooms that Italians call *porcini.* Some are native to American woods—

Grilled Fresh Porcini Mushrooms (continued)

I have had *porcini* from California, Washington state, Georgia, Vermont; some are imported from Italy. A warning: Do not pick mushrooms in the woods on your own until you have learned to distinguish clearly the *edulis,* which means edible, species from the poisonous; buy them only from a knowledgeable vendor.

No fresh mushroom, and no other wild mushroom, morels and chanterelles included, remotely approaches the bosky flavor and satin texture of *porcini.* And no cooking method liberates so much of that flavor as grilling or sautéing with olive oil and garlic. Whether on the grill or in the skillet, *porcini* must cook slowly until tender throughout. High heat stuns the flavor and withers the texture. Good olive oil is indispensable. Butter is the doom of *porcini*: You might as well be cooking *champignons* if you are going to cook them in butter.

In the recipe you will find chestnut leaves listed as an optional ingredient. I don't know if they are ever found in America. But if you should be cooking in Europe, try them. It is the Genoese way of doing it, and it enhances the mushrooms with an aroma most congenial.

For 4 persons if served as a side dish;
if served as a full course, double the quantity

1 pound fresh *porcini* mushrooms
5 or 6 chestnut leaves (optional, if available)
⅓ cup extra virgin olive oil
2 teaspoons chopped garlic

1 tablespoon chopped parsley
Salt
Black pepper in a grinder

1. Turn on the broiler, if cooking indoors, or light the charcoal. The coals will be ready for cooking when they have become evenly coated with white ash. They should be medium, rather than flaming, hot.

2. With a paring knife trim away from the mushrooms' stems any part that has soil attached. Wash the mushrooms rapidly under running water and pat thoroughly dry with paper towels.

3. Detach the stems from the caps and cut the stems lengthwise into slices about ½ inch thick.

4. Put both the mushroom caps, with their round side facing up, and the stems, in a single layer, on a grilling rack and place the rack about 8 inches away from the source of heat, in the broiler or over the coals.

5. After 5 to 7 minutes, depending on the thickness of the caps, turn the caps and stems over. Rotate their place on the rack if you find that some are cooking faster than others. Cook for 4 to 5 minutes more.

6. *If you are using a rack and broiler pan indoors:* Remove the rack from the pan. Place the optional chestnut leaves on the bottom of the pan, brushing them lightly with olive oil. Put the mushrooms on the leaves (or on the bottom of the pan if you have no leaves) with the caps' round side facing down. Pour the remaining olive oil over the mushrooms, then sprinkle with the chopped garlic and parsley, salt, and generous grindings of pepper. Return to the broiler for another minute or two.

If you are grilling over coals: Season the mushrooms with the olive oil, chopped garlic and parsley, salt, and grindings of pepper and cook for 1 to 2 more minutes, depending on the thickness of the caps and the heat of the coals. About half a minute before removing the mushrooms from the fire, moisten the chestnut leaves (if you have them) with olive oil and place them over the mushrooms. Serve the mushrooms on top of the leaves.

ALTERNATIVE METHOD USING A SKILLET

Fresh *porcini* can be just as delicious when done in a skillet. Use the same ingredients and follow the cleaning procedure of the above recipe. Coat the bottom of the skillet lightly with olive oil, put in the mushrooms with the caps' round side facing up, and turn on the heat to medium low. After 5 to 7 minutes, turn the mushrooms over and sprinkle with salt and pepper. In a little while you will find that the mushrooms release liquid. Turn up the fire for as long as it takes to evaporate that liquid. Then season the mushrooms with the remaining olive oil, the chopped garlic, and the chopped parsley and cook for another 2 to 3 minutes. If you have the chestnut leaves, moisten them with olive oil and place them over the mushrooms for half a minute while they finish cooking. Serve the mushrooms piping hot on top of the leaves.

Spinaci e Ceci

SPINACH AND CHICK-PEAS
WITH OLIVE OIL AND LEMON

*I*T WAS in the home of my mother-in-law, Julia Hazan, that, newly married, I became acquainted with an Italian cooking of which, until then, I had known nothing: the cooking of Italian Jews. While some of Julia's dishes came from the same Bolognese tradition I had grown up close to, others took familiar ingredients, but phrased them with an accent new to me, that of the eastern Mediterranean. No one who was treated to Julia's delicious cooking, or to the tenderness with which it was dispensed, forgot either. The spinach and chick-peas recipe given here is one of the dishes that reminds me most vividly of her.

Except for cleaning the spinach—and it is essential here to use only fresh

Spinach and Chick-peas with Olive Oil and Lemon (continued)
spinach—it is an effortless dish to prepare. Its plush layers of satisfaction rest on the reciprocally flattering qualities of chick-peas and spinach, enriched by olive oil and, with a touch typical of the cuisine, quickened by lemon juice.

NOTE: Those who would like to know more of this many-flowered branch of Italian cooking should get themselves a copy of *The Classic Cuisine of the Italian Jews* by Edda Servi Machlin, a cookbook to treasure.

For 4 to 6 persons

1½ pounds fresh spinach
Salt
19-ounce can chick-peas

½ cup extra virgin olive oil
¼ cup freshly squeezed lemon juice

1. Wash the spinach as described on pages 55–6, but do not chop it.
2. Put the spinach in a pot with 2 tablespoons of salt. Add no water except for that which clings to the spinach. Cover and cook over medium heat until the spinach stems are slightly softened but not too limp. Drain.

3. Drain the chick-peas and squeeze off their peel, one by one.
4. Put the spinach, chick-peas, olive oil, and lemon juice in a saucepan, cover, and cook over medium heat for 10 to 15 minutes. Stir occasionally. Taste and correct for salt. Serve while still hot.

➤ SAUTÉING ZUCCHINI: ➤ THE DEFT ITALIAN TOUCH

With a grasp of the Italian way with vegetables, a cook could nearly stretch zucchini's prodigious natural endowments to make a whole cuisine. Think of the *antipasti,* the soups, the *risotti,* the pasta sauces, the fish and meat courses with zucchini. They are past numbering. The group of four recipes that follow demonstrates how, with slight variations in seasonings and cooking vehicles, the basic sautéing method can produce dishes significantly individual in flavor and presentation.

In the first recipe, the flavor base is onion and parsley cooked in olive oil and butter. To keep the taste subtle, the onion is softened, but not allowed to become colored. The zucchini are cut into sticks and cooked with the base, adding thyme for fragrance and crumbled bouillon to round out the savor.

In the succeeding recipe, the richer flavor base is olive oil, onion, and bacon, the onion sautéed until lightly colored. The zucchini is cooked in it with no other seasoning than salt and pepper.

The third version leads to spry, savory zucchini that is equally endearing as a vegetable course or a sauce for pasta. This time, the flavor base is butter and garlic, the garlic sautéed to a pale gold. The rounds of zucchini cook in it until they are done, and basil and Parmesan are stirred in.

In the last recipe of the four, a suavely aromatic one, zucchini is cut into sticks and, over high heat, *insaporiti*—coated with a flavor base of olive oil, sliced garlic, and sage. White wine is added gradually and the zucchini are cooked until tender and gleaming.

Zucchine Trifolate al Timo

SAUTÉED ZUCCHINI WITH THYME

For 4 to 6 persons

1½ pounds fresh, young zucchini, soaked in water for 20 minutes
4 tablespoons extra virgin olive oil
2 tablespoons butter
⅓ cup onion chopped fine

⅓ cup chopped parsley
1 bouillon cube, crumbled
Salt
Black pepper in a grinder
2 teaspoons thyme

1. When the zucchini have soaked the recommended amount of time, wash them in several changes of cold water, rubbing them with your hands or with a stiff brush to dislodge all grit.

2. Trim away both ends from each zucchini and cut into sticks about 3 inches long and ½ inch thick.

3. Put the oil, butter, onion, and parsley in a sauté pan and turn on the heat to medium. Cook, stirring from time to time, until the onion wilts, but without letting it become colored.

4. Add the zucchini sticks, the crumbled bouillon cube, a pinch of salt, grindings of pepper, and thyme. Stir well and cover the pan. Cook, stirring occasionally, for 20 to 30 minutes, depending on the youth and freshness of the zucchini, until they are tender. Serve at once or even lukewarm.

Zucchine con la Pancetta Affumicata

ZUCCHINI WITH BACON

For 6 persons

1½ pounds firm, young zucchini, soaked in water for 20 minutes
⅓ cup extra virgin olive oil
1½ cups onion sliced very thin
¼ pound bacon, cut into strips ⅛ inch wide
Salt
Black pepper in a grinder

1. When the zucchini have soaked the recommended amount of time, wash them in several changes of cold water, scrubbing their skin with your hands or with a stiff brush to dislodge all grit. Trim away both ends from each zucchini and slice the zucchini into disks about ¼ inch wide.

2. Choose a lidded sauté pan that can subsequently accommodate all the zucchini rather snugly. Put in the olive oil, onion, and bacon and turn on the heat to medium high. Cook, stirring from time to time, until the onion becomes colored a pale gold.

3. Add the zucchini, turn them over once or twice, cover the pan, and turn down the heat to medium. Cook for 12 to 15 minutes, uncover the pan, add a little salt and a few grindings of pepper, and cook for another 2 to 3 minutes in the uncovered pan, stirring frequently. Serve promptly.

AHEAD-OF-TIME NOTE: The entire dish can be prepared several hours in advance and reheated gently just before serving.

Zucchine Saltate col Basilico

SAUTÉED ZUCCHINI WITH BASIL

For 4 to 6 persons

2 pounds young zucchini, as small and fresh as possible
1 tablespoon chopped garlic
6 tablespoons butter
Salt
Black pepper in a grinder
1 cup fresh basil leaves, torn by hand into small pieces
2 to 3 tablespoons freshly grated *parmigiano-reggiano* (Parmesan) (⅔ cup if using as a pasta sauce)

1. Soak the zucchini in cold water for at least 20 minutes.

2. Wash them in several changes of cold water, rubbing them with your hands or with a stiff brush to remove all soil. If the skin still feels a little gritty, peel the thin outer layer.

3. Remove both ends from each zucchini and slice the zucchini into very thin disks.

4. Choose a lidded sauté pan where the zucchini can fit later with little or no overlapping. Put in the garlic and butter and turn on the heat to medium high.

5. Sauté the garlic until it becomes colored a very pale gold, then add the zucchini, turning up the heat to high. Cook the zucchini, turning them over frequently, until they become colored a light brown on each side.

6. Turn down the heat to medium low, add salt and pepper, mix thoroughly, and cover the pan. Cook, stirring from time to time, until the zucchini are tender but still firm.

7. Uncover the pan and, if the zucchini have thrown off any liquid, raise the heat and quickly evaporate the liquid, stirring frequently.

8. Add the basil, stir, and turn off the heat.

9. If serving it as a vegetable dish, mix in 2 to 3 tablespoons of grated cheese and serve immediately. If using it as a pasta sauce, when tossing the zucchini with the cooked pasta add 2/3 cup of grated cheese.

Zucchine alla Salvia e Vino Bianco

SAUTÉED ZUCCHINI WITH SAGE AND WHITE WINE

For 4 persons

2 pounds young, firm zucchini, as small as possible, preferably 1 inch in diameter
1/3 cup extra virgin olive oil
4 medium garlic cloves, peeled and cut into thin disks

7 or 8 fresh sage leaves, or 4 or 5 dried leaves, chopped
1 cup dry white wine
Salt
Black pepper in a grinder

1. Soak the zucchini in cold water for 20 minutes.

2. Wash them in several changes of cold water, rubbing them with your hands or with a stiff brush to dislodge all grit.

3. Trim away both ends, split the zucchini in half lengthwise, then cut them into thin, short sticks about 1/2 inch thick and 3 inches long.

4. Choose a sauté pan large enough to contain all the zucchini later with little or no overlapping. Put in the oil, garlic, and sage leaves and turn on the heat to high. When the oil is very hot, add the zucchini. Cook, stirring frequently, until the zucchini become lightly colored. Altogether, this step should take less than 3 minutes.

5. Add the wine, 1/4 cup at a time, turning down the heat to medium high. Stir frequently, adding more wine as it evaporates. Sprinkle with salt and grindings of pepper. Cook until the zucchini are tender but still firm and their surface becomes glossy and all the wine and any watery liquid have evaporated. Serve immediately.

Parmigiana di Zucchine

ZUCCHINI, PARMESAN STYLE

IN THINKING about zucchini, it occurred to me that there was no reason one couldn't cook them *alla parmigiana,* like eggplant. Basically, that is what this dish is, with some changes I thought suit the zucchini. I have eliminated oregano; instead of baking the dish with uncooked tomatoes, I first made a light tomato sauce with olive oil, onion, and parsley; finally, I enriched the grated Parmesan with beaten egg. Its taste is neither superior nor inferior to eggplant *parmigiana:* It is different, perhaps more polished and urbane.

For 6 persons

1½ pounds zucchini, soaked in water for 20 minutes

Vegetable oil for frying

4 tablespoons extra virgin olive oil

3 tablespoons onion chopped very fine

¼ cup chopped parsley

1⅔ cups canned Italian peeled plum tomatoes, cut up, with their juice

Salt

Black pepper in a grinder

2 eggs

½ cup freshly grated *parmigiano-reggiano* (Parmesan)

An oven-to-table baking dish of any standard size

10 ounces whole-milk mozzarella, cut into thin slices

1. When the zucchini have soaked the recommended amount of time, wash them in several changes of cold water, scrubbing their skin with your hands or with a stiff brush to dislodge all grit.

2. Trim away both ends from each zucchini and cut the zucchini lengthwise into slices ¼ inch thick.

3. Put enough vegetable oil in a skillet to come ¾ inch up the side of the pan. (The oil will be discarded later, so it would be more economical to use a small skillet and fry the zucchini a few at a time in several batches.) Turn on the heat to high. When the oil is very hot, slip in as many slices of zucchini as will fit very loosely. Cook them on both sides until they become colored a light golden brown. Using a slotted spoon or spatula transfer the zucchini to blot on a plate lined with paper towels or to a draining rack.

4. When all the zucchini are done, discard the oil in which they were fried, wipe the skillet clean, and put in the olive oil and chopped onion. Turn on the heat to medium.

5. When the onion becomes colored a pale gold, add the parsley, stir once or twice, add the tomatoes, sprinkle with salt and several grindings of pepper, stir well, and turn down the heat to medium low. Cook for about 20 minutes, stirring from time to time, until the oil separates from the tomato and floats free.

6. Turn on the oven to 400°.

7. Beat the eggs in a small bowl. Set aside 1½ tablespoons of the grated cheese and beat the rest into the eggs.

8. Spoon a little bit of the tomato sauce into an oven-to-table baking dish, spreading it evenly over the bottom. Cover the bottom with a layer of fried zucchini, cover the zucchini with mozzarella slices, spread some sauce over the mozzarella, and top with some of the egg and cheese mixture. Repeat the procedure, building up layers in the same sequence. Top with a layer of zucchini lightly daubed with tomato sauce, sprinkling over it the remaining 1½ tablespoons of grated cheese.

9. Bake in the uppermost level of the preheated oven for 30 minutes. Allow to settle out of the oven for at least 10 to 15 minutes before serving. It is also excellent when served at room temperature.

AHEAD-OF-TIME NOTE: The entire dish can be made up to 1 day in advance and reheated in a 300° oven until it is warm, but not piping hot.

Frittelle di Zucchine

ZUCCHINI FRITTERS

*I*F ONE can do everything else with zucchini, why not fritters? What I especially like about these fritters is their texture: The vegetable is shredded along its length, producing fine zucchini filaments that cook quickly yet maintain their firmness. Aside from the zucchini themselves, the fritter batter consists of garlic, parsley, Parmesan, egg, and bread crumbs, a composition clearly familiar to Italian cooks.

The fritters are fine on their own, but they are even lovelier with a sauce of fresh tomatoes, onion, and butter, as indicated below.

For 4 to 6 persons

Zucchini Fritters (continued)

1 pound zucchini, as young, small,
   and fresh as possible, soaked in water
   for 20 minutes
3 tablespoons chopped parsley
1 teaspoon garlic chopped extremely fine
1/2 cup freshly grated *parmigiano-reggiano*
   (Parmesan)

3 eggs, not too large
1/4 cup fine, dry, unflavored bread crumbs,
   plus 1 cup spread on a plate
Black pepper in a grinder
Vegetable oil
Salt

1.   When the zucchini have soaked the recommended amount of time, drain the zucchini and wash them in several changes of cold water, rubbing their skin with your hands or with a stiff brush to dislodge all grit. Trim away both ends from each zucchini and, using a grater or food processor disk with large shredding holes, shred them lengthwise.

2.   Put the shredded zucchini in a bowl with the parsley, garlic, and grated cheese.

3.   Beat the eggs in a small bowl and add them to the zucchini. Add the 1/4 cup of bread crumbs, a few grindings of pepper, and mix thoroughly.

4.   In a skillet or sauté pan put enough vegetable oil to come at least 1/2 inch up the side of the pan. Turn on the heat to medium high.

5.   When the oil is hot, add salt to the zucchini, mix quickly, and form flat patties about 3 inches in diameter and 1/2 inch thick. Dredge the patties in the bread crumbs on the plate, and slip them into the pan. Cook, turning them over, until they have formed a crust on both sides. Transfer them to a plate lined with paper towels or to a draining rack to blot. Do not fry more patties at one time than will fit loosely in the pan. Serve hot, warm, or at room temperature.

NOTE: Do not salt the patty mixture before you are ready to fry or it will throw off some liquid.

AHEAD-OF-TIME NOTE: The fritters may be cooked a day or two in advance, refrigerated in plastic wrap, and served with the fresh tomato sauce that follows.

Frittelle di Zucchine col Pomodoro Fresco

ZUCCHINI FRITTERS WITH FRESH TOMATO SAUCE

For 6 persons

1/2 pound fresh, ripe, firm plum tomatoes
3 tablespoons butter
1 cup onion chopped very fine

Salt
Black pepper in a grinder
1 recipe Zucchini Fritters (preceding recipe)

1.   Use the tomatoes, butter, onion, salt, and pepper to make the sauce described on page 143.

2.   When the sauce is done, add the fritters to it, turn down the heat to medium, and warm up the zucchini in the sauce for 4 to 5 minutes, turning them over from time to time. Transfer the fritters, together with the entire contents of the pan, to a warm platter and serve.

Il Fricandò di Casa Mia

MIXED SLOW-COOKED VEGETABLES

*T*HE French word *fricandeau* describes a veal dish with sauce. In the dialect of Rome, transliterated into *fricandò,* it came to mean a medley, a hodgepodge, and, metaphorically, a messy situation. From there it became the name of a dish of widely assorted vegetables, no longer related to the original French cooking term. A "mess" it may be, but a gloriously exuberant one.

It is a preparation so susceptible to improvisation and individual style that nearly every family I know makes a *fricandò* of its own. The one given here is mine. The vegetables I like to use are peppers, fresh tomatoes, eggplant, green beans, and zucchini. The flavor base is olive oil, onion, and garlic, chopped coarse. The vegetables cook together in a single pot, but as you will find in the recipe, they go in at different times. Basil and hot pepper provide the finishing touch of fragrance and spice.

For 4 to 6 persons

1 sweet bell pepper, preferably yellow, but if unavailable, red
3 small or 2 medium zucchini
6 tablespoons extra virgin olive oil
2 cups onion sliced thin
2 garlic cloves, chopped rather coarse
1½ pounds ripe plum tomatoes, or 1½ cups canned Italian peeled plum tomatoes, drained

1 medium eggplant or ¾ pound small eggplants
½ pound young green beans
8 to 10 fresh basil leaves
½ teaspoon hot red pepper, or to taste
Salt

1.   Remove the bell pepper's core and seeds, skin it raw with a peeler, and cut it lengthwise into ¼-inch-wide strips.

2.   Soak the zucchini in cold water for 20 minutes.

3.   Put the oil and onion in a 12-inch sauté pan and turn on the heat to medium. When the onion is halfway to being tender, add the garlic. Stir, cook for 4 to 5 minutes, then add the bell pepper. Turn over all the ingredients once or twice.

4.   While the vegetables are simmering, bring

Mixed Slow-Cooked Vegetables (continued)

a pot of water to a boil. Drop in the fresh tomatoes, boil for 1 to 2 minutes, then drain and set aside to cool. (Omit this step if using canned tomatoes.)

5. Wash the eggplant in cold water, cut off green stem, cut into 1-inch cubes, add to the pan, and turn down the heat to medium low.

6. Trim both ends off from all the green beans, wash the beans, and add them to the pan. Turn over with the other ingredients.

7. Drain the zucchini and scrub them under running water with a rough cloth to remove any grit embedded in the skin. Trim away both ends from each zucchini, cut the zucchini into 1-inch pieces, and add them to the pan. Turn over all the vegetables 2 or 3 times.

8. Peel the fresh tomatoes, cut them into large pieces, and add them to the pan. (If using canned tomatoes, cut them up and put them in the pan.) Turn up the heat to medium and turn over all the vegetables.

9. Wash the basil, shake it dry, tear it into small pieces, and add it to the pan, mixing it with the other vegetables.

10. Add the hot pepper, stir, add salt, stir again 3 or 4 times, and taste and correct for seasoning. The moment all the vegetables are tender when pricked with a fork, the dish is done. If there is more liquid in the pan than seems desirable, raise the heat and boil it away while stirring the vegetables. Allow to cool for 3 to 4 minutes before serving.

AHEAD-OF-TIME NOTE: The entire dish may be completed up to 1 day in advance and reheated just before serving.

Salads

*N*EARLY everyone I meet who is tasting Italian food on its home ground for the first time is affected by the sparkling good flavor of salads in Italy. In salads, the chief characteristics of Italian cooking are conspicuously displayed: the simplicity of seasonings, the sure feel for compatibility of ingredients, the shunning of fussiness. You will notice that in none of the salads in this chapter is any other oil used but extra virgin olive oil; there are no herb or other flavored vinegars, only pure wine vinegar; there are no fruits, except for citrus; no cream cheeses; no sticky, treacly dressings. Clean, clear, vivacious taste is what Italian salads aim for.

Insalata di Finocchio col Peperone Rosso e el Olive Nere

FINOCCHIO SALAD WITH RED PEPPER AND BLACK OLIVES

*C*RISP white *finocchio* rings, glossy black olive wedges, firm strips of red bell pepper—all sprinkled with parsley—give this simple salad a liveliness of appearance, texture, and taste that more complex compositions seldom equal.
For 4 to 6 persons

2 medium to large *finocchio* (fennel)
½ sweet red bell pepper
6 or 7 black Greek-style olives
Optional: 2 teaspoons of the preserved hot
  peppers from the recipe on page 48

½ teaspoon chopped parsley
3 tablespoons extra virgin olive oil
Salt
Black pepper in a grinder
2 teaspoons wine vinegar

1. Cut off the tops of the *finocchio* and discard any of the stalks that are bruised, discolored, or wilted. Trim the base, cutting off a slice about ⅛ inch thick. Cut the *finocchio* horizontally, across its length, into the thinnest slices you can, to produce ¼-inch rings. Soak the slices in 2 or 3 changes of cold water, drain them, and dry them thoroughly, using a salad spinner or simply

Finocchio Salad with Red Pepper and Black Olives (continued)

wrapping them in a towel and shaking them sharply. Place the *finocchio* slices in a salad bowl or deep serving platter.

2. Remove all seeds and any of the whitish core from the ½ pepper. Pare away the skin with a peeler, as described on page 21. Cut the pepper into strips about 1 inch long and ¼ inch wide. Add these to the salad bowl.

3. Cut the olives into very thin wedges. Discard the pits and add the olives to the bowl. Put in the optional hot peppers. On top sprinkle the chopped parsley.

4. Just before serving, toss the salad with the olive oil, salt, generous grindings of pepper, and the vinegar.

Insalata di Limone, Cetriolo e Peperone

LEMON, CUCUMBER, AND PEPPER SALAD

*T*HE only fruits used in Italian salads are either oranges or lemons, because of their citric tartness. The refreshing coolness of both the taste and the prevailing colors in this salad is particularly welcome after a fish course. Also see the orange and cucumber salad on page 414 of *More Classic Italian Cooking*.

For 4 to 6 persons

2 or 3 lemons (depending on size)
Salt
1 sweet red bell pepper
2 cucumbers, preferably the so-called
   English variety without seeds

Extra virgin olive oil
Black pepper in a grinder
1 tablespoon parsley chopped coarse

1. Wash the lemons and slice them, with the rind on, as thin as possible, but no thicker than ⅛ inch. With the tip of a paring knife pick out all the seeds you can, in particular the cut ones, which secrete a bitter oil.

2. Put the lemon slices in a small bowl and sprinkle liberally with salt.

3. Cut the bell pepper lengthwise along its creases. Remove the stem, core, and seeds. Skin the pepper with a peeler as described on page

21 and cut the flesh into the thinnest possible strips, no more than ¼ inch thick. Set aside.

4. Using a mandolin, the single long slit of a four-sided grater, or the thin slicing disk in a food processor, slice the cucumber paper thin, leaving the peel on. If using a regular cucumber, first wash it under a strong jet of cold running water, rubbing it vigorously with a rough cloth. Set the sliced cucumber aside.

5. When ready to serve, choose a very shal-

low bowl or deep serving dish where the ingredients can be spread out. Line the bottom with cucumber slices. Drain the lemon and put the slices over the cucumber, allowing a border of cucumber to show. Repeat the concentric arrangement with the peppers, placing them over the lemon. Sprinkle with olive oil, pouring it in a thin stream in a figure 8 pattern to distribute it evenly. Add a few grindings of pepper and top with the chopped parsley. Just before serving, but not earlier, sprinkle with salt.

Insalata di Pomodori, Cetrioli, Cipolla e Basilico

TOMATO, CUCUMBER, ONION, AND BASIL SALAD

*T*HE salad tomatoes we use in Northern Italy are usually underripe, even partly green, a practice that shocks most visitors from America. I have never known anyone, however, to have suffered from eating them. The reason we choose tomatoes that are not fully ripened is that we prize their firmness and slightly tart, sprightly taste. On the other hand, in Central and Southern Italy, from Tuscany to Sicily, it is the tender, sweet, well-ripened tomato, the kind Northerners would be more likely to use for sauce, that is preferred for salads. Whether you do it the Northern way or not, tomato, cucumber, onion, and basil are the components of the fundamental Italian salad to which one assigns the traditional palate-cleansing role toward the close of the meal. In this salad, and whenever else it is used raw, onion is soaked in several changes of cold water to sweeten it.

For 4 to 6 persons

1 cup red Bermuda onion cut into very thin slices
1 pound slightly underripe, firm tomatoes
1 cucumber
6 or 7 fresh basil leaves

¼ yellow bell pepper (optional, if available)
⅓ cup extra virgin olive oil
Salt
Black pepper in a grinder (optional)
2 tablespoons red-wine vinegar

Tomato, Cucumber, Onion, and Basil Salad (continued)

1. Put the sliced onion in a bowl with cold water to cover. Squeeze the onion gently in your hand—but do not crush it—forcing some of its sharp acid out into the water. Let soak for 7 or 8 minutes, drain, refill the bowl with fresh water, and put the onion back into the bowl. Repeat the operation until the onion has soaked for about 30 minutes in at least 4 changes of water. Drain the onion, drying it in a salad spinner or blotting it on paper towels, then put it in a salad bowl.

2. Wash the tomatoes, skin them with a peeler, cut into ¼-inch-thick wedges, remove any seeds embedded in runny or gelatinous pulp, and add the tomato to the bowl.

3. Wash and peel the cucumber, trim off the ends, cut it into very thin rounds, and add it to the bowl.

4. Wash the basil in cold running water, shake it as dry as you can, tear it into small bits, and add it to the bowl.

5. Remove the core and seeds from the optional ¼ yellow pepper. Skin the pepper with a peeler as described on page 21 and cut it into very thin strips. Add it to the bowl.

6. Dress the salad only when ready to serve it. Add the oil, salt, optional grindings of pepper, and the vinegar—in that order—to the bowl. Toss repeatedly to season all the ingredients uniformly. Taste and correct for oil, salt, pepper, and vinegar. Serve at once with good, crusty bread on the side.

Insalata Cotta e Cruda di Melanzane, Peperoni, Pomodoro e Cipolla

COOKED AND RAW SALAD WITH EGGPLANT, PEPPERS, TOMATOES, AND ONION

ROASTED eggplant and bell peppers are the only cooked ingredients here. The spicy taste of the eggplant that perks up this salad comes from roasting it whole over a gas burner. If you don't have gas, it can also be done under a broiler or in an oven heated to its maximum setting.

For 4 persons

½ large red Bermuda onion, sliced very thin
1 pound eggplant, preferably small,
    young ones
Salt
2 sweet bell peppers, preferably yellow,
    but if unavailable, red

4 fresh, ripe, firm plum tomatoes
Black pepper in a grinder
½ cup extra virgin olive oil
2 tablespoons wine vinegar

1.   Place the sliced onion in a bowl of cold water. Squeeze the onion tightly with your hands, drain after 7 to 8 minutes, refill the bowl with fresh water, and put the onion back in water. Soak for at least 30 minutes—the longer the better—in several changes of cold water.

2.   Wash the eggplants, but do not trim them of their stems. Place over a burner and turn on the heat to high. (If you do not have gas burners, see introductory remarks above about using the broiler as an alternative.)

3.   Roast the eggplants on all sides, using the stems or 2 spoons to turn them. Do not puncture the skin. In about 10 minutes, when the eggplants feel soft if pressed with a spoon, they should be done. Remove from the heat.

4.   As soon as the eggplants are cool enough to handle, peel, discard the stems, and cut the flesh into lengthwise strips about ½ inch wide. Sprinkle with salt and set aside.

5.   Roast the peppers over the burner in the same manner as the eggplant, charring the skin on all sides. Place them in a paper or plastic bag and twist it tightly closed. Before the peppers cool completely, remove them from the bag, peel them, split them lengthwise to remove the core and seeds, and cut the flesh into lengthwise strips about ½ inch wide. Set aside.

6.   Skin the tomatoes raw with a peeler and cut them into ¼-inch wedges. Pick out most of the seeds with the tip of a paring knife.

7.   Place the strips of eggplant along the bottom of a serving bowl. Over the eggplant arrange the tomato wedges in a sunburst pattern. In the center place the peppers.

8.   Drain the onion, dry it by shaking it in a cloth or a salad spinner, and spread it over the other ingredients in the bowl. Sprinkle with salt, grindings of pepper, the olive oil, and the vinegar. Bring to the table, toss, and serve.

AHEAD-OF-TIME NOTE: The salad may be prepared and composed even a day in advance, in which case hold back the salt until ready to serve. When prepared in advance, the tomato becomes a little softer, but absorbs the agreeable flavors of the other ingredients.

Insalata di Patate
con la Pancetta Affumicata

POTATO SALAD WITH BACON

DICED browned bacon, with all its browning juices, is tossed with sliced boiled potato in this stout-flavored salad. It is best served after marinating for several hours.

For 6 persons

2 pounds boiling potatoes
¼ cup extra virgin olive oil
½ pound slab bacon, diced into ¼-inch cubes

Salt
1 tablespoon chopped parsley

1.   Wash the potatoes in cold water, put into a pot with enough water to cover amply, cover, and bring to a boil. Cook until tender, then drain. Peel the potatoes as soon as they are cool enough for you to handle. Slice them thin after they have cooled off a little longer so that you can cut them into compact slices. If they are too hot, the slices will crumble.

2.   Put 2 tablespoons of the olive oil and the diced bacon in a skillet and turn on the heat to medium high. Brown the bacon, turning it from time to time, but do not let it become crisp.

3.   Pour the entire contents of the pan over the potatoes together with a sprinkling of salt. Toss well and allow to rest before serving for at least 1 hour or up to 4 to 5 hours at room temperature.

4.   When ready to serve, add the remaining 2 tablespoons of olive oil and the chopped parsley, and toss well.

Insalata di Lenticchie e Cetriolo

LENTILS AND CUCUMBER SALAD

THE interesting combination that lentils and cucumbers make is even more fascinating when it is served with the lentils still slightly warm.

For 6 persons

1 cup lentils
⅓ cup extra virgin olive oil

Salt
Black pepper in a grinder

1½ cups cucumber shredded into fine strips
1 tablespoon red-wine vinegar, or more
    to taste

1 onion, preferably the red variety, sliced very
    thin and soaked in cold water as described
    on page 22

1.   Put the lentils in a pot together with 3 cups of water, cover, and turn on the heat to medium. When the water comes to a boil, turn down the heat to low and cook at a gentle simmer for 15 minutes. The lentils are done when they are tender but firm and with their skins intact.

2.   Drain the lentils and put them in a serving bowl. Dress them immediately with olive oil, salt, and a liberal grinding of pepper.

3.   When the lentils are lukewarm, add the cucumber, the vinegar, the onion, toss well, and serve.

NOTE: The salad may also be served at room temperature instead of lukewarm. In that case, add the cucumber and vinegar only when ready to serve; otherwise the cucumber will throw off liquid as it steeps in the salt and become soggy.

Finocchi in Insalata con Salsa Piccante

COOKED FINOCCHIO SALAD WITH SAVORY DRESSING

W*HEN finocchio* is boiled, it develops sweetness and its anise fragrance becomes light as a whisper. The dressing that complements it so well is an unusual one of parsley, anchovies, and grated Parmesan.

For 6 persons

3 large *finocchio* (fennel)
5 tablespoons parsley chopped fine
8 flat anchovy fillets chopped fine
Salt
Black pepper in a grinder

2 tablespoons wine vinegar
2 tablespoons freshly grated *parmigiano-reggiano* (Parmesan)
½ cup extra virgin olive oil

1.   Cut off the *finocchio* tops down to the bulb. Trim away a thin slice from the flat bottom of the root end. Discard any blemished or discolored outer leaves. Thinly peel the thickest outside leaves to remove some of the threads.

Soak the *finocchio* in cold water for about 15 minutes, then rinse in 2 or 3 changes of water.

2.   Bring 4 to 5 quarts of water to a boil and drop in the *finocchio*. Cook until the root end feels tender but firm when pricked with a

Cooked Finocchio Salad with Savory Dressing (continued)

fork. Drain and set aside to cool completely.

3. In a small bowl put the chopped parsley, anchovies, salt, pepper, vinegar, and grated cheese. Mix thoroughly, beating the ingredients together with a fork until they become blended into a homogeneous pulplike consistency.

4. Trickle the olive oil into the bowl in a thin stream, beating it into the dressing with a fork.

5. Squeeze the *finocchio* gently with your hands, forcing out any water. Cut it in half lengthwise, then into wedges about 1 inch thick. Place the wedges on a platter and pour the dressing over them. Serve at room temperature.

Insalata di Fagiolini Marinati

COLD, HERB-FLAVORED MARINATED GREEN BEANS

ONE of the vegetables that marinates best is green beans, absorbing seasonings without compromising the beans' firmness. Note that the beans are put into the marinade while they are still hot and thus most receptive to the vinegar and the other flavorings.

For 4 to 6 persons

2 tablespoons chopped parsley
8 to 10 fresh basil leaves, chopped to yield
   2 tablespoons
1 teaspoon oregano
5 tablespoons wine vinegar
2 tablespoons onion chopped very fine

2 garlic cloves, peeled and crushed
1 pound green beans
⅓ cup extra virgin olive oil
Salt
Black pepper in a grinder

1. Choose a bowl large enough to accommodate the green beans later and put in the parsley, basil, oregano, and vinegar. Let steep for 10 minutes.

2. Add the onion and garlic, mix, and let steep for at least 30 minutes.

3. Snap off the ends of the green beans, rinse them in cold water, and drop them into boiling salted water. Drain when still very firm.

4. Add the green beans, while still hot, to the bowl and marinate for a minimum of 1 hour and as much as 5 or 6. Mix thoroughly from time to time.

5. Serve the beans at room temperature, adding the olive oil, and season with salt and grindings of pepper to taste just before serving.

Insalata di Rinforzo col Cavolfiore

CAULIFLOWER SALAD WITH RED PEPPER, OLIVES, AND ANCHOVIES

*T*HIS IS A SICILIAN salad traditionally made to be consumed during the week between Christmas and New Year's. More of it is made than can be eaten the first day, and each day thereafter fresh ingredients are added to replenish the ones consumed. That is the explanation of the name *insalata di rinforzo,* "reinforced salad." The original version has pickles, which I have replaced here with red bell pepper. It is admittedly less seasonal, but I found the pepper's mildness desirable in a salad that can become quite sharp.

For 4 to 6 persons

1 head cauliflower, about 1½ pounds
2 tablespoons capers
4 flat anchovy fillets, chopped coarse
½ cup sweet red bell pepper, peeled, cored, and cut into strips

10 black Greek-style olives, pitted and halved
Salt
Black pepper in a grinder
⅓ cup extra virgin olive oil
2 tablespoons wine vinegar

1.   Discard the large outer leaves of the cauliflower and rinse it in cold water. Cut a cross into the root.

2.   Bring at least 6 cups of water to a boil. Add the cauliflower, cover the pot, and cook until the stem of the cauliflower is easily pierced by a fork, 20 minutes or more, depending on the cauliflower. Drain and let cool.

3.   When the cauliflower is cool, break up the clusters into bite-size pieces or slightly larger and put them in a salad bowl.

4.   Add all the other ingredients, toss well, taste and correct for seasoning, and serve.

Insalata di Riso con Verdure e Fagioli

RICE SALAD WITH VEGETABLES AND BEANS

O*NE* of my favorites among all rice salads. The cooked ingredients— cranberry beans and diced boiled zucchini—are mingled with tomatoes, cucumbers, and bell peppers. The brisk olive oil and lemon dressing includes basil, garlic, and oregano.

For 6 persons

2 medium zucchini
1 pound fresh cranberry beans
   (unshelled weight); or ½ cup dried,
   soaked overnight; or half a 19-ounce can,
   drained
Salt
1¼ cups long-grain rice
5 tablespoons extra virgin olive oil
¼ cup freshly squeezed lemon juice
½ teaspoon garlic chopped very fine
1 teaspoon oregano

Black pepper in a grinder
1 cucumber, peeled and diced into
   ¼-inch cubes
4 to 6 ripe plum tomatoes (depending on size),
   skinned raw with a peeler, seeded, and
   diced into ¼-inch cubes
1 yellow or red sweet bell pepper, quartered,
   seeded, cored, skinned raw with a peeler,
   and diced into ¼-inch cubes
6 to 8 fresh basil leaves, cut into narrow strips

1. Soak the zucchini in cold water for at least 20 minutes.

2. If using fresh beans, shell them and wash the beans in cold water. If using dried beans, drain them of their overnight soak and rinse them in cold water. Put either fresh or soaked dried beans in a pot and pour in enough water to cover by at least 3 inches. Do not add salt. Cover the pot and bring to a slow, steady simmer. Cook until tender, then drain and set aside to cool. If using canned beans, drain and set aside.

3. Drain the zucchini, rinse them in cold water, and scrub them vigorously with a rough cloth to remove all grit from the skin. Do not

cut off their ends. Put them in a pot of water without any salt and boil until just tender but still firm. Drain and set aside to cool. When cold, trim away both ends and dice the zucchini into ¼-inch cubes.

4. Bring a pot of water to a boil, add salt, and, as the water resumes boiling, put in the rice. Cook until the rice is tender but firm. Drain, transfer to the bowl in which you will subsequently serve the salad, and toss with 1 tablespoon of the olive oil.

5. Put the remaining olive oil, the lemon juice, chopped garlic, oregano, and several grindings of black pepper in a small bowl. Beat with a fork until the ingredients are blended

into a homogeneous sauce for dressing the salad.

6. Add all the diced vegetables and the beans to the bowl containing the rice. Pour the dressing over them, add the basil, and toss thoroughly. Serve after 1 hour or even several hours later.

AHEAD-OF-TIME NOTE: The salad is excellent, or even better, served the following day, slightly chilled.

Bagnet

GREEN PIEDMONTESE DRESSING
FOR RAW TOMATOES, BOILED POTATOES,
OR BOILED FISH

*T*HIS earthy, parsley-green specialty of Piedmont is as good on fish as it is on salad. In addition to the parsley, it is composed of vinegar-soaked bread, garlic, hard-boiled egg yolk, and anchovies. All of it is liquefied in a food processor or blender, which does a job superior to the old Piedmontese hand-chopped method.

2 cups

½ cup crumb (the soft, crustless part) from
    good-quality country-style bread
½ cup red-wine vinegar
½ tightly packed cup parsley leaves
½ teaspoon chopped garlic

1 hard-boiled egg yolk
2 or 3 flat anchovy fillets
¾ cup extra virgin olive oil
Black pepper in a grinder
Salt

Green Piedmontese Dressing for Raw Tomatoes, Boiled Potatoes, or Boiled Fish (continued)

1.   Cut up the crumb and put it in a small bowl. Pour the vinegar over it. Let the crumb steep until it is thoroughly soaked, then squeeze the vinegar out of it with your hand.

2.   Put the crumb, parsley, chopped garlic, egg yolk, and anchovy fillets in a food processor. Turn the processor on and, with the motor running, trickle in the olive oil in a very thin stream.

3.   Transfer to a small bowl, add liberal grindings of pepper, taste and add as much salt as it requires.

ADDITIONAL SERVING SUGGESTIONS: For boiled fish or shrimp, serve on the side in a sauceboat. (See page 178 on boiling fish in the Italian manner.)

For boiled potatoes, spread some *bagnet* on the potatoes after they are sliced, but still warm, and reserve some to serve on the side.

For raw tomatoes, choose, ripe, firm plum tomatoes, split them in half lengthwise, remove the seeds, and fill the cavity with *bagnet*.

AHEAD-OF-TIME NOTE: Bagnet can be prepared 2 or 3 days in advance and refrigerated. Return to room temperature and stir before using.

Sweets, Fruit, and Ice Cream

Torta di Amaretti e Cioccolato

AMARETTI AND CHOCOLATE CAKE

*H*OW this recipe got into my files I no longer recall. It had been there for years, and, when I finally got around to trying it, I wished I had done it sooner. I ought to have known that *amaretti* and chocolate make an ideal match, neither one too sweet, both with that fine, faint touch of bitterness so bracing on the palate. This is not a cake that rises much, but it is moister than its low profile might lead one to suspect. There are few desserts that a topping of homemade whipped cream does not do some good to, and on this one, I think, it would be particularly apt.

Up to 8 portions

½ pound butter, softened to room
temperature, plus 1 tablespoon for
smearing the baking pan
1 cup granulated sugar
A bowl for beating egg whites—preferably,
but not indispensably, a copper bowl
washed with vinegar and salt, rinsed
thoroughly, and dried
5 eggs

½ cup flour, plus 1 to 2 tablespoons
for dusting the pan
10 pairs of *amaretti* (Italian macaroons),
full size (about 4 ounces unwrapped), not
the miniatures, ground to a powder in a
blender or food processor
2 ounces semisweet baking chocolate, grated
fine
A 10- to 12-inch springform baking pan

1. Combine the softened butter and the sugar in a bowl and beat until the mixture becomes creamy and fluffy.

2. Break an egg, put the white in the copper or other bowl, and add the yolk to the butter and flour mixture. Beat the yolk in rapidly with a whisk. Repeat the operation with the remaining eggs, beating in 1 yolk at a time.

3. In a separate bowl mix the ½ cup of flour and the ground *amaretti*. Add to the butter,

sugar, and egg mixture, beating in a little at a time until it is all thoroughly incorporated.

4. Add the grated chocolate to the mixture, mixing it in thoroughly.

5. Turn on the oven to 350°.

6. Beat the egg whites until they form stiff peaks. Gently stir 3 to 4 tablespoons of beaten egg whites into the cake mixture to loosen its consistency slightly, then fold in the remaining egg whites.

7. Smear the inside of the baking pan with the tablespoon of butter, dust with the 1 to 2 tablespoons of flour, turn the pan upside down and give it a knock against the work counter to shake off excess flour.

8. Pour the cake mixture into the pan and bake in the uppermost level of the preheated oven for 1 hour. The cake is done when a toothpick poked into it comes out dry.

9. Loosen the side of the springform pan and, when the cake has settled a little while, detach it from the bottom of the pan.

NOTE: While baking, this cake will sometimes swell and then subside. It is nothing to be concerned about.

Bünet

*F*OR this specialty from her native Piedmont, not published in any of the sources I have seen, I am indebted to my friend Graziella Torti. *Bünet* is smooth, dark, and delicious, somewhat like a pudding in consistency, but so much silkier and buoyant than puddings ever seem to be. It is best served chilled.

About 8 portions

For the caramel:

⅔ cup granulated sugar
2 tablespoons water

A 10-inch ring mold

---

1 dozen pairs of *amaretti* (Italian macaroons)
2 cups milk
7 tablespoons granulated sugar
4 extra large eggs
3 tablespoons unsweetened cocoa powder

2 tablespoons rum
1 tablespoon Amaretto liqueur
Whipped cream topping made with 1 cup heavy cream and 1 teaspoon granulated sugar (optional)

1. Make the caramel: Put the sugar and water in a small, preferably thin-bottomed saucepan. Turn on the heat to high and melt the sugar until it is a dark brown color. Do not stir, but tilt and rotate the pan to keep the sugar from sticking while it is melting.

2. The instant the sugar has become caramelized to a dark brown, pour it into the ring mold, turning and tilting the mold to coat it evenly with sugar.

3. Turn on the oven to 375°.

4. Crumble the *amaretti* and put them in a mixing bowl.

5. Warm up the milk in a saucepan over medium heat. When it comes to a simmer, pour it in the bowl over the *amaretti*, together with the 7 tablespoons of sugar. Let the *amaretti* steep in the hot milk until thoroughly soaked; then, using a wooden spoon, mix to a creamy consistency, making sure that

the sugar has completely dissolved.

6. In another bowl beat the eggs with a whisk until they are soft and foamy.

7. Add the cocoa powder to the eggs, stir well, then add it to the *amaretti* and milk mixture, mixing it in thoroughly.

8. Add the rum and the Amaretto liqueur, mix well, then pour the entire contents of the bowl into the caramel-coated mold.

9. Choose a baking pan large enough to accommodate the mold comfortably, put some water in the pan, and set the mold in the water. Place over a burner and, over medium heat, bring the water to a gentle simmer. Transfer the pan together with the mold to the middle level of the preheated oven.

10. Bake for 40 minutes, but test for doneness after 35 minutes. If a knife inserted into the *bünet* comes out dry, the dessert is done and should be removed from the oven. If the blade comes out moist, it will need the additional 5 minutes.

11. When the *bünet* is done, remove it from the oven and remove the mold from the pan. When cool, place the mold in the refrigerator for a minimum of 2 hours—it is best to leave it in overnight.

12. To unmold, place the mold again in a pan with some water and bring the water to a boil over a burner. Remove from the heat, loosen the dessert from the mold by sliding a knife blade all around the sides, then turn over onto a serving platter. When ready to serve, top with the whipped cream, if desired.

Bomba di Mandorle alla Veneziana

VENETIAN ALMOND CAKE

VENETIAN recipes for almond cakes would fill a not-too-little book: Every family, every pastry shop appears to have a version of its own. This one is among the least common. Its appearance is supposed to suggest a halved cannonball bristling with almond and citron "shrapnel"—hence the name *bomba*. The batter, in addition to almonds, citron, and raisins, features the quickening presence of the grated peel of an entire lemon.

About 8 portions

Venetian Almond Cake (continued)

½ cup seedless raisins, soaked in water for
    30 minutes
1 cup shelled, unpeeled almonds, blanched
    and peeled
3 ounces candied citron diced very small
10 tablespoons butter, softened to room
    temperature, plus additional butter for
    smearing the baking sheet
⅓ cup granulated sugar

2 eggs
1⅔ cups flour
Grated peel of 1 lemon (outer skin with none
    of the white pith beneath)
½ cup milk
1 ounce fresh cake yeast, or 1 package active
    dry yeast
Salt

1.   Drop the almonds into boiling water. Remove them after about 1½ minutes, draining them well. Put the almonds on a damp cloth towel, close the towel over them, and rub the almonds vigorously with the towel. The friction will remove the skin from all or most of them. If any almonds are left with the skin still on, squeeze it off with your fingers. Pat the skinned almonds dry with a fresh towel.

2.   Put half the peeled almonds and half the citron in a food processor and process until ground very fine, or chop by hand.

3.   Put the butter in a large mixing bowl, add the sugar, and mix with a wooden spoon until the butter becomes creamy.

4.   Add 1 whole egg and the yolk of the other egg, reserving its white for later. Continue to mix until well amalgamated with the butter.

5.   Add the flour, mixing it in thoroughly a little at a time.

6.   Add the grated lemon peel, mixing well to distribute it uniformly.

7.   Warm the milk slightly until it is just lukewarm, then dissolve the yeast in it. When the yeast begins to bubble, add the milk to the bowl together with the chopped almonds and citron, mixing them in evenly.

8.   Drain the raisins, squeeze as much liquid as possible out of them, dust them very lightly with flour, and add them to the batter in the bowl, together with a pinch of salt, mixing them in uniformly.

9.   Cover the bowl with a clean cloth and place in a warm corner of the kitchen to let the batter rise for about 1 hour.

10.   Turn on the oven to 375°.

11.   Chop the remaining almonds into coarse pieces.

12.   Smear the bottom of a baking sheet with butter.

13.   Rework the batter for a minute or two, using the wooden spoon. Shape it into a ball with your hands—you will find it a bit sticky— and place it on the baking sheet. Smooth the surface of the ball as well as you can with a moistened spatula.

14.   Beat the remaining egg white lightly and brush it over the surface of the ball.

15.   Stud the ball with the cut-up almonds and the remaining diced citron, distributing them over the entire exposed surface and pressing them in firmly.

16.   Place the baking sheet in the middle level of the preheated oven and bake for 40 minutes. Test the cake by probing with a long thin skewer. If it comes out dry, the cake is done.

17.   Remove from the baking sheet and transfer to a cooling rack.

NOTE: In studding the cake, candied orange peel can be substituted for the citron.

Torta di Cioccolato con Uvetta e Pignoli

CHOCOLATE CAKE WITH RAISINS AND PINE NUTS

*T*HIS low-rising, compact chocolate dessert somewhat resembles firm fudge or brownies, to which the raisins and pine nuts bring a distinctly Mediterranean flavor.

For 8 persons

⅓ cup seedless raisins
1 cup granulated sugar
8 tablespoons butter, softened to room temperature
3 eggs, separated
5 tablespoons milk

1⅔ cups flour, plus 2 tablespoons for dusting the raisins and pan
2½ tablespoons unsweetened cocoa powder
½ cup pine nuts
Salt

1. Turn on the oven to 350°.
2. Soak the raisins in lukewarm water for 20 to 30 minutes.
3. Put the sugar and softened butter in a mixing bowl and beat them with a whisk to a foamy consistency.
4. Add the egg yolks to the bowl and then the milk, in a very thin, slow stream, mixing all the ingredients thoroughly.
5. Mix in the 1⅔ cups flour a little bit at a time.
6. Drain the raisins and pat them thoroughly dry with kitchen towels. Dust them with the 2 tablespoons of flour, shake them in a strainer to remove excess flour, and add them to the mixing bowl, together with the cocoa and the pine nuts. Mix until all the ingredients are well amalgamated.
7. Whip the egg whites with a pinch of salt until they form stiff peaks, then fold them lightly into the mixture in the bowl.
8. Lightly grease the bottom of a 10-inch springform pan with butter, dust it with flour, then turn it upside down and knock it once or twice against the work counter to shake away excess flour. Pour in the cake batter and level it with a spatula. Place the pan in the uppermost level of the preheated oven. Bake for 50 minutes, or until a toothpick inserted into the cake comes away clean.

Torta Ricciolina

ANGEL HAIR NOODLES AND ALMONDS PIE

*T*ORTA RICCIOLINA is a pastry cook's interpretation of noodles *alla bolognese*. It looks like pasta, indeed it is pasta, but it is nonetheless a dessert — the most charming one, I think, Bolognese bakers have created. The noodles, cut into the thin strands known as angel hair, are put in raw. If you are making your own pasta, cut the noodles by hand because the narrow cutter on the pasta machine makes them too broad for this recipe. If you buy them ready-made, make sure they are still pliant, not dried.

To complete the pasta conceit, a mixture representing Bolognese sauce is made with chopped almonds and citron combined with cocoa. Layers of fluffed-up noodles are then alternated with the almond and cocoa "sauce."

When baked, the top layer of noodles and almond mixture turns dark and crisp; the inner layers stay moist, and the flavor is dense. The consistency and taste are not unlike those of some Middle Eastern sweet, but *torta ricciolina* is far less cloying. My thanks go to Margherita Simili for the recipe.

8 to 12 portions

For the piecrust:

1½ cups flour
⅓ cup confectioners' sugar
Pinch salt

2 egg yolks
6 tablespoons butter, softened to room
    temperature

For the pie:

7 ounces almonds, blanched, peeled,
    and dried, about 1½ cups
2 ounces candied citron, about ⅓ cup
½ cup plus 1 tablespoon granulated sugar
½ teaspoon unsweetened cocoa powder,
    preferably Droste's
Grated peel of 1 lemon (outer skin with none
    of the white pith beneath)

Angel hair (very thin noodles) made with
    2 large eggs and about 1½ cups flour, as
    described on pages 93–5; or 1¼ pounds
    fresh, store-bought angel hair noodles
8 tablespoons butter
½ cup good, dark rum

1.   Prepare the dough for the piecrust: Make a mound on a work counter mixing the flour, confectioners' sugar, and salt. Make a well in the center and into it put the egg yolks and the softened butter cut up into small pieces. Draw the sides of the well together, kneading the flour with the eggs and butter. Do not knead past the point at which all the ingredients have been amalga-

mated into a smooth and uniform ball of dough. Wrap the dough in plastic wrap and refrigerate for at least 1 hour before proceeding with the recipe.

2. Chop the almonds and citron together with the granulated sugar in a blender or food processor. If doing it by hand, chop the almonds and citron, then mix with the sugar. They need not be chopped particularly fine or uniformly, but no piece should be larger than twice the size of a grain of rice.

3. Transfer to a bowl and mix with the cocoa and grated lemon peel.

4. Turn on the oven to 375°.

5. If making your own pasta, knead it and thin it as directed on pages 94–5. Thin it out to the next to last setting on the machine, then cut it into the skinniest possible strands by hand. Proceed at once to assemble the pie while the pasta is still moist.

6. Smear an 8-inch springform baking pan thinly with butter, dust with flour, and rap the pan smartly upside down on the counter to dispose of excess flour.

7. Flatten the ball of dough between 2 sheets of wax paper and roll it out in a round sheet about ¼ inch thick. Line both bottom and side of the pan with the dough.

8. Take ⅓ cup of the almond and cocoa mixture and set it aside. Divide the remainder into 2 equal parts.

9. Divide the butter into three parts, one of 4 tablespoons and two of 2 tablespoons each.

10. Divide the pasta into 3 equal parts. Take 1 of the parts and put it in the pan, loosening it up with your hands to make it fluffy.

11. Over the pasta sprinkle 1 of the 2 large parts of the almond and cocoa mixture. Dot with 2 tablespoons of the butter. Cover with a second layer of pasta, loosening it up as before. Sprinkle over it the remaining large part of the almond and cocoa mixture and dot with 2 tablespoons of the butter. Top with a third layer of pasta, spread loosely, over it sprinkle the ⅓ cup of almonds and cocoa, dotting with the 4 tablespoons of butter.

12. Place the pan in the uppermost level of the preheated oven. After 15 minutes, remove from the oven, cover with wax paper or aluminum foil, then return to the oven and bake for 25 minutes more.

13. Remove from the oven, discard the covering paper or foil, and sprinkle immediately, while it is still very hot, with the rum. Serve a day later, or up to 2 weeks later.

AHEAD-OF-TIME NOTE: The pie can be completely assembled, up to the time it is ready to bake, 2 or 3 days in advance and refrigerated covered with plastic wrap.

Dolce di Mele con le Mandorle e l'Uvetta

APPLE TRIFLE WITH ALMONDS AND RAISINS

*A*T *PAST* ninety years of age, my mother still springs surprises. With my manuscript nearly finished, she came up with a recipe I could not fail to include. It is for a most unusual apple trifle, delightfully tender and light: There is no flour in it except for the negligible amount needed to dust the raisins. The cool fragrance of the peel of 1 lemon plus 2 tablespoons of lemon juice add sprightliness to the bittersweet combination of *amaretti*, nuts, and raisins. It comes to mind that it is very like an autobiographical portrait of my mother, in dessert form.

About 6 portions

3 ounces seedless raisins, soaked in a bowl of
     lukewarm water for 20 to 30 minutes
1½ pounds Golden Delicious apples
7 tablespoons granulated sugar
2 ounces (about ⅓ cup) shelled,
     unpeeled almonds, blanched and peeled
     as described on page 302
4 pairs of *amaretti* (Italian macaroons), about

1½ ounces unwrapped
5 eggs, separated
Grated peel of 1 lemon (outer skin with none
     of the white pith beneath)
2 tablespoons freshly squeezed lemon juice
1½ ounces (about ¼ cup) pine nuts
1 tablespoon flour
1 tablespoon butter

1. Wash the apples, peel, core, and slice them very thin.

2. Put the slices in a pot with 2 tablespoons of the sugar and ½ cup of water. Cover and turn on the heat to medium. Cook for 30 minutes or more until there is no more liquid in the pot and the apples are extremely soft, nearly mushy.

3. Purée the apples through a food mill, inserting the disk with the smallest holes. Set aside to cool.

4. Chop the almonds very fine, together with the *amaretti*, in a food processor or blender.

5. Turn on the oven to 375°.

6. Add the remaining 5 tablespoons of sugar to the egg yolks and beat them until they form soft, pale yellow ribbons.

7. Add the puréed apples to the yolks, mixing them in a little at a time.

8. To the mixture add the grated lemon peel, then trickle in the lemon juice, drop by drop, while stirring constantly and gently.

9. Mix in the chopped almonds and *amaretti*, together with the pine nuts.

10. Drain the raisins, squeeze them dry in kitchen towels, put them in a strainer, and dust them with the flour, shaking the strainer to elimi-

nate excess flour. Mix them into the egg batter.

11.   Beat the egg whites until they form stiff peaks, then fold them gently into the batter.

12.   Smear the bottom of a 10-inch springform pan with butter. Cut out a disk of wax paper of the same diameter as the pan, place it inside the pan, and smear it with butter.

13.   Pour the batter into the pan and place the pan in the uppermost level of the preheated oven. Bake for 50 minutes, or until a toothpick inserted into the trifle comes out dry.

14.   Unmold when lukewarm. Serve either lukewarm or at room temperature.

Budino di Patate e Mandorle

POTATO AND ALMOND BAKED CUSTARD CREAM

FOR the past decade, out of the smallest restaurant kitchen I have ever seen, Dante's in Bologna, has come some of that city's most surprising and refined cooking. This potato custard is an example. When Dante suggested I try it, I was as skeptical as you may be. Yet if you try it, you will find, as I did, that the common potato makes an elegant custard with a lively texture.

8 to 10 portions

½ pound boiling potatoes
2 cups milk
¼ pound (about ¾ cup) shelled, unpeeled almonds, blanched and peeled as described on page 302
1 cup granulated sugar, plus ½ cup for the caramel
3 eggs

Grated peel of 1 lemon (outer skin with none of the white pith beneath)
1½ tablespoons Amaretto liqueur
A soufflé dish, stoneware if possible, 3 inches high and 7½ inches in diameter, about 1½ quarts' capacity

Potato and Almond Baked Custard Cream (continued)

1. Wash the potatoes, peel them, and shred them very fine, about as broad as a grain of rice is thick. If using a grater with different perforations, the most suitable would be the next to smallest hole or, in a food processor, the finest shredding disk.

2. Put the milk in a saucepan and bring it to a boil. Add the shredded potatoes. Cook for 30 seconds after the milk returns to a boil. Empty the contents of the pan into a bowl and let cool completely.

3. Dry the almonds thoroughly with an absorbent towel, then chop them fine, but not to a paste, in a food processor or blender.

4. Turn on the oven to 375°.

5. Put the ½ cup of sugar and ¼ cup of water in a small, light saucepan and turn on the heat to medium. Melt the sugar and cook it until it becomes colored a medium brown. (For a more detailed description of caramelizing sugar, please turn to page 329.) Pour the caramelized sugar immediately into the baking dish and tilt the dish in several directions to spread the caramel evenly over the side and bottom.

6. Break the eggs into a bowl, add the 1 cup of sugar, and beat them until they swell, forming soft, pale ribbons.

7. Add the chopped almonds, grated lemon peel, Amaretto liqueur, and mix well.

8. Add the potatoes and milk, when they are cold, and mix thoroughly to obtain a homogeneous mixture—otherwise the potatoes may settle to the bottom.

9. Put the potato and almond mixture into the dish. Choose a flameproof pan that is wider and shallower than the baking dish. Place the baking dish in the pan and pour into the pan 1½ inches of water, more or less, depending on the height of the pan. Place the pan, with the baking dish always inside it, over a burner and turn on the heat to medium. When the water begins to come to a simmer, transfer the whole thing to the uppermost level of the preheated oven. Bake for 1 hour.

10. When done, remove the dish from the pan and let cool completely before unmolding. To unmold, place the dish with the potato custard once again in a pan of water. Heat gently over a burner until the dish begins to be warm, about 1 minute or so. The objective is to warm up the caramel beneath and along the side of the custard just enough to make it flow. At this point, remove the dish from the pan, run the blade of a slender knife between the side of the dish and the custard, and invert the dish over a cake platter whose rim or shape will keep the liquefied caramel from spilling over.

Torta di Carote

CARROT CAKE

*T*HE outstanding features of this butterless, flourless carrot cake are its consistency—firm, but not leaden, satisfyingly chewy, yet moist; and its flavor —nutty, aromatic, and fresh.

6 to 8 portions

9 ounces shelled, unpeeled almonds
1 cup plus 2 tablespoons granulated sugar
9 ounces carrots, peeled and cut up into
    1-inch pieces
¼ pound ladyfingers, made crisp in a 325°
    oven for 20 minutes
1 teaspoon cream of tartar (sold by
    drugstores as potassium bitartrate) mixed
    with 1½ teaspoons bicarbonate of soda,
    or 2½ teaspoons baking powder

1 tablespoon Amaretto liqueur
¼ teaspoon salt
4 large eggs, separated
A 10-inch springform pan
1 tablespoon butter for greasing the pan
Whipped cream topping made with 1 cup
    heavy cream and 1 teaspoon granulated
    sugar (optional)

1.   Turn on the oven to 350°.

2.   Put the almonds and sugar in a food processor or blender and chop very fine. Transfer to a mixing bowl large enough to accommodate later all the other ingredients.

3.   Chop the carrots as fine as possible in the processor or blender and add to the bowl, mixing them with the almonds.

4.   Break up the ladyfingers into small pieces and chop them in the processor or blender until very fine, then mix with the other ingredients in the bowl.

5.   Add the cream of tartar and bicarbonate mixture or the baking powder together with the liqueur and the salt and mix thoroughly.

6.   Mix the egg yolks with the other ingredients in the bowl.

7.   In a separate bowl, beat the egg whites until they form stiff peaks. Take 1 or 2 tablespoons of beaten egg white and mix it into the cake batter in the bowl to soften it a bit. Then fold in the remaining egg whites gently.

8.   Grease the bottom of the springform pan with butter and pour in the batter, leveling it without pressing it. (Note: If you are not using a springform pan, line the cake pan with buttered wax paper before pouring in the batter. This will make it easier to remove the cake when baked.)

9.   Place the pan in the uppermost level of the preheated oven and bake for 50 to 60 minutes. Begin checking for doneness after 50 minutes by inserting a knife in the cake. When the blade comes out dry, the cake is done.

10.   When the cake is lukewarm, remove it from the pan. Serve at room temperature, with whipped cream, if desired. If it is not consumed the same day, wrap the cake, when completely cooled, in aluminum foil. It will keep up to a week, without refrigeration.

Riso Nero

BLACK RICE CAKE

WHEN I came across this recipe from Western Sicily, I was intrigued to find so many apparent similarities with one of my favorite traditional Italian desserts, the Easter cake from Bologna (see *The Classic Italian Cook Book,* page 428). Both have rice boiled in milk, both have almonds and chopped citron. That, however, is where the similarity ends. In the Sicilian cake the flavor of dark espresso, both the grounds and the brew, and of chocolate takes over. It is these two ingredients that are responsible for *riso nero*'s striking, almost inky black appearance. The rice becomes so closely bound to the almonds that some of my friends, upon trying it for the first time, were startled to be informed that it was a rice and not an almond cake. Moreover, *riso nero*, unlike the Bolognese cake, is not baked.

6 to 8 portions

4 ounces whole, shelled almonds, peeled as described on page 302
3 or more cups milk
½ cup Arborio Italian rice
1⅓ cups strong espresso coffee
⅔ cup granulated sugar
Pinch salt
2 ounces semisweet chocolate, grated

2 ounces (½ cup) citron chopped fine
Grated peel of 1 lemon (outer skin with none of the white pith beneath)
1 tablespoon espresso, very finely ground
½ tablespoon butter
Whipped cream topping made with 1 cup heavy cream and 1 teaspoon granulated sugar

1. Chop the peeled almonds fine, by hand or in the food processor.

2. Put the chopped almonds in a saucepan together with 3 cups of milk, the rice, the brewed coffee, sugar, and salt. Turn on the heat to medium, bring to a slow boil, and cook, stirring frequently, for about 1 hour, until all the liquid has evaporated and the mixture is compact. Taste to make sure that the rice is very tender. If it is not, and there is no liquid left, add ½ cup of milk and continue cooking, stirring steadily, until all the milk has either evaporated or been absorbed and the rice is well done.

3. Turn off the heat and add the grated chocolate, chopped citron, grated lemon peel, and coffee grounds. Mix thoroughly to a uniform consistency.

4. Choose a cake mold into which the mixture can be spread to a thickness of no more than 1½ inches. A rectangular mold is best because if the cake is spread too broad it has a tendency to become too dry. Line the mold with wax paper greased with the butter. Pour the rice batter into it, leveling it and pressing it down firmly. Refrigerate for at least 24 hours. It can stay in the refrigerator for as long as 4 days before serving.

5. Unmold over a serving platter and top with whipped cream.

Crema al Marsala

CUSTARD CREAM WITH MARSALA

WHEN I come in out of a cold, snappish winter day, I find zabaglione comforting. On most other occasions, however, I find it heavy and oversatiating. This custard, made with the basic zabaglione ingredients, offers comparable flavor, without the heat and the weight.

4 portions ·

3 egg yolks
⅓ cup granulated sugar
3 tablespoons flour

½ cup dry Marsala
1½ cups milk

1. Put the egg yolks, sugar, and flour in a saucepan. Off heat, beat the ingredients until they are evenly amalgamated without any lumps.
2. Add the Marsala and mix well to a smooth consistency.
3. Put the milk in another saucepan over medium-low heat. Bring the milk to the start of a simmer, but do not let it boil. Pour it all at one time into the saucepan with the egg mixture, while stirring constantly and thoroughly.
4. Put the saucepan over medium heat and cook, stirring steadily, for 8 to 10 minutes, until the mixture is dense, creamy, and smooth.

SERVING NOTE: The custard cream can be served cold as dessert, or warm over biscuits or sponge cake or crumbled *amaretti*, or with fresh berries.

Crema di Albicocche

APRICOT CREAM

ALTHOUGH this apricot cream was formulated as a filling for the stuffed crepes in the recipe that follows it, it makes a most agreeable fruit dessert just by itself.

For 6 persons

Apricot Cream (continued)

1½ pounds ripe apricots

7 ounces granulated sugar

2 tablespoons freshly squeezed lemon juice

1 egg

1 tablespoon butter

1.   Wash the apricots, split them to remove the pit, and cut them each into 4 or 5 pieces.

2.   Put the apricots with the sugar in a food processor and blend to a creamy consistency.

3.   Transfer to a saucepan, add the lemon juice, and turn on the heat to medium. Bring to a low boil and cook for 10 minutes, stirring constantly.

4.   Transfer to a bowl. When the apricots are cool, break the egg into a small bowl and beat it well. Add it to the apricots, beating it in thoroughly.

5.   Add the butter and return the mixture to the saucepan, turning on the heat to low. Beat constantly until the cream is uniformly blended and warm. Do not let it boil; otherwise, bits of the egg white will separate and harden.

6.   Pour into 6 serving cups, let cool completely, then refrigerate. If you prefer, it can be poured into a single serving bowl instead of individual cups.

Fazzoletti della Nonna con la Crema di Albicocca

SWEET BAKED CREPES WITH APRICOT CREAM STUFFING

*H*ERE is a sweet version of *fazzoletti della nonna*, the stuffed crepes customarily served as a pasta course. Please see page 144 for a full description.

For 6 persons

A 9- by 12-inch oven-to-table baking dish or its equivalent

½ recipe Apricot Cream (preceding recipe)

The crepes from the *fazzoletti* recipe on page 144

3 tablespoons granulated sugar

2 tablespoons butter

1. Turn on the oven to 450°.
2. Smear the bottom and sides of the baking dish with butter.
3. Stuff, fold, and place the *fazzoletti* in the baking dish as described in step 6 of the recipe on page 146. Use about 1½ tablespoons of the apricot cream for each of the *fazzoletti*.

4. Sprinkle the sugar on top, then dot with the 2 tablespoons of butter, making sure there is a dab of butter on the peak of each of the *fazzoletti*.
5. Bake in the uppermost level of the preheated oven for 20 minutes, or until a golden crust forms on top. Serve warm.

Fragole all'Aceto Balsamico

MACERATED STRAWBERRIES
WITH BALSAMIC VINEGAR

*O*N *A VISIT* to the West Coast, I had agreed to prepare a menu for the food editor of a major California daily. The dessert was strawberries with balsamic vinegar. Unhappily, I had ignored my own principles and had committed myself to strawberries before seeing them, with the result that I had to make do with the only strawberries I could find, pale and unripe. When the editor saw them she said, "Forget about them. I am not fond of strawberries even when they are perfect. We can do without a dessert." "If they are not good we won't eat them," I replied, "but you are going to taste them." When the strawberries were done, the balsamic vinegar had erased every trace of greenness, and they tasted as though they had been penetrated by the most ardent of summer suns. We not only tasted them, we finished them. Although it is a good recipe to remember whenever you are stuck with less than ripe berries, balsamic vinegar on strawberries at their peak of ripeness is an experience not to be missed.

For 6 to 8 persons

2 pounds strawberries
4 to 6 tablespoons granulated sugar,
    depending on the ripeness of the berries

2 tablespoons *aceto balsamico*
    (balsamic vinegar)

1. Wash the strawberries, leaving the stem on so that water does not filter in.
2. Remove all the stems and cut those berries that might be thicker than 1 inch at their broadest point into two pieces. Put all the berries in a serving bowl.

3. An hour before serving, add the sugar and toss gently but thoroughly. The sugar will dissolve and form a thin syrup.
4. Just before serving, add the balsamic vinegar and toss delicately several times.

Arancini alla Sorrentina

MARINATED ORANGES WITH ORANGE PEEL
AND CARAMEL

*S*UBTLY spiced and lovely to look at, these oranges from Sorrento will bring any dinner to a triumphantly refreshing close. They are also to be considered as an elegant alternative to ice cream, on any occasion that it might be served at home.

The peel and the sliced orange are marinated separately for about two days, the latter with cloves and cinnamon. When it has finished marinating, the peel is sliced into very fine julienne strips, coated with dark caramel, and drenched with the spiced, aromatic juices of the orange marinade. The orange slices and the caramelized wisps of peel are then combined. The dish is ready to serve after a few hours of refrigeration, but it will also keep for several days.

For 6 or more persons

6 medium oranges
Round toothpicks
1¼ cups granulated sugar

4 cloves
1 cinnamon stick

1. Peel the oranges, taking care to remove only the outer orange skin and none of the white pith beneath.

2. Put the peels in a bowl with enough cold water to cover amply and place in the refrigerator to marinate for 36 to 48 hours. Replace the water with fresh cold water at least twice a day.

3. Remove the white pith surrounding the oranges and cut these into slices ½ inch thick or less. Slice across, not along, the sections. Recompose the orange, skewering together the slices with toothpicks.

4. Put the orange slices in a bowl together with ½ cup of the sugar, ½ cup of cold water, the cloves, and the cinnamon stick. Cover the bowl and place it in the refrigerator for the same length of time as the peels.

5. When ready to complete the recipe, drain the peels, pat them dry with a kitchen towel, and cut them into long strips about ⅛ inch wide.

6. Put the remaining ¾ cup of sugar and ¼ cup of cold water in a small, lightweight saucepan and turn on the heat to high. Allow the sugar to melt without stirring. When it becomes colored a dark brown, turn off the heat. Add the orange peels and stir vigorously.

7. Remove the cloves and cinnamon stick from the bowl containing the sliced oranges. Pour the liquid from the bowl into the caramel. Stir steadily until the caramel dissolves to a flowing consistency. Pour the caramel with the peels over the oranges. Refrigerate and serve from several hours to several days later. Remove the toothpicks when serving.

Pere Cotte con Alloro e Amarone

BRAISED PEARS WITH BAY LEAVES AND RED WINE

*T*HESE pears are braised, not poached, an important distinction that I have found, when teaching the dish, many people overlook. First they are sautéed in butter, a step that establishes the base for their finely articulated flavor. Subsequently, bay leaves add their distinctive aroma and, of course, the final significant element is the red wine. You should make every effort to use Amarone because of its intensely concentrated fruitiness and faintly raisiny quality. Of all alternatives to Amarone, the most highly recommended would be a late-harvest Zinfandel.

When the pears are done, there must remain no wine in liquid form, but only a dense syrup that dyes the fruit deep purple and forms a caramel-like coating on it. To favor the reduction and evaporation of the wine, it is necessary to use a broad, low pan, rather than a tall, narrow one.

For 8 persons

4 firm, not overripe pears
1 tablespoon butter
4 to 6 tablespoons granulated sugar
6 to 8 bay leaves

2 cups dry, full-bodied red wine: The ideal choice is Amarone; other mature, full reds such as Barbera, Chianti Riserva, or Zinfandel are suitable.

1. Peel the pears, slice them in half lengthwise, and remove the core. If they have the stem, leave it attached to half the pear, for it looks attractive in the finished dish.

2. Choose a lidded sauté pan that can later accommodate all the pear halves lying flat without overlapping. Put in the butter, leaving the pan uncovered, and turn on the heat to medium high.

3. Heat the butter until its foam subsides, but take care not to let it become colored; otherwise, the pears will acquire a disagreeable burned-butter flavor.

4. Put in the pear halves flat side down. Brown them lightly on one side, then turn them over and do the other side.

5. Add the sugar, judging the quantity according to the ripeness of the pears (the riper the pear, the less sugar one needs). Spread out the bay leaves in the pan and pour in the red wine. Cover the pan, keeping the cover slightly askew, and turn down the heat to medium.

6. Cook the pears, turning them from time to time, until they are easily pierced with a fork. They should be just tender, but still firm enough to maintain their shape compactly.

7. If, when the pears are done—and the time varies depending on the variety of pear and degree of ripeness—the cooking juices in the pan are not yet reduced to a dense, syrupy consistency, uncover the pan and raise the heat to evaporate excess liquid. On the other hand, if

Braised Pears with Bay Leaves and Red Wine (continued)

the cooking juices are already dense while the pears are still hard, add a little water and continue cooking, with the cover on and askew, until they are done.

8.   Transfer the pears to a serving platter, placing them flat side down. They look most attractive in a round dish with their narrow ends meeting in the center.

9.   Remove as much of the bay leaves as you can from the pan. Allow the cooking juices to cool slightly until they are just fluid enough to be poured, but not runny. With a spoon pour the syrupy juice over the pears, covering them as completely as possible.

10.   Serve the pears as soon as they are cool, or several hours later, but do not refrigerate.

⤫ *LA FRUTTA AI FERRI* ⤬
Grilled Fruit

ON *PICNICS,* after we were done with barbecuing fish or meat and vegetables, it seemed a shame to let the coals' last heat expire unused, so I would drop whatever fruit we had on the grill. Good as it was—and I don't think fruit can get any better—I accepted it as the fire's parting gift without thinking of it as a deliberate approach to preparing fruit. When we installed a charcoal grill in one of our terraces in Venice, I began to produce on it complete meals for our friends, barbecuing everything from the *antipasto* to the dessert. The dessert, of course, was fruit, and, as I paid attention, I found there could be more to it than just throwing it on the grill. I didn't get into anything fancy, but with a few simple procedures I discovered I could draw substantially more varied flavor from each kind of fruit. Others trying their hand at it could certainly come up with variations of their own. The instructions below are an account of what has worked out well for me.

THE FRUIT. Fresh peaches, apricots, apples, plums, pears, bananas, figs.

EQUIPMENT. A narrow mesh double gridiron, hinged on one side, and a charcoal grill.

PREPARING THE FRUIT FOR GRILLING.
Peaches: Choose the freestone variety whose flesh comes easily away from the pit. Slice them in half; separate the halves, rotating them in opposite directions; and remove the pit. In the hollow left by the pit, put ½ teaspoon of sugar in each peach half.
Apricots: Prepare exactly like the peaches.

Plums: Do not cut or puncture; keep them whole. Handle figs the same way.
Apples: Cut them in half and scoop out the core. Score the flesh of each half apple with 3 or 4 cuts about ¼ inch deep. Put ½ teaspoon of sugar in the hollow of each half.
Pears: Prepare exactly like the apples.
Bananas: Make an incision the length of the banana, following its curve, but taking care not to cut through to the other side. Do not peel the banana. Sprinkle 1 teaspoon of sugar into the cut. Reserve 1 tablespoon of rum or Cointreau to use later.

GRILLING THE FRUIT. 1. Allow the coals to burn down until they form a thick layer of ash and are no longer fiery.

2. Place the fruit skin side down on one side of the gridiron. Swing the other side down over the fruit. Place the gridiron, with the skin side of the cut fruit facing the fire, about 12 inches above the heat.

3. After about 7 to 8 minutes, depending on the heat's intensity, when the sugar has melted and the fruits' skin has become slightly charred, turn the gridiron over so that the cut side of the fruit now faces the fire. After 2 to 3 minutes, turn them over again and cook for 2 minutes longer. As you turn them over, if you are grilling bananas, pour the rum or Cointreau into the cut.

4. Transfer the fruit to a serving platter and allow to settle for 1 to 2 minutes before serving. It is best when still warm, but it is also good at room temperature.

NOTE: If you are grilling apples and pears with other fruit, start them 3 to 4 minutes earlier and remove them from the heat 3 to 4 minutes later.

ITALIAN ICE CREAMS, SORBETS, AND SEMIFREDDI

THE ITALIAN ICE CREAM TASTE. To all but the most recent generations of Italians, the coming of the warm season was associated with the welcome call of the ice cream man's bell, and with the delicacies he dispensed from his pushcart: clear tasting, fluffy, and light, mixed in a hand-turned freezer only hours before. Today people push buttons instead of turning cranks, and pushcarts have been replaced by glossy shops of granite and chrome. But the flavor of good Italian ice cream still springs from the same source—fresh, unlabored handling of ingredients that are natural, unprocessed, and not overrich.

One of the most entrancing properties of ice cream in Italy is its lightness. It is an attribute that we owe to the modest means of our friend the pushcart man, and of his predecessors. Having to sell their product at a trifling price, they ignored such expensive ingredients as cream and butter. Their necessity was our good fortune. To attain lightness, ice cream must absorb air and swell as it is beaten in the freezing machine. Heavy fats hamper this process. When made by home methods, very rich ice cream is ponderous. Commercial manufacturers may resort to injecting it with air, as one does shaving cream. The recipes in this section, you will find, never call for butter, cream only sometimes, and then only if it is diluted with milk or fruit juice.

Lightness, then, along with freshness of preparation and uncomplicated flavor, are the attributes of ice cream made in the Italian style. Happily, they are more easily achieved at home than in a commercial plant; in your own kitchen, with just one special piece of equipment and the simplest ingredients, you can make better ice cream than you can buy.

ICE CREAM, SORBETS, AND SEMIFREDDI: A DEFINITION. The Arabs gave us both the ice and the word for it. Sorbet or sherbet— *sorbetto* in Italian—comes from the Arabic *sharbah*, an acidulated fruit drink. Hence, a sorbet is made from liquefied fruit to which lemon or orange juice and/or water may be added. There is no milk or cream in sorbets.

Whenever milk or cream is used, it becomes ice cream.

Semifreddo means partly cold. It refers to a frozen dessert part of which may or may not be beaten in an ice cream freezer, and which may be combined with such nonfrozen ingredients as biscuits, cake slices, candied fruits, meringue, or whipped cream. It is customarily presented either in a loaf shape or in wedges, although in this section you will find a round one. The nonfrozen components, and the generally high proportion of sugar or cream a *semifreddo* contains, produce a sensation on the palate slightly less cold than ice cream. Therein is the reason for its name.

ICE CREAM MACHINES. For years, the only machine I had at home was an inexpensive one that went into the freezer compartment of my refrigerator, to be plugged by means of its long cord, into an outside receptacle. Although slow, particularly with such dense mixtures as chocolate, it gave me much satisfaction. Recently I bought one of those self-contained units that freeze the ice cream as they beat it. It is fast, it makes close to 2 quarts at one time, and it does an exceptionally good job. Such machines are bulky and expensive, but if neither the size nor the cost is a problem, they are a marvelous tool to have.

Gelato di Panna

CREAM ICE CREAM

A LOOK at the list of ingredients for *gelato di panna* may give you an idea of its flavor. No *gelato* I have ever had has a taste so pure, nor so true a claim to the name ice cream.

About 6 to 8 portions

1 cup milk
1 cup heavy cream

4 tablespoons granulated sugar

1. Put all the ingredients in a small saucepan, turn on the heat to medium, and bring to a low, controlled boil.
2. Cook, stirring constantly, for 10 minutes.

3. Transfer to a bowl and allow to cool completely.
4. Place in an ice cream maker and freeze according to the manufacturer's instructions.

Gelato di Crema

CUSTARD ICE CREAM

*T*HE restaurant Diana in Bologna is justly famous for the handmade pasta from which it fashions its rigorously classic *tortellini* and green *lasagne*. No less extraordinary is its own custard ice cream, the recipe for which I have generously been given permission to publish. In a city where breathtakingly good ice cream is as common as, say, hot dogs in Times Square, this one may be the very best of all. Diana serves it with hot bitter chocolate sauce, but it is no less good plain.

About 6 to 8 portions

6 egg yolks
¾ cup granulated sugar
2 cups milk

Peel of ½ orange (outer skin with none of the white pith beneath)
1 tablespoon Cointreau

1. Put the egg yolks and sugar in a bowl and beat until the yolks become pale and form soft ribbons.
2. Put the milk and orange peel in a saucepan, turn on the heat to medium, and bring the milk to a low simmer, but do not let it break into a boil.
3. Add the milk to the egg yolks, pouring it in a thin stream through a strainer. Add the milk a little at a time, stopping briefly to beat it into the yolks.
4. Add the Cointreau, stirring it in well.
5. Transfer the mixture to a saucepan, turn on the heat to medium, and heat it, beating constantly, without letting it come to a boil.
6. Let the custard mixture cool completely, then freeze in an ice cream maker according to the manufacturer's instructions.

Gelato di Cappuccino

CAPPUCCINO ICE CREAM

*F*OR most Italians *cappuccino* is breakfast: Its strong, dark taste lingers, pacifying the palate until the long midday pause for lunch. After many trials, this was the only recipe that gave an ice cream with an equally gripping, persistent flavor. It is particularly enjoyable served with the cream ice cream on page 318. The amount of sugar is moderate in proportion to the coffee. It

Cappuccino Ice Cream (continued)

suits my taste, but if you find it too austere, increase the sugar gradually until it is just sweet enough for you, without letting it become cloying.

About 4 portions

2½ cups milk
½ cup espresso, regular grind

2 small egg yolks
¼ cup granulated sugar

1.   Put the milk and coffee grounds in a saucepan and turn on the heat to medium.

2.   When the milk comes to a boil, let it bubble for 5 minutes, stirring steadily.

3.   Line a strainer with 4 layers of cheese-cloth and set it over a bowl. Pour the milk and coffee solution into the strainer. It will drip very slowly, separating the liquid from the grounds. When the rate at which it drips becomes very intermittent, help the liquid through the cheese-cloth by stirring it with a spoon. At the end, pick up the ends of the cloth and twist, applying gentle pressure, to force through as much of the remaining liquid as possible.

4.   Beat the 2 egg yolks together with the sugar until they form pale, foamy ribbons.

5.   Pour the milk and coffee solution into the beaten egg yolks in a slow, thin stream, beating constantly with a whisk or fork. If at the end you see a deposit of grounds, stop pouring.

6.   Set aside to cool completely, then freeze in an ice cream machine, following the manufacturer's instructions.

Il Gelato di Cioccolato del Cipriani

THE CIPRIANI'S DARK CHOCOLATE ICE CREAM

*I*F ONE judges chocolate ice cream by how sumptuously concentrated, how close to chocolate essence it is, the one made by the Cipriani Hotel in Venice must take an absolute first place. When Franco, the pastry chef, at last released his recipe to me, I discovered the secret: deep brown caramelized sugar added to the cocoa and bittersweet chocolate to intensify both color and flavor. To obtain a suitably dark caramel, it may be helpful to read the note on *croccante* on page 329.

About 6 to 8 portions

4 egg yolks
2/3 cup plus 2 tablespoons granulated sugar
2 cups milk

3 1/2 ounces semisweet baking chocolate
1 1/2 ounces unsweetened cocoa powder

1. Put the egg yolks and 2/3 cup granulated sugar in a bowl and beat with a whisk until they are creamy and form pale ribbons.

2. Bring the milk to a boil in a saucepan, then add it to the beaten yolks, trickling it in slowly and steadily and mixing it in with the whisk.

3. Melt the chocolate in the upper half of a double boiler, then pour it into the bowl containing the egg yolks and milk mixture, mixing it in thoroughly with the whisk.

4. Add and mix in the cocoa.

5. Transfer the contents of the bowl to a saucepan, turn on the heat to medium, and stir with a wooden spoon until all the components of the mixture are well amalgamated.

6. Put 2 tablespoons of sugar in a saucepan with 2 teaspoons of water, turn on the heat to high, and melt the sugar until it is dark brown. Add it immediately to the egg and chocolate mixture, mixing it in thoroughly with the whisk. If it crystallizes, don't worry: It will dissolve as it is whisked.

7. Transfer the mixture to a bowl. When it is cool, place the bowl in the refrigerator for at least 20 minutes. Put the mixture in your ice cream maker and proceed according to the manufacturer's instructions.

Gelato di Limone

LEMON ICE CREAM

AROMA is the clue to successful lemon ice cream. Here it is extracted from the rind, which is boiled with water and sugar to make a syrup.

About 6 portions

3/4 cup water
Peel of 2 lemons (outer skin with none of the white pith beneath), about 1/4 cup, tightly packed

1/2 cup granulated sugar
1/3 cup freshly squeezed lemon juice
1/3 cup heavy cream

1. Put the water, lemon peel, sugar, and lemon juice in a small saucepan and bring to a boil. Boil for 2 minutes, then strain the syrup into a bowl. Let it cool completely.

2. When ready to put it into an ice cream maker, stir in the heavy cream, then freeze immediately in the ice cream maker according to the manufacturer's instructions.

Gelato di Fichi

FIG ICE CREAM

*I*N *ITALY* we peel figs before eating them and, automatically, I peeled them before using them for ice cream. Subsequently, I wondered what effect the peel would have had. A most agreeable one, I found when I tried it, deepening the color to a lovely pastel green and putting a keener edge on the taste. Without the peel, figs make a mellower ice cream. It is so simple to do, when fresh figs are available, that you may want to try both ways and choose for yourself.

About 6 portions

1 pound fresh, ripe figs
⅔ cup granulated sugar

⅔ cup water
⅔ cup milk

1. Peel the figs and put them in a food processor or blender together with the sugar. Purée to a creamy consistency.
2. Add the water and milk and process a few moments more.
3. Transfer to an ice cream maker and freeze according to the manufacturer's instructions.

VARIATION WITH UNPEELED FIGS

1 pound figs
⅔ cup granulated sugar

⅔ cup water
1 cup milk

1. Wash the figs, remove the protruding stem, but do not peel them.
2. Process exactly as described in the preceding recipe and freeze in an ice cream maker according to the manufacturer's instructions.

APRICOT, PEACH, ⌘ APPLE, WATERMELON AND LEMON, AND ⌘ POMEGRANATE SORBETS

Please note that a citric juice, either lemon or orange, is used with all the following sorbets. It not only makes their taste more refreshing, but the acid in the juice also favors a clearer expression of the fruit's own fragrance. It is the lemon, for example, that makes the watermelon taste of itself; without it it tastes of little more than frozen water. Sorbets taste best when they are consumed within a few hours after they have been made.

Sorbetto di Albicocca

APRICOT SORBET

About 6 portions

1 pound fresh, ripe apricots
½ cup granulated sugar

½ cup freshly squeezed orange juice

1. Wash the apricots well in cold water. Split them to remove the pits and cut each into several pieces. Do not peel them.
2. Put the apricots with the sugar and orange juice in a food processor or blender and blend until liquefied.
3. Place the mixture in an ice cream maker and freeze, following the manufacturer's instructions.

Sorbetto di Pesca Bianca

WHITE PEACH SORBET

About 6 portions

1½ pounds white peaches
½ cup granulated sugar

2 tablespoons freshly squeezed lemon juice

1. Wash the peaches, peel them, and cut them into several pieces, discarding the pits.
2. Put the cut-up peaches and the sugar in a food processor. Blend until liquefied.

3. Add the lemon juice, letting the processor's blade turn a few moments longer.
4. Transfer to an ice cream maker and freeze, following the manufacturer's instructions.

Sorbetto di Mela Golden

GOLDEN APPLE SORBET

About 6 portions

3 Golden Delicious apples, about 1½ pounds
2 tablespoons freshly squeezed lemon juice

1 cup granulated sugar, or 1 to 2 tablespoons less if you like it tarter

1. Wash the apples, peel them, quarter them to remove the core, and cut them into pieces.
2. Put the apples, together with the lemon juice and the sugar, into a blender or food

processor and blend to the consistency of applesauce.
3. Place in an ice cream maker and freeze, following the manufacturer's instructions.

Sorbetto di Cocomero e Limone

WATERMELON AND LEMON SORBET

About 6 portions

3 pounds watermelon (gross weight with the rind), or 2 pounds net weight with the rind removed

¾ cup granulated sugar
¼ cup freshly squeezed lemon juice

1. Cut away and discard the watermelon rind. Cut the watermelon into 1-inch cubes, picking out all the seeds.
2. Put the watermelon with the sugar and lemon juice in a food processor or blender and blend until liquefied.
3. Strain the liquid through a medium mesh strainer and freeze in an ice cream machine according to the manufacturer's instructions.

NOTE: The sherbet is best the moment it is done, but will keep well in a freezer for 24 hours. After that it becomes too hard and icy.

Sorbetto di Melagrana

POMEGRANATE SORBET

About 6 portions

4 pomegranates, about 3 pounds, yielding about 6 cups of juice seeds
3 tablespoons granulated sugar

1 tablespoon freshly squeezed lemon juice
6 or 7 medium-size fresh mint leaves, torn by hand into 2 or 3 pieces each

1. Remove the pomegranates' rind to extract their seeds.
2. Mash the flesh-coated seeds through a food mill fitted with the disk with the smallest holes, collecting the juice in a bowl.
3. To the bowl add the sugar, lemon juice, and torn mint leaves. Stir until the sugar has fully dissolved. Let the mixture rest for about 30 minutes.
4. Pour the mixture through a strainer with a fine mesh to separate from it the mint and any tiny pomegranate seeds that may have passed through the food mill.
5. Freeze in your ice cream machine, following the manufacturer's instructions.

Zabaglione Semifreddo

FROZEN ZABAGLIONE CREAM

*A*LL my Bologna students who visited Parma will remember this dessert. It came at the end of the midday banquet that rewarded them for a long, albeit instructive, morning in a local dairy studying the production cycle of *parmigiano-reggiano* (Parmesan).

This is an example of a true *semifreddo,* made without an ice cream freezer. You will note that each layer of the *semifreddo* is spread on the other after the preceding one has solidified, to prevent the two from running together. It wouldn't affect the taste if they did, but it would spoil the appearance.

The restaurant that devised it is Stendhal, at Sacca di Colorno, about ten miles outside Parma, where the Po River separates Emilia-Romagna from the Veneto.

About 8 portions

5 eggs
2/3 cup granulated sugar
A double boiler (bain-marie pan)
2 tablespoons dark rum
2 tablespoons Cognac
1/4 cup dry Marsala

2/3 cup heavy cream, kept very cold
2/3 cup confectioners' sugar
1/4 cup strong espresso coffee
2 ounces semisweet baking chocolate, grated
A 1 1/2- to 2-quart loaf pan

1. Separate the eggs, keeping for this recipe all the yolks and 4 whites.
2. Put the yolks and the granulated sugar in the upper part of a double boiler. Beat them off heat until they become colored a pale yellow and form ribbons.
3. Combine the rum, Cognac, and Marsala in a pouring cup and add the mixture to the egg yolks, beating it in a little at a time.
4. Put water in the lower half of the double boiler, turn on the heat to medium, and slip into place the upper half of the pan containing the egg yolks and spirits mixture. Beat it constantly with a whisk until it becomes a soft foamy mass. Remove it from the heat and allow it to cool to room temperature.

5. Beat the cold heavy cream. When it swells and stiffens, incorporate it with the egg yolk mixture.
6. Beat the egg whites in a separate bowl. When they begin to become firm, add the confectioners' sugar a little at a time and continue beating until the whites form stiff peaks. Add 1 or 2 large dollops of beaten egg white to the cream and egg yolks, mixing them in. Then add the remaining egg whites, folding them in gently.
7. Transfer one-third of the mixture to another bowl and mix in the coffee.
8. Add the grated chocolate to the bowl containing the larger part of the mixture, mixing it in uniformly.
9. Line a 1 1/2- to 2-quart loaf pan with wax

paper. Put in half the mixture containing the grated chocolate, level it off with a spatula, and place it in the freezer.

10. Put the 2 bowls, one containing the coffee mixture, the other the remaining mixture with chocolate, in the refrigerator.

11. After 1 hour, remove the loaf pan from the freezer and the bowl with the coffee mixture from the refrigerator. Transfer the coffee mix-

ture to the loaf pan, level it off with a spatula, and return the pan to the freezer.

12. After another hour, remove the pan from the freezer and the remaining bowl from the refrigerator. Transfer the chocolate mixture from the bowl to the pan, level it off, and return the pan to the freezer. Freeze for at least 24 hours before serving.

Semifreddo al Cioccolato

CHOCOLATE SEMIFREDDO

*O*NE of the simplest of *semifreddi* whose disarmingly homey flavor makes it one of our own family favorites. It is nothing more complicated than whipped cream and grated chocolate frozen into a loaf.

8 to 10 portions

2 cups heavy cream, kept very cold
1¼ cups confectioners' sugar
4 ounces semisweet baking chocolate, grated

6 egg whites
A 1½- to 2-quart loaf pan

1. Whip the cream. Before it stiffens, while it is still the consistency of buttermilk, add the confectioners' sugar a little at a time and continue whipping.

2. When all the sugar has been incorporated, and you have whipped the cream until it is stiff enough to form peaks, add the grated chocolate, mixing it in thoroughly.

3. Beat the egg whites. When they are stiff fold them into the cream and chocolate mixture.

4. Line the loaf pan with wax paper, and pour the mixture into the pan. Place in the freezer overnight. To serve, unmold it over a flat platter and slice it, as though it were meat loaf, into individual portions.

Semifreddo di Crema e Amaretti

AMARETTI AND CUSTARD CREAM SEMIFREDDO

*H*ERE is a two-layer *semifreddo* made partly with ice cream. One layer of custard ice cream is mixed with espresso and powdered ladyfingers, the other with ground *amaretti* cookies. Remember to freeze the first layer in the pan before topping it with the second.

6 to 8 portions

½ pound ladyfingers
⅔ cup strong espresso coffee
Double the Custard Ice Cream recipe on
    page 319
A 10-inch springform pan

Wax paper
16 pairs of *amaretti* (Italian macaroons),
    full size, not the miniatures, ground to a
    powder in a blender or food processor

1. Turn on the oven to 325°.
2. Spread the ladyfingers on a cookie sheet and put the sheet in the oven when it reaches the preset temperature.
3. Remove after 15 to 20 minutes, allow the biscuits to cool, then grind them to a powder in a blender or food processor. Mix the powdered biscuits with the espresso and set aside.
4. Place half the custard cream mixture in an ice cream machine and freeze according to the manufacturer's instructions.
5. While the ice cream maker is going, line the bottom of the springform pan with wax paper cut to fit and place the pan in the freezer.
6. When the ice cream is done, fold into it the ladyfingers and coffee mixture. Remove the pan from the freezer and spread the ice cream on the bottom. Level it with a spatula without pressing hard, thus keeping it fluffy. Return the pan to the freezer.
7. After 1 hour, place the remaining half of the custard cream mixture in the ice cream maker. When the ice cream is done, mix the *amaretti* powder gently into it.
8. Remove the pan from the freezer and spread the second batch of ice cream over the previous layer. Return the pan to the freezer. The cake is ready to serve when it is firm enough to slice neatly; it will keep for several days.

PRALINES WITH PINE NUTS AND WITH ALMONDS AND ORANGE PEEL

Italian praline—*croccante*—is darker than other pralines; it needs that firm thrust of bitterness to break through the otherwise sticky, compact sweetness of the sugar. One can go too far, of course—I am not talking about black, unpalatably bitter caramel. A dark, warm, distinctly brown color is what one should aim for. It is all a matter of timing, of judging when in another second or two the color will irretrievably cross the threshold from brown to black; before that happens, add the nuts.

Two recipes are given here, one with pine nuts, the other with almonds and orange peel. You can develop your own combinations of nuts and flavorings. Hazelnuts too make a good *croccante*. There is no finer homemade candy than a nice dark piece of *croccante*. When ground up, it is a happy addition to ice cream, custard, and other soft desserts.

Croccante di Pignoli

PINE NUT PRALINE

A light, thin saucepan about 8 inches in diameter
1 cup granulated sugar
1/4 cup water

5 ounces (1 cup) pine nuts
A baking sheet lined with heavy-duty aluminum foil
A washed, unpeeled potato

1. Put the sugar and water in the saucepan and turn on the heat to high. Let the sugar melt without stirring. When the sugar becomes lightly colored, tilt the pan in different directions to keep the sugar moving.

2. When the sugar darkens to the color of bitter chocolate, put in the pine nuts and stir with a wooden spoon. At first lumps will form because the cold pine nuts cause the sugar to congeal, but as you stir you will see that the sugar liquefies again. Continue stirring until the pine nuts are evenly distributed and any lumps have dissolved. Pour over the aluminum-lined baking sheet.

3. Cut the potato in half at its narrower part. Discard one half. From the other half pare away about 1/2 inch of peel close to the cut. Use the flat, cut side as a trowel to spread the sugar and pine nuts thinly and evenly over the aluminum foil.

4. When cold, peel away the *croccante* from the foil and break into irregular bite-size or larger pieces. Serve after dinner, or at any time as candy.

NOTE: When kept in a dry, snugly closed container, *croccante* keeps virtually indefinitely.

Croccante all'Arancio

ALMOND AND ORANGE PEEL PRALINE

½ cup orange peels, soaked in water for
    36 hours as described below
6 ounces shelled almonds peeled as described
    on page 302

2 teaspoons vegetable oil
1 cup granulated sugar
A washed, unpeeled potato, cut in half

1.   Prepare the orange peels, taking care, as you peel the oranges, not to cut into the white pith beneath the skin, which is bitter. Soak the peels in a bowl filled with cold water for 36 hours, changing the water 5 or 6 times. Drain and dry thoroughly with kitchen towels.

2.   Turn on the oven to 400°.

3.   Spread the peeled almonds on a baking sheet and dry them in the oven for 2 to 3 minutes.

4.   Chop the almonds and orange peels together, using a food processor or blender. Do not overchop. The consistency ought to be coarsely granular and ricelike, not powdery.

5.   Unroll a 2-foot length of heavy-duty aluminum foil and lay it flat on a work counter, marble if possible. Grease the surface lightly but evenly with the tip of a towel or a brush dipped into the vegetable oil.

6.   Put the sugar in a light saucepan together with 2 tablespoons of water and turn on the heat to medium high. Melt the sugar without stirring,
just tilting the pan from time to time with a slight rotary motion.

7.   When the sugar becomes colored a medium brown, the shade of walnut, add the chopped almonds and orange peel.

8.   Cook, stirring constantly with a wooden spoon. At first, the mixture will feel stubbornly gummy because the sugar hardens at its contact with the almonds and orange peels, but in a little while, as it begins to simmer, it will liquefy again.

9.   When the liquefied almond and caramel mixture becomes colored a walnut brown again, pour it over the aluminum foil. Cut and pare the potato as in step 3 of the preceding recipe, and use it to spread the mixture evenly and thinly over the foil.

10.   If you want to end up later with regularly shaped pieces of brittle, cut it before it cools into squares, rectangles, or diamonds, as you prefer. When completely cool, the brittle will lift easily from the foil. It keeps indefinitely.

I Zalett

BOLOGNESE POLENTA COOKIES

*I*N BOLOGNESE dialect, *zalett* means "little yellow ones." It is *polenta* flour that gives these cookies that color and their name. They have a marvelous crunch to them and true, warm corn fragrance. On their own, they are a superior crisp cookie, and they are excellent with ice cream, with zabaglione, with custards, and with the pears in red wine from page 315. My husband likes to dunk them in *grappa*. This is another of Margherita Simili's recipes.

100 to 120 cookies

2 cups plus 1½ tablespoons *polenta* (cornmeal) flour
1 cup plus 2 tablespoons all-purpose flour
⅛ teaspoon baking powder
1½ cups plus 2 tablespoons confectioners' sugar

10 tablespoons butter, softened to room temperature and cut up
⅓ cup lard, softened to room temperature
Grated peel of 1 lemon (outer skin with none of the white pith beneath)
⅛ teaspoon salt

1. Put the *polenta* flour, the all-purpose flour, and the baking powder in a bowl and mix thoroughly.

2. Pour the contents of the bowl onto a work surface and make a mound with a well in the center. Put all the other ingredients in the well. Draw the flour over the well and amalgamate thoroughly with all the ingredients, without, however, kneading the dough.

3. Divide the dough into 2 parts, wrap each in wax paper, and refrigerate for at least 1 hour or even overnight.

4. Turn on the oven to 350°.

5. Dust the work surface and a rolling pin with flour. Unwrap one of the balls of dough and roll it out with the pin to a thickness of ¼ inch.

6. Using a round cookie stamp 2 inches or slightly less in diameter or a wineglass or other suitable tool, cut the sheet of dough into disks. Place the disks on an unbuttered cookie sheet and bake in the uppermost level of the preheated oven for 7 to 8 minutes, until they become colored a deep gold.

7. Press the leftover cuttings together into a ball, wrap in wax paper, and place in the refrigerator.

8. Remove the other ball of dough from the refrigerator, unwrap, roll out, cut into disks, and bake, following the same procedure employed for the first batch of cookies.

9. Combine the second set of leftover cuttings with the first, roll out, cut, and bake for a third batch of cookies.

10. When cold, store the cookies in a tin box with a tight-fitting cover.

Index

A Note About the Author

Marcella Hazan was born in Cesenatico, a fishing village on the Adriatic in Emilia-Romagna, Italy's foremost gastronomic region. After receiving her doctorates from the University of Ferrara in natural sciences and in biology, she lived and traveled throughout Italy. In 1967 she and her husband, Victor, an Italian-born American, came to New York, and shortly thereafter Mrs. Hazan started giving lessons in Italian cooking in her New York apartment. With the publication of *The Classic Italian Cookbook,* her reputation as America's premier teacher of Northern Italian cooking spread throughout the country. Her second cookbook, *More Classic Italian Cooking,* was published in 1978 to broad acclaim, and the school she opened in Bologna, Italy, drew students from throughout the world. Mrs. Hazan now divides her time between New York and the sixteenth-century palazzo in Venice whose top floor she and her husband have restored.

A Note on the Type

The text of this book was set in a film version of Baskerville. The face is a facsimile reproduction of types cast from molds made for John Baskerville (1706–75) from his designs. The punches for the revived Linotype Baskerville were cut under the supervision of the English printer George W. Jones. John Baskerville's original face was one of the forerunners of the type style known as "modern face" to printers—a "modern" of the period A.D. 1800.

Composed by Superior Type, Champaign, Illinois.
Printed and bound by Halliday Lithographers,
West Hanover, Massachusetts.
Typography and binding design by Virginia Tan.